Separated by War

An Oral History by Desert Storm Fliers and Their Families

Ed Herlik

TAB **AERO**
Division of McGraw-Hill, Inc.
Blue Ridge Summit, PA 17294-0850

FIRST EDITION
SECOND PRINTING

Library of Congress Cataloging-in-Publication Data

Herlik, Edward C.
   Separated by war : an oral history by Desert Storm fighters and
their families / by Edward C. Herlik.
     p.   cm.
   ISBN 0-8306-4481-4 (h)
   1. Persian Gulf War, 1991—Aerial operations.   2. Persian Gulf
War, 1991—Personal narratives.   I. Title.
   DS79.72H475   1993
   956.704'4248—dc20   93-14695
                                                CIP

Acquisitions Editor: Jeff Worsinger
Editorial team: Charles Spence, Editor
                Susan Wahlman, Managing Editor
                Joanne Slike, Executive Editor
Production team: Katherine G. Brown, Director
                 Sandra Fisher, Proofreading
Book Design: Jaclyn J. Boone
                Brian Allison, Associate Designer
Cover: Carol Stickles, Allentown, Pa.
Front Cover Photographs (clockwise from top right): top and
   lower right, photos courtesy of J. Scott Walsh, left photo,   TAB2
   © Julie Habel/Westlight   4443

We dedicate this book to
Art, Rick, Spike, BJ, Donny, Teak,
Weeksy, McTavish, Buick, BC, Syph, Hicksy,
Chicken Man, Dale, Dave, Woody, Trey,
and the other airmen
who flew through the eye of the storm.
Their places at the bar
remain empty and unfillable.
This one's for you, guys.
We hope you like it.

To paraphrase the song, Heaven's got
one hell of a flying squadron.

You know, it's true.
Freedom has a sweet taste
to those who've fought for it
that the defended can never know—
they haven't had to pay the price.
And that's just fine with us.

Contents

Foreword

A tired old cliché goes something like this: "The more things change, the more they stay the same." That's certainly true in combat aviation. Over North Vietnam, I used maneuvers that were developed by men flying wood and cloth fighters in World War I. The F-4 Phantom II would have been barely recognizable as an airplane to those first combat fliers, but the moves and spirit they developed contributed to the difference between my coming home as an ace and not coming home at all. This book shows that technology continues to evolve while the fliers keep the qualities and characteristics I saw in Southeast Asia more than 20 years ago. To live and excel in this arena requires a person who is a risk taker: one who has the education, skill, training, attitude, determination, and tempered aggression to operate right up to the edge of his or her capabilities and the capabilities of the machines. Due to the complicated, deadly nature of the business, there's no room for anything less than highly trained professionals with the discipline to do the right thing every time. The planes change but the fliers stay the same.

The most important constants in combat aviation have more to do with professionalism and teamwork than anything else. For example, some 200 people were directly involved in the launch and recovery of a flight of the F-4s we flew in Vietnam. Thousands of other people were indirectly involved in getting us into the air and back safely. Had it not been for those individuals, who were proud of their work and performed it in a professional and outstanding manner, I certainly would not be a fighter ace and I might not even be alive. When you read these stories, keep in mind that even the pilots in single-seat fighters are team members representing the professionals who made their flight possible.

While that professionalism hasn't changed, the training that goes into the making of a combat flier is very different from my experience. As good as our training for Vietnam was, it was inadequate, especially in the air-to-air arena. Despite having the best training available as a com-bat-experienced Fighter Weapons School instructor, the first time I fought anything other than another F-4 was in combat against a MiG-21 near Hanoi! That serious problem was partly due to the feeling that it was unsafe to train the way we would fight, so we were not allowed to practice fighting other kinds of airplanes. We now realize that safety is using your head, being smart, and training in a realistic manner. Training the way we plan to fight will never be completely safe, but the flying en-vironment is already risky even before combat threats are added. Desert Storm fliers trained as they would fight and the results are now history.

There's been one other critical change from my experience. The fliers in this book were free of the senseless limitations placed on those of us who fought over Vietnam by the politicians. Many of this genera-tion's politicians didn't support Desert Storm, but at least they stayed out of the way. Too many of my friends paid too dearly to prove that politi-cians and combat don't mix.

True to a constant in the military fraternity, Ed Herlik kept in touch with his many friends who flew in the Gulf War. He eventually con-cluded that their stories should be told and could only be told by some-one who spoke the language of combat aviation. He's right, but that was only part of the story. The battle on the homefront has been largely ig-nored; families go through a different but still intense hell in time of war. No Desert Storm story can be complete without both viewpoints.

This book conveys human experiences in that inhuman situation better than any other I've seen on the Persian Gulf War. It's not a narrow book about wars or the fliers who fight them. It is, rather, the gripping stories of people living their lives at the focus of titanic forces.

I highly recommend these stories to you. They'll take you through the worlds of combat aviation and the military family as you've never seen them before. If war can have a human face, you'll see it here.

Steve Ritchie
Colonel, USAFR

Colonel Ritchie is the only Air Force pilot ace from the Vietnam War.

Preface

An inevitable consequence of any war is the avalanche of books by various experts. True to tradition, many people have written many books about the Persian Gulf War. Most of that work falls into two categories: the coffee-table picture book or the instant analysis by, frequently, someone with an ax to grind or a reputation to bolster. This book is neither.

It is, instead, a finely detailed look into both modern combat aviation and the timeless apprehension known to the families of men, and now women, in combat. This is a people book. Unique in blending the experiences of combat fliers with the significant others they left behind, this book tells the deeply human stories of ordinary people in an extraordinary time.

On another level, these experiences will take you beyond filtered accounts cleared by the public relations folks to the unvarnished truth in many corners of the Persian Gulf War. It is not meant to be comprehensive or to draw conclusions, but you'll see that, like all wars, this one was neither clean nor easy. It was not the high-tech video game some analysts made it out to be.

With the experience of three wars spent both in the air and at home, I know that the basics of the combat flier's life don't change much. The fear of missing the fight followed by the fear of the fight are as timeless as the war on the homefront. Technology changes, but the people who are the soul of any nation's defense never do.

We all lived the Persian Gulf War on television. With this book, you now have a chance to find out what really happened in the air. Read it.

Chuck Yeager
Brigadier General, USAF (Ret.)

Acknowledgments

Thirty-four very special people lived this book; all I had to do was record their experiences. Thanks again, everybody. Getting to know you was worth far more than the two years it took to print your stories. Please keep in touch and call me when you have an open seat in the cockpit.

Several of my friends have remarked at how difficult it is to get a book written and published and, therefore, how significant an accomplishment this is. Now that I've done it, I don't agree. Swapping "war stories" with fliers certainly isn't work as far as I'm concerned. The hard part was finding talented people like my agent, Fritz Heinzen, and the people at TAB, Jeff Worsinger, Susan Wahlman, and Debbie Polsin, to drag me through the process in spite of my ignorance. With patient experts like them on your side, publishing is easy.

Introduction

This is not a book about war: this is a book about people at war.

The Persian Gulf War—Desert Storm—was one of those events that mileposts individual lives and changes the mood of entire nations. Each of us will remember where we were when the air war started just as the bombing of Pearl Harbor and Kennedy's assassination are remembered. The American people came together like we haven't done since World War II, and we shook the Vietnam hangover, finally. The world's six-week addiction to that video war turned Any Service Member[1] into a close cousin. But the cutting edge of the air war couldn't be filmed, so we never knew what our fliers were really doing.

Spike, Teak, Buick, Weeksy, McTavish, Syph, and the rest joined our families as we hung on their words and swelled with pride at their cocky competence. They were the guys and gals on the pointy end of the sword. They were the best. They were us. It was the 1980 U.S. Olympic hockey team all over again. Except this game was for keeps and there was no silver medal.

---

[1]Any Service Member—the address on letters and packages sent by Americans to deployed service personnel.

We sat up nights to fly with them, we marveled at their skill, and we cursed the missiles that clawed for their lives. We cheered over their shoulders as those kids next door catapulted into the maniac's den. Our prayers nursed their crippled jets home, most of them. . . .

This book of their experiences also includes the never-easy war on the homefront. You'll hear the mesmerizing stories of the moms and dads, the wives, the fianceés, the brothers and sisters left at home. Until now, they've been forgotten because the spotlight hasn't penetrated the shadows of the combat aviators.

You'll also find controversy between these lines in that the facts do not always agree with official statements. Here are details on which aircraft worked and which didn't; which preparations made sense and which caused unnecessary deaths; who led and who only commanded.

I wrote down their stories simply because it had to be done and it could be done only by a flier. It had to be done because far too many people believe the Gulf War was somehow easy and sterile, like a huge video game. Some people were lulled by our thankfully low losses into believing Iraqi defenses were not serious. We never saw the weapons effects beyond bomb-impact videos. We never saw fliers fighting for survival. We never saw them cry when their closest friends lost those fights. The friend I flew my last OV-10 mission with died in Saudi Arabia. War is never easy.

Please don't read this book: hear it. Listen to the fliers and their families as they talk to you in their own language. I've included footnotes to help with the translation and ask your patience through the early chapters. They must be heavily footnoted as you learn the language of combat aviation. Throughout the book, I'll speak to you in italics, and radio calls will be transcribed in capitals. Everything else is the same first-person narrative you'd hear in a squadron's bar or around the kitchen table. You can't get closer to our lives without putting on a flight suit and going for a hop.

My access to fliers and my understanding of our lives left me with little choice but to tell their stories. The experiences are theirs. The mistakes are mine. We hope a new understanding will be yours.

Part One:

Getting There

A Mother's Letter and
a Soldier's Bullet

He's every mother's dream
but he's in the desert now.

An American soldier's mother
moves along in her usual routine.

An American soldier's enemy
moves along in his usual way.

The stationary is plain
but more than adequate
for a quick note.

The bullet is ordinary,
poured like a million others
and cast to specifications.

She sits down to write,
sure to cover all the local goings on,
and then she slips the letter
into the envelope.

The soldier sits down with his weapon
and covers all the procedures to account for it
and then he slips his ammunition
into a pouch attached to his waist.

The letter fits snug in its envelope.

The bullet fits snug in its brass casing.

Then, on a gray winter morning,
she walks out to the mailbox.

Then, on a brisk sunny evening,
the soldier pulls out his weapon.

She looks one last time
to make sure
the envelope has her son's name on it.

The soldier takes one last glance at the bullet,
unaware of whose name is on it.

She opens the mailbox
and pushes the letter inside.

The soldier opens the cylinder
and pushes the bullet into its chamber.

No one heard the last sound
that letter made
as it was slipped into the mailbox.

No one heard the last sound
that bullet made
as it was slipped into the chamber.

It is the thirteenth day of January
and there is a letter in the mail
with an American soldier's name on it.

It is the thirteenth day of January
and there is a bullet in a gun
with an American soldier's name on it.

He's every mother's dream
and he sits alone in the desert
unknowingly waiting
for the letter,
for the bullet.
Which one will he receive first?

My brother and I
are American soldiers in the desert.
We love you Mom.

David Hafer   13 Jan 91
Air Force pilot
Riyadh

1

The Commander's
a Lady

Air Force Captain Anne Armstrong is a living argument in favor of women in the military. Her ambition took her from an upper-class neighborhood near Washington, D.C., to jet pilot training, to wartime command of America's largest airplane. There's even a case to be made that missions run more smoothly when the commander is a lady.

Captain Armstrong's jet was the Lockheed C-5 Galaxy strategic airlifter. It's hard to comprehend the C-5's size. The largest free-world airplane, it weighs more when completely empty than the C-141 Starlifter weighs fully loaded. With a payload of more than 240,000 pounds, the C-5 could easily lift an empty B-52 or most fully loaded civilian airliners. The cockpit windows are three stories above the ground, and the tail is another three stories above that. C-5 pilots practice landings in empty Galaxys that still weigh more than fully loaded DC-10s. It's a truly amazing airplane.

Combat complicates the airlift mission but doesn't change it significantly. So, for Captain Armstrong and the other airlifters, the war really began with the first deployments on August 4th, 1990. Twenty-four hour duty days with 10-hour breaks became the norm in a physically grueling routine that was exceeded only by the B-52s. And the war didn't end with the cease-fire. For our forces in the Persian Gulf area and any of the world's other hot spots, strategic airlifters will always be the link with home.

Captain Armstrong:

At the ripe old age of six weeks, I was adopted by my parents in Chevy Chase, Maryland. That was clearly the best thing that had happened in my albeit then short life. They sent me to a private school and I eventually received an Air Force ROTC[1] scholarship and an appointment to the Air Force Academy. I took the scholarship to Vanderbilt University and earned dual degrees in geology, with a minor in history, and anthropology, with a minor in English. Vanderbilt is a very fine school and afforded me a terrific education. It is, however, extremely conservative, so I didn't get along very well with some of the administration's policies. I was commissioned through the ROTC program at Tennessee State University and went to UPT[2] at Columbus AFB, Mississippi.

I wanted to be an astronaut. When I was six or seven years old, I turned on the television and Captain Kirk sailed across the screen. I said, "That's what I want to do." So that's what I fought to do. Military flight is a stepping stone to the astronaut program, so that's why I went.

With aspirations to be an astronaut, I obviously don't agree with the restrictions against women in various military jobs. The complaint that women can't pull their weight is malarkey. For example, it seems that the people who wonder if women can kill in combat assume that the woman would be beamed into the cockpit without having thought about her mission. That's garbage. She would have fought to get a fighter airplane like men do now, she would have been through all the training, and she would know exactly what pulling that trigger means. We've been through difficult desegregation problems in the military before, and we can rise above this one too. I firmly believe we're professionals, and being professional is what it's all about.

The integration problems I saw with women at flight school resulted from stereotyping. If one woman resembled whatever prejudiced view was in fashion, her actions reflected on all women. For example, one girl was more promiscuous than the guys thought she should be— she behaved like they did. Because of her, all female pilots were suspect. Double standards are common. If "Joe" is a terrible pilot and can't find his fanny in the radar pattern, that means Joe is terrible. If "Betsy" is terrible, that means all women are terrible. Women have only flown military jets for about 15 years, so it's still a matter of time until everybody's used to having us around.

---

[1]Reserve Officer Training Corps (ROTC)—Military scholarship program that pays for college and leads to a commission as an officer.

[2]UPT—Undergraduate Pilot Training. Air Force pilot training program. Primary training is flown in the Cessna T-37, a very mild and forgiving jet, while advanced training is flown in the supersonic Northrop T-38.

I earned my wings in 1984 and was assigned a C-23 Sherpa light transport until it was given a combat role. Since women didn't fly combat, I was reassigned to a C-21 Learjet but switched to the C-12 King Air executive transport because that got me back into the air two months quicker. I ended up as an evaluator in the C-12 at Langely AFB, Virginia.

I planned to apply for test pilot school because it's almost required for the astronaut program. The only square I didn't have covered[3] was the high-performance jet time, so I seriously considered returning to the T-38[4] in the Air Training Command[5]. But I was uncomfortable in ATC; I liked MAC[6] much better. My other choice was to move to the C-5 and take a chance that the test pilot requirement would go the way of the dinosaurs as the shuttle program became even more routine. But shortly after I accepted the C-5 assignment, the Challenger exploded. That ended my hope of getting into the shuttle because they would only take test pilots forever after that crash.

The C-5 was terrific. It is a great airplane with a great mission and I loved the people I worked with. I especially thrived on commanding the airplane. My briefing as aircraft commander before each mission set the tone, I hope, that I expected professionalism on the job, I expected people to do their jobs, and I expected them to be safe. Off duty, I expected everybody to let their hair down, enjoy themselves, and complain. Complaining is therapeutic. I never had any problems with any of that. The people I worked with in the 9th MAS[7] and the 709th ALS[8] were professional and safe. I certainly believe in letting people who know their jobs do 'em.

It seemed that female ACs[9] had an advantage in that the men would verbally spar with each other over what to do next but nobody ever sparred with me. The stereotype that women are better at compromise and consensus may be true, or it could have been the personalities of

---

[3]filling squares—Meeting requirements, as in marking off the square blocks on a checklist.

[4]T-38 Talon (38)—Supersonic Air Force advanced trainer. Every Air Force pilot trained in that Northrop jet fell in love with it.

[5]Air Training Command (ATC)—Air Force command that handles all pilot training among many other training functions. As a nonoperational, stateside command, ATC became stagnant with an overemphasis on tradition and politics.

[6]Military Airlift Command (MAC)—The Air Force transport aircraft people. Superseded by the Air Mobility Command.

[7]MAS—Military Airlift Squadron, a unit of MAC.

[8]ALS—Air Lift Squadron; superceded MAS as a squadron designation.

[9]aircraft commander—AC. The individual responsible for the aircraft, crew, and its mission. He or she commands an aircraft just as a captain commands a ship.

the men involved. I don't like sweeping generalizations, and there are a lot of qualifiers in a stereotype like that, but I never had a conflict while reaching a decision as an AC.

The most obvious difference between active-duty flying and Reserve[10] flying was that the Reserves had the big picture. They have a much more reasonable view of pilots and of what professional pilots and officers can handle. Fliers on active duty are often treated like children and led by the nose through everything. We were only allowed to train on one airplane at a time and couldn't live very far from the squadron. I didn't like being treated like a child and found that rather insulting. Reservists are commonly current in two jets at the same time (civilian and military) and are trusted to be where they're supposed to be even if they choose to live on the other coast. I really preferred being treated like an adult.

Reservists came at the C-5 with a perfectly fine attitude: "An airplane's an airplane, and I know how to fly an airplane." But they were considered bastard children by the active-duty people who didn't seem to be aware of the tremendous experience on the Reserve side. Active duty fliers thought they were the backbone of MAC who did things right while the Reservists just tried not to kill themselves.

Anyway, in early August 1990, I was in a week of simulator training when I heard of Iraq's invasion on the news. I thought, "Oh my God, there's some work coming down for us over this one." Many crews pulled bravo alerts[11] that first week while we finished with the simulator. I chomped at the bit and wanted to get involved with the airlift. As soon as the simulator refresher ended, I was thrown right into the fray and flew almost constantly to the end.

I flew 920 hours in the next ten months[12].

The early days of the airlift war (August 1990) were complete mayhem. It was run very poorly; crews were taken advantage of; there was no command and control; we were totally unprepared for the specifics of that operation. We had generic plans that had to be adapted, but they didn't

---

[10]Air Force Reserves—The American Air Force comes in three parts—active-duty forces, the Reserves, and the Air National Guard. Reserve and Guard fliers handle 35% or more of transport and tanker operations in their spare time while holding civilian careers too. When called to active duty for Desert Shield, Reserve and Guard fliers carried 60% of the transport load.

[11]bravo alert—Airlift contingency status that keeps a crew ready to lift off in less than three and a half hours for 48 hours at a time.

[12]Transport pilots routinely log 400 hours in a year. MAC fliers flew at nearly three times their normal pace, while the jets logged seven years' worth of flying in those 10 months.

work. As the war went on[13], things progressed from complete idiocy and mayhem to, "Hey, we're starting to get a clue!", to clockwork at the end. We really had it down. Once everything was ironed out, the job was easy.

At first, we flew air refueling missions direct from the States to Saudi Arabia. After that first week, we usually took off for somewhere stateside and loaded up with Army equipment before carrying it to Torrejon Air Base, Spain, or Rhine-Main Air Base, Germany. Another crew would take the plane from there—sort of like the pony express in reverse: instead of the pony being tired, the riders were tired. Transports are always the first ones in during a crisis, so the war started for MAC in August.

A typical mission for me was a launch from bravo alert to Pope AFB, North Carolina, where we loaded up full of cargo and full of fuel to fly across the pond[14]. In the heat of the mid-afternoon, we were supposed to take off on that short runway[15]. It was classic poor planning on MAC's part and we had to wait until evening to get off. Then we heard on the radio that our destination, Torrejon, was a total nightmare. There was no water, everybody slept in the gym on cots, there was no food and crew rest[16] was only ten hours, which is completely illegal. I said, "Crew, we're not going to Torrejon." Then I called the MAC controllers and told them we were stopping at the Azores for gas so that we could reach Frankfurt (Rhine-Main). They said okay, because they had no idea where any of the planes were going anyway. We got to Frankfurt and found that there was nowhere to stay and just finding food was hard. Still, conditions were better than at Torrejon. All those problems were entirely understandable since nobody could be ready for what happened.

From Frankfurt, we were supposed to fly down to Thumrait, Oman, and return—a 20-hour day after 27 on the way to Germany. We had to wait six hours at Thumrait as they put 200,000 pounds of fuel[17] on the airplane with their thin fuel hoses. Just as we were ready to start, the command post[18] called with news that we were going to fly cargo to

---

[13]Transport fliers saw little difference in their operations when the fighting started. Their war ran from August 1990 to May 1991.

[14]pond—Ocean. Usually the Atlantic Ocean.

[15]Lift and jet engine thrust are reduced by heat and altitude. Combine that with a short runway and the jet may be unable to take off.

[16]crew rest—The mandatory rest period a flier must have between duty days. Twelve hours off is required, although transport crews lived on 10-hour breaks for part of the crisis.

[17]pounds of fuel—Jet fuel is often measured by weight. The type used by most of these jets weighs 6.5 pounds per U.S. gallon, so 200,000 pounds was about 30,800 gallons.

[18]command post—Command and control center on a base that handles the flow of aircraft, keeps track of the crews, etc.

King Fahd on the way to Germany. Fahd was an incomplete international airport with no lights at all, no instrument approaches, no control tower, and no C-5 had ever been there before. I said, "We're going to get there at night, without lights, and we're tired. You're crazy!"

Then they got a general in Riyadh on the phone who said, "Blah, blah, blah, this is an order, humph, humph, humph." In the meantime, they loaded our plane with two school buses and the fire trucks that weren't at Fahd yet either. I pointed out that we could land at Dhahran, an established C-5 base, and drive those vehicles the 20 miles to Fahd. The general wouldn't hear it. He was typical of the command and control from Riyadh through the entire war. If it was on the orders, you did it whether it made any sense or not. They wouldn't listen to safety concerns or better ideas. They were very, very rigid and wouldn't listen to anybody.

I asked the more-experienced pilot with me, who said we ought to do it. That swayed me since I really wanted to get the wheels in the well[19] and get away from those whackos. We found Fahd with our inertial navigation systems and it turned out they had some lights on the runway. The copilot and I were both qualified in tactical arrivals, so we flew a visual pattern over that black hole and taxied in on only the airplane's taxi lights. Those were also the only lights for our totally unauthorized, engine-running offload[20] before we got the hell out of there. It had been a long damn day by that time.

I called the controllers in Germany and told them we were going to stop at Sigonella, Italy. If they wanted the airplane, they could come down and get it.

Somebody tried to kill us with stupid decisions a couple of other times too. An aircraft commander went to the command post at Torrejon to say he couldn't fly at the weight he was carrying because it was too hot to make the minimum climb gradient for a safe takeoff. The controller said, "Of course you can, MAC has waived the requirement for that climb gradient[21]." The engineer was a crusty old senior NCO[22] who had been with the airplane for a million years. He leaned into the window and said, "Son, you can't waive gravity." But they did waive every-

---

[19]wheels in the well—To retract the landing gear into the wheel wells after takeoff.

[20]engine running offload/onload—Most military transport airplanes can load or unload in a hurry with the engines running.

[21]Most procedures and safety rules became waiverable. Such corner-cutting sometimes made sense and sometimes was simply unsafe.

[22]NCO—Noncommissioned officer. Senior enlisted person who does most of the work in the military, while allowing officers the ego-saving illusion of control.

thing else, and I had controllers try to get me to take airplanes that were unsafe.

For example, my crew was sent to Andrews AFB, Maryland, once to pick up a plane that diverted there for weather[23]. When we got to the airplane, the engineers called me to the tail because it had been tail-scraped on landing. There was 15 feet of exposed sheet metal on the aft pressure doors, fist-sized holes in the skin, and shredded speed tape dangling from the damaged area. It turned out that three days prior, the tower reported a rooster tail of sparks when that plane made a night landing at Torrejon. But the cargo was classified (a captured Scud[24] missile) so the maintenance people weren't allowed inside to inspect the damage. A crew was alerted to fly it to the States but turned it down as unsafe. The command post at Torrejon then violated the regulations by alerting another crew who also turned it down. As I understand it, the MAC Commander eventually ordered a crew to fly it back in spite of the damage. We were supposed to fly it back to Dover for repair. That comes under the heading of stupid people trying to get me to kill my crew. We took a bus home.

As for support at home, I got back to the States very little and then for only 12 hours at a time, so I didn't see any of the support firsthand. My entire war was spent with CNN in hotel rooms and the BBC on the airplane's short-wave radio. I don't like to watch television at all, so I probably doubled my lifetime television viewing hours with that time watching CNN. But I still felt that the American support back home was marvelous, overwhelming. There was never a doubt in my mind that they supported us.

When we got to the hotels in Frankfurt or Madrid, I'd put my name on the phone waiting list to call home and let my family know what was going on. We talked about daily life mainly and didn't dwell on what I was doing beyond some of the places I'd been. My mom especially tried to put the war on the back burner to cope.

As I flight planned[25] to leave Dover yet again, I saw a story on the television monitor that said we'd lost a C-141 and they showed a picture

---

[23]weather—(noun) Specifically, bad weather that obscures vision such as fog, rain, or clouds. Fliers mention weather only when it's a significant consideration, as in lots of clouds, thunderstorms, bad visibility, etc. It can be a real showstopper.

[24]Scud—Russian-built, militarily useless terror weapon based on captured German V2 rockets.

[25]flight plan—(verb) To check the weather, notices, fuel requirements, routes, etc., and complete a flight plan. (noun) Standard form listing mission information and route of flight.

of a 141. Then they corrected themselves and said we'd lost a C-5—typical media mistake. Mom and Dad didn't know where I was, so I called my mother right away and said, "Mom, you're going to hear on the news that we lost a C-5. I don't know the particulars but it wasn't me."

I'm surprised we didn't lose more heavy airlift airplanes[26] than we did. Chronic fatigue sets in after flying for 24 hours with 12 hours crew rest; 24 flying, 12 hours crew rest; 24 flying, 12 hours crew rest over and over and over again. After a while, you just can't function. I'm convinced fatigue crashed that C-5 at Ramstein. They were fatigued by that routine and then sat on the ramp[27] for 10 hours before takeoff. I don't believe the safety report that blamed a mechanical problem.

We didn't crash as many C-5s as we expected to, but there were some really close calls. Of all the C-5 Air Medals to come from the war, Major John Haszard's was the most deserved. The irony is that it went to a man who had 23 already from Vietnam. His situation is the nightmare every pilot is afraid of: heavyweight, full of gas, a cargo of bombs, and lots of people on board when they hit a flock of birds. Losing one motor that way won't necessarily kill you but losing two motors will.

This mission started off like so many others. The 709th Military Airlift Squadron crew formed around Major John Haszard as the aircraft commander. They gathered early for his formal briefing on the mission, cargo, destination, etc., before splitting up to prepare for the first flight of the day. The loadmasters under Chief Master Sergeant Steve Pennypacker checked the 141,000 pounds of high-explosive bombs loaded onboard. The flight engineers under Master Sergeant Syd Redmond conducted the preflight inspection[28] and Technical Sergeant Sam Davidson served as the scanner[29]. The AC and copilot, Major Jim Jordan, handled the flight planning. Most of these men had gone through this routine hundreds of times before so preparations were handled quickly and efficiently. Situation normal.

In the following transcript, radio transmissions are capitalized and each crewmember is identified by the job he performs. We pick up the cockpit tape at the point where the C-5 was cleared for takeoff:

---

[26]Heavy airplanes—Heavies. Usually refers to transports, tankers, or bombers.

[27]ramp—Multiple-acre concrete expanse where airplanes park.

[28]preflight—The aircraft inspection made prior to engine start. The preflight of a fighter takes the pilot a few minutes. The preflight of a C-5 takes both flight engineers about an hour and a half.

[29]scanner—A fully qualified flight engineer who moves around the airplane to check on trouble spots.

Tower: MAC 90016, WINDS TWO SEVEN ZERO [degrees] AT ONE FIVE GUST TWO ZERO [nautical miles per hour], CLEARED FOR TAKEOFF.

Copilot (CP): CLEARED FOR TAKEOFF, MAC 90016.[30]

Pilot (P): Cleared for takeoff, checklists complete. Advancing throttles now to 95.8 [percent engine RPM[31]]. Copilot, adjust the throttles please.

Engineer (E): Fifteen. Twenty. Time.[32]

CP: Go.[33]

Do you see those birds?

P: Yeah. I'll let us drift off to the left of the runway to avoid 'em. Gear up[34].

CP: Gear up.

A flock of birds, startled by the roar of the heavy transport's engines, rose from the grass beside the runway and flew into the C-5's flightpath.

Tower: 90016, TOWER, LOOKS LIKE YOU HIT SOME BIRDS SIR.

P: Yeah we did! We hit the suckers.

CP: ROGER. WE MAY HAVE SOME DAMAGE TO NUMBER THREE (engine). WE'RE GOING TO COME BACK AROUND AND LAND. I'LL CALL YOU BACK.

P: Aw shit!

Tower: MAC 90016 ROGER. ARE YOU DECLARING AN EMERGENCY SIR?

CP: THAT'S AFFIRMATIVE!

Tower: SAY YOUR SOULS ON BOARD AND FUEL REMAINING.

P: Tell him to wait.

CP: JUST STANDBY. WE'LL CALL YOU BACK.

E: It is number three. It sounds like we've got a lot of noise and vibrations out of number three.

P: Yeah, it really sounds bad. Scanner, take a look at the right side of the plane and let me know what you see.

Scanner (S): Scanner's on his way. [*The scanner had to go down a*

---

[30]The pilot not flying makes all the radio calls.

[31]RPM—Revolutions per minute. Measure of the power being generated by a jet engine.

[32]On the C-5, the flight engineer calls off the elapsed time as the copilot adjusts the throttles to the takeoff power setting. "Time" means the throttles cannot be moved again while the engineer confirms the health of the engines.

[33]go speed—On heavy aircraft, the copilot calls "Go" at a predetermined speed, meaning the aircraft is committed to takeoff.

[34]gear—Landing gear. The wheels. "Gear up" means retract the wheels.

20-foot ladder and work his way back around the bombs to one of the portholes.]

CP: It looks like the number three fuel flow's[35] going over limits.

P: I'm going to turn left into the visual pattern for landing. We'll stay at about fifteen hundred feet off the ground.

E: Number three really sounds bad.

P: How's it look, scanner?

S: I can see some visible damage under the fan area (the front) on the bottom of number three engine. I can't tell if anything's wrong with number four.

P: I'm sure we hit those birds, so let's shut it down. Confirm number three fire handle[36] pulled?

CP: Confirmed number three.

P: Fire-fighting agent's not required. Copilot, start the emergency engine shutdown checklist for number three. I'm going to turn downwind[37] now. We're still getting a lot of noise out of there, scanner. Are you sure number four's okay also?

S: Number four looks clean. I don't see any evidence of damage to number four.

CP: (*From the checklist*) Fire handle's pulled. Agent's not required. Throttle?

P: Number three, idle.

CP: Fuel and start ignition switch?

P: Confirm number three? Stop.

CP: Engine scan?

S: Engine scans clean.

CP: Rudder limit switch—min Q [an emergency setting]. Engineer's report?

E: Check completed. Fuel remaining, two hundred forty four thousand pounds[38].

CP: Emergency engine shutdown checklist, completed.

---

[35]fuel flow—A measure of how much fuel is being pumped to an engine. The fuel is supposed to be burned normally, but, if the engine is damaged, raw fuel may be pumped into the engine area, causing an extreme fire hazard.

[36]fire handle—An emergency engine shutdown system that cuts off all fuel, fluids, and ignition. On a plane with more than one flier, both confirm that the proper engine is being shut down to avoid getting that deafening silence from the wrong engine.

[37]downwind—The part of a normal landing pattern that is parallel to the runway but flown in the direction opposite to landing, en route to the base turn.

[38]Just for comparison, 244,000 pounds of fuel is about 38,000 gallons, or more than all but the largest civilian airliners weigh when they're fully loaded. At this point, the C-5 weighed just under three quarters of a million pounds, or about 380 tons.

P: Okay, engineer, what's our two-engine ceiling?

E: We don't have one. [*i.e., the plane won't fly on two engines.*]

P: Let's not dump fuel yet. We're just about back on the runway. We're on downwind now. Troop compartment[39], pilot.

Troop (T): Troop, go.

P: Keep all the guys calm back there. We just hit a flock of birds and shut down number three. We're goin' to be landing here in just a couple of minutes. We're on downwind for two three[40]. Pass it on to everybody.

T: Roger sir.

E: Overheat in number four! Overheat in number four!

P: Aw shit! Engineer, we're going to have to dump fuel. We're over an isolated area so get that started.

E: Are you going to pull back number four at all?

P: No. We can't shut it down right now 'cause we can't fly on two engines. Let it burn! We'll shut it down when we get on the ground.

E: Scanner, engineer. Verify fuel dump[41].

P: Tell tower we're comin' in and make sure they got the fire trucks there.

CP: TOWER, MAC 90016. WE'RE TURNING BASE[42].

S: Fuel dump confirmed.

Tower: MAC 90016 ROGER. CHECK GEAR DOWN. WINDS TWO SEVEN ZERO ONE FIVE GUST TWO ZERO. CLEARED TO LAND RUNWAY TWO THREE.

CP: CLEARED TO LAND, ROGER. CONFIRM FIRE TRUCKS ARE OUT?

Tower: SIR, CRASH AND FIRE EQUIPMENT IN PLACE.

C: ROGER THAT. 90016, WE HAVE TWO HUNDRED AND FORTY-FOUR THOUSAND POUNDS OF FUEL ON BOARD, SIXTEEN SOULS, TEN AFT AND SIX FORWARD. BE ADVISED, OUR NUMBER FOUR ENGINE IS OVERHEATING, BUT WE'RE LEAVING IT RUNNING AT THIS TIME.

Tower: 90016 ROGER.

P: Okay, the runway looks good. I'm just a little bit lower on glide-

---

[39]The C-5 has a 75-passenger seating area, the troop compartment, above the cargo area and just forward of the tail. Loadmasters ride back there for passenger safety and answer the intercom as "Troop."

[40]Runways are labeled according to the direction they point, so runway two three points 230 degrees on the compass, or southwest.

[41]The scanner can look out a porthole to see 1400 gallons of fuel pour out of the wings each minute when fuel is being dumped.

[42]base—That part of the normal landing pattern perpendicular to the runway, just before the turn to final approach.

path than I'd like to be. We'll go ahead and turn final[43] and get the gear. We'll leave the flaps at forty percent until landing is assured. Gear down, before landing checklist.

S: Pilot, scanner. We've got damage to the right inboard flaps from number three coming apart.

P: Roger.

CP: Gear down. [*The copilot lowered the gear handle. The flaps were already partially down from the takeoff.*]

P: Okay, I think we've got it made.

S: Pilot, scanner's coming upstairs.

CP: [*From the checklist*] Landing gear down and aligned, crosswind positioning is not installed, flaps forty percent and slats extended, GPWS[44] is on, brake pressure normal. Engineer, did we miss anything on that checklist?

E: Negative. Before landing checklist completed. Do you want to select the alternate brakes?

P: Negative, number four hydraulic system's still intact. Keep an eye on it 'till we get on the ground. If we lose number four, we'll go ahead and select number one hydraulics.

P: Flaps landing.

CP: Flaps landing. [*The copilot lowered the flaps the rest of the way.*]

Four and a half minutes after takeoff, Major Haszard landed the crippled jet.

CP: Nice touchdown.

P: Spoilers. Reversing number two. Looks like we're okay. The fire trucks are up there on the right. We'll just taxi on off the end of the runway and shut down by the fire trucks.

CP: Tower, MAC 90016, we'll shut down number four with the fire handle when we get off to the fire trucks.

Tower: MAC 90016 Roger.

P: Here are the fire trucks so we can go ahead and shut down number four. Number four fire handle, pulled.

CP: Roger.
Tower, 90016 is shutting down number four at this time with the fire handle.

Tower: 90016 tower copies. Fire chief requests you shut down number one and two.

---

[43]final (approach)—Last part of a landing pattern before touchdown. Last part of a bombing attack before weapons release.

[44]GPWS (Ground Proximity Warning System)—Safety System on a C-5 that sounds a warning when the aircraft is too low.

E: Copilot, engineer: You need to select alternate brakes with number four shutdown.

CP: Roger.

P: Scanner, you're cleared out. Go ahead and chock[45] the nose gear.

Troop, get the people down and move them to the crew entrance door.

After landing checklist.

P: Okay, ready engineer?

E: Ready. We're on the right [side] APU[46].

P: We'll shut down number two then number one, finish up the checklists and get out of here.

Major Haszard's crew was awarded the Air Force Association President's Award for airmanship in recognition of the skill they displayed by averting what would have been a very serious accident. They also got the rest of that day off.

Captain Armstrong continues:

It was the most brilliant C-5 flying I've heard of, and thank God we don't have to hear of brilliant flying like that very often.

Toward Christmas and the start of the war, when MAC started getting its act in gear, they initiated something called the pilot pool. We were still working on the pony-express concept where the rider got off and the pony continued with a new rider. Pilots were the restricting factor because we had enough engineers, crew chiefs, and loadmasters to handle the system (they worked very hard). A pool of pilots hung around in Rhine-Main and Torrejon crew resting until they were selected to fill out a crew for the 24-hour flight downrange[47] and back. Those homeless pilots then went back into the pool until their next trip 12 hours later. Pilot poolers logged so much time because they were on trips nearly 24 hours out of every 36.

We had fatigue limits on how much flying we could do. I hit those limits, burned out, about eight times during the war including right at the end of December. I got back to Dover on the 23rd and so got to go home to my parents for Christmas Eve. I was jet-lagged and exhausted

---

[45]chock—(noun) Block of wood or plastic wedged under a tire to prevent it from rolling. (verb) To put the chock in place.

[46]APU—Auxiliary power unit. A small jet engine in the fuselage of a plane that supplies electric, hydraulic, and pneumatic power for ground and emergency operations.

[47]downrange—Final destination. In this case, it refers to the Persian Gulf area of operations.

but at least I was home. Then I went back overseas on the 26th and was over France for New Year's.

Somebody came up with the terrific idea of mailing Christmas cards to Any Soldier, but it backfired. We had planeloads of highly supportive cards that caused the guys offloading to weep at all the extra work. All they could do was push them off to the side until somebody eventually distributed the cards. It was a mixed blessing.

We were over the Adriatic when the BBC announced the start of the war and the first Scuds hitting Israel. In the hotel later, I got to see tape of that marvelous footage of the fight over Baghdad. The only change for us was a few days on the ground as the war started and transports were kept away. When we picked up again, we carried missiles, missiles, missiles, lots of Patriot missiles. The ground crews downrange were very tense and nervous but the operation ran fairly smoothly in spite of the griping and grousing about the poor command and control.

I was fully behind the President. I thought he was a terrific leader during the war and I enjoyed working for him.

One time, we flew to Tel Aviv and picked up some mine sweepers that we had given the Israelis years ago. Mind you, they were getting hit with Scuds and were being really good about not retaliating. But we had to fly those mine sweepers to Frankfurt where somebody else flew them downrange because the Saudis would not accept a plane or cargo direct from Israel, even then.

I can't remember how I heard that the bullets stopped flying. It was a gradual winding down for the C-5s so nothing changed at the end of the fighting. Our mission didn't change for the start of combat or the end of combat. We just kept on flying.

For me, the war is a gaping black hole out of my life spent flying the C-5.

George Armstrong introduced his daughter to flight and supported her in her ambitions ever since. The fact that those ambitions took her to jets and a military career was icing on the cake.

George Armstrong:

I entered Princeton University in the fall of 1941. The war came along, so I went off as a private in the Army for three and a half years. After the war, I went back to college, got married, and then joined the CIA. I then became an automobile dealer in 1960 and sold my business in 1979.

My partner in business taught me to fly in his Piper P12; my wife, Jane, was horrified. Anne came out to fly with me in a Cessna 150 a couple of times and seemed to like it. She was about 14 and almost scared me half to death. I thought, "This child will never, never learn anything about flying." Then she took a couple of lessons and got the bug for flying. I was delighted.

I went to her college graduation and didn't know if I should stand at attention and call her sir or madam when I gave her the lieutenant's bars. That was quite amusing and I was very, very proud of her.

I've always wanted to fly and thought the Air Force was a terrific opportunity for her, especially since she really loved it. That is kind of ironic since I was such a poor soldier. And I was very much impressed with the training she got in Columbus, Mississippi. I was very much impressed with the attitude of the training officers there toward everybody and especially toward women. Anne and the other women were treated just like the men. I thought her flying jets was great.

Jane and I attended her graduation from pilot training, which was really something. So she was launched off on a career in the Air Force.

Anne's being in the Air Force and doing what she wanted, especially flying, was absolutely marvelous. I had had a pretty good career in the CIA and then a very confining career in the automobile business. It kept me working at something I really didn't like for years, but Anne didn't have to face that. Furthermore, she could fly those hot airplanes, it didn't cost her anything, and she would see the world. I went even further in my mind's eye and thought that there were certain advantages to being a woman in the Air Force. There were opportunities for a bright girl that weren't found in other lines of work.

My wife's dominant thought, of course, was the danger of flying. She was brought up in a generation when her parents never flew, ever. I was brought up to look at airplanes as exciting, so that's the way I looked at Anne's flying. It gave me great pleasure to see that she'd done well and was well-treated in training. I had to swallow my own pride at her mastering those skills that were way beyond me.

I would have sided with her if she had really hankered after flying one of those fighter airplanes. I frankly approved of keeping women out of combat, but I have since modified my view about that. There are all kinds of problems with women and men being that close together in real bad combat situations.

When Anne started flying the C-5, I thought it's kind of ridiculous to think of a 5'8" girl flying an airplane that looks about as big as the Eiffel Tower. It doesn't make any sense. Half the people we tell don't seem to believe that our daughter flew the biggest airplane in the free world.

When Kuwait was invaded, I figured right away that she would be in the thick of it. Her mother was really upset, of course. I figured Anne was going to have a hell of a good time flying and she wouldn't have to do the chickenshit things around the office that she didn't like. I thought that was great because I'm a firm believer in being busy at what you want to do. I wasn't apprehensive about the first part, the build-up, though there was apprehension about chemicals and missiles later.

Anne stayed in Europe most of the time and didn't come home very much. But she's a great telephoner and said she was happy, busy. She had a lot of command duty, which I thought was great. She apparently handled it very well. What more could you want?

I kept telling my wife that there was very little danger, that her airplanes were pretty safe, and that Annie had said they flew way to the south and west of Kuwait. There was a lot of work and discomfort, sleeping in hotels, but they also drank a lot of beer in officer's clubs—I liked the thought of that myself.

She described some of the snafus that happened and was quite bitter about some of the things that had gone wrong with administration. I told her that that was just the way it is in a war.

In a situation like that, I felt sorry for the ones who were left out. Anne was right in the middle of it, and that was the place to be. You can't ask anything more than to be right in the middle of it which was a great privilege, I thought. I sensed from Anne's voice that she was very busy, very enthusiastic about what she was doing, and glad to be where she was. Years earlier, I wouldn't have missed the Second World War for anything.

We saw the start of the war on television. After that first broadcast from Baghdad, with all the stuff going up in the air, I grew a little apprehensive about Anne. We didn't know where she was. The only thing safeguarding her would be the distance she could put between herself and Iraq. There was the chemical warfare and Scud missiles to worry about, so we were very, very glad when most of that didn't materialize.

Neighbors and friends asked, "Aren't you very proud of your daughter?" and, "Isn't she in great danger?" Of course we were proud, but flying the fighters was much more dangerous than flying C-5s. She was in more danger from the crowded skies than from the Iraqi air force.

My wife handled the war by consciously trying not to think about it. She put it out of her mind. I would reassure her and then Annie would call and say she went to Sicily and drank a lot of beer or she went to Turkey and bought a rug for us. That helped.

My attitude on women in the military has changed a little bit. I think it would be fine if women were allowed to fly fighters. I'd be all for it; whatever Annie wanted to do would be fine with me.

Part Two:

After Five Months in the Desert, It's Personal—Day One

Lost and Found

I found a passport yesterday
as I walked through the gutted passenger terminal
at Kuwait International.
Laying next to it was a ticket
dated 2 August 1990.
Both were just left behind
on that day.
I thumbed through the passport
only to find the picture of a little girl
from Sri Lanka.
She was traveling alone.
I know because there was a note
from her parents.
I couldn't bear to hold the passport
so I just put it back where it was left.
I hope she is safe,
but I will never know.
I hope I did the right thing.

David Hafer   11 Mar 91
Air Force pilot
Riyadh

2

Solo against the SAMs[1]

Navy Lieutenant Phil Gardner, Chauncey, was an unlikely fighter pilot. Very few Harvard men from privileged backgrounds pass on the chance to make their fortunes in favor of the military. But fighter pilots are born, not bred, so he answered the call of an intense profession that is a full world away from the boardroom.

Chauncey's jet was the F/A-18 Hornet. Arguably the most agile fighter in the world, the Hornet is the only American jet that really does everything well. Armed with radar and heat-seeking missiles plus the Vulcan cannon, it's a formidable fighter. With a realistic bomb load nearly three times that of the F-16, plus antiradiation missiles, the Hornet also excels in attack[2]. And it's a joy to fly. Some may wonder, however, at

---

[1]SAM—Surface-to-air missile. Missile fired from the ground and guided to the target by radar, heat, laser, or some other energy. Soviet SAMs are designated "SA" and a number (such as SA-6); the higher the number, the newer and more deadly the missile. When plotted on a flier's map, the max ranges of these weapons form rings of defended territory. SAMs and their control systems were the targets of early Desert Storm attacks.

[2]attack—Though generically known as fighter pilots, attack pilots bring the fight directly to the enemy forces on the battlefield. Not fighters dueling high out of sight or bombers leveling whole acres, attack pilots fight in the teeth of the air defenses and often within easy sight of the friendly troops. One attack pilot was paraphrased as saying aerial combat was simply the irritating delay attack pilots have to put up with as they shoot down any fighters that try to interfere with their real mission of hitting ground targets. A pair of USS *Saratoga* F/A-18s dispatched a pair of Iraqi MiG-21s just that way before delivering their bombs as planned.

the judgment of fliers who throw their bodies onto pitching carrier flight decks[3], at night, in bad weather, for lieutenant's pay.

Lieutenant Gardner:

I was born into an upper-middle class family in Morristown, New Jersey, in 1963. I lived in a big, white house in the suburbs until I went to a little boarding school called Groton up in Massachusetts. I then studied at Harvard College in Cambridge for four years to major in political science with some work in economics.

At the end of college, I looked at everyone going into investment banking and decided that I-banking wasn't what I wanted to do right then. At that time in the eighties, everyone from Harvard went to Wall Street.

My grandfather was in the Navy during World War II and my father was also in the Navy for two or three years—subs. Joining the Navy for a couple of years after college was becoming a family tradition. I knew that I wanted to fly jets ever since I was a little kid and flying for the Navy off a carrier was probably the best way for me to get into combat. So I was mostly attracted by the excitement and the danger of flying on and off an aircraft carrier day and night.

I showed up at Pensacola, Florida, in September 1985, got all my hair shaved off and began AOCS[4]. After graduating near the bottom of my class because my military standards were so bad, I went to Corpus Christi, Texas, to fly the T-34 basic trainer. What a fun little aircraft. I graduated at the top of my class and selected Beeville, Texas, for primary and advanced jet training. The jet you fly out in the fleet is determined by your training grades, so I really busted my hump those 20-plus months in Corpus and Beeville.

It was at the end of the T-2 Buckeye syllabus that I first did some carrier work. My first carrier landing is something I'll remember for as long as I live. I came aboard the USS *Lexington* 65 miles off Key West. I remember orbiting overhead the boat, solo, and being amazed that I was actually going to land on that postage stamp. All I could think about was not screwing up; I was too busy to get nervous. I remember lining up in the groove[5] for my first real landing and thinking how small and rickety the ship looked. The real thing was so different from our practices back

---

[3]flight deck—On a carrier, the flight deck is the flat part on top covered with the semicontrolled chaos of flight operations. Aircraft take off and land on the flight deck.

[4]AOCS—Aviation Officer Candidate School. Fourteen weeks of basic military training by Marine drill instructors. See *An Officer and a Gentleman.*

[5]groove—Glidepath to a landing on a carrier.

at the field. My landings went surprisingly well and the catapult (cat) shots were just awesome. I flew back to Texas with my shins and shoulders all bruised up from the traps[6]. Pretty amazing.

As advanced jet training finished, I had to put down my preferences on what jet I wanted to fly in the fleet. I put down F/A-18s on East Coast as my first choice and was ecstatic when I was told that I was headed to Cecil Field in Jacksonville, Florida, to fly the Hornet.

I showed up at Jacksonville in December 1987. It was in my six-month RAG[7] stint that I made my first night carrier landing. Flying off a carrier is not bad until it gets dark, then it can get ugly really fast. I finally showed up in my squadron, VFA-81, the Sunliners, in the spring of 1988. The squadron had just transitioned from the A-7 Corsair so it was a brand new VFA[8] squadron. I got in on the ground floor and was a Sunliner for almost three years before Desert Storm.

All squadrons go through extended workup cycles in preparation for cruise so we went through our training track in anticipation of our scheduled August 1990 deployment to the Mediterranean. The idea behind workups is to first train the individual squadrons and then have all the different squadrons of an air wing, F/A-18s, F-14s, A-6s, S-3s, etc., come together and learn to fight as a team. Our air wing, CVW-17 with the USS *Saratoga*, would replace another carrier and air wing for our six month turn in the Med as part of the 6th fleet.

The workup schedule starts almost a year prior to the cruise and wraps up with some very intense war games off Puerto Rico. During those war games, I flew an incredible amount—three or four times a day. I became so tired that I almost fell asleep up on CAP[9] station the last night guarding the ship. I remember groggily coming aboard the ship at dawn and sleeping for 16 hours after that night.

The air wing and the ship had a real slow start to workups—we just weren't doing many things right. But as the year progressed, the air wing

---

[6]trap—To land on a carrier and be stopped, trapped, by the arresting gear.

[7]RAG—Replacement Air Group. Navy and Marine units that train qualified pilots in the specific missions of their new squadrons.

[8]VFA—Navy and Marine squadrons are designated according to their missions and equipment. V means heavier than air, F means fighters, A means attack, M means Marine and H means helicopter. So VFA-81 is a naval heavier-than-air squadron that flies both fighter and attack missions.

[9]CAP—Combat Air Patrol. Interceptors roaming assigned areas looking for trouble. Interceptors sweeping in front of a strike to clear the skies of enemy aircraft. Fighter patrols to gain and maintain air superiority. Allied fighters did a spectacular job and never lost an escorted friendly to an enemy fighter.

really got its act together and the flight deck started to work well. We were ready for cruise.

After workups, cruise is supposed to be a piece of cake and the *Saratoga* was scheduled for a love boat cruise. We were going to bounce around the Med spending most of our time in exotic ports in France, Italy, and the eastern Med. That all changed on August 2nd. When the Iraqis moved into Kuwait, our beautiful Med plans were scrapped and the *Saratoga* was ordered to buster[10] to the Middle East to show the flag. We ended up spending most of Desert Shield and all of Desert Storm doing figure eights in the northern Red Sea just south of the Suez Canal. It wasn't pretty.

As officers, fliers lived in staterooms with one or two other guys stacked up in the same tiny cubicle. The enlisted men lived with sometimes 75 to a room. I lived directly underneath the bow catapults with another guy. The noise and banging when they launched jets was horrendous, but, like anything else on the ship, you just got used to it. The living conditions were pretty bad. The *Saratoga* is an old boat; she'd been in salt water since the mid 1950s and showed her age. Coming home from a day flight, you could always find the Sara by the huge oil slick she left in her wake.

My typical Desert Shield day started with a wake up at, say, eight or nine in the morning after getting to bed between one and two. I'd go through a flight briefing and then launch at 11 or 12. We'd typically fly a low level and drop some practice bombs or play with the F-14s or the EA-6B, our jammer plane. We also did a lot of night flying to stay current and sometimes ran profiles against destroyer or cruiser escorts to give them some practice defending the battle group. Luckily, the weather in the Red Sea was almost always good.

In normal cyclic operations, the ship catapults a batch of aircraft off the front end to fly their hour-and-thirty-minute missions. While they're out, another batch of aircraft is readied for launch. At the end of their missions, the first group of aircraft orbit overhead the ship waiting for the deck to clear as the second group of aircraft shoots off for their missions. The orbiting aircraft then recover back aboard the ship. Little trucks, called yellow gear, drag the planes to the back of the ship because deck space is at an absolute premium. The planes are chained down, armed, and fueled while we preflight them. When its time to start shooting jets off the front end again, the plane captains[11] take all the

---

[10]buster—Hurry. Signal to go to full speed. Used by attack pilots when entering the target area or when bandits are present.

[11]plane captain—Enlisted man responsible for the care and feeding of a Navy or Marine aircraft. See crew chief.

chains off and you taxi up to one of the catapults. This is all part of a big orchestration that ensures the right planes get to the right catapults, in the right order, at the right time. The process continues on and on as the rearmed aircraft are catapulted to make room for the returning missions. It's an amazing show to watch in such a small space.

After we had been out at sea for a while, all the antiskid material wore off the flightdeck so it became as slick as an ice-skating rink. During the war, we had to be unbelievably careful because the nose wheel steering was basically worthless. We had dozens of 45,000-pound combat-loaded jets skidding around the deck trying to get somewhere without ending up over the side. It was a dance with 22-ton ballerinas.

There's a group of pilots who stand on a platform on the back end of the ship and ensure that you don't kill yourself getting back aboard. They're called LSOs[12], landing signal officers. They grade each landing and it's a real point of pride to come aboard the ship, not only safely, but looking real good too. As soon as you hit the deck, you go to full power in case you miss the arresting wires or your hook[13] skips the wires. If you miss the wires, you go around the pattern and try it again.

Naval aviation is just eye watering. I am continuously amazed that we can condense the activity of Newark Airport onto a metal deck 60 feet above the water.

During Desert Shield, we practiced a number of the strikes[14] that we would later fly into Iraq. We called those practices "mirror images." We flew them just like the real mission only, as we approached Iraq, we'd bend everyone back to the south and finish the run over Saudi Arabia. Those practice strikes were enormous with upwards of 40 jets and five tankers in one piece of sky.

During Desert Shield, we had the feeling that we were fairly well supported back home but we didn't know for sure. We were really isolated from the rest of the world as we sat in the middle of nowhere with the BBC as our only up-to-date news. The Brits had a great slant on everything. They were supportive and always took events in a more humorous vein than we did. I also enjoyed listening to the BBC because it was more fact-filled and objective than our news. It gave us the European perspective and reported on the coalition's political bickering.

---

[12]LSO—Landing signal officer. Specially trained flier on duty at the back of a carrier to ensure all landings are safe and to grade the landings.

[13]hook—Arresting gear tailhook on the back of a carrier-based airplane.

[14]strike—Long-range bombing attack made deep in the enemy's territory.

We got mail infrequently out there on the back end of the supply pipeline. Not only did the mail have to go through New York to Saudi Arabia, it had to be dragged all the way across Saudi Arabia to Jeddah and then make its way out to the ship. So we didn't know much about our support from home until Desert Storm started.

That's when support from home became just unbelievable. I was writing to six or seven grade-school classes at one time and was swamped with care packages from friends of friends. It was just unbelievable. We plastered the inside of our stateroom with kids' drawings of planes landing on the carrier and of Saddam Hussein. We had custom made fifth grade wallpaper. I really enjoyed the mail and it really helped our spirits.

As the January 15th deadline rolled around, we really had no idea when the kickoff was planned. It was hard to discern what was political posturing and what was real preparation for war. I was lounging in my rack on January 16 at about 7:30 A.M. when my squadron skipper[15], "Spock" Anderson, called and said that we had a target time. We were to be overhead Baghdad that coming night at 4 A.M.

I got up, showered, and headed down to CVIC[16]. I basically had very little final strike planning to do before the 9 P.M. brief time; all we had to do was fill in a couple of blanks on our kneeboard cards. We had spent literally hundreds of hours during Desert Shield planning every single detail of the mission.

I tried to sleep in the afternoon but ended up staring at the ceiling for two hours. I just lay in bed and sweated. I wasn't particularly scared right then but I was incredibly wired up and jumpy.

Spock briefed the strike at 9:00 that night in the CVIC. We had mirror imaged this strike so many times that the brief was pretty standard by then. But, obviously, that night was different. The admiral was there, the captain of the ship was there, CVIC was jammed with people. It was after the CVIC brief, when we headed back down to our ready room and pulled out the revolvers, that I started to get really wired up and scared. Sitting around waiting to walk to the flight deck was always the worst part of any mission.

The President and the Joint Chiefs picked a good night to start the festivities: it was really dark on the opening night. There was an overcast layer over the Red Sea so we got no moon or starlight.

I preflighted as much of my jet as I could but, as usual, most of the back end was hanging out over the water. I did get a good chance to

---

[15]Skipper—Commander. The Boss.

[16]CVIC—Carrier Intelligence Center. "CV" stands for carrier, fixed wing.

preflight my HARMs[17] and check out my Sparrows[18] and Sidewinders[19]. The deck crews were incredibly pumped up knowing that we were going to start delivering some of the weapons that they had been loading on our jets for so long. The ordies[20] had covered each one of my HARMs with grease-pencil graffiti addressed mainly to Saddam, his mother, and his camel.

The Sara launched 10 Hornets for the "wild weasel[21]" mission, A-6s with MK-84s[22], EA-6Bs for jamming, and F-14s for high value unit[23] CAP protection of the Prowlers. I made a full blower[24] launch as scheduled at about 0130 with three HARMs, a full air-to-air load and two drop tanks.

After uncaging my brain from the heavy cat shot[25], my first job was to check in with our Red Crown radar controller as I entered the MEZ[26]. I was worried about getting shot by our own guys almost as much as by the Iraqis that first night.

Our flight of KC-135[27] tankers showed up early at the rendezvous point over Saudi and we started to get the strike package together. There was a really rough chop[28] at 21,000 feet. The basket[29] jumped around so

---

[17]HARM—High-speed anti-radiation missile. Very fast, very lethal air-to-ground radar homing missile used to kill radar sites. Follow-on to the Shrike carried by the original Wild Weasels in Southeast Asia.

[18]Sparrow (AIM-7)—Radar-guided, air-to-air missile used at long range.

[19]Sidewinder (AIM-9)—Heat-seeking, air-to-air missile used in a dogfight between gun and radar missile ranges. Very lethal.

[20]ordies—Ordnance specialists. Weapons loaders. The guys who arm the airplanes.

[21]Wild Weasel—F-4G Phantom II anti-SAM fighter. Descended from the F-100 and F-105 Wild Weasels, these fliers display the solid brass parts of their anatomies by hunting surface-to-air missiles. Other aircraft, such as the F/A-18 Hornet, have a limited Weasel capability also. Imagine trolling for Jaws.

[22]MK-84—("mark eighty-four") General-purpose, 2000-pound, high-explosive bomb.

[23]high value unit—HVU. Navy term for an airborne asset worth protecting with its own escort.

[24]blowers—Afterburners. Cans. Reheat.

[25]cat—Catapult

[26]MEZ—Missile engagement zone. One of the defensive rings around a naval battle group, the MEZ is an extremely dangerous place for hostile or unidentified aircraft or any aviator who's recently insulted a radar operator. See Robocruiser.

[27]KC-135—Tanker or refueling aircraft based on the Boeing 707 airframe. Any aircraft with a "K" prefix is a tanker. They were some of the unsung heroes of the war.

[28]chop—Light turbulence, like driving on a rough road.

[29]basket—Aircraft that use probe and drogue refueling, like Navy and Marine aircraft as well as helicopters, plug into a cone-shaped receptacle, the basket, on the end of the refueling hose.

much that I could hardly get into the thing. When the air is rough, tanking off the 135 is an incredible amount of work. Right on schedule, the tankers broke out of the rendezvous track and started dragging us north toward the Iraqi border. We broke the Iraqi's high EW[30] line at about 0230 while slightly east of Al Jouf airfield in Saudi.

My first HARM shot was at 0400 and 15 seconds just to the east of Al Taqaddum airfield, which is about 25 miles outside Baghdad. The winds at altitude were over 100 knots[31] from the west, so I hung on the Saudi-Iraqi border for a minute after the tankers left us. The last thing I wanted was to be blown up to Baghdad early by the wind and have to orbit waiting for my HARM shots. I went through the combat checklist step by step and as methodically as I could. I wasn't that nervous but was incredibly wired. I was so busy making sure that I didn't get killed that I didn't have time to get nervous.

At about 0320, I pushed north and crossed the border. I shut my mode one, my mode three and my mode charley squawks[32] off and shut my lights out. My air-to-air radar and RWR[33] systems were on: the radar had lots of contacts (friends) and the RWR was spiking a lot. I never realized how much I was going to rely on the ALR-67[34]. It was a godsend.

Passing over Mudaysis airfield in Iraq, I could see the remnants of a B-52 strike. The whole southern part of Iraq lit up from that strike. The B-52s basically pounded that field into oblivion.

As I proceeded north, I had some nasty RWR spikes that I never really could confirm. Anytime I heard anything out of my RWR, I punched out some chaff[35] and moved the jet around. I just couldn't figure out who was locking me up.

With the big westerly winds, I kept on having to throttle back and slow down. That was really uncomfortable, but I figured it was better to

---

[30]EW—Early warning radar.

[31]knot—Nautical mile per hour. A knot equals about 1.14 miles, so 480 knots equals about 550 mph.

[32]squawk—(noun) Electronic transponder that identifies an aircraft. (verb) To intentionally transmit that identification signal.

[33]RWR—Radar warning receiver. Sensors that give fliers the direction and identity of radars that are looking at them. Very sophisticated radar detector that works on surface and airborne radars. Provides both audible and visible warning. To a flier in Indian country, this display of bad-guy radars is the neatest thing since hangover remedies.

[34]ALR-67—RWR system on an F/A-18 Hornet.

[35]chaff—Radar-reflecting strips of metallic foil released in bunches to confuse radar. Bundles of chaff are released in clouds designed to blind enemy radar and decoy radar-guided missiles.

go slow down in the south, and then speed up as I got in towards Baghdad, than to enter the fight slow. I found a couple scud[36] layers to hide out in. My game plan that night was to hide as I drove up towards my shot point. Pretty stupid game plan in retrospect but that's what I did.

There was an enormous amount of chatter on the radios. The number two (back) radio was on a Navy flight common frequency[37] with the number one radio tuned to the E-3 AWACS[38], callsign CHOCTAW. The AWACS controller made bull's-eye[39] calls off of a cluster of islands in the big lake to the south and west of Baghdad. When I first dialed up the AWACS freq, I heard calls like, "BOGEYS[40] CAPPING OVER BULL'S-EYE" and knew that it was going to get colorful. There was supposed to have been an F-15 sweep[41] to clean those guys out but, for some reason, the bandits[42] were orbiting—just waiting for us. It was weird. The radio calls sounded exactly like the ones we'd heard in our training at Fallon (Nevada). Unfortunately, this time it was the real thing.

There was some real buffoonery[43] on the back radio. An EA-6B got separated from his F-14 escort and garbaged up the whole back radio with their yelling and screaming trying to find each other. That crap on the radios denied all of us the situational awareness[44] we could have

---

[36]scud—Here, scud means thin cloud layer, not the missile.

[37]Navy common—Frequency used together by all Navy aircraft in an operation. Air Force slang for the emergency frequency all military aircraft must monitor, but only the Navy seems to use to chat. See Guard.

[38]AWACS—Airborne Warning and Control System. Heavily modified Boeing 707 airframe sporting a radar disk on top that monitors huge volumes of the sky. Used to spot enemy aircraft and control the battle from behind friendly lines.

[39]bull's-eye—Common geographic reference point. Usually refers to the common reference used by radar controllers to point out enemy aircraft such as, "Bandit, bull's-eye one six zero (degrees) for 30 (nautical miles), heading South at 35,000 feet, 700 knots."

[40]bogey—Unidentified and possibly hostile aircraft. Could be friendly, neutral/civilian, or hostile. Treated as hostile for monitoring but will not be attacked unless confirmed hostile. See bandit.

[41]sweep—To clear the sky. What interceptors do to the sky ahead of the strike formations they protect, as in "sweep the sky of MiGs."

[42]bandit—Confirmed hostile aircraft.

[43]buffoonery—To behave like a lower primate (apologies to those buffoons who know the real correlation between fighter pilots and even hairier primates). Some would say flying fighters isn't exactly smart in the first place, so comparing the low points to ape behavior is considered insulting by real buffoons.

[44]situational awareness—SA. How well an airman knows what's going on around him or her. The critical, unteachable, unmeasurable quality that good airmen have and poor airmen don't. Most fliers have it, while some—the lucky or the dead—don't. Opposite of clueless.

given each other by talking. Those crews deserved the shit they got when they returned to the Sara that morning.

As I approached my shot point, Spock Anderson, in a much elevated voice, announced: "CHOCTAW, I'VE GOT A FAST MOVER LOCKED UP[45] ON MY NOSE FOR ABOUT 15 MILES DOING (mach[46]) 1.2!" CHOCTAW couldn't identify him and the ROE[47] didn't allow Spock to shoot the MiG. Spock called: "I HAVE A MiG ON MY NOSE[48] AT SEVEN MILES!" That's a hairy situation, especially at night. It turned out that a division[49] of MiG-25s got airborne and they were raising cain. But they were basically clueless. I think they got airborne just prior to a strike on their field and had nowhere to land. With their Soviet training, those guys were idiots without GCI[50] and we jammed their controllers. So they just flew around at the speed of heat causing trouble. In fact, one MiG-25 went right over the A-6 strike package and scared the crap out of them. The Deputy CAG[51], who was leading the A-6s, kept on saying: "SOMEBODY SHOOT THAT SON OF A BITCH!" over the second radio. I certainly thought about it but it was like everyone was scorching around at mach speed inside a fishbowl. It was just too hard to keep track of everything and be sure to shoot the right jet.

As I approached my shot point, there was a lot of chatter from the A-6 guys as they got close to their target, Al Taquaddum airfield. As the A-6s approached, the lights were still on at the field and I could clearly see the lights of Baghdad just off my right wing.

As the first A-6s dropped their MK-84s, I could see bombs detonate

---

[45]lock—Radar lock-on. To highlight a target by radar just prior to killing it.

[46]mach—Aircraft speed relative to the speed of sound. Point 94 mach, for example, is 94% of the speed of sound.

[47]ROE—Rules of engagement. Who can shoot what, when, and how. A sore point with the military because politically imposed ROE allowed the Koreans, Chinese, and Vietnamese to use sanctuaries in past wars.

[48]nose—Front of the airplane. "The targets are on/off the nose" means directly in front of the airplane.

[49]division—Navy and Marine term for four aircraft in formation. See four ship.

[50]GCI—Ground-controlled intercept. Under the Soviet system, fighters are held on a short leash by radar controllers and become very dependent on directions over the radio. Western fliers, conversely, are barely controllable in the best of times (sic) and so need only be pointed in the right direction with permission to fire. Western pilots are selected for initiative and individual skill, giving them a distinct advantage over pilots dependent on GCI. That also partially explains their formidable and well-deserved egos.

[51]CAG—Carrier Air Group. Unit composed of all aircraft stationed on a carrier. "The CAG" usually refers to the wing commander who leads all the aircraft assigned to his carrier.

plus secondary explosions[52]. About that time, the triple-A[53] went absolutely bonkers. It looked almost comical and reminded me of a cheap county fair where the lights blink in sequence. There were arcs of different colored tracers flying all over the place. My ALR-67 picked up missiles over on the right hand side but I never got locked directly by anything.

I got to the shot point on time, 0400 plus 15 seconds, and hosed a HARM off on my SA-2 target. The HARM launch was unbelievably spectacular. It blasted off with a very bright flash and then, about 2000 feet in front of the jet, went into its roll program and blasted into the ionosphere. The HARM left the jet with this prolonged WHOOOSH sound. Pure speed. Some of the bombers broke[54] on our HARMs thinking that they had SAMs coming at them. I shot my second HARM a couple of miles closer to the target and that one took off like a scalded ape as well.

There was so much stuff in the air by then that I just couldn't digest it all. The Iraqis were barrage-firing from their SAM sites (shooting everything they had), triple-A was everywhere, and we were shooting back with tons of HARMS.

After my second shot, I planned to orbit outside the target SAM envelopes[55] and save my last HARM for any direct threats to the A-6s or the British Tornados that were scheduled to follow them. I started my orbit and went to the scan option on the HARM. "Jesus Christ," I remember muttering to myself, "this is insane. I'm doing lazy circles over Baghdad!" CHOCTAW was still talking about airborne bogies, MiG-25s, arcing around and there I was asking one of them to cornhole me south of the target.

The HARM scan option didn't help me much because *everything* was up. Missile guidance signals, target trackers, you name it and I had it. So I decided to switch to the target tracker and right away came up with an SA-2 site. The SA-2 was so strong that I decided to take him and actually had to drop the nose of my Hornet to shoot him. I could see a little white light at the SAM site with the HARM box right over it quivering just like a Sidewinder that's found a heat source. The HARM box was going just bonkers over that SA-2. I couldn't have been more than a cou-

---

[52]secondary explosion—Detonation of something on the ground caused by an attack.

[53]triple-A—Anti-aircraft artillery. Guns that shoot at airplanes. Everything from rifles to 130mm radar-directed cannons with time fuses. Over 80% of aircraft losses are usually due to triple-A. It was the primary reason coalition aircraft fought the war from above 10,000 feet. The nightly light show over Baghdad was triple-A.

[54]break/broke—(verb) As in "break turn," the act of making a max-performance, last-ditch, everything-she's-got turn to avoid being hit by a missile.

[55]envelope—Flight regime of an aircraft or missile as in the altitude, airspeed, and range capabilities.

ple of miles from the site—well inside his envelope. In fact, I started hearing the RWR squawk just as I lowered my nose. I assume he was locking me up at just the same time. I smashed my thumb on the pickle button and unloaded the last missile. That shot was awesome. The HARM left my wing and went straight for that SA-2—it didn't even bother to pitch up. As I looked at the light on the target, the rocket motor hurled right toward it. Unbelievable. I have never seen speed like that in my life.

I watched it for a couple potatoes and then said to myself: "WHAT THE HELL ARE YOU WATCHING THIS SON OF A BITCH FOR? GET THE HELL OUT OF HERE!!" I yanked the jet left to the north and, about halfway through the turn, realized that I was turning the wrong way around rather than the simply turning to the south. Navy pilots always turn left because traffic patterns over the ship are always to the left. I said to myself "You dumb shit. . . ."

I started kicking the ponies but didn't light the cans[56] 'cause I didn't know if the MiG-25s were still arcing around. CHOCTAW was talking about other bandits to the west so I decided not to highlight myself with burner plumes. I locked the throttles full forward, which gave me almost mach.

As I headed out, the triple-A went absolutely bonkers. The sky over Baghdad and south of Taquaddum was lit up with bizarre-looking, overlapping, fluorescent spaghetti. The Iraqis must have done a ton of damage to themselves with all that stuff settling back down on their heads.

I looked back over at Baghdad and saw big old SAMs rising but really not guiding on anybody. There were plenty of SAMs rising from Taquaddum too. I was picked out by Iraqi radar a couple times on the way home but kept putting chaff out and maneuvering. I figured the farther south I moved, the better off I was.

I got to the exit point at 27,000 feet and, as briefed, turned my squawk back on. My lights went on full bright near the Saudi border, so the F-15s wouldn't shoot me, and I checked in with CHOCTAW. He had me in radar contact so I felt like I could get back into Saudi airspace without getting zapped. That was a scary egress[57], a real scary egress. I checked in with Skipper Spock on the second radio and told him I made it out all right.

As we all approached the KC-135 tanker south of the border, we realized Scott Spiecher wasn't with us. We'd lost him.

The air in the refueling track was fairly smooth but I still had a

---

[56]cans—Afterburners. Reheat. Blowers.

[57]egress—To leave the target area.

tough time. I was pretty rattled, and, in fact, fell out of the basket once and had to plug in again. The skipper was real low on gas after playing with that MiG-25 up north, so he refueled first. Sitting on the tanker's wing, I asked our E-2 and the other guys on the second radio if they had heard from Spike. No one had heard anything. None of us could figure out what to do other than make sure that everyone was aware of his potential loss.

The autopilot took me south as I tried to relax. I headed for the entrance point to the MEZ and, with another 200 miles to go, tried to settle down as much as possible. I even unstrapped and took a leak though I really didn't need to. For some reason, taking a leak in the cockpit always seems to cool your nerves a little bit.

As I approached the MEZ entrance point, I called up Red Crown for clearance. I made real sure that Red Crown had the proper squawk and position on me. The last thing I needed was for some Aegis playing Robocruiser[58] to start lobbing Standard missiles at me.

As I went feet wet, Red Crown handed me off to the Sara's approach controllers, who did a real nice job of slowly vectoring us down to get us aboard. I told them, "Hey guys, I'll need some time on the final bearing tonight to get my act together." They were real helpful and gave me five miles on final to settle down. I was really tired but had a ton of adrenaline pumping. The last thing I wanted to do was kill myself getting back aboard the ship.

As I approached three miles, I told the LSOs to *talk*; meaning I basically wanted a talkdown. The LSOs gave a lot of "sugar" calls as I got inside of a mile from the ramp. They knew how shook up and tired we were after five hours in the air.

I started my pass a little high but worked it off OK for a three wire[59]. I have never had a better feeling than the tug in the straps when I caught that wire. I was incredibly happy to be aboard and alive but was also really bothered that we didn't know about Spike.

The sun was just coming up when I finished debriefing the flight-deck chief on the little mechanical glitches that I had in flight. When I walked below, the ordies already had bombs loaded under the wings of the jet for the next sortie.

I went through almost two hours of debriefing and incredible swings of emotion. One swing was jubilation: I was overjoyed to be alive and to know that I had done some real good work in killing Iraqi

---

[58]Robocruiser—Guided missile cruiser with the Aegis system capable of shooting down everything in the sky almost simultaneously.

[59]three wire—Aircraft carriers have five arresting wires strung across the touchdown zone. Catching the third wire indicates a good landing and is a point of pride with pilots.

SAM sites. Then came a down cycle where I asked myself what those poor slob SAM operators had done to me to justify throwing molten steel cubes on their heads. I killed a number of people that first night. Then it was back to jubilation: "I'm alive! I can't believe how lucky I am to be alive and how proud I am to be a Navy pilot!" Then I thought of the Scott Speicher and sank again. I was so wired up that I didn't get to sleep until noon.

Throughout Desert Storm, I saw people perform incredibly well out there. It really brought out the best in a lot of people and you quickly learned who you could really trust, who you could really depend on. We were lucky in that we had a squadron of very, very aggressive and talented pilots. Very brave too.

Skipping ahead, we knew things went very well with the ground campaign. In fact, the Red Sea side of the house was kept out of the ground business, which was fine. We continued to hit strategic targets in Iraq by finishing off Saddam's chemical and nuclear capability to make sure those facilities were gone when the war ended.

The end of the war wasn't a singular event like a sudden capitulation. For us, it was a slow winding down of the conflict as we launched fewer strikes. We continued to CAP overhead the ship and that was it.

My skipper released me as soon as the fighting stopped since I'd already been extended in the squadron for the war. I caught a helo off of the ship and dragged all around Egypt until I wound up in the cargo bay of a C-130 going to Sicily. I took a C-141 through the Azores to Norfolk and arrived at 6:00 in the morning. We were kind of ratty lookin' after not sleeping for a couple days but the nice group of little old ladies waiting to welcome us couldn't have been more accommodating. I took a five-hour bus trip through rural Virginia to get to Washington and finally got home to Deborah late in the afternoon.

Deborah Gardner is one of those intelligent, independent, and capable women who are so badly stereotyped on programs such as L.A. Law. Unmarried at the time, she'd had almost no contact with the military when her man went to war. She didn't have the benefit of the military family support system, though she certainly had to deal with all of the anxiety.

Deborah Gardner:

I'm from Newton, Massachusetts. Phil and I met during our senior year at Harvard, and, when we graduated, he went into the Navy and I went to law school. Though we lived in separate cities for many years, we saw each other often and made a commitment to speak on the phone almost daily.

Phil was already scheduled to board the *Saratoga* for a routine tour in the Mediterranean Sea when Kuwait was invaded on August 2, 1990. Ironically, as I left Phil in Jacksonville, all I thought about was the damn airline's cancellation of my flight and the consequential inconvenience as I scrambled to file some documents at my Boston law firm.

Deep in our hearts, however, we both knew that this "routine" tour would be far from routine. The planned port stops might be delayed or canceled and the tour might be extended. Nobody knew. So, I just tucked those thoughts in the back of my mind and said good-bye hoping we would see each other soon in some far-away place. I had no experience with the military and probably used a lot of denial.

As time went on and August rolled into September and then October and November, those patient thoughts of romance and adventure gave way to anger and frustration. There was so much uncertainty. Glimmers of optimism were dashed daily as the news diminished all hopes of a port stop or an on-time return to the United States. Separation grew painful while I clung to the hope that Phil would be home by January. All those parties that I attended alone; all those nights when I couldn't share my innermost thoughts and feelings; the absence of someone who formed another part of my identity began to wear on me. Mail was infrequent and never informative. Plans were always subject to change. There was so much uncertainty that I had a hard time dealing with our separation, but I still clung to the hope that Phil would be home by January or that I could visit him somewhere, anywhere, in December.

A war seemed impossible. Somehow, the conflict had to end diplomatically.

Meanwhile, Desert Shield, and later Desert Storm, made me aware of just how self-involved I was. Though the country buzzed with talk of the arms build-up, border skirmishes, and the ceaseless shuttling of troops to the Gulf, my thoughts concentrated on Phil and me. If Phil had been killed or even injured in combat, the war would not have been worth it to me. Lofty aims such as depriving Hussein of nuclear capabilities, securing our oil supply, and protecting Kuwait could not divert my mind from one thought—the possibility of life without Phil. To me, the Navy was an inconvenience, a never-ending disruption in my life, a bureaucratic entity that had to be constantly skirted. The war seemed like just one more dirty trick.

Finally, in December, the *Saratoga* made a port stop in Haifa, Israel. Though many Americans were concerned about terrorist threats in the U.S. and particularly in the Middle East, I was determined to see Phil. I eagerly met him in Israel, where we spent two weeks exploring before meeting again in Turkey. Once again proving the shortness of memory, I quickly forgot all worldly concerns and settled right into life with Phil. The Israelis and the Turks were incredibly friendly, offering reduced rates at hotels and generously lending assistance. Tour guides in Israel were ecstatic to guide a Navy pilot.

That little respite seemed no different than all those other holiday adventures snuck in between Navy deployments. However, Phil and I gained new appreciation for each other. Though we had both been very independent in pursuing our own careers and making our own friends, the difficult few months between August and December had made me realize what an important and intricate part of my life he was.

Then a ferry shuttling members of the *Saratoga* from the ship to Haifa sank. All Navy personnel were called in for a head count just after Phil and I checked in to a quaint hotel north of the city, eager to explore some ruins the next day. Phil worried that the ship had been bombed; I worried that Phil was going to board the *Saratoga* and not come back off. All the uncertainty and anxiety that I had felt before coming to Israel returned.

Strangely, the return to Haifa and the funeral ceremony for those who died made me see the Navy community in a very different way. I had been amazed to see how passive the wives were. In contrast, I was hysterical and upset that the Navy once again deprived Phil and me of precious moments. Then I realized that those wives were simply relaxed and easy-going while waiting for the message informing them of the Navy's plans. As I got to know some of the women, I became impressed with their independence, selflessness, and courage. Many of them managed jobs and families while their husbands were off at sea. The ferry incident was time for support rather than a cause for frustration.

I stayed on after Phil went back to sea and was able to get to know some of those other women, becoming particularly close friends with one of them. It was nice to be able to share the feelings of uncertainty and anxiety with others who were similarly situated.

When Phil and I met again in Turkey, we explored ruins and toured the countryside. We became engaged at a beautiful site of old Roman ruins on a cliff overlooking the ocean and two points of land. As we said good-bye two days later, I thought only of our future together. At some point, Hussein would give in to reason and recall his troops. Then Phil would come home.

I was in Washington, D.C., searching for an apartment when the war started. I remember watching a news report at 10:07 one night that a Tomahawk missile had just been launched. What a historic moment that was, watching the beginning of a war as if it were the Olympic games. At midnight, the news reported that the allied airpower had demolished many of the communications centers, strategic buildings, and Iraqi aircraft. I went to sleep oddly exuberant. Maybe it would be over soon.

I awoke the next morning to the telephone. My mother called to tell me that an F-18 from the *Saratoga* had been shot down! The war suddenly seemed so close as if it were leaning on my shoulder whispering, "Wake up!" I began to imagine life without Phil. Other concerns that had been so important paled when I thought of going through life without him. Looking at people that day, I wondered how life went on. Jobs, apartments, politics—it all seemed so insignificant. Didn't people realize what was going on?

On the second night, they announced that another Navy plane was down. In tears, I telephoned my mother, hanging on the phone in the early hours of the morning reconstructing our memories of Phil and desperately hoping that that was not all we would have to remember.

Other sleepless nights followed. Each day, I avidly listened to the Defense Department briefings and read every article on the war. I called the Navy hotline many times seeking reassurance that Phil had not been shot down. Each time, my heart sank as I waited for a response, my eyes tearing in relief when I learned that Phil was still alive.

Phil was supposed to come home immediately after the war stopped because he was overdue for his next assignment at the Pentagon. One day, he called from Saudi Arabia to say that he was coming home. The next day he arrived. He was worn out, but at least he was home.

3
Leaders of the Pack

Marine Captain Dave Deist, Dyno, was a bombardier/navigator (B/N)[1] in VMA(AW) 224 at MCAS[2] Cherry Point, NC. That means he did every-thing but fly the jet. B/Ns find the target, lock onto it for the kill, and then point the way home through whatever the enemy can throw at them. The pilot-B/N team functions smoothly, with virtually no words, and is as tight a bond as a man can have. Get one of their wives started and she'll complain that the other flier seems to know her husband better than she does. And she's often right.

Dyno's pilot on this mission and throughout the war was Captain Paul Andrus, callsign Droid. He was 31 and Dyno was 27 when they led the entire Marine Corps strike on this first mission of the war.

The A-6 first tasted blood in Vietnam. It's an old machine by any standard and has been the subject of nostalgic films for several years now. But it can sure do the job. Routinely lifting 6-ton bomb loads and delivering them spot on, Intruders[3] are the equally lethal cousins of the F-111, the Tornado, and the F-15E. The big difference between those air-

---

[1]bombardier/navigator—B/N. Half of an attack jet's flight crew, the B/N is responsible for everything but the piloting. B/Ns navigate to the target, find it on radar, designate it with the laser, clear the pilot to release the weapons, and then find their way home.

[2]Marine Corps Air Station (MCAS)—Marine Corps flying base.

[3]Intruder (A-6 Intruder)—Navy and Marine Vietnam-era medium bomber. Subsonic, two-seat, very accurate, all-weather workhorse also flown as a four-seat electronic warfare jet (EA-6B Prowler).

craft is survivability. The F-111 is one of the world's fastest aircraft, while the F-15E and Tornado are top fighters. But the Intruder is unarmed and relatively slow. Their aircrews continue the tradition of wooden ships and iron men to get the job done.

Captain Deist:

I grew up in New Castle, Delaware, and graduated from William Penn High School. The Naval Academy at Annapolis was next and I graduated in the Class of '85. I chose the Marine Corps because Marines just seemed like a tighter bunch, more competitive. The Marine Corps seemed to be a bit more elite than the other services. I didn't have the eyes to be a pilot, so I signed up to be a Marine B/N. I went through The Basic School[4] right after graduation, like all Marines, and then waited for my flight school to start around May of '87.

NFO[5] flight school is similar to the pilot course: you start off with weather, communications, navigation, instruments, and aircraft systems for the T-34. You fly the T-34 to get into an airplane with Tacan[6] approaches and squirrel cage[7] stuff. From there, I went to the T-2 for instrument training and ACM[8].

Through the whole NFO program, the instructor in the front seat acts like a voice-actuated autopilot. So if you're flying an approach or ACM, you'd say something like, "Come left to zero nine zero and climb to seven thousand." He'll do that. If you're doing a high yo-yo[9], you'd tell the pilot to come hard left, get the nose up, reverse, etc., and he'll do exactly what you tell him. Then I went into the T-47, which is a Cessna Citation equipped with a radar.

The Navy decides which airplanes people will fly as they go from T-2s to T-47s. Guys who are going to S-3s, EA-6s, and A-6s go to a T-47 with a ground radar. You learn to interpret the radar and navigate with it through the mountains and over flat terrain. We did that flying in the

---

[4]The Basic School—TBS. Marine Corps basic officer training. All Marines start out at TBS and are trained infantrymen. The fliers have a very good idea what the guys they're supporting are going through.

[5]NFO—Naval flight officer. Navy or Marine flier who is not a pilot; B/Ns, for example.

[6]Tacan—Ground-based navigation system that allows fliers to navigate and find a runway without seeing it. In the air-to-air mode, it's used to measure the distance between aircraft.

[7]squirrel cage—Basic acrobatics flown in a defined block of sky. From the outside, the plane looks like a squirrel running around inside a cage.

[8]ACM—Air combat maneuvering. Fundamental dogfighting maneuvers.

[9]yo-yo—Dogfighting maneuver that resembles the up and down movement of a yo-yo as the attacking fighter tries to get behind a rapidly turning target.

East Coast mountain ranges from West Virginia on down and also over the flat areas southeast of Memphis to the coast. I got my wings out of Pensacola and then went up to Whidbey Island, Washington, for eight months of A-6 specifics.

I finished at Whidbey in February of '89 and came right out here to North Carolina. I checked in at the end of March to VMA(AW) 224 and then left on April 4th to WestPac[10] for six months at Iwakuni, Japan. I just had time to put the boxes in the rooms they belonged in and move some furniture around in our new house before I left.

Being the new guy, I got to go on all the dets[11] for training. I got to go to Cubi (Philippines) every time the squadron went down there and to Australia for a couple weeks. I flew as much as anybody in the squadron, which was nice. I finally settled in here at home in North Carolina after that WestPac tour.

We were in a MCCRES[12] in August '90 when things started happening in Kuwait. That exercise was supposed to be our big test before going back to Iwakuni in October '90. We were just starting our preparations when we got the word to forget about the MCCRES 'cause we were going to the Middle East. We'd already started thinking about the possibility of going on the afternoon of August second; leave[13] was cancelled, that type of stuff. We could see it coming.

A lot of the work to get ready to go was already done since we were supposed to go to Japan in October. The big part of getting ready to go was trading some of our G-limited[14] airplanes for unlimited ones from other squadrons so that we had 10 good jets when we left.

I went over there in an A-6. We had some aircraft problems trying to go with the squadron on August 22nd so my pilot and I ended up going three days later on our own. We launched and joined up with a KC-135 out over the ocean to go across, just one A-6 and the KC-135. We joined a couple of AV-8s at Rota, Spain, and finished the trip to Shaikh Isa Airbase on the southern part of Bahrain. The officers ended up liv-

---

[10]WestPac—Western Pacific. Marines routinely deploy to Iwakuni, Japan, on six-month tours for training in Korea, Japan, the Philippines, etc.

[11]dets—Detachments. Deployments from the main unit or base for temporary operations somewhere else.

[12]MCCRES—Marine Corps Combat Readiness Evaluation System. As-real-as-possible test of a unit's combat readiness. Similar to Air Force Operational Readiness Inspection.

[13]leave—Vacation.

[14]G-limited—Flight restriction on the acceleration, Gs, an airplane can stand. Such restrictions are usually the result of old wings beginning to crack at the end of their useful lives. No flier wants to go into combat in a limited jet.

ing in Bahraini barracks with air conditioning, but the rest of the squadron slept out in ordinary tents. The Air Force had air conditioners for their tents but the Marines didn't.

We went on alert about four days after we got to Bahrain. Once our support caught up, we started flying more to rehearse our reaction for when the Iraqis came across the border. We thought there was a pretty good chance of them pressing on through Saudi Arabia. We got the initial planning done for the reaction and started flying practices of the plan.

We considered a triple-A piece in everybody's backyard to be pretty high threat if you're below 10,000 feet. We developed some new high-altitude tactics for deep air strikes to get above the guns since that's not really what A-6s are trained to do. We train to go low through mountains at night but there weren't any mountains to hide behind. If you go high, you have all the SAM rings out there to deal with, but the SAMs were pretty dispersed. We had a pretty good idea where the SAMs were and felt we could pick our way through 'em until we got to the target and didn't have any choice. We considered triple-A to be the big threat. We counted on darkness and the F-18s and F-15s to take care of the air threat.

It didn't take long at all to figure out that we had a lot of support from home. There was more Any Service Member mail than you could answer by October. There were huge bins of mail that guys would grab by the handful. Some guys were writin' up to 70 people they'd never met, while some guys didn't want to write any 'cause they had enough friends and family members to write. The mail and support we were getting was just overwhelming.

There was a lounge area in the chow hall with a large-screen TV. It was just Bahraini TV at first, which wasn't real informative about anything other than what the Shaikh of Bahrain was doing. Once the war started, they showed CNN 24 hours a day on one of the Bahraini channels. If you had time, you'd go watch CNN to get the big picture of what everybody else was doing during the war.

Paul and I had both graduated from WTI[15] as weapons and tactics instructors earlier in '90. That made us the weapons and tactics experts in the squadron, so the skipper put Paul and me in the plans section. We were involved in the planning from the very beginning back at the end of August. We had folders made by September with routes to the targets, weapons loads, support, and all that. We had briefed the plans by the middle of September, and, by early October, we were flying practices of

---

[15]WTI—Weapons and Tactics Instructor school. "Doctorate" in combat flying (British and U.S. Marine Corps term). See Fighter Weapons School.

those strikes. Between then and January, the targets changed but the basic missions pretty much stayed the same.

We knew our targets for at least the first three days of the war by the middle of December. Day one, wave one was the first night attack and we were going to hit Tallil airfield. It's on the Euphrates River about halfway from Kuwait to Baghdad.

Paul was the mission commander for the entire Marine Corps package on day one, wave one, and I was mission commander for the A-6s. We sent aircraft to Tallil airfield, to the Nasiriyah power plant, and to Qurnah airfield. We planned to take six MK-83s[16], an ALQ-167 radar jamming pod, and a 300-gallon drop tank on each A-6.

At about 1730 on the 16th, everybody who was involved in mission planning for all the waves got together and went over the last details on the special instructions. At the end of the meeting, we were told the day one, wave one missions would launch that night. Our TOT[17] was between 0405 and 0415 on the 17th. That was the first time we knew for sure that we were going.

Day One, Wave One. Captain Paul Andrus, Droid, joins the narrative:

Droid (Pilot): On the morning of January 16th, they told us we'd rehearse the mission. That was plausible since we'd rehearsed it about five times already. Then they said we'd fly it with live ordnance. That was plausible too, because they'd been talking about exercising the trucks and trailers and cradles and hoists to load up the bombs. Then they said we'd launch, go up to the border, and turn around. Even that was plausible 'cause we figured George Bush would want to make Saddam sweat a little bit before they actually kicked it off. But we weren't stupid either. We knew what day it was so, by about 1600, our attitude was, "Yeah sure, we're just going to go practice tonight." But, like Dave said, we were officially told at 1730.

Dyno (Bombardier-Navigator): We knew the 15th was the deadline for them to get out, so on the 16th, Paul and I had everything ready. We had kneeboard packets for the guys. We had charts ready to hand out to the aircrews. The whole targeting folder was put together. The overhead slides were done for the brief. All we had to do was add the times. We really had everything done. So, when they told us at 1730, we just filled in the blanks, got some dinner, and tried to get some sleep.

---

[16]MK-83—("mark eighty-three") General-purpose, 1000-pound, high-explosive bomb.

[17]TOT—Time on target. Exact time the bombs will detonate (interdiction). Timing is the primary means of ensuring safety from "friendly" explosions, and crews count on the effectiveness of earlier attacks to pave the way for their missions. Entire raids fit into 90 seconds or a few minutes.

Droid (P): I ran the mass brief in a plywood and concrete slab room called the barn that we'd just built a few days before this thing. There were 48 planes involved in the strike, but not all of them were there. The tankers and Tornados came from other bases. Imagine 50 guys there sittin' on camp stools with big fold-out charts all around to brief off of. I got up, introduced myself, and went through the brief just like at Red Flag[18]. Our whole experience proved that exercises like Red Flag, Cope Thunder, and Carolina Combat made us really well prepared for what we came up against. It, no kiddin', went just like we trained.

Dyno (B/N): I'm not sure the troops, the enlisted Marines, were really sure we were going to launch day one, wave one—that we were really going to come back without the bombs. They got a pretty good feel for what was going on just by looking at us and how spooled up we were.

Droid (P): We did a couple things different this time that they saw. We took all our patches off, we took the blood chits[19], and gave the flight equipment guys all our personal stuff. Officially, the Skipper got all the guys together after we were gone and told them it was for real.

Dyno (B/N): I'll tell you how well the troops had a feel for what we were doing. We were gettin' high fives all the way out to the plane. Every flier who wasn't going lined up to shake hands with the guys headed out to the planes. The whole 8000-foot-long taxiway was lined with enlisted troops cheering as we went by. Being in a foreign country, we couldn't have flags out. But when we got to the end of the runway where the Weasels had their revetments, we saw a huge American flag with a spotlight on it.

Droid (P): The next thing I remember is doing the off count. We had to keep count to be sure we had the minimum number of planes required to get the job done. Thirty-seven airplanes launched at 10-second intervals from Shaikh Isa for just our package. Everybody else was flying too.

Dyno (B/N): Watching all those jets launch at night was pretty impressive. And there weren't any radio calls at all. In fact, the only radio calls were to AWACS to tell them we were going into Iraq and then again to tell them we were back out.

Droid (P): We taxied onto the runway and went down to the nine-

---

[18]Red Flag—Largest air war and interdiction exercise anywhere. Run many times a year on the instrumented ranges north and west of Las Vegas, this realistic training gave Allied pilots a real edge.

[19]blood chits—Leaflets with phrases printed in many languages promising rewards for helping downed airmen.

board[20] with the other section[21] lining up at the ten-board. They signaled with their landing lights that they were ready so we ran the engines up and took off with the same 10-second interval. We got airborne and got whoever we could on board the formation before we ran into some clouds. The division got together above the clouds so we went to work on navigation, updates, and timing to be on time at the target. We had different types of aircraft coming in from different altitudes and different directions, plus only a short period of SEAD[22] protection, so we absolutely had to be right on time. And all with no radio calls at all. If we were off by a few seconds, I don't know which way it was.

Dyno (B/N): We had always trained with 60-second's separation at night; 7 or 8 miles between airplanes. When we started the planning for this, we realized that wasn't going to work. We had to get the planes closer together. That planning was a lot of the work building up for Desert Storm, but it had to be done. We planned to have aircraft from the same formations spread 15 seconds apart over the target with 30 seconds between different formations. So four F-18s would cross the target in 45 seconds and then, 30 seconds later, four A-6s would do the same thing.

Droid (P): And all lights out. Really black. We were flying in formation on minimum, minimum lights—glow from the instruments, strip lights, and star light 'cause there was no moon. Later on, the wingman flew a preplanned separation maneuver running into the target and we were on our own from there.

Dyno (B/N): We went out at 24,000 feet taking navigation updates from any known place on the ground that was radar-reflective. I watched the returns on the ground-mapping radar to recognize our update points like the highway cloverleaf we used as the first one.

In the meantime, the jets in our division started having problems. We'd briefed that certain systems were required or that jet wouldn't cross the border. One airplane had generator problems and another guy had a problem with the ECM[23] self-protection jammer. So we ended up crossing the border with two A-6s after starting out with four.

---

[20]board—Runway length-remaining marker. All runways have signs showing how much runway is left, so the nine-board indicates 9000 feet remaining.

[21]section—Navy and Marine term for a formation of two aircraft. See two ship.

[22]SEAD—Suppression of enemy air defenses. Reducing the threat to attacking aircraft. An attack is often led by aircraft that engage the enemy missiles and triple-A to protect the rest of the aircraft.

[23]ECM—Electronic counter measures. Fighting electrons with electrons. Much of a modern war is fought with "electrons." This war of radars, radios, and jammers is critical to putting bombs on target.

It took some convincing to get them to leave. Paul had to tell one guy more than once to go home but he eventually did. You can imagine that the guys wanted to stay and were willing to go into Iraq with only one wing if that's what it took.

Droid (P): This one guy wanted to go and at least get rid of his bombs just north of the border on the Iraqi positions. There was plenty of air defense around and I did not want him going up there without any defensive ECM at all. So I sent him home.

Dyno (B/N): We knew what they had for defenses, what they had for equipment, we just didn't know how well they could work it. They had some pretty capable equipment. They had sixes (SA-6)[24] and eights (SA-8)[25] and every size of triple-A right there on the border.

We got to about 10 miles from the border, as the first airplanes in, and saw the whole border defined by tracers coming up. The oil wells were on fire already too. You could see where the Republican Guard was by the trace of their triple-A and SAM launches on the ground. There were ribbons of tracers coming up and falling back down. Wherever there was population there was triple-A and SAMs being fired.

The A-6 only has a very weak RWR so we essentially didn't have any way to know who was looking at us or who was shooting at us other than with our eyes. That's kind of a bad feeling flying over SA-6s without a RWR.

Droid (P): Our final approach was 13 miles long so, at 480 knots or 8 miles a minute, it was a minute and a half or so. We use an IP[26] to key ourselves to complete the combat checks in the cockpit. At that point, we showed our hand by radiating with the radar and jammers.

Dyno (B/N): The heading we flew just before the IP wouldn't let the radar see Tallil, so I kept it off until we made that last turn. I had about 60 seconds to find the target.

Droid (P): We hit the IP exactly on time. You can't get but only so screwed up in 13 miles if you try so we knew we were at the right place, at the right time, and things looked really, really good. Our SA (situational awareness) was up to the point where we accelerated before the turn to compensate for the 30 knots of wind we'd face on final. We had to keep our ground speed the same for timing. Dave selected the weapons stations the bombs were on and armed the dual fuses. The master arm switch was last and then we were set.

---

[24]SA-6—Soviet-built, low- to medium-altitude, radar-guided, surface-to-air missile. Bad news.

[25]SA-8—Soviet-built, low-altitude, radar-guided, surface-to-air missile.

[26]IP—Initial point. Known geographic reference from where the final attack run begins.

Dyno (B/N): Tallil was a pretty big blob on the radar. I had to break out certain buildings right there in the middle of the airfield complex. That's what the A-6 was designed to do.

Our first choice was to find the target on the Forward Looking Infrared system. It had been a nice night for it up to that point but there were clouds and fog from the Euphrates River over the field. So I had to bomb radar only.

We can use an offset where the radar locks onto something that's radar reflective and distinct and then uses the known distance and bearing to the target to put the bombs on it. From the pictures and all we had, we worked out what we thought the radar picture would look like and made the plan on that.

Droid (P): We knew the airfield had a square fence around it and that there were literally a thousand triple-A pieces there. When we got there, we saw a perfect square of triple-A: there was absolutely no doubt in our minds that we'd made it to our target. All of the empty space inside the fence was filled with triple-A.

It was one thing to look at a little rectangle of fire from up high and another to push over so that it was transposed up to the windscreen. There's a lot of difference in your mind between looking down at it and having it in your face. To this day, I still remember that as the most unnatural act in my life. Imagine turning a stove on high and forcing yourself to slap your hand onto it. That's what it felt like.

I imagine that's about what a duck sees on opening day.

We had to dive on the target but the radar's mechanical limits won't follow a roll-in just 10 or 15 seconds from release. All I could do was push the nose over so there was only a half a G on the airplane. It's a little uncomfortable as dust flies off the floor and the maps come out of the map case, but it's over in a few "potatoes" (seconds).

Dyno (B/N): Flying around above twenty-some thousand feet watching all that triple-A arc up, knowing that we were pushing the nose over into it, made the push even more uncomfortable.

Paul pushed the plane over into a 30-degree dive at about 8 miles out. I locked onto the offset point and told Paul I had what I was looking for. We both checked the armament panel about a dozen times to be absolutely sure the bombs would come off. As we came down the chute[27], I looked for the target building a couple times but finally stuck with the offset. I was pretty busy tuning the radar for a better picture and trying different modes.

I had my head in the boot—it's a black plastic tube that protects the

---

[27]chute—Diving attack flightpath. Probably a reference to everything coming together in one direction, as in a coal chute.

radar screen from glare, so I lost a lot of SA on what was going on out-side and how close we were to weapons release. Paul told me the bombing cue was close so I locked the bombing solution in for the last time and kept trying to refine it.

When I was sure I had the target, I hit the attack button on the slew (left hand) stick on my side. That makes the computer run a little faster as it figures out attack solutions and is my consent to drop. The pilot has a trigger on his stick. When he squeezes it, he tells the computer that he's pretty confident in what I'm doing on my side, so the computer re-leases the bombs on its own at the right time.

The next thing I knew, I felt at least a four-G pull with the nose coming up so I knew Paul was coming off target. My first thought was, "Where's he going? We've got to put the bombs on target!" Then I looked over and saw that the bombs were off the plane. It happened real quick.

The bombs went on target. It was a Scud storage building that we saw on the damage photos had a stick[28] or two or three of bombs through it.

Droid (P): We had a "clever" plan for coming off target[29]. We'd get the nose back down to the horizon and complete the turn to the pre-planned egress heading that would get us back to the border. We would maintain altitude and laterally displace from the triple-A. On target, I changed my mind 'cause I wanted to get back up as high as I could above that flak. I was wildly displacing the airplane to avoid the triple-A.

Dyno (B/N): As soon as I realized the bombs were gone, I looked outside to watch for a missile launch. We knew there were a lot of SA-6s so I was lookin' back over my shoulder for anything that might be pointed at us.

When we pulled off target at about 12,000 feet, I looked up to see the nose comin' up through the horizon with about four Gs on the plane. I didn't care what Paul did with the plane as long as he was on the right heading outta there. I made sure of that too!

I looked back inside the plane and we were at 30,000 feet. I thought, "That works for me!" About that time, I saw a bluish streak in the distance start near the ground, come up along the wing and start moving up the canopy. It could've been a missile or an F-18 in burner or a HARM shot or just about anything. I told Paul about it and looked around again.

When I looked back into the plane the next time, we were at 15,000 feet again. I could see that Paul was doing a great job of getting us

---

[28]stick (of bombs)—More than one bomb dropped at a time.

[29]off—Done with the attack and moving away. "Lead is off the target."

around to a lot of places in the sky. The next time I checked, we were back up to our egress altitude of 28,000 feet and about 30 miles from the target. That looked pretty good to me!

When we got to the quiet spot between Tallil and the border, and could breath a little easier, Paul and I simultaneously thought, "Where's our wingmen, Screw and Roogs?"

Droid (P): But the air-to-air Tacan was still ticking so they were still with us. They ended up about 12 miles behind us.

Dyno (B/N): We could still see all that triple-A from Tallil. About that time, the British GR-1 Tornados went through at low altitude. We couldn't imagine, after seeing all that triple-A, anybody going in low and coming back out. We were absolutely amazed to hear that those guys had gone in there, did what they were supposed to do, and got back out. They didn't lose anybody on our strike though they did lose other Tornados doing exactly that.

Droid (P): Our next concern was making it through the friendly air defenses in one piece. We jumped on our published return route and, once across the border, we turned all the lights and IFF[30] on, called AWACS, and slowed way down. Slowing down was okay 'cause we were having the times of our lives. We were off target, we were alive, we were going to enjoy the flight home!

It was only a minor madhouse getting back to our runway. Besides being real durable and able to get us out of the target after being hit, the Intruder goes a long, long way without refueling, so we got back to base with lots of gas and checked in without a care in the world. We got in line and landed.

We pulled in, opened the canopy and hit each other with a high five. We'd made it!

We got out of the airplane, climbed down, and everybody crowded around us talking at a hundred miles an hour. The ground crews were utterly excited and we all started lookin' at the airplane right away to see if it had been hit. There wasn't a ding on it anywhere.

Dyno (B/N): Then we started the debriefs with the Intell[31] guys and the thousand people asking, "What did you see? Do you think that was a missile? What size triple-A did you see? What color was every tracer you saw? What did the target area look like? Did you hit the target?" We also ran around the barn trying to get our hands on the leaders of the other divisions to see if everybody made it back.

---

[30]IFF—Identification Friend or Foe. Electronic identification system.

[31]Intell—Intelligence. Department that briefs intelligence information to fliers. People who brief intelligence information. Intelligence information itself.

About the only thing we did wrong that night was ignore the girl from CNN when she asked if we just got back from flying. But we didn't want to be on camera and say something stupid. We might have been famous.

Droid (P): The sun was coming up so we went to the chow hall. CNN was on the TV and they had a map of Iraq up with our targets on it.

Dyno (B/N): Goin' to the chow hall was a pretty good feeling. They told us where we were going the night before so that had been a pretty quiet dinner. You'd have to have been an idiot to look at the aircrews eating dinner and not know that we'd just been told we were going to bomb Iraq. Everybody sat there not saying anything, just eating dinner. On the way to the airplanes, everybody was saying, "Hey, I'll see ya at breakfast." You're thinking, "Yeah, I hope I see every one of these guys at breakfast." So that was kinda nice sittin' there in the chow hall eatin' your coco puffs or chocolate-covered sugar bombs and seeing everybody else come in. They watched CNN saying, "Yeah, I did that!"

We wouldn't bet our lives on anything we heard on CNN, but it was interesting to hear how everybody else was doing. When we came back from the first night, we knew how everybody on base did but turned CNN on to see Baghdad blowing up. You could hear CNN talking about an F-18 getting shot down someplace or that there weren't any planes down in other places.

Dyno (B/N): After breakfast, I came back and called Vicki. She said, "What's new?!" I said, "Are you watching TV?" "Yes." "Are you watching the news?" "Yeah." "Do you know we just bombed Iraq?" "Yeah." "Well I just landed." That was kind of a shock to her.

Droid (P): People have a way of shutting things out. I commented to my wife and mother that I was tired of being shot at. They both said, "They're shooting at you?!" They hadn't even considered that. It's probably a natural reaction to shut that out.

Dyno (B/N): After the war was over, we were told first in, first out like everybody else. But we still maintained alerts even after we'd torn everything down. I left on a 747 with the main group of Marines on about 24 hours notice.

I was one of the first guys off when we got back to Cherry Point and Vicki came running up to me right away. My parents were there too, watching our son, James. It was probably the same as all the other homecomings with the bands and the banners and the decorations all over the hangers.

At least they didn't make us form up and march in. That's the one thing that worried me, speeches and all that wasting time. I just wanted to be home.

Captain Dave Deist and Captain Paul Andrus earned Distinguished Flying Crosses in the flak-filled skies over Tallil.

Vicki Deist grew up in southern Delaware and then attended the University of Delaware. She went to the Naval Academy for a dance, organized through her all-girls dorm, figuring to meet a bunch of midshipmen for the dance and that'd be it. Instead, she met a guy who was also from Delaware and whose parents lived 15 minutes from the college. They went out when he was home and the rest, as they say, is history.

Her family is typical in that they have a young child and are living in their first long-term house. Vicki was already used to the separations that are part of a Marine family's life. But war was different.

Vicki Deist:

Military family life is exciting, always uncertain. People ask me if we're back to our normal routine and I say, "Yes, if you could call it normal." We travel a lot and try to go to see Dave wherever he is on long deployments. You never know how long you'll be in one place. You just have to be real flexible.

Dave's deployments have been unusual in that he left for six months as soon as we got here, was back for three, went away for two, came back for one, went away for one, came back for two, left for seven, and now he'll be back for three before leaving for six more months. The war meant he was gone a lot more than he should've been.

I grew up in one place until I went to college so this life was something new to me. It's helped me grow a lot to travel and meet people from all different parts of the country. It's broadened my horizons.

I don't really remember what I was doing when I first heard that Iraq had invaded Kuwait 'cause it didn't seem important to me when it happened. Then we started hearing about sending troops and Bush saying Kuwait was of vital economic and strategic importance to us. People were asking if Dave was going to go and, for awhile, I was saying, "No, I don't think he'll go." He was never allowed to say what was really planned but then it got to the point where he came home one day with a power of attorney for me. There are just little signs you start to recognize before something like this happens. Even though I'd never been through a deployment like this before, I got the feeling things were different.

One day I finally asked him, "Are you going?" He kind of said, "Well, probably." I don't think they were allowed to say definitely whether they were going or not. They finally went about a week later than they expected.

I wasn't too happy about them leaving, but they were supposed to go to Japan anyway so I was prepared for a separation. I dealt with it by telling myself that nothing had really happened over there yet. He even told me that they'd probably sit there for awhile before anything happened. The politicians said we've gotta give the economic sanctions time to work. So I just dealt with it as a regular deployment until the war actually started.

There was a little bit more of an element of . . . I remember saying to him, "You better come back! I just hope you come back!" So there was a little more emotion this time but a lot of the planning was pretty much the same.

We went out to dinner without James one night before he left. Then James and I went to the squadron and watched the planes take off—the kind of things we do normally. We called a lot of people on the phone, like his family. They wanted to know when he was leaving, but he couldn't tell them.

Desert Shield was pretty much like a normal deployment. I went and visited my family a couple of times and they visited me once. I got together with my friends like we always do when the guys are gone.

The community of Havelock had a fair to support the military families just after they left which I thought was really nice. The general feeling of support from this military community was really good.

James knew something different was going on. Before he would go to bed, when David used to sit down with him to share a bowl of ice cream, he was kind of sad. But he was too young to really comprehend all of it. That made it a lot easier for me since he wasn't old enough to ask a lot of questions.

I was at my parents' house when the war started. We had gone out to dinner and my dad immediately turned on the radio when we got back in the car. I could tell he thought something was up. The announcers said something like, "We're not sure but we think something's happening in Iraq." We turned on CNN when we got home and sure enough, there was Peter Arnett saying, "It looks like the Fourth of July in Baghdad!"

I was almost excited in a way. I knew something was going to happen and wanted to just go ahead and get it over with. Once the deadline was set, I was resigned to the fact that we were going to war so we might as well just start and get it over with. So I was kind of excited in a way watching TV from about 7:30 until we went to bed around 11:30. That whole time I was thinking the A-6s were not involved 'cause the TV reports didn't talk about them. I really wasn't worried and it's probably good that I didn't know. I'm sure the denial was a way to deal with it.

He called about 12:30 that night and I heard my mom say, "David?" I was relieved then 'cause she was talking to him so everything was

OK. When the phone first rings like that you're worried that it's not him calling . . .

I said, "Hi, what's new?" I didn't mean, what's new with the world 'cause I'd just watched it all on TV. I meant, what's new with you? He said, "I just landed," and proceeded to tell me what had happened. That was really amazing 'cause I'd just watched it all like the rest of the American public had with the war pretty much right in the living room. Then I got a phone call from my husband who'd been involved in it.

The next day, no one could believe it when I told them. My nephew got to school and the teacher asked if they knew what happened. He said, "My uncle dropped a bomb on Iraq."

When the war first started, I watched CNN from the time I got up in the morning to the time I went to bed. My mom described me as a zombie. We were invited to a friend's place for dinner that first weekend and by that time I needed a diversion. That was really nice. It gradually tapered off so that I watched TV when I got up in the morning, before I went to bed, and then maybe a Pentagon briefing in the afternoon. I had to get back to a normal life.

I was at my parents' house until early February so it was nice to have family around for support. I really was a zombie in the beginning and, if it had just been me and James at home alone, he would've really felt neglected.

By the time we got back to Cherry Point, I'd adjusted to the fact that we were at war and he was flying in combat. It really helped that he called about once a week. And the wives kept a message machine updated with what was going on. That was wonderful. Being able to call that machine whenever you wanted to without bothering somebody was really good.

That phone system was run by the "key wives." In the Marine Corps, we're used to deploying for six months at a time. The key wives are women in the unit who help the wives that are having problems, so that system was already there. We could call that machine anytime to get an update on what the guys were doing.

Before the war, a lot of people were against the idea of fighting but once it started, they figured, "We're in this and can't change it so let's rally behind the troops." That was good. The lack of support from Congress upset me the most. I mean, I really resented the fact that my husband was over there in the Middle East, waiting to go to war, away from his family for Christmas, and Congress waited until right before the deadline to debate the situation. They waited until they got back from their long Christmas vacations with their families to think about supporting our people who'd just spent Christmas in the desert. They knew perfectly well that President Bush had set the deadline, and, if they really wanted to debate, they should've gotten together back in November or December. Once we did go to war, they couldn't even pass a quick resolution to support the troops because they couldn't agree on the way it should be worded. It took them two or three days to pass a resolution to support the troops.

I just really resented that! They're our elected officials but they couldn't even say they supported my husband when most of the American public was doing everything they could to be patriotic and support the troops.

People who have time on their hands tend to go out and protest. They got so much publicity because people who supported our being there weren't out demonstrating. Then somebody along the line decided to have rallies to support the troops. That really caught on. We had one here in Havelock in February. That was a change when the war started. People went from saying they supported the troops to getting out and showing it.

I was really excited when the war ended. David called and said all the flights were cancelled for that night which was *the* best news I could hear. When that happened, I still didn't think he was coming home right away but I was convinced he was out of danger. That was good news!

I got the house ready and learned to use the new breadmaker to get ready for him to come home. It went really fast once he knew he was coming home. James and I made banners for the house and the kids in the neighborhood put one up on the garage that said; "Welcome Home Mr. Diest." I put yellow ribbons up.

The key wives organized everybody to make posters for the hangar but we didn't see them in all the excitement. That just wasn't the important issue that night. I kept saying I'd believe it when I saw him. And then I did.

The next day we just went shopping and did normal things. Normal, that is, except for Dave waking his mom up while wearing a gas mask and helmet saying, "Scud alert! Scud alert!"

That's not really normal—even for my Marine.

4
Master of All Trades

Captain Mark Koechle, Coke, was a Hog driver[1] so his job was close air support[2]—period. That deceptively simple description makes his most lethal, intense, and demanding specialty sound almost benign. But war is most personal to a CAS pilot. He talks to the men he supports while flying just a few hundred feet above them and has likely served with them on the ground. Theirs is not a fight between million-dollar missiles and million-ruble radars: The A-10's weapons are all aimed by eye, and strafe[3] is as up-close and personal as it gets. Desert Storm added some new missions to the Hog's bag of tricks while reaffirming that close air support is one of the toughest jobs a flier can draw. There's no faster way to win a posthumous Medal of Honor.

Hollywood's shimmering image of air combat centers on the whorl of split-second moves by small teams of big egos in the air-to-air world. An air-to-mud fight, however, is a barely controlled meat grinder where the most common and lethal weapon is still the canon. A dogfight resembles pro karate while CAS resembles a prison riot.

---

[1]Hog—Warthog. A-10 Thunderbolt II's more common nickname.

[2]close air support—CAS. Attacks in very close proximity to, and in direct support of, friendly ground forces. This job is the toughest a fighter pilot can draw with the greatest chance of being shot down, killing friendly troops, or earning the Medal of Honor. Both Air Force Crosses won in Desert Storm were earned on attack missions.

[3]strafe—(verb) To attack a ground target with a gun carried by an aircraft. (noun) The gun attack itself.

Coke's jet was the Fairchild A-10A Thunderbolt II. Named after the Thunderbolt of WWII fame, the Warthog is a big, heavy, tough beast with 30mm fangs and is built to take the punishment that's unavoidable when bringing the fight directly to the enemy. In fact, grunts[4] have an understandable misperception that the A-10 simulator is an iron dumpster that the operators throw rocks at. But those same grunts breathe easier with Hogs around and are bitterly amazed when told that most of the A-10s have already been mothballed.

Captain Koechle:

I'm an Air Force brat. My dad was life-long SAC[5], tankers, so I grew up moving around and ended up graduating from Maconaquah High School in Bunker Hill, Indiana. I graduated from Purdue University in '83 and went to pilot training at Columbus AFB after taking my ROTC commission. I got my second choice airplane out of pilot training and went to Bentwaters, England in the A-10. After three and a half years there, I went to Weapons School[6] on the way to England AFB in Louisiana.

I had just taken over as the 74th Tac Fighter Squadron (Flying Tigers) Weapons Officer and B Flight Commander when Kuwait was invaded. My job was to keep the squadron as tactically oriented as possible because the wing at England tended to focus on the BDU Olympics[7] as opposed to tactics. My big push was the Maverick missile[8] and tactics.

Our deployment was on-again, off-again, as the F-15s and F-16s left. We had our bags packed and were ready to be there within a week of the invasion but the Air Force leadership changed the plan. At my level, we got the impression that General Horner, 9th Air Force Commander

---

[4]grunt—Infantry.

[5]SAC—Strategic Air Command. One of the Air Force's major commands before the latest restructuring. SAC's mission was nuclear deterrence. They owned all of the Air Force's strategic nuclear weapons and the means to deliver them.

[6]Fighter Weapons School—FWS. The Air Force "doctorate" program in combat flying based at Nellis AFB, Las Vegas, Nevada. Similar to the Navy's Top Gun program, though twice as long and more detailed than that school. Renamed simply USAF Weapons School.

[7]BDU Olympics—Intramural bombing competition using practice bombs (BDUs) on small, nontactical weapons ranges.

[8]Maverick—AGM-65A/B/D/G. Short, stubby, TV- or infrared-guided air-to-ground missile carried almost exclusively by the A-10. Most have 125-pound shaped-charge warheads, but the G-model has a 300-pound blast warhead. It's a Maverick on steroids. Extremely lethal, the Maverick and the Sidewinder are sometimes referred to as "I wish you were dead" missiles.

and CENTAF[9] commander, wanted to spend more resources getting F-15s and F-16s over there so he swapped the deployment schedule around to get those fast jets in first. Then Schwarzkopf jumped in and said, "If I'm going to have guys on the ground fighting, I want the A-10s to protect them! Now!" Once we got out of the deployment flow, it was hard to get back in.

We finally left at the end of August with the first stop at Myrtle Beach, South Carolina. The next hop was 13 hours into Moron, Spain—no fun. I led a cell of six airplanes as the tanker we were following took us right through a big thunderstorm at night. The lightning blinded us for three or four seconds each time so that I couldn't see the tanker a few feet away. Then I got struck by lightning. I felt a ZAP! through my helmet and the guy next to me had his hand blown off the throttles by another bolt. Lightning hit a guy on the other side of the tanker, too, just as they ran into some sort of a micro burst that dropped them several thousand feet. Then the tanker got hit, decided he'd had enough and ran away from us. When we popped out of the thunderstorm, there were A-10s all over the sky. The tanker finally 'fessed up that he had weather radar problems and unintentionally dragged us through it. We pressed on and landed at Moron nine hours later. After two more days and a short 10½-hour flight from Moron, we got to King Fahd.

The base was really barren but had beautiful runways, the best runways I have ever flown off of. There were two parallel strips, 300 feet wide and 14,000 feet long. I opened up the canopy, got hit with a blast of hot air and thought, "Okay, which engines are running and blowing their exhaust my way?" It was like standing behind a jet engine, but it had already cooled down to about 120 degrees on the ramp. Our wing commander handed me a hot Pepsi and said, "Welcome to Saudi Arabia."

Everybody worked pretty hard to set up a typical flying operation from nothing. We also established our squadron operations, filled sandbags, and put up barricades. We weren't worried about the Iraqis invading without us seeing their build-up, but we were concerned about terrorists—the guy driving in with a truckload of dynamite. But it was just too hot to do anything outside in the middle of the day, so, if you weren't flying, there wasn't much to do besides sit around and read.

Our only unclassified news from the outside world came in four-day-old *Stars and Stripes* newspapers with news that was three days old when they printed it. News delivery improved when we eventually got a TV cable hooked up just in time for the Super Bowl.

---

[9]CENTAF—Central Air Force. Command headquartered in Riyadh and McDill AFB, Florida, that controlled essentially all Allied flying in the Kuwaiti theater.

The Any Serviceman's letters were just amazing—we couldn't believe the support we had. There was so much mail that we didn't know what to do with it. They all said the same thing: "We really support you and we hope you come home safe." Each of us pulled out as many letters as we felt we could answer and wrote back. I made a pen pal. She was Britany Pitzer, a nine-year-old in Bloomington, Illinois. I sent a letter to her class and she ended up writing me back herself. She sent me cookies and a picture of her family. Her letters were my favorites after Carol's.

It began to look like we'd need some low threat[10] tactics so we got to work developing them. With a squadron from Myrtle Beach, we also developed night tactics since there were basically none for the A-10. We were chomping at the bit to get in, get it over with, and get home.

We wanted to paint the jets some sort of a sand color like the Brits did. But we were told, "No! Shut up; sit down; no-no-no!" Our squadron leadership got really ticked 'cause we kept asking them about that obvious need. I don't know if they were directed from higher than the wing level or what but changing camouflage made sense. We could be seen from well over 10 miles away in the desert. Several of the New Orleans jets were repainted before they deployed but then somebody higher got wind of that and said, "Paint them back or you're not taking them!" Camouflage was one of our big after-action gripes since it was a big factor in our losses. Dark jets were a lot easier to see. Every A-10 that got hit was hit by an optically aimed weapon even if it was terminally guided by something else.

The weapons officers planned the first few day's fight and had an idea it would start sometime on the 16th or 17th of January. All that was top secret at the time and we'd never seen top secret stuff before. The guys in the squadron knew I was working on something 'cause I would disappear for a day and a half at a time with: "Sorry, I hate to say this, but I can't tell you."

We finally got clearance to brief our squadrons on the 15th since we knew the war was going to start. Individual flight leads[11] planned their tactics and were ready to go on the morning of the 17th. The guys were excited.

As a fairly experienced weapons officer, I was given one of the

---

[10]low threat—Measure of the enemy's defenses, meaning "not too bad." Generally assuming an absence of radar-guided missiles or enemy fighters, low threat tactics are flown above ground fire versus high threat tactics, which are flown below radar coverage.

[11]flight lead(er)—Pilot in command of a formation of aircraft. Combat aircraft usually fly in fours or pairs with one flight lead commanding the whole formation and an element or section lead commanding the second pair if in a four ship or division.

higher priority targets: a GCI site[12] about 80 miles inside Iraq. It sat right on one of the major air routes from Saudi to Baghdad so they wanted it taken out to help the night guys get up there with less warning. My wingman was Captain Steve Barbour, number three was Captain Jim Tillie, and number four was Captain Dave Feehs. Scott Kelly and Paul Johnson each led two ships against other GCI sites. So, on the first morning of the war, A-10s flew around, in daylight, in Iraq, with no escort. And our GCI site was 7 miles south of a main divert base for Iraqi fighters. It's not supposed to happen that way but it worked[13]. Hog drivers had some heartburn with the planners in Riyadh saying we couldn't survive while sending us on nonstandard missions like that one. I was concerned about that airstrip, of course, but it was fragged[14] to be hit by three B-52s, Strike Eagles, Tornados, and F-111s.

The solid undercast broke up as we approached our target and attacked from the East, comm out[15]. Each of us fired two G-model Mavericks, which is an infrared guided missile with a 300-pound warhead, and dropped four CBU-52s[16], cluster bombs with softball-size bomblets.

I took out one of the troposcatter microwave transmitters with a Maverick to open up, and then we worked through the list of priority targets. Both Three and I shot Mavericks with delay fuses into the commander bunker. I rolled in on a high 60-degree diving delivery from about 20,000 feet and pickled my CBUs, which ended up hitting short of the radar that I was aiming for but hit another radar[17]. As I pulled off target, I looked back and saw a little white cloud in the air. I thought, "What's that? It wasn't there before." Then another one appeared and it

---

[12]GCI site—Radar station whose controllers direct fighters very closely on intercepts. Key part of the inflexible Soviet-style air defense system and vulnerable to disruption. See GCI.

[13]A-10s are assumed to be vulnerable to "real fighters" since they're slow and would have serious problems coping with a good airborne radar missile attack. But, as many fighters have realized while looking down the barrels of the largest Gatling gun in the air, picking on an A-10 is like getting into a knife fight in a phone booth, except the Hog wears armor and carries a short sword.

[14]fragged—To be assigned a mission that is listed in the frag, or fragmentary order.

[15]comm out—Without communications. Executing a plan without using radios so as to reduce the chance of detection.

[16]CBU—Cluster bomb unit. Lots of little bomblets within one bomb casing. CBUs are further specified by their numerical designation, such as CBU-58 or CBU-87.

[17]Until recently, A-10 bombing systems were never modified with computer sights. That made bombing very difficult and really no different than it was when George Bush did it back in WWII. Hogs have been fitted with a safety modification designed to save some of the many that fly into the ground. This modification also allowed computer bombing. None of the improved jets went to war.

dawned on me that they were shooting at us. So I told the other guys and strafed one of the triple-A sites as the last of the bombs hit. We destroyed four radars, three microwave transmitters, the command center, and a bunch of assorted buildings.

We egressed south while looking for interceptors. I was real concerned about them and had checked the frag to find out where the nearest CAP would be in case Iraqi fighters showed up. Our nearest CAP was 100 miles south, a four ship[18] of Eagles. But the Iraqis didn't show so the flight home was uneventful.

It felt like a training mission until they started shooting at us. The triple-A drove home the point that there was somebody down there trying to kill us, too.

You train and you train and you train and you always strive for the perfect mission. We planned and worked so hard on that specific mission that I was just ecstatic when it came off so well. We landed, got together, and shook each other's hands with smiles all around. Then it was back to business.

My second day's mission was to hit a smaller GCI site. We had G-model Mavericks again and six MK-82s[19], 500-pounders with airburst fuses set to go off 15 feet above the ground. They were showstoppers. My wingman then and for the rest of the war was Lieutenant Don "O" Henry. He got to Saudi about the middle of November, brand spanking new out of pilot training with 100 hours as a Hog wingman. What a way to start your career. We had some down-to-earth talks after several sorties but he learned a lot and came along real well.

The weather was really bad. As we popped into the weather, I got a call on guard[20] from our controllers diverting us to look for three mobile Scud launchers somebody spotted on their way home. So there I was, in the weather, trying to plot the Scuds, with O doing a real good job of hanging on my wing. The Scuds were about 10 miles southeast of the GCI site we hit the day before.

O went lost wingman[21] so we looked for each other and worked out an attack plan. I popped down through the clouds at about 13,000 feet and saw three big "semi trucks" 5 miles south. I got so excited that I was ready to roll in and shoot them right away but realized I needed to find my wingman for mutual support.

---

[18]ship—Airplane. A four ship is a formation of four airplanes.

[19]MK-82—("mark eighty-two") General-purpose, 500-pound, high-explosive bomb.

[20]guard—Common emergency frequency that all NATO aircraft monitor.

[21]lost wingman—Planned and rehearsed turn away from the formation that wingmen use when they lose sight of their leaders in clouds.

We got back together again and dropped down through a hole in the clouds to commence with the attack. I rolled in and fired on a Scud with a G-model Maverick. It kicked up the dust right at the base of the Scud. It was a dud[22]. Of the 36 Mavericks I fired, that was the only one that didn't work as advertised. Don rolled in on another Scud but his Maverick wouldn't come off the rail. We had eight perfect Mavericks the day before but were oh for two so far. I rolled back in and shot my second Maverick, which blew up one of the Scuds. It was a very nice explosion so we were happy again. O came back around and blew up the same target he couldn't shoot at the first time with another very nice explosion. Somewhere in that sequence, we lost sight of each other again.

The winds were pretty strong out of the east. As we got back together, I was blown about 7 miles west of the target and happened to pop out of a hole above seven other Scud or Frog[23] launchers. Man, we hit the jackpot. I went back to the first target, found O and set up to drop my bombs on the last Scud. I dropped the bombs on a really nice pass but I got the winds wrong. The last bomb hit about 100 meters short of the launcher, which at least peppered it[24]. I was really pissed off by that time because I'd used a Maverick and six bombs on that thing and couldn't hit it. So I pulled back around and rolled in with the gun to put a 300-round burst on that Scud. It was kind of beat up when we left.

Those were the first Scuds anybody had found, so, that afternoon at the military briefing, Schwarzkopf said Air Force airplanes had found some mobile Scuds that had been firing on Israel and Riyadh.

We went looking for somebody to hurt 'cause I was still upset at the weapons problems. It turned out that O couldn't get his bombs off at the second target, he had a loose wire in his armament control system, so we strafed the Frogs until we hit our no-kidding bingo[25]. We heard later that we'd found an Iraqi artillery battalion that supposedly had Frog missiles.

The Hog was making a name for itself. Hog drivers have always known we would do well, that the A-10 would do a good job.

We also knew that if we got hit we would probably survive and get home. Hogs were hit 70 times, including 24 serious hits. But we only lost four behind the lines and two that crashed on the runway after flying home. One jet had over 500 holes in the tail from a missile warhead and

---

[22]dud—Weapon that does not detonate when it should.

[23]Frog—Soviet-made, short-range, ballistic missile.

[24]That problem with the winds would not have happened to an airplane equipped with a computer bomb sight.

[25]bingo—Radio call meaning, "I'm out of fuel and must go home now." A low fuel state.

another had a missile blow up inside a wing—they both got home. When the first guys came back with battle damage, it increased our confidence in the jet. F-16s almost never made it back after being hit. So we had great confidence in our airplane, but I think the F-16 guys knew how fragile their jet was.

The Hog was finally taken seriously. For example, word came up from Riyadh that there were only three sources Intell would believe for target location and damage assessment: satellite photos, photo reconnaissance, and A-10 pilot reports. We were real happy to hear they took our word as to what we killed. But that meant we were picked for oddball missions like flying over the Tawakalna Republican Guards at low altitude to look down into the revetments and see what was there. We said, "Wait a minute! How 'bout your satellites and RF-4s?[26]" Nope, we were it.

So we took a look and found that about 75% of the revetments were full but only 10 to 20% of those had good targets. The others were old rusty vehicles, farm tractors, decoys, and plywood boxes. Then the Guards opened up with 23mm triple-A and shoulder-fired SAMs, so it was time to get out.

None of us were close to the first missile launcher except its Hog target so the Hog driver rolled in himself and strafed the guy who shot at him. Taught him a lesson. The fast movers would light their burners and run when they were engaged which was smart since they can't turn very well. But we couldn't run away. The gun and the Maverick allowed us to outduel anybody except the SA-8 or SA-6 so, when somebody shot at us, they became the primary target. For example, if three or four 57mm triple-A sites opened up and we pumped a Maverick into one of them, the rest always quit shooting for some reason. The Iraqis learned that lesson very quickly. That was our policy: anybody who shot at a Hog, died. Period.

We dumped our bombs and Mavericks on the triple-A sites and left.

We figured they asked us to do those oddball missions because we were fairly successful at everything they tasked the Hog to do. That was not the F-16's war since the ground fire kept them up high, but they don't have precision-guided weapons, so they're not very accurate up there. We went in with Mavericks on targets they'd missed several times.

Me and Paul Johnson, PJ, went to Riyadh to meet Defense Secretary Cheney and General Powell since we had flown several significant missions. We were the only Air Force guys there except for lots of generals. Schwarzkopf sat behind me and three chairs over. Cheney and Powell were real friendly, very, very intelligent, and very knowledgeable. I was

---

[26]RF-4—Tactical reconnaissance version of the F-4 Phantom II.

shocked by how knowledgeable they were about individual systems. They knew about the Maverick, they knew what the A-10's gun did, they knew about Navy systems that I had no clue about.

Each guy took 5 to 10 minutes and told his story. When it was our turn, we were asked, "What can we do better, what do you guys need?" I wanted more photo imagery. They asked how our gun was doing. I said, "Well sir, I can tell you for a fact that we can destroy a tank from 10,000 feet above the ground and 2 miles away because I've personally blown up several of them that way." They were very, very interested in what we had to say and seemed to take it to heart. It seemed like they'd gotten all the eye wash[27] from the generals and wanted words from the guys in the trenches.

My squadron then switched to nights and carried both ground and parachute flares, infrared Mavericks, and bombs. We had 10 underwing weapons stations loaded; and, though it wasn't supposed to work, we used the Maverick to find targets. Darkness allowed us to orbit as low as 3000 feet above the ground. The first Mavericks got something burning so we could drop the bombs and then strafe. Iraqi tracers were nice because they marked themselves as we rolled in to take care of 'em. Then they wouldn't shoot anymore. We fired the last Mavericks on the way out.

There was a lot of confusion on our limits. The day guys were allowed no farther north than North Kuwait and could not strafe in an overreaction to some losses. Can you believe that? A-10s not allowed to strafe? The night guys, who have a tough time seeing anything, could strafe, but not the day guys. Those restrictions didn't go over well at all.

Anyway, we found a 200-plus vehicle convoy trying to run north from Kuwait on the very last night of the war. We wanted to destroy as many vehicles as we could before the cease-fire. When we attacked, the Iraqis jumped out of their vehicles and ran while we went to work so there were relatively few casualties. Some were burning when we got there but, after our two missions, there were a whole lot more burning when we left.

We knew the cease-fire was coming and it was kind of an anticlimax. When you win the Super Bowl, you expect a big victory celebration. But it turned out that we simply quit flying. "Okay, what do we do now?" There was no big hurrah. Part of me was happy because it was over and the other part was kind of upset because the job wasn't finished.

We immediately got into the paperwork by writing out the medals and citations and all that. We emptied a lot of sandbags, cleaned up, and didn't fly except to keep the jets in shape and the pilots current.

---

[27]eye wash—Window dressing. More glitter than substance.

Each one of us got one ride over Kuwait at 3000 feet, a lot lower than we flew during the war in daylight. It was awesome. There were trenches everywhere you looked. The Iraqi army had buried themselves in the sand and the trench network was immense. I saw lots of tanks and artillery that we had blown up. The oil trenches still had oil leaking out on the sand.

We left on March 20th and stopped at Sigonella, Italy, the Azores, and Myrtle Beach. We brought 24 jets in to land at England AFB in front of about 5000 people. The whole ramp was full of them. Each of the wives and families had their own golf cart sitting on their pilot's parking spot. Each pilot had picked up a couple red roses for our wives so I climbed down the ladder, gave my wife a rose, and had kids hanging all over me. That was some happy homecoming.

My kids wouldn't let me out of their sight for about four days; they hung all over me that long.

Coke earned two Distinguished Flying Crosses for his first two combat missions.

Carol Koechle had the advantage of experience going for her. She under-stood the military life and had been through many separations by the time Desert Shield was forced on her. She was also a flight commander's wife, which added the unwritten responsibility to take care of the less-ex-perienced families. This deployment was different, of course, especially for the children.

Carol Koechle:

I lived in Indiana until I married Mark. We met in government class in high school and got married after our sophomore years in college. I like the military life because it's so different from the way I grew up. We travel and get to do more than just visit new places. Even within the United States, regions, languages, and cultures are different, and I enjoy getting to know the people in the different places we've lived.

In the first few days after Kuwait was invaded, it didn't occur to me that Mark would go there. I figured somebody else would go. Then he came home one day and said, "I think we're going to Saudi." That was a surprise though there was no apprehension.

The date they planned to leave seemed to change every day. "We're leaving in three weeks . . . We're leaving in two days! . . . False alarm, we're leaving in two weeks now . . ." It went back and forth like that for three weeks. As much as I hate to say it, I was ready for him to go just to end the stress. I wasn't worried because deploying is his job.

We took care of the unpleasant details like figuring out where Mark wanted to be buried should he not come back and he made some tapes of stories for the kids to listen to before bed.

We've gone through many deployments and that one really didn't seem different. The reality of the situation hadn't set in because the consensus here was that there wouldn't be a war. The guys would go over there, flex their muscles, so to speak, and the Iraqis would go away. So the one real difference was the media with their hype when the guys took off.

Our squadron alone had six wives who had been married for two months or less. They were new to marriage, they were new to the Air Force, and they were not happy about their husbands leaving, much less going to war. They went back and forth from being okay to being not okay or maybe even hysterical. At least I had adjusted to the Air Force and what it's all about. Many of them didn't know what they were getting into and then had a war thrown in.

My routine changed in that I kept up on the news more and read the papers through.

The base and the towns of Pineville and Alexandria were very, very supportive. People went out of their way to help and I got as least three calls a day offering to help for the whole time Mark was gone. My neighbors were always there checking on me.

The pilots who were left here were disgruntled. They were really good about helping the wives out around the house but they were obviously unhappy that they didn't get to go. They felt left behind and mostly stayed away from the wives' functions. There's nothing worse than a whining fighter pilot (sic).

Steven was five and Matthew was three at the time. Steven especially was very aware of what was going on. He watched the news with me because he wanted to and always asked questions. He knew all the names, who everybody was, and what was happening. They talked about it at school, at church, and even in cartoons. Even the kids couldn't stick their heads in the sand and ignore it if they wanted to. He was very upset about the whole situation.

Kids at school asked Steven, "Is your dad going to die in Saudi Arabia?" His teachers said he always had a good answer, he knew that was a possibility. But we also prayed every night that his dad would come home safe.

The kids are usually very good for me when Mark deploys but there were a few differences that time. One of the biggest problems was that they would stay awake as long as I was up. They thought they had to sleep with me because I was lonely. Worrying about the kids and their reactions was the hardest part for me. I felt more stress and was less patient with the kids. I gave more of my attention to the phone or the TV instead of to them, which is where they think my attention should be.

The wives speculated the whole time on when the guys would come home and whether or not there would be a war. We spent a lot of time talking about things like that when we couldn't make a difference anyway. Wives would even get into pointless arguments over when the guys would come home. The stress showed.

As I walked out the door on my way to church that Wednesday evening with my friend Karin Yohe, a neighbor called to say the war had started. We turned the TV on and decided to stay and watch the fireworks. Even though I knew it was coming and really wasn't surprised, I almost couldn't believe it happened. We'd been told that the A-10s would not go in for three days and so assumed our husbands were not in any immediate danger, which was nice. Ignorance is bliss.

The squadron commander's wife, Sherry Green, called each wife the next morning to say that all of the guys had flown and were back safe. After that, she called the flight commander's wives with news and we called our girls. That was our regular chain of information.

I felt it was important for the kids to keep the same routine at school and at home. I didn't notice the change in them that I expected when the war started. They went to school in the morning and then music class or McDonalds with friends in the afternoon. The wives had an activity one or two nights a week. Most of us kept our routines during the war.

Most of the newlyweds cried and were upset, afraid, when the war started, but they did okay. Two of them were in my flight so I talked to them at least once every day, and they each had someone to get together with.

I didn't get to talk to Mark for the first month he was gone and then only once a month for most of Desert Shield. We didn't talk about the war or what he did at all. I knew there were questions he couldn't answer and that he couldn't talk about their plans so we avoided the subject all together. We talked about day-to-day life instead and complained about the slow mail. His letters took 12 to 14 days to get to me.

If anything, support increased even though they were very supportive from the start. The city put flags on all the flagpoles along MacArthur Drive, the main street; people had signs in their yards saying they supported our troops; stores had signs in their windows. The schools all had support rallies. Fort Polk and Camp Beauregard are both also near here and sent people to Saudi. With the people from England AFB, this is a big military community.

When Mark found those Scuds, I got to see him on CNN, which was really nice. I also got nearly 50 phone calls that night and was called by the local paper and radio station for interviews. But I was not pleased with the national press during the war. They asked questions they knew wouldn't be answered like, "When is the war going to start? Where will it be? What are we going to do?" It was frustrating watching them dig for that kind of information when they're supposed to be on our side.

About halfway through the war, Steven said, "I don't want to watch the news any more. If something important happens, tell me, but I don't want to watch the news any more."

Before the war, we were told that we would be notified of any A-10 crashes before the press found out. But three out of four times, we saw it on CNN first. That was really hard: all we knew was that an A-10 had gone down so it could have been any of them. The commanders didn't know anything about the crashes that quickly. It was an upsetting way to find out and not the way it was supposed to work.

When we lost an A-10 from Alex[28], we heard it on CNN first while the local commanders had no information. We assumed they would know if it was one of ours and so thought it wasn't. Then I got a call from Sherry saying it was a jet from another squadron and the pilot was presumed dead. That brought the reality of war a lot closer, especially for the wives in that other squadron 'cause he was well-liked. Thankfully, he came home with the POWs.

We anticipated the end of the war but I was still real excited when President Bush came on to announce the cease-fire. I screamed when he said that and Steven came out of his room: "Why did you scream, mom?" It was a happy scream so we hugged and he watched the news with me. The phone calls started again with everyone saying how glad they were that it was over. Then our focus turned to their coming home.

The next month was very long. The war was over, there wasn't as much news, and we were afraid the war might start again. We went through another period of rumors on when they would come home, who would come home first—the regular uncertainty.

The day Mark got back, I took the kids to the base in the little flight suits they wanted to wear—they were real excited. There were 5000 people there and it was a neat, sort of patriotic feeling to watch the planes fly over in full squadron formations. The guys finally got out of the planes and the boys and I ran up to give Mark a big hug. There was a band and speeches but we skipped all that by staying out at the plane.

The boys stayed physically attached to him for the rest of the day, and I think Mark spent the next two weeks playing baseball in the back-yard with the kids. Since the war, Mark's had more time for family than he ever had before.

---

[28]Alex—England AFB near Alexandria, Louisiana.

Part Three:

First, We're Going to Cut It Off . . . The Air War

If you could see
through my eyes
what I have seen,
what stories would you tell?
What memories would you hold?
When I wipe away the sweat of war unseen,
all that remains
are stains of blood.
Now look at my eyes,
into my eyes,
the blood is not mine.
Only the stories and memories.
I can wash away the blood
but I cannot forget
the human cost of war.

David Hafer   3 Feb 91
Air Force pilot
Riyadh

5

No Cake Walk

First Lieutenant Greg Walters, Chase, was typical of the natural pilots who are assigned the best new fighters fresh out of pilot training. The son of a fighter pilot, he saw much of the world as he grew up. It should have been no great surprise that he worked harder than he'd ever worked in his life so that he, too, could choose fighters.

His jet was the F-16. The Fighting Falcon to public relations people but the Viper to her pilots, the F-16 is such a joy to fly that euphoria is actually a safety problem. Vipers were designed for the close-in visual dogfight and so are lightweight, high-thrust, tight-turning machines. Speed is life and F-16s depend on speed more than most because there's no room for armor, self-sealing fuel tanks or an extra engine. Single-seat and single-engine, Vipers are built the way fighters were meant to be.

First Lieutenant Walters:

I was born in Alexandria, Virginia, the second son of a fighter pilot. We moved to Charleston, South Carolina, when I was eight so I grew up there after my dad went to fly airlines. Once I made up my mind, he backed my choice of the Air Force 100% and I'm sure he's glad I did. Fighters are something I can go home and relate to him about and he always understands. I took ROTC in college but really had to fight for a pilot slot since I needed two waivers for my eyes.

I moved to Columbus AFB, Mississippi, for a year of pilot training. I had to work pretty hard to do well but I knew that one year of my life would decide what I'd do for the next six or seven years. So I decided that, no matter what, nothing would interfere with pilot training. Even so, it was, no kidding, one of the most fun years of my life.

I was an experienced wingman when Kuwait was invaded. I had been in the squadron at Torrejon, Spain, for six months and was at the point where I could walk out to the airplane and feel comfortable with it. I had enough flying hours in the F-16 to be confident whatever the mission.

Around the 21st of August 1990, we were told to prepare to deploy to Greece. We packed up the squadron and were ready in 24 hours. Then we were put on standby. Then we were told to prepare for Aviano, Italy. Then we went on standby again and back and forth until, finally, it got no-kidding serious. Nobody knew exactly where we were going but we were very ready. We launched for Doha, Qatar, on August 29th.

The flight down there was kind of spooky. We were used to peacetime flying but all of a sudden our mode fours[1] were being tickled all the time and we listened to the Navy ships we had to steer clear of or they might shoot us. Things were serious and almost spooky. The terrain was also really odd. Egypt was just sand for as far as I could see. The Nile was pretty neat and then it was back to the desert.

We flew armed with four AIM-9Ms (Sidewinders) and a hot gun. The trip was a 7½-hour hop with tankers.

Our living conditions at first were great even though it was 120 degrees at 5:00 in the afternoon. There was no base, no unit had ever deployed there before, so we went to the Gulf Sheraton Hotel. That lasted about 10 days until we got the order to move out immediately. We had one hour to move into the Qatar enlisted dorms, two to a room. The Emir of the country seemed hurt that we left and offered to pay for the two hotels on either side of us and to have a boat patrolling on the water in front of the hotel at all times to handle the terrorist threat. They really took it personally that we would not stay in their hotel.

The flying was excellent 'cause we didn't have the 2000 foot minimum altitude restriction the Spanish put on us. Because of that problem with Spain, we didn't have much experience flying low. So we had to train ourselves to fly at 150 or 100 feet. That was the great part of being deployed to a war situation: fewer rules and restrictions.

I thought it was great to be a lieutenant on a wartime deployment. I had a great position at a great time in my life and I get to enjoy what I've done for the rest of my career.

We also ended up with close to 30 Mirage F-1s[2] to use as adver-

---

[1]mode four—Classified part of the Identification Friend or Foe system that electronically identifies an aircraft to properly equipped radars (like those connected to missiles).

[2]Mirage—Family of fighters built by France.

saries. The Iraqis fly them too, so what better training could we have than to fight the actual airplane that we'd probably fly combat against? We could put together an eight or sixteen ship and fight eight F-1s on the way to the target. You couldn't beat it. Then the Canadian F-18s arrived so our air-to-air training got really good 'cause the Canadians are tough. The training was unbelievable.

Even at $14 for three minutes, I called my parents fairly often to find out what was going on in the States. Julie, my wife, was eventually able to call too, so she also let me know how people back home reacted to Desert Shield. It didn't take long to figure out that we had a ton of support. We got Any Service Member mail with all kinds of cakes and food and all that stuff so we knew everybody was behind us. We also pitched in and bought a TV and VCR to see news tapes that were maybe two weeks old. That good communication lasted until they turned the phones off about a week before the 15th of January.

I opened a letter from a kid that was funny as hell. It said: "Dear soldier, I don't know why you joined the army. I would not join the army for $100. You are stupid. Your friend Minesole. P.S. Write back, butthole." I thought that was funny so I made copies and sent it to some of my friends.

I also listened to a tape from a super sincere guy who said he sat up all night to record some songs for us. He was really patriotic and wanted to know what he could do, how he could help us out. He filled a 90-minute tape asking what he could do for us. He went into detail about his family and how they would help us and just write for whatever we needed. He was about 40 years old, lived in a trailer in Michigan and was going through some hard times himself financially. His job was on the down side because of all that was going on in the Middle East. But you can only eat so many cookies so we didn't need anything. I wrote him back to say thanks.

The first two days of the war were pretty benign. We dropped bombs and saw some bullets coming at us but there weren't a whole lot of SAMs. We thought, "This isn't so bad." But on the third day of the war, the 19th of January, we were scheduled to go to Baghdad. That was a jolt. I looked at the map with the SAMs plotted and there were so many that I couldn't even comprehend them. Baghdad was just a big red spot covered in SAM rings. I got a really bad feeling in my gut,

Then I started rationalizing: "It probably isn't that bad. They wouldn't just send us up there blindly." And, of course, nobody would say, "No, I'm not going to Baghdad."

The guy next door came over to talk before we went to sleep. We were kind of looking forward to it for the excitement. A bunch of guys said they had trouble sleeping that night but I was always so tired that I hit the sack and got a good night's rest, no kidding. I was always tired those first couple of weeks, just drained.

I thought about getting shot down. If that happened, I wanted to at least have eaten and been well hydrated, so I always ate before a mission. I also always wore my jacket when I flew. Everybody looked at me funny as I burned up on the ground but it got down into the 40s on the ground in Iraq.

We got to the intelligence part of the pre-mission briefing and there were the SAMs again. I hoped the guy would say: "Well, these missiles are gone and the Weasels got those and the rest are unconfirmed." But he didn't. They were all still there, waiting for me.

The guys who flew the morning go to Baghdad got back. They had aborted for a lot of reasons. The Weasels and the F-111s didn't show up, a tanker didn't show up, the weather was solid to 39,000 feet; it was a nightmare. We could get above that weather but it's not very smart since you'll never see a SAM coming. My squadron commander was so aggressive that it was amazing to see him return with all his bombs.

Our launch went normally and yes, the weather was really cruddy. We couldn't go under it, and, right at the border, it was solid up to 28,000 feet. One of the tankers didn't show so Tico went looking for it with his four ship[3]. The mission started off fairly disorganized and not as professional as we were for the rest of the war. We weren't helter-skelter but we weren't in the groove either. Then four guys turned around and went home with a variety of aircraft problems. We were getting frustrated, which gave me a bad feeling; we're much more professional than that.

And we ended up with only half of the Weasels we expected. We found out that wasn't nearly enough.

A single huge black cloud from a very heavy triple-A gun marked the border at 30,000 feet in front of us.

The clouds north of the border were much lower, about 10,000 feet, and thin in places. We passed over Talill airfield just before sunset and its triple-A looked like firecrackers, a ton of them. That threat reminder sprung us into gear. We had to get squared away or go home. So we spread out and settled down as things seem to go smoothly again.

My four ship went after the air force headquarters that you saw on CNN. There was Nips and myself and then Hobbs and M.R. The southern guys could barely see their targets through thin clouds but ours was obscured. When their bombs went off, SAMs started flying everywhere! We didn't know it at the time but the Weasels had bingoed out[4] and left

---

[3]four ship—Four aircraft in formation fighting as a team. See division.

[4]bingoed out—Left for home after reaching the bare minimum, bingo, fuel.

without a radio call. We might have done things differently if we'd known our SAM suppression was gone, but hindsight is 20/20.

It was time to get out of there. Then I got a SAM launch indication on my RWR so I was really scared. I looked to my right for the missile and saw M.R. blow up about a mile and a half away. It looked to me like the tail of his airplane was blown off and I thought, "That guy's dead." I didn't know who it was at the time but it sure looked to me like the airplane disintegrated.

I jettisoned my bombs and gas tanks to get some speed and broke left to stay on my flight lead. He called, "Just hang with me!" The radio was completely trashed with everybody screaming: "SAM launch! SAM launch here! SAM launch there!" We lost all mutual support basically because everybody was spread out doing everything they could to get away from the SAMs. The elements[5] ended up on their own with some single ships like me trying to catch up.

I was in full afterburner chasing my leader but, whenever I got a missile launched at me, I couldn't care about anybody but myself. He had to do the same thing so we had a hard time getting back together.

Another missile passed through the cloud of turning jets and detonated off Tico's left wing. It was such a helpless feeling listening to Tico call that he was hit and had no engine. But what could we do? If we went back and orbited around him we'd get shot down real quick. Then he called, "I've got an engine. I'm all right!" He was leaking fuel and burning a lot of oil, smoking really bad, but at least he was flying at about 300 knots. He had to disregard any other SAMs 'cause he couldn't maneuver.

It seemed like it took hours, just forever, to get out of there. It actually took two to three minutes; the whole thing was over in less than three minutes. The Iraqis fired 20 to 25 missiles including nine at E.T. His dodging those SAMs took him below 10,000 feet and he's lucky he didn't get hit by bullets. He just didn't give up and made it home. We called him Dodger after that. He was a hero on base after the crew chiefs[6] saw his videotape. They were amazed.

Tico made it almost 150 miles south of Baghdad. Then his engine quit, the airplane went out of control, and he jumped out. It was really grueling to listen to Tico as his jet died though he was very calm and certainly handled it better than I did. We got one radio call from Tico that he was on the ground and surrounded.

---

[5]element—Air Force formation of two airplanes within a larger formation. A two ship.

[6]crew chief—Enlisted person who "owns" and babies a jet. When given a darn good reason, crew chiefs grudgingly lend their jets to fliers, who invariably break something that the long-suffering crew chief must fix before the next ham-fisted flier shows up. See plane captain.

The tanker guys were unbelievable. It was the third day of the war with a Fulcrum[7] in the area but they still flew north of the border to help out. I climbed to 45,000 feet to save as much gas as I could. I was pretty much by myself though I could see some F-16s in the distance. I was too low on gas to try to catch up and the tanker was already north of me by then.

I tried to digest what had happened as I cruised home high and slow. It was tough to think about M.R. because I assumed he was dead. And his wife was pregnant, due in two weeks. In the hour from the border to Doha, I went back and forth from being okay to tears of frustration because I couldn't help him.

I landed with 700 pounds of gas, barely enough to light the engine. Then I almost taxied into a C-130. My mind was Jello.

It was strange how normal everything was. We lost two jets, but there were the normal forms, the maintenance debriefing, and that kind of stuff. I found my flight commander and apologized for almost hitting the C-130 but he just looked at me and broke into tears. Everybody was in tears for a few minutes, the whole group of fighter pilots.

We had had a little trouble getting along with our support troops. I guess some people there had chips on their shoulders 'cause we were pilots, lived indoors while they had tents, and got some special privileges. There was some tension between the fliers and everybody else from the chow hall to the laundry guys to the transportation officers. For example, I stopped by the laundry tent on my way back that night. I just wanted my laundry but I had the white slip instead of the pink one. The clerk said, "No sir, you're suppose to have the pink slip." We could see my laundry on the shelf but he wouldn't give it to me. I'd had enough for one day and walked out.

Then word got around that we lost two airplanes; this fight was for keeps. Attitudes changed. That laundry guy asked another pilot in line, "What's wrong with him?" The pilot said, "In case you don't know, we're fighting a war. We lost two pilots today." So that laundry guy grabbed my bundle and found me to deliver it. Pilots weren't coming home all of a sudden, and the base pulled together. We finally became a team.

Thereafter, the maintenance guys, weapons guys, crew chiefs, everybody, would gather around when we walked out to the airplane: "Okay, let's see your target. What are you going after?" There were even more people around when we landed to see how we did. And they sure didn't want to see you bring "their" bombs back. The crew chiefs would act depressed when that happened.

---

[7]Fulcrum—MiG-29. Latest-generation Soviet fighter bomber. Roughly similar to the F-18 and the best fighter the Iraqis had.

Those losses brought a feeling of unity to the whole wing that wasn't there before. I don't think you can experience that kind of thing in peacetime.

It turned out that M.R. punched out too but got captured instantly. We got them both back on March 5th.

The war ended at the end of February and we were ready to get out of there. Then we got M.R. and Tico back so we were whole again and it was time to go. We were a couple planes short but so what. That's why God made taxpayers (sic).

After a couple delays and missed dates, we left on March 29th. The reception at Torrejon was very small compared to the States but it was still great. The "important" people gave their speeches before most of the guys arrived and then left. We didn't care as long as our wives were there.

There's more than a grain of truth to the contention that military wives hold the toughest jobs in the military. If you have any doubts, ask one. Julie Walters was introduced to that new life when she left her extended family in the Old South to join her fighter pilot in Spain. Her lesson turned extreme when, a few weeks after the wedding, her pilot went to war.

Julie Walters:

I knew nothing at all of the military life before we were married. I was born and raised in Charleston and was really leery of all the moving I'd seen the military kids do. We got married in June 1990 while Greg was stationed in Spain and I got to our apartment on the Spanish economy a month before the first deployment false alarm. There were several more false alarms while he ran around trying to get powers of attorney, wills, and all that stuff. I couldn't even sign checks in his checkbook yet. The squadron finally deployed but they wouldn't tell us where they were going.

There was no point staying on the Spanish economy alone so, after my parents took a vacation in Spain, I went home to Charleston and filled in at Sea-Land where I had worked before I got married. They were busy with shipments of military supplies. I talked to people in Spain every three or four days to trade information, but the military wasn't telling them anything I didn't already know.

My brother, my best friend, and I were standing in the kitchen making spaghetti when a TV announcer said, "The liberation of Kuwait has begun!" That just set my mind running about what was going on, and I stayed up all that night watching television while the phone rang and rang and rang. People wanted to make sure everything was okay and asked about Greg. They wanted to know about his job, did he fly air-to-air, did he fly air-to-ground. I couldn't answer most of them 'cause I didn't know. We'd been married for nine months and together for less than two. Greg called after the war started so I learned a lot more. They only flew during the day, which was a huge relief for some reason.

It was good to go to work 'cause it kept my mind off it and me away from the TV. You could get addicted to watching it. I also knew he was asleep while I worked so there was nothing to worry about. I tried to catch the 10:00 A.M. Pentagon briefing each day because it was the most informative.

All but about five of the squadron's 20 wives went to the States so we set up a telephone chain. I got a call one afternoon and the first thing she said was, "It's not your husband." That was the first thing out of her mouth. "We've lost a pilot but we don't know his situation. They thought they saw an ejection seat but no parachute." Then I got a call with the same news from the pilot's mother-in-law. I was at a total loss for words to say to her. At least we were notified before the media released the story.

The red, white, and blue flags really came out when the war started and I think people were even more interested in what was going on. The debating stopped and we all became one. I'd go shopping on King Street and get accosted by people who were full of questions, I mean just hundreds of them. Both our families have been in that community a long time so we have a huge network of friends who checked on us.

Greg played down the winding down of the war because I got too excited. It wasn't truly over yet and he didn't want me to get my hopes up. When the war did end it was kind of anticlimactic.

I returned to Spain two weeks prior to his arrival. The people on the base were super. The colonels really catered to the wives and took care of emergency leave flights on MAC, housing, everything.

We decorated the squadron and made lots of food. The firefighter trucks sprayed water as the airplanes taxied in so it was real dramatic.

We went to the Canary Islands a couple days later to get to know each other again.

6

You're Never Too Old for a Fight

Captain Frank Ochello went to war in a B-52 that was his senior. Built in the fifties for a starring role in World War III, BUFFs[1] are cramped, uncomfortable, and a bear to fly. Their long, relatively thin wings were designed for very high altitude penetrations of the Soviet heartland and so made for a wild ride down in the weeds[2]. BUFF pilots arguably had the most physically demanding missions of the war, given 14-hour, multiple refueling flights, at night, in an antique. But, when the job is to obliterate a large target, there's no substitute for the very best. The BUFFs proved that good jets with even better crews really are never too old for a fight.

Captain Ochello:

I reported to my new squadron at Barksdale AFB two months before the air war broke out. Pam and I were happy to get to Barksdale because I'm originally from New Orleans and went to Louisiana State University while she's from Mississippi. I'd lived in Louisiana my entire life and had never been out north until the Air Force decided to send us to the farthest northest spot in the country, lovely K. I. Sawyer AFB, Michigan. I didn't know there was that much snow in the world. I had about eight

---

[1]BUFF—Big, Ugly, Flying, um . . . Fellow. "Affectionate" nickname for the B-52 Stratofortress.

[2]in the weeds—Really low. If your job is to penetrate radar defenses and you aren't scaring squirrels out of the trees, you're doing something wrong.

months as an aircraft commander at K. I. Sawyer before they opened up a few more south rotations to get some of us out of the tundra and back to civilization.

I barely had time to join a crew and get checked out before we started seriously talking about deploying for the probable war. That was approximately January 3rd, 1991, and the deadline was on the 15th. Deploying looked inevitable. My wife was kind of dragging her heels because she didn't want to believe anything was going to happen. I said, "Look, you're going to have to start doing a lot of things on your own." I got some life insurance without a war clause[3], put our paperwork in order, and started packing. It was really tough making those plans, but everybody had to do it. I had to be sure Pam would be well taken care of if I didn't come back.

Predeployment training started getting serious. SAC finally let us use live war loads in training, which was amazing since I'd never seen more than nine weapons (bombs) at a time and had never dropped a full load. We practiced some high altitude stuff because we hadn't bombed from high level in a while and usually glossed over it. We still concentrated on low altitude though since Iraq had quite a complement of SAM systems and early warning radars—probably right behind Russia in terms of numbers and quality. After practicing all phases of a mission, each crew flew two nice short 8- or 9-hour sorties to the test ranges in Nevada to put it all together.

Nobody on base believed it was gonna come down to a shootin' match even though we already had a few crews deployed to Diego Garcia[4]. But as the deadline started gettin' closer and it started gettin' a little more serious, people were forced to see what was coming. There was already a tremendous amount of support for the deployed folks and we didn't get complaints in the local area even though we were flying at all hours of the night. The local community was real supportive.

The shock of our deployment orders still hit my wife pretty hard because you really can't prepare for it. I think it's better to be sent on no notice so you don't dwell on the risks for two months.

A call put us on telephone standby. I called the guys in the crew and told them to pack their bags so we could meet in the squadron the next day. We couldn't fly our jet over because Spain didn't want to let us in until the war started. We had to travel as passengers on a KC-135

---

[3]war clause—That line in most life insurance policies that voids the coverage during war. Military fliers have a hard time finding commercial life insurance that covers hostilities and crashes.

[4]Diego Garcia—British island in the southern Indian ocean. It served as an unsinkable aircraft carrier for bombers, tankers, and transports.

tanker to be ready for the bombers when they were finally allowed in. The multiple good-byes while all that was diplomatically sorted out were tough on the families.

When we first got to Moron, Spain, we were concerned about how much protesting was going on back home and how much support we would actually get from Congress. I remember the media dwelling on 2000 protesters in a city of 1 million. There were only 2000 protesters but that's all you saw on the news. Then the media started showing the other side, the folks who said, "Nobody wants to kill, nobody wants to see folks get killed, but we're gonna support our troops." For example, we were worried that the Super Bowl might be canceled. We wanted it to go on because America doesn't stop for Saddam. We watched the game and were amazed at the amount of support we had right from the get-go. We really enjoyed that game. From what I could gather, the support was really building across the country and that helped us a lot.

Most of the ground troops lived in tents with floors. The aircrews had dorm rooms that were real nice compared to how the rest of the folks were being housed. We had three fliers to a small room that was probably designed for one person, so it got a little cramped with our extra gear in there. SAC crews stay together normally so we'd see each other as much as we'd see our wives day to day. Being squashed into dorm rooms was no big deal.

As an aircraft commander with about 1800 hours in the B-52, I had a little more experience than the average guy we sent over there since quite a few young folks deployed.

We needed the three or four days before the war kicked off to get used to the local area and local flying. The B-52 community doesn't deploy to Europe a lot so I'd never dealt with foreigners trying to speak English. Other than that, we spent time studying our targets, other potential targets, and the egress areas. There was a big argument going on about what tactic we should use: should we go in high or low? We finally said to heck with it, the first cell is gonna launch and split up high and low.

In fact, we were working on those details at about midnight on the 16th when Colonel Marcotte stuck his head in and passed the word to our squadron commanders that the war had kicked off. We turned on the TVs to see what was going on. We knew airplanes were enroute to us from Barksdale loaded with bombs. We were just going to put fuel on them and launch.

We had a great crew: the co-pilot was Lieutenant Gary Forhan, the radar navigator was Captain Mark Carbo, the navigator was Lieutenant Mike Dilda, the electronic warfare officer was Captain Mark Laflamme, and the gunner was Staff Sergeant Ray Helms. We didn't actually fly the first mission that night even though we were a spare crew and were prepared to fly. We started up our BUFF and watched the six mission birds get off with no problems.

We also had problems with one of our local allies, Turkey, because they didn't want us flying B-52s through their country. B-52s have an ominous connotation to some folks. That diplomacy really hurt the timing of the first mission and coordination with our support package of F-4 Wild Weasels, F-15 CAP, F-111s, and EC-130s[5].

The seriousness of our mission really hit home as I watched six of my buddy bomber crews take off while we were ready to jump in. I prayed for them all to come home 'cause we were gonna do it the next night. They ended up aborting the mission after the first air refueling because the diplomatic clearance from Turkey came so late that the support package fell through. They brought the bombs back.

The next evening, we launched six B-52s followed by six KC-10s with one minute spacing between each launch. I'm told that was pretty impressive. We were number six, which was number three in the low cell.

We fought headwinds in the climb and so burned too much fuel. We were immediately concerned about getting to the target with no fuel and so called the KC-10s. Their support was tremendous: they said, "We'll give you every drop we've got even if we have to divert somewhere." They were really gonna hang it out for us.

I had never taken on more than 25,000 pounds of gas during practice refueling. We took on 190,000 pounds that time and I was on the boom[6] for about 30 minutes since my young co-pilot wasn't refueling-qualified. Refueling is one of the more challenging parts of flying the B-52 because your gross weight increases as you take on gas and the underpowered G-model[7] we had really struggled to keep up toward the end. One hundred ninety thousand pounds is more than the B-52 weighs empty. B-52s hadn't taken on that much gas since the combat missions in Vietnam.

We finished refueling near Sicily and about four hours from the Iraqi

---

[5]EC-130—E (for electronic warfare) version of the C-130 light transport that jammed enemy radar and communications. They were a real showstopper for the Iraqi defenses.

[6]on the boom—Connected to the refueling probe (boom) that extends from the back of a tanker. Refueling in the air is formation flying at its most challenging in a large aircraft.

[7]G-model—Aircraft variations are designated with suffixes, so a G-model B-52 is newer than a D-model but older than an H-model. All B-52s older than the H-models are equipped with ancient turbojet engines and are underpowered. The H-model has very good turbofans and actually held a world time-to-climb record. Jet pilots can never get enough power in their aircraft or cars, so they don't appreciate gutless engines.

border. Guys started thinking about getting into enemy country. A couple of the crew members had Kevlar vests and were stacking the extra parachutes against the fuselage next to their stations as additional flack protection. Not a bad idea. We checked our guns and made sure everything was shipshape. I was gettin' a little nervous and we still had a few hours to think about it before crossing the fence[8].

We finally got our clearance into Turkey and split into high and low cells. Our low cell descended into the weather at the mountains and that's when training took over. We don't practice tactical flying in the weather and definitely not that low—in the mountains—with weather—at night. The clouds started at three to five hundred feet above the ground in that area of southern Turkey with mountain peaks between eight and nine thousand feet. We flew manually using our TA set[9], which is not a true terrain following system like on an F-111. We started at 500 feet above the rocks to get the pilots ready for the real low altitude work while the navigator kept us masked[10] from Iraqi radar. I'm sure they knew we were comin'. So the radar navigator[11] directed us and the co-pilot backed him up. Everybody got real quiet as the radar navigator talked and I followed his direction, putting the airplane where it needed to be.

As we warmed up, I started relaxing because I trust Mark and he trusts me. You've got to trust each other. He was tense as he worked real hard. Even though his voice was tense, it calmed me down. But I shouldn't have been calm since I'd only flown blind in mountains like that in the simulator.

I took it down to 300 feet where we stayed until we got into Iraq. Our mission called for us to stay in country for an hour and three minutes, definitely not a five-minute job. The terrain flattened out so I blew for the ground and got back in the dirt again. There were several divisions of Iraqi troops in front of us that some F-111s woke up so bullets were flying everywhere. Thank goodness they used tracers, which helped us see the barrage fire[12]. The co-pilot called out the flak while I

---

[8]fence—Boundary between the good guys and the bad guys. As John Wayne would've said, "When you cross the fence into Indian country, partner, you'd better have your guns loaded and your feces consolidated."

[9]TA set—Terrain avoidance radar. Radar display of the terrain in front of an aircraft that enables the pilot to manually avoid the "rocks."

[10]terrain masking—Flying "behind" terrain to avoid detection by radar.

[11]On a crew-served airplane, crew members are referred to by the position they fill. So the radar operator is "radar," the aircraft commander is "pilot," the other pilot is "copilot," etc.

[12]barrage fire—Unaimed anti-aircraft artillery fired in the air to create a lethal barrier over the ground unit.

watched a radar scope and tried not to look outside. Visibility was really low that night and we couldn't even see with the night vision goggles the co-pilot was using. He called out the triple-A and I actively maneuvered the airplane—horsing it around so as to not present a stable target for any of those gunners. Most of it was barrage fire but quite a bit of it was being directed[13]. We had to figure out which areas were defended because our intelligence briefings weren't very good. They depended on photo satellites, which didn't work when the weather was bad.

Number one made his run with the second bomber a minute behind him. By the time we came through last, every gunner in that valley was awake.

That's when it got really hectic: the octaves in our voices went up and guys screamed, "Break left! Break right!" The electronic warfare officer piped up saying an SA-6 was lookin' at us. We tried to stay down at 200 feet on the radar altimeter[14] and not hit the ground. I got a little low one time and the guys downstairs[15] let us know about it as we touched 50 feet: "That's too low! Climb!" We maneuvered all the way to the target area trying to avoid the triple-A. It was really intense. The jockeys[16] and some of the fighter guys nicknamed that area near the town of Mozul: Happy Valley.

They must have gotten a deal when they bought their bullets 'cause they sure had a lot of them. Some colonel made a comment that there must have been a blue-light special on cannon shells at K Mart. But they were evidently not duck hunters because they missed us.

The co-pilot was outside the aircraft[17] making sure we didn't run into the ground or get hit by the triple-A. The electronic warfare officer pointed out radars that were lookin' at us and called out what we should do to avoid them while the navigator figured out the attack heading. They were both downstairs working the scopes and radar just like a training mission. I'm glad they didn't have a window to see us trying to stay out of the dirt at 200 feet.

---

[13]aimed (directed) fire—Anti-aircraft fire deliberately aimed at a specific aircraft, as in shooting skeet.

[14]radar altimeter—Simple radar pointed down that displays exact altitude above the ground.

[15]downstairs—Lower level of a B-52 cockpit. Two crew members ride in the lower level and eject downward. They don't like to fly too low.

[16]jockey—Airplane driver. Flier.

[17]outside the aircraft—Figure of speech meaning attention was focused outside the cockpit while leaving the instruments, displays, weapons, etc., to other crew members.

The radar asked what we could see out there. We were still down at 200 feet and I said, "I can't see shit—it's dark!" That kind of drew him back a little bit because he thought we were seeing things outside. He was a pretty experienced navigator but he had never flown that low without the pilots being able to see out the windows.

We maneuvered off track quite a bit and had to get over to the IP. We had to keep the airplane steady from then on so I just blocked it all out to get the bombs on target. Sixty seconds out, I saw that we were still too low and so yanked the airplane up to about 500 feet. I didn't want to come all that way and drop a bunch of duds or frag[18] our own plane. The number two B-52 was a minute ahead of us and dropped a full load of fifty-one 750-pounders. The night turned to day. I wanted the fireworks to fade real quick but it didn't because the target was on fire. We were lit up by fires from the chemical weapons facility we were attacking. As if that wasn't bad enough, I had my doubts about flying right over a burning chemical weapons research plant.

The high guys came in from different ground tracks to spread bombs all over the target and so did we. The first jet in the cell came in from the right, number two flew up the middle, and we came in from the left. There was a minute between each bomber so we wouldn't arrive at the same time. That timing became pretty critical because somebody would fly through the bomb blasts otherwise. The frag hung in the air for about 25 seconds and there were 51 bombs on each jet.

We got to the target area and radar-dropped the weapons—scratch one chemical weapons factory. It was destroyed, totally destroyed. It would have been neat to sit back and watch six guys working as a team like that.

Our next concern were the SAMs out there looking for us. I got us back down into the dirt and, since the weapons were gone, it was the electronic warfare officer's job to keep us abreast of the missiles and triple-A being shot at us. We used the radar to look for terrain to hide behind. I remember one comment comin' from downstairs after some of the triple-A died down: "I don't have anything lookin' at us, is anybody shootin at you?" "No." "WELL THEN CLIMB GODAMMIT!" That got a chuckle out of everybody and relaxed us a little bit. We climbed a few hundred feet.

We still had 33 minutes of flying and a range of mountains to cross on the way out of Iraq. The G model is underpowered so you've really got to look out ahead of you and plan your climb early. At about seven

---

[18]frag—(verb) To be hit with fragmented pieces of an exploding warhead. (noun) Fragmentation. High-velocity metal parts from a bomb casing.

miles from the mountains and at 500 knots, I firewalled[19] the throttles, yanked the airplane up, and traded airspeed for altitude[20]. I would have felt a hell of a lot better if we could have seen something outside. We don't practice terrain avoidance at night and in the weather for obvious reasons.

Mike piped up to say we were out of the country. I was so happy to be out of there that I could have kissed every one of those guys. We climbed to a couple thousand feet above the terrain and relaxed. We'd used every ounce of adrenaline, there was no more left.

We got behind the other BUFFs during the bomb run so the other aircraft were waiting anxiously for me to pipe up 'cause they were really worried that we didn't come out. I wasn't going to report up while we were still in country so they were real happy to hear my voice when we reached Turkey.

We had already flown approximately eight hours with an hour in combat when it came time for the second refueling. I was exhausted but the co-pilot was new and couldn't refuel. My left arm was worn out so I had the co-pilot handle the throttles while I switched to my right arm. He had never tried refueling so I talked him through it.

Then came the tough part—staying awake. I'd never been that tired before in my life and kept falling asleep on top of the yoke[21]. The autopilot brought us home.

We didn't call home that night but got hooked up after other missions with a bunch of ham radio operators in the States. On their own time, effort, and money, they would connect us to the Sprint phone network. Sprint let us call home free so each member of the crew would take turns. The only problem was that the whole world listened as you talked to your wife so you had to watch what you said. I called home to hear Pam's voice one more time just in case. We couldn't say much but I think the wives could tell there was a change in our voices. I held back since I didn't want Pam to know how frightened I was after flying a mission. I just wanted her to know we were home. As the war drug on a bit

---

[19]firewall—Reference to the fire barrier between the engine and the cockpit on old piston-engined fighters. Throttles were usually rods that stuck out of that firewall, so firewalling the throttle meant pushing it all the way to the stops without regard to the damage full power might do to the engine. It's better to bring back damaged engines than to not come home at all.

[20]Flight is largely energy management. Kinetic energy (airspeed) and potential energy (altitude and engine power) must be traded for each other, so an underpowered jet always loses speed in a steep climb.

[21]yoke—Aircraft control wheel. Most large aircraft have control wheels, while fighters have sticks.

and POWs were paraded on the news, I realized that I didn't really prepare her for that. I didn't talk to her about it.

There was no attempt to show off how tough we were 'cause every damn one of us was scared.

We landed, checked the aircraft for chemical contamination, and downed a couple of beers pretty quick. I remember kissing the ground, shaking everybody's hand, and being happy to be alive. Then we went through debriefing, which stretched a 16-hour sortie into a 24-hour day. But your buddies were up next so you let them know anything you learned. The bombing from our base went around the clock with somebody taking off every three hours.

The Iraqis really wanted to shoot a B-52 down and had some very heavy triple-A. But, for some strange reason, the SAM threat wasn't there. They were apparently afraid to turn the radars on 'cause our Wild Weasel buddies were doing a great job. So we shifted to high-altitude attacks and our crew flew about every other night for the rest of the war.

We hung around for eight or ten days after the war and learned that even fliers can only drink so much. We didn't know if the war was going to stay over and we wanted to go home.

As part of the original contingent from Barksdale, we were allowed to fly one of our eight bombers home. We flew straight over the Atlantic, over Boston, refueled inflight and continued nonstop to Barksdale.

On the way, we radioed the same ham operator from Indiana. We got to talk to our families again with his help. A lot of folks appreciated what he was doing. I don't know what their day jobs were but those guys ran their radios all night. We could hear everybody else call home and it tugged at my heart to hear what the other fliers were saying. I don't know how he did it. He couldn't stop saying how proud he was of what we were doing over there, and we said we couldn't have done it without guys like him.

We got back over Barksdale with eight bombers in formation and circled Shreveport before landing. There were lots of dignitaries shaking hands, but I just wanted my wife. I didn't want to shake anybody's hand or deal with the cameras or talk to the media. I just wanted to see my wife and go off and relax for awhile. I didn't want to think about it.

There were people I didn't even know shaking my hand and saying how proud they were of us and how happy they were that we were home alive. But nobody was happier than me. The wives were supposed to wait behind some line, but they said to heck with that and broke through as soon as we shook the last dignitary's hand. I won't forget that day for the rest of my life.

Captain Ochello earned the Distinguished Flying Cross on his first com-bat mission.

Pam Ochello has had to put up with quite a bit during her short time as an Air Force wife—and that's saying something given the unique lifestyle of military families. Born and raised in Mississippi, she moved to the Upper Peninsula of Michigan after her wedding. Even moving back south near home proved a mixed blessing when her husband went to war be-fore they'd even unpacked all the moving boxes.

Pam Ochello:

I met Frank while we were both in Columbus, Mississippi; he was in pi-lot training and I attended Mississippi University for Women. Moving from Mississippi to the snow in Michigan was quite a change for me, but being away from family and friends was tougher. I like moving around now even though it was tough being away from home at first. But you can't be a momma's baby in the Air Force and I wouldn't give it up for the world now.

We had been married about a year and a half by the time Frank's new squadron began planning to deploy. We knew deploying was a real possibility when we took the PCS[22] to Barksdale AFB 'cause people had already deployed from there.

Frank was assigned a crew on the day he checked in and went to work right away. Of course, we were still in the process of trying to find a home and move in. Combat flying is his job, though, and it was just a matter of time before he had to go. Joining a unit that was deploying for war was a risk, but just being in the military is a risk. And I want him to do what he enjoys 'cause if you don't enjoy your job, you're not happy. If Frank's not happy then I'm not happy. It's not something you look for-ward to or want to happen but at least we were closer to where we call home when he left.

I found out Frank was deploying while I was still at work when someone else got wind of it. After the initial shock, I had to shake it off because there were things to do. Frank couldn't get it all done himself. We had handled a lot of little things just in case, but we still had to get him all packed up and ready. He got a call putting him on telephone standby on a Thursday evening while we were eating dinner. We weren't sure exactly how much time we had so we packed him up that evening. I went out the next morning as quickly as possible to grab bat-teries and that kind of stuff. We had new power of attorneys and all the

---

[22]PCS—Permanent change of station. Permanent move from one base and assignment to another as opposed to a temporary assignment and return.

paperwork was updated. That's standard. Frank left on the next Saturday.

I work as a pension specialist for an actuarial consulting firm here in Shreveport. It's an 8:30-to-5:00 job that takes a lot of concentration. I couldn't keep my mind on work at first but everybody in the office was very patient with me and I was at work every day. It was great to be away from the concentration on military life and to hear the everyday goings-on with other people in the office.

People at my office were very supportive and real inquisitive. They asked a lot of questions I could not answer, either because I did not know or just couldn't say. We were not allowed to give out our guys' location, for example. The public seems to think they need to know stuff like that but it's better for our guys' safety if they don't.

I'd get up in the morning, go to work, and run errands on the way home. I took on a lot of the extra household jobs that come with purchasing a house so that there would be less on Frank's mind. He needed to concentrate on his work. So my days were full of ordinary things to keep my mind busy.

I came home the Wednesday evening after Frank left, turned on the TV and heard the news that the war had started. I'd been telling myself that it wasn't going to happen, that he wasn't in danger. We have a clue about what's going on when the guys fly training missions but, once the war broke out, we had very little contact with them. I quickly got to the point where I didn't want to know if he was flying that day 'cause it just kept me preoccupied at work when I was trying to use my work to distract me.

The people around me changed a lot. They were even more concerned, and they had a lot more questions that I still could not answer, like where he was and what he had hit. I had no way of knowing anyway. They were also trying to be very comforting by telling me B-52s don't do this and they don't do that. How would they know? I just didn't feel like talking about Frank's missions.

I finally got into a routine, but I was very unsettled and did not sleep well. I had been used to the safety of living on an Air Force base but now I wasn't. I probably caused some of my stress by thinking I wasn't as safe as I had been when we lived on an Air Force base.

I didn't sleep well and the days ran into each other.

My neighbors were real helpful and checked to see how I was. If they saw something strange around the house, they'd call to check on me. It was nice to have somebody who wasn't so close to the military to talk to. I'd come in from work and stop and chat for a little while about nothing in particular—especially nothing related to the war.

I couldn't hear from Frank much. His first call was only three minutes long and he caught me at the office with a million and one things to say that didn't get said. That was the day the war broke out and he just wanted to say that he was fine. We tried to come up with a schedule to catch him at the dorm. I would get up at 4:00 in the morning and then usually dial until 6:00 without even getting through to the operator in Spain. I was very excited when I was able to announce that he had a new niece during one of those radio calls on their way back to base. That news was so positive and so totally away from the war that it was very good for him to hear.

Tankers often brought their letters to Barksdale and put them in the local mail so we normally got them in three to four days. He wrote that the missions were extremely long, that it took them a long time to get where they were going, and then it took them that long to get back after they'd done their work.

We hadn't met many people before Frank deployed, but he ended up on an all-married crew which was kind of unusual. The six of us wives on the crew[23] got to know each other pretty well. We phoned and tried to get together as much as we could to swap rumors about how the guys were. We tried to take care of each other. We also wanted the guys to know that we were keeping in touch and that, if one of us needed something, we knew we could call on the other five.

I didn't like a lot of what I saw on TV. Frank and I are both private types, and we don't like the way the media hounds people. We were told not to speak with them, not that we had anything sensitive to tell them anyway. I wish the media understood that the families were just as much in the dark as the public. They would report locations and details that didn't need to be broadcast. It didn't take much to figure out that B-52s from Spain had to come through northern Iraq, for example. Frank doesn't go into much detail on what he does for a reason.

As the war went on, I got real tired. I wasn't sleeping well. But we didn't want the guys to worry and even sent a videotape so that they could see that we were okay. We wanted them to focus on what they were doing and take care of themselves.

Life was real empty at home. I started working through a list of things I could do around the house to give me something useful to do. The war seemed like it went on forever when it was actually extremely short. Not having children simplified things for me; my girlfriends got questions from their four-year-olds that made things a lot more difficult for them.

Frank's mother doesn't understand a lot of what Frank does though

---

[23]Whole military families, not just the service people, are "on the crew," "in the squadron," or "in the Navy," etc. It really is a way of life, unlike less-intense professions.

he tries to explain. He's her first child and she's very, very proud of what he's done. The war was very difficult for her. She would hear things on the news that she didn't understand, and it was hard for her to comprehend that much of what they said didn't relate to Frank. For example, she wasn't well versed on the locations over there and so didn't know that the one B-52 we lost went down 8000 miles from him. And I was not telling Frank's location anyway. I hated to keep people in the dark but, like I said, it was for his safety.

I was on the phone with one of the other girls on the crew when the President announced a cease-fire. There was a lot of excitement here at home but it still wasn't over. It had taken several months to get those people there so we didn't know how long it was going to take to get them back. And we knew it was just a cease-fire—somebody could mess it up.

But we were still all excited and everybody had to call everybody. All six of us called each other and jammed the phones.

Frank sounded very relieved when we finally talked. He had reason to be a lot more relaxed by then. The missions had been very tiring for him with his relatively new co-pilot. It takes a lot for an aircraft commander to learn a new co-pilot's capabilities and develop trust. His co-pilot obviously came through for him. Frank was also the new guy on the crew so they had their questions about him too. He had been under a little pressure over that, naturally.

There wasn't a lot of time to prepare for their return and the calls to Spain never got easier. One of the wives got another call through the ham radio operators—the guys were in the air. Then it was just a matter of being very anxious and waiting and hoping that they weren't going to be delayed for any reason.

The crew's wives were together for the homecoming. We could see the planes holding in the distance so we counted them to be sure they all got home. All the children had little American flags and were jumping around in their excitement. The planes flew their fly-by and then landed one by one. We had to wait while they unloaded and the VIPs got their pictures taken with our guys before they could come to us.

It was hard to believe they were actually home. We'd been told they were okay and they'd said so too, but we had to see them for ourselves and actually touch them to believe it. We were so happy, we cried. Then it was neat to watch the daddies with their little children 'cause the children were so excited. They hadn't thoroughly understood what was going on but Daddy was home, that's what counted. The little babies didn't recognize Daddy at first, they weren't sure. But it didn't take 'em long to figure it out.

7

Laser Tag[1]

Captain Merrick Krause, Genghis, always wanted to fly. Starting with Junior ROTC in high school, he followed that dream through the Air Force Academy and pilot training all the way to his evaluator qualification in the F-15E Strike Eagle. Many young people dream of flying but few pull it off as well as he did.

His jet was the bombing version of the F-15 that retains all of its air-to-air punch while adding a weapons system operator[2] and a solid dose of magic. With the F-117, the Strike Eagle is the most sophisticated bombing platform in the world, and it's getting better. Its sensors found the targets anytime and under any conditions to bring back videos as proof of their impossible precision.

Captain Krause:

I've always wanted to fly.

I got a civilian flying license during high school back in Pittsburgh and then went to the Air Force Academy. After graduation in 1984, I

---

[1]laser tag—Hitting a target with a laser-guided weapon. Also, modern battlefield exercises are scored by computers and lasers. Each weapon has a laser mounted on it, plus an array of laser sensors to declare "kills."

[2]weapons systems operator—WSO ("wizzo"). U.S. Air Force flier who runs the navigation and weapons systems while the other flier flies the airplane. B/N, RIO, RAF navigator, pitter, backseater.

learned to fly jets at the EuroNATO Joint Jet Pilot Training Program at Shepherd AFB near Wichita Falls, Texas. Then it was off to Holloman AFB in Alamagordo, New Mexico, for Fighter Lead-In[3] followed by F-4 training at George AFB in Victorville, California. I flew F-4s at Moody AFB in Georgia until 1988, when we moved to Seymour-Johnson AFB, North Carolina. I ended up in the first group that converted from F-4s to Strike Eagles with the 335th Tac Fighter Squadron there.

In July, 1990, we finished a wing exercise with the one and a half F-15E squadrons and one F-4 squadron that we had at the time. Then the Iraqis rolled over the fence into Kuwait and we deployed the 336th squadron with their Strike Eagles to Saudi. I was an air spare[4] and flew about halfway to the Azores before turning around. A few of the spares were flight leads and instructors, like me, so we sat around for a week-long piss-and-moan session when it looked like we would sit out the war. We knew everybody in the 336th squadron since we had flown with them for a couple years and felt we should be in Saudi with the boys. That was pretty depressing, but we jumped into the training we had to run to get new guys qualified to deploy.

For a while, there were only two instructors left in the wing, the 335th Squadron Commander and me, so we flew our butts off. I flew just about twice a day, every day, and then usually ended up staying afterwards with the paperwork. The constant flying was great, but we all wanted to be in Saudi. We still made sure, though, that every guy got the full training so he would at least have a decent chance for survival.

From August to December, we spent our free time complaining to each other over beers about being left behind. Our wives were ready to just kick us out the door; they wanted us to go there, get it out of our systems, and get back. We spent a lot of time gritting our teeth, instructing, and waiting for our chance to go.

Watching the changing opinion polls at home was interesting. I got a real kick out of seeing how the President's popularity ratings increased; how everybody seemed real supportive and proud of the troops. That was good to see, especially when I figured I was going to be there sooner or later. It was nice to know that people back home had a good attitude and were in a good mood.

---

[3]Lead In Fighter Training (LIFT). All "baby" fighter pilots in the Air Force go through LIFT at Holloman AFB, New Mexico, to learn basic fighter and attack maneuvers in the attack version of the T-38.

[4]air spare—Airborne backup airplane. On critical deployments, spare airplanes and crews stand by to fill in for scheduled airplanes that drop out for any reason. Air spares take off with the group and fly to a predetermined point where, if they're not needed, they turn around and return home.

In the meantime, we went through several points where we thought we would get shipped to Saudi any day. We were always ready. We always had a mobility bag in the car ready to go. Finally, in mid-December, we got orders to leave on the 27th with the full squadron of 24 jets. We flew in one hop from Seymour-Johnson all the way to Al Karj, Saudi Arabia. The deployment was perfect, no aborts. It was a night mission with bad weather over the mid-Atlantic, but we're fairly used to nights and everybody was pumped to get overseas. We sure had some good maintenance on the jets—24 jets took off from Seymour and 24 landed 14 hours later with no emergencies or diverts at all.

The tent city was pretty decent by the time we showed up. We had shells of tents waiting for us with furniture in boxes that we put together with our Swiss Army knives. As time progressed, we got mosquito netting to segment the tents into separate small rooms.

We got there about two and a half weeks prior to the war and spent that time on familiarization training and the last couple upgrades. We practiced flying low over the desert to see how our systems performed in that environment. Most of us had a gut-level feeling things were going to heat up, though we weren't given that word until just before fighting started.

It took a long time to start getting letters so that was kind of tough. But we were able to get into the town for phone calls a couple times before they sealed off the base. You could only talk in general terms: "The weather's fine." "I'm okay." We couldn't say where we were or what we were doing.

As the war progressed, and besides the daily letters from my wife, Shari, and many notes from my family, I got some letters from strangers and from the children of classmates I hadn't seen in 11 years. One of my favorites was a letter from the daughter of a couple I knew in high school. Everybody in her grade school class signed it and told me that I had to write back. I got a real kick out of that and I wrote them back a couple of times. They sent me a picture and a couple of little presents as the war continued.

My first night's mission was near Tallil airfield, where I led a flight that hit a communications center from low altitude. It went just like clockwork. We avoided the triple-A, the Iraqis didn't fire any missiles at us, and we were too low and too fast for the MiGs.

But my most memorable flight was on the second night of the war. We planned a six ship and I led the second element as number three. We were pumped up from the first night but our place in the middle of the package made it obvious we were in for a real tough one.

We weren't going to be able to sneak in because we were attacking near Basra, which was a real hot spot, one of the major command centers. There were several airfields and a couple Republican Guards divisions so it was a pretty high threat area—very high threat. We knew it would be tough to get in, so we planned to go in low and come out low to avoiding most of the SAMs and the heaviest part of the triple-A. The weather was also bad enough to be a factor. Each of us had twelve 500-pound bombs to drop on one pass while using infrared pods to precisely identify our targets at night.

To avoid the defenses and cities in Kuwait, we planned to leave the tanker, drop down and follow the western side of the Kuwaiti border around to attack the Basra area from the northwest and then get out the same way. There were other flights working the other areas near Basra, so we needed to stay out of their way. Just get in and get out.

The leader of our flight was "Chairman" Mouw and he flew with "Radar" O'Reilly. My personal callsign was Genghis, and my back seater, who was also my flight commander, was Joe Seidl, callsign No Cap. We flew the night before and had a pretty good idea how each of us handled the stress. We were comfortable working with each other; he's an excellent aviator.

We briefed and then suited up in life support. No Cap's main survival gear was a pack of cigarettes and maybe a spare water bottle. I felt like carrying tennis shoes because, as soon as I hit the ground, I planned on running to the nearest border. Seriously, I ended up carrying extra maps and pointy talky translators that I could pull out and point to what I wanted to say. Like a lot of us, I had a personal 9mm pistol, extra knives, and water bottles strapped in every available pocket.

Our mood was pretty somber. No Cap and I had seen high threat areas the night before and we knew what was coming. We had no illusions, and I think we were both pretty well prepared for it. But neither of us wrote home saying it might be the last letter because we didn't feel that way. We were going to accomplish the mission while keeping ourselves and our wingmen alive. That was my goal during the whole war.

The jets were configured with the 12 Mk-82 bombs plus a targeting pod and a navigation pod. The navigation pod gave us terrain-following radar and a Forward Looking Infrared (FLIR)[5] picture. The targeting pod contained the laser and also gave us a close-up picture of the target from some distance. We had a couple bags of gas[6] and conformal fuel tanks[7]. The launch went normally.

---

[5]Forward Looking Infrared (FLIR)—Imaging system that produced an infrared view for fliers. That image was seen often on bombing video.

[6]bag—External drop tank for extra fuel.

[7]conformal tanks—External fuel tank that are molded, or conformed, to the sides of an airplane. Most common on the F-15E.

There were a lot of clouds and the tankers were in them with most of their lights off. Refueling that way was pretty exciting, especially at night, in the weather, and after not sleeping much. Some guys had a lot of trouble with spatial disorientation, but everybody finally got their gas and got their heads on straight.

We made a combat descent from 30,000 feet. Some guys roll over to pull down to 30 degrees nose low, just like dive bombing, and recover from the dive at a thousand feet or so. That got us into the low-altitude environment, and we pushed into Iraq.

We flew in a train, a string of airplanes behind each other but offset to the left or right so nobody was directly behind the guy in front of them. You didn't want to run right into the bullets meant for the guy in front. As we crossed into Iraq, some triple-A opened up near number two but it was pointed straight up. As we got closer, the gunner started leading us as if he had night-vision goggles. It was a smaller caliber, probably a 23mm, and looked like a red stream from a garden hose or a whip. There was no where to pull but up and away so I flew a barrel-roll type maneuver around it—not something you'd normally want to do at low altitude, especially at night. Joe was pretty surprised but it worked! I unloaded the last half of the roll[8] so we wouldn't pull into the ground and let down to 500 feet. We drove right over the gunners and could see light reflecting off their helmets below us. They couldn't swing the guns fast enough to follow us through the maneuver. They must have been impressed—I was. We caught our breaths and moved forward.

The low level was only 15 or 20 minutes long. We flew west of Basra and hooked[9] through some swamps to attack the oil-storage area south of Basra from the northwest. It was unfortunately right in the middle of two divisions of Republican Guards and three different airfields with all the SAMs and triple-A they could muster. No Cap ran the ground radar and sensors while I monitored the air-to-air radar, our position on the moving map display, and the FLIR to make sure we didn't hit either the ground, some triple-A, or one of the jets in front of us.

Chairman and Radar reached the target and really stirred 'em up. By the time we got there as number three, the triple-A was pretty thick. Their tracers blended with reflected light from the burning targets plus the town and various power plants to turn the bottom of the clouds into a movie screen. The triple-A created red, orange, and some yellow

---

[8]unload—To push on the control stick and reduce, or unload, the G forces on the plane. A plane unloaded to near zero G will stay pointed in the same direction while rolling.

[9]hook—To turn around in a pattern that resembles a fish hook.

streams of fire that went into the clouds and then back down. It looked like the big whipping stream from a fire hose, especially when a ZSU[10] opened up.

The glow from the reflections off the clouds a couple thousand feet up made them as bright as the ground. That made flying a hard turn to get away from the triple-A really tough because it was almost impossible to tell which way was up and which was down. Tracers streamed up, reached apex, and fell back down again so we had tracers going up, down, and all different directions at the same time. There was no time to say anything other than the required crew coordination such as my calling triple-A at left nine o'clock or Joe calling it at right five.

The defenses at an airfield in front of us really opened up after number two went by. We had to break out of the formation and, as planned if that happened, flowed to the back of the package to follow the rest of the guys in. As Joe and I pitched out of the fight, that triple-A followed us a for little bit and then died off enough for the next guys to get past. We decided to press in for another attack even though it was a high-threat environment. We felt we had to stop their supplies or a lot of our guys on the ground were going to die. We watched on our radar as numbers four, five, and six came down the left side of the scope. When number six passed off the left side, we came back hard left to roll in three or four miles behind him. We thought we could hack another run down the gantlet.

I radioed number six and told him to call leaving the target because he wasn't last anymore. I could see him on the FLIR but you can't tell distance that way. As long as he was in front of us, I could concentrate on the triple-A and making sure that we didn't hit the ground.

We headed straight towards the same damn airfield that made us break out the first time. Joe had to get the sensors locked on and other attack directions were blocked by airfields and the guys coming off target. All the vehicles on the roads had parked and were shooting up at us. What a mess! I waited until the last second and turned away from a group of triple-A pieces about the time Joe froze the map and said, "You're clear to turn!"

Now pointed at the target, I could see it in the HUD[11] FLIR and out

---

[10]ZSU—ZSU 23-4 Shilka. Soviet-built, four-barreled, radar-directed, 23mm, mobile, armored, anti-aircraft gun system on a tank chassis. Bad news.

[11]HUD—Heads up display. Small glass screen on top of the instrument panel that displays critical flight and weapons data. Allows the pilot to fly and fight without the potentially fatal distraction of looking inside the cockpit. Allows "heads up" rather than "heads down" flight. The rapidly moving symbols seen in gun camera film were projected on the HUD and used by the pilot to control the aircraft.

the windows. It was burning like something out of Dante's Inferno. My field of view was filled with bubbling, oozing fires, and I had to turn up the brightness on my sights because the fire in front of us blanked out my screens. Joe went to the targeting pod and designated our specific target as I tried to keep an eye on the triple-A arcing over the canopy. The gunners could see us against the bright overcast and tried to lead us. We were going more than 500 knots, which was too fast for them to get a good bead on us.

Number six called off target just before we popped, so I knew he was well clear of the target area. In the meantime, Joe had the target designated and called the pull-up point for our loft attack[12]. It was up to me to fly the jet on course until the computer released the bombs at the desired point. I tried to follow the steering commands on the heads-up display as we climbed toward the clouds. The triple-A was really heavy since, as we got closer to the clouds, we became a lot more visible. I couldn't use the afterburners[13] because they would light us up like a Christmas tree. If we kept going up, we would've flown right into the triple-A.

It probably would have been a good idea to have jettisoned the bombs and tanks and pulled off the target run. But we had gone so far, under so much fire, that we were both pretty pissed off. We came all the way downtown[14] and were going to hit the target.

As we pressed in, I decided that was enough for me. I chose to disregard the computer and rolled the jet upside down into direct pop[15]. Strike Eagles have 10 or 15 different switches on both the stick and throttles so I "played the piccolo" to change bombing modes. I changed from the automatic computer delivery mode to a more manual bombing mode and picked one of the oil facilities we were supposed to hit. The bombs came off, and it was everything I could do to escape the triple-A coming at our nose.

I punched off[16] the tanks, which had finally run dry, as we got close

---

[12]loft attack—To release bombs while climbing so they fly a ballistic arc to the target like artillery. Designed to increase the distance between the bomber and a high threat target.

[13]afterburner—Aft section of a fighter's engines that injects raw fuel into the exhaust for a very fuel-expensive burst of power. Reheat. Can. Blower.

[14]downtown—Metropolitan Baghdad or another heavily defended area. Fliers in Southeast Asia referred to a flight over Hanoi as "going downtown." Desert Storm fliers used the same term for heavily defended areas.

[15]pop—Pop-up attack. Climbing then diving maneuver that takes a bomber from low altitude to a diving attack. Pops usually include a turn toward the target, so a direct pop is one flown straight at the target without turns.

[16]punch off—To drop or turn off. You can punch off (jettison) external fuel tanks to strip down for a fight or punch off a radio to silence it.

to another airfield that had opened up with their own triple-A. I avoided most of that by getting low while No Cap used our radar to pick up the other guys. Chairman wanted to make sure everybody was still there so he ordered a check-in on the radio. Six didn't check in. We didn't know exactly what had happened, but we had a bad feeling about it. In any case, we had to get out of the target area first, then we could find them.

We headed west and were going to hook south all the way around Kuwait. As we turned south, we called for a rescue for number six because we still couldn't get him to check in, and I felt he had gone down.

About then, we got an indication that a missile radar was following us and Joe said, "Break left!" I turned hard and the Roland missile[17] flashed over the right wing and blew up close in front of us. We thought five had been hit because we saw that explosion in front of us. The flight leader tried to call everybody and now got responses from two, three, and four, but not five or six.

We called the AWACS again for search and rescue. They needed the general coordinates from the last time we heard from number five as well as number six. As we got farther out, number five came up on the radio again real broken and started talking to Chairman. It turned out that his radio went dead just as the Roland missile blew up in front of us.

We got out of Iraq and through the clouds before we could finally slow down for the ride home. That return flight was pretty tough because one of us had gone down. We were still very tense; it had been a tough flight with a lot of triple-A at low altitude. There wasn't a whole lot of chatter in the cockpit other than radar contacts and other business. Joe and I didn't chat as buddies going home that night.

No Cap and I took a lot of ribbing throughout the rest of the war about that reattack in Basra. It seemed like the thing to do at the time because we wanted to accomplish the mission, and we thought we could do it and stay alive. We did.

But losing those guys hit all of us pretty hard, and I still think about it everyday. They did the best that could have been done at the time and their sacrifice was very honorable. They did their duty regardless of the consequences, and they sure helped save a lot of our guys on the ground by hitting the target. They did their duty and sacrificed more than anyone else in the squadron. Heroes.

It was ugly. It was an ugly mission.

As the air war progressed, we went from those real high-threat missions to Scud-busting. We'd go looking for them but had backup targets like radar sites, ammo dumps, or railroad yards to hit if we didn't find

---

[17]Roland missile—Very good, radar-guided, surface-to-air missile built by a French and German consortium.

any Scuds. Several of those target areas ended up with nicknames. An area near the Syrian border was called SAM's Town. We lost another airplane there in the first week (they were captured) and just about everybody who flew in that area had a couple SAMs shot at them. Right next to it was Triple-A Alley, because, guess what, there were all kinds of high-caliber triple-A guns there. They were protecting mobile and fixed Scuds plus lots of different facilities.

On the Kuwaiti front, we did a lot of tank-busting and attacked convoys. Artillery pieces were often highest on the target list with tanks next. Toward the end, we'd send out one laser designator pod with two airplanes and a total of 16 bombs. We'd hit 16 out of 16 unless there was a weapons malfunction or a cloud in the way. The sensors could tell the difference between artillery, tanks, Scuds, etc., and we'd wipe out whole columns of tanks, one right after the other.

Joe and I were stepping out[18] on one of those tank busting missions when we were diverted to cut off the Iraqis' big retreat from Kuwait City. We needed to choke off the retreating troops so they wouldn't regroup in Basra and reattack. I sent our wingman up high to drop his bombs through the clouds on a highway intersection while I descended under the clouds with No Cap just north of Kuwait City, near Aljar. We made five passes on that area. I wish I had the cockpit tape: Joe said, "We have a missile at six o'clock, but I don't think it's on us, and we've got triple-A at left nine." I said, "Yeah, we've got triple-A at right three and also at twelve—we're in for another pass." We had quite a few missions by that time, and, though we were still afraid of the triple-A, it wasn't a surprise anymore. They fired six SAMs at us that night but none guided. We knew if we kept moving and kept our eyes open, we had a good chance. The target pod video showed the dumb bombs[19] impacting on the road and trucks. It helps to get in close to hit your target when dropping without the computer or automatic delivery.

As far as we were concerned, the war didn't end when the fighting stopped. The ground war ended but we were part of the residual force and had to keep flying to make sure they didn't come back. We flew all sorts of combat air patrol missions. Sometimes we'd fly with mixed air-to-air and air-to-ground loads in case the Iraqis tried to attack.

The first-in, first-out policy made sense, and nobody had any problems with that. But just as our turn to go home came up, they froze all Air Force redeployments. They finally released half of our squadron in

---

[18]step—To leave the life support section in flight gear and go to the jet (U.S.). See walk.

[19]dumb bombs—Bombs without guidance. Opposite of laser-, TV-, etc., guided smart bombs.

May, but the rest of us stayed until the end of June. I had had enough by that point—I was definitely ready to get home.

After flying for 300 or 400 hours in the desert, I couldn't comprehend the colors we saw as we crossed the East Coast. Amazing. We taxied in, shut down our engines, and popped open our canopies at the same time so it looked fancy for the wives. Shari ran to the jet and I climbed down as a couple guys grabbed my hands and shook 'em. Shari waited for me all dressed up looking very lovely and just laughing. It was a very happy occasion, especially since the war had been over for four months by the time we finally got home. Our return was so long overdue that the war almost seemed like ancient history, but the base still put on a great welcome.

Then we just hung around the house. I mowed the grass. It was great. We spent a lot of time talking and getting reacquainted, but Shari had had no problems. She was pretty strong through the whole thing. I think she held up better than me.

Genghis and No Cap earned Distinguished Flying Crosses for their attack near Basra.

Shari Krause seems to handle life just a little better than most people. She married her high-school sweetheart only after he'd finished some of the most intense training you could want (not a bad idea at all), adjusted to the constant moves and separations that define the military life, and has earned her doctorate. That cool, calm, and collected personality served her well when the fliers in "her" squadron were being shot down.

Shari Krause:

I was born and raised in Pittsburgh, where I met Merrick. We were both in high school Junior ROTC, so I always knew he wanted to go to the Air Force Academy. I had set my sights on becoming an airline pilot, so I majored in aviation at Metropolitan State College in Denver while he was in the Academy. We then got married after UPT. I had never been closely associated with the military, but hanging around the Academy for four years gives some idea of what it's about.

There have been two big differences from civilian life. We consider ourselves very lucky if we're at one place for at least three years and very, very lucky if it's four years. The other difference is that your social life and work are intertwined. In the civilian world, you may never socialize with the people at work. But in the military, 95% of your friends are in the squadron, so we have monthly functions that are totally unknown in the civilian world. I find that rather unique.

I was finishing up my master's degree in aviation operations the week

Kuwait was invaded. We weren't sure if Merrick would go in the response or not. His eventual deployment was a lot easier for me than the uncertainty of August. It was obvious: the President said he was sending troops, the 15E was going to be involved, so who would it be? One night, he came home for dinner and said, "I'm only going to be home for an hour, then I'm going back to the squadron." That one statement put the chill up my spine because I knew then that somebody was going. It could be him.

He came back home late that night still not too sure if he was going or not. For the next four days, he left every morning with his mobility bag and didn't know if he would head off to the desert or come home for supper. That was very tough. Every day was a good-bye. And every night he would come back frustrated. The guys were on an emotional roller coaster since that deployment was what they had trained to do. They were so pumped up and heated up that the attitude in the squadron was, Go, Go, Go!

Then Merrick was an air spare for the first deployment. I went out by the runway on that miserable, rainy, overcast day and stood there to see them take off. I was pretty sure Merrick was one of them, but I didn't know which one. They disappeared within seconds into the overcast. I just stood out in the rain. I was very proud and excited and sure he would go all the way over. Then he called, "Hon, I'm home."

The same thing happened to two of our very good friends, so, that night, the three guys sat on a friend's porch, drank beer, and blew off steam—wives not included. I finally got a phone call, "Come on down." We sat around the kitchen table venting our frustration. We all needed to hear the guys' perspective, the disgusted feeling at being left behind.

When the President set the January deadline, we knew it was only a matter of time before the rest of the guys would go. The departure was eventually set for December 27th. It went pretty much like a normal deployment. As for the war, we had to take it a step at a time. A war might be thrown into that situation but there was no telling.

Public support was great, especially in Goldsboro. I'm sure most military towns had yellow ribbons, flags, and bows everywhere and people wearing lapel pins. During Desert Storm, it seemed that everybody was unified and got into flag waving. When total strangers heard Merrick was a fighter pilot, they'd say, "Tell him we're thinking of him and we're behind him." Being a fighter pilot was different.

I saw the start of the war on TV, as I'm sure millions did—the whole shooting match over Baghdad. It wasn't a total shock because the deadline had passed. But I sat there for a minute sort of mesmerized. Then Merrick's mother called from the office. The TV was blaring in the background, papers were flying, and she was trying to get home. She called just to hear my voice.

After that, quite honestly, I read Psalm 91 and Psalm 140 and prayed for his safekeeping. I called a pilot friend who hadn't deployed yet and asked if he thought Merrick was flying that first night. He said, "Probably." That's what I thought, too.

I was in my doctorate program and so didn't have time to dwell on the news. I tried to listen to scheduled military press conferences, but other than that, I would watch news in the morning to see what had happened the night before and then go about my business. I knew he flew at night, so when I was sleeping, he was also coming back, having breakfast, and going to sleep. I didn't really have sleepless nights because I knew he was sleeping too.

I had four very close friends and we decided we were not going to become basket cases. We would not panic and that was that. I didn't have any tolerance for the wives who sat up literally all night watching CNN, not sleeping, not functioning, not being able to go to work for days on end. Some of them looked at me as if I was unfeeling or naive. But the guys were safe and asleep while they panicked. What was the point?

Like any other group of civilians, the folks I taught in college were pro-military. They thought the Air Force was just great and said, "Your husband's really doing an awesome job." It hadn't occurred to them that he was a fighter pilot before the war too even if those were practice missions. I guess they thought he just flew around.

Our first loss came on the second night of the war. It blew everybody away after the emotional highs of the TV reports saying, "Victory in the skies!" We thought a million things could have happened. They could be POWs; they could be evading and would be rescued. I considered anything except that they might be dead. Then it happened again when a second plane from the squadron went down a couple days later.

Now we had four wives with missing husbands. Their very close friends spent literally 24 hours a day at those homes to answer the phone because it had become a media circus. The other wives were very supportive. I was in the support group and coordinated meals. There were so many phone calls that it wasn't practical to individually offer to cook—we simply coordinated jobs like that.

Some of the more experienced wives seemed more shaken up than the younger ones. I had one wife call who lived a half mile from an MIA's home and honestly could not remember how to drive over there. She was that upset. Even the younger wives who had never met them felt a bond—"We're all in this together. It could have been my husband." I thought the support for the wives was tremendous.

One morning we turned on CNN and there were Dave Eberly and Tom Griffith. You don't wish POW status on anybody, but we all breathed a sigh of relief that at least they were alive. We kept hoping for the other two.

Merrick and I wrote every day, well over a hundred letters in all. Later, we talked a lot on the phone—expensive therapy! He was disgusted with the devastation and the oil fires. He was tired of the Saudis. They wanted us to come over and save them but only at their convenience. Even after the war, the guys couldn't go downtown at certain times; there were lots of cultural restrictions on Americans. They couldn't even fly very far from the base after the war unless they were on a mission.

I heard of the cease-fire on CNN, but I was hesitant. I thought they had stopped too soon. I wasn't privy to what Merrick knew, but I didn't think enough damage had been done to Saddam. So I was skeptical.

Nothing really changed for us. The 336th squadron came home in March, but our guys still sat there. With rumors of everyone coming home and then the partial return of the 335th in May, we went through the same predeployment ups and downs again. By the time Merrick came home at the end of June, it was great for us, but it was almost anticlimatic since even many military people didn't know that people from Seymour-Johnson were still over there. That was disheartening because our guys didn't get the same welcome the earlier guys had.

The squadron wives planned to welcome them back with a pizza party and something like a thousand green and white balloons, our squadron colors. We were ready and then waited and waited and waited through all the rumored return dates. Even though I was emotionally exhausted by those ups and downs, I still got goose bumps when the music played as the jets pulled in. There was so much emotion—it was just really great.

Families discovered that bad marriages were hurt by the separation and good marriages were made even stronger. That's how I felt with Merrick. The second I gave him that big hug at the jet, a six month wide missing piece of my life just slid right back. I had never felt anything like that before. As far as our relationship went, it was like nothing had happened. It was great.

We went home and our dog and I followed Merrick around the house while he went into every room and rediscovered home. He thought it was great to be back in civilization and just wanted to turn up the air conditioner and get drinkable water.

8

Bloody Amazing!

Flight Lieutenant Ian Teakle, Paddy, was a Tornado GR-1 navigator in the Royal Air Force.[1] He is unique to this book in several ways besides representing the British experience. He was commissioned in the RAF without attending university and served as a navigator on bombers and tankers before converting to the Tornado. Just 31 years old when the war started, he already had 13 years of flight experience and more than 1000 hours in the Tornado, making him the most experienced combat flier in this collection.

Paddy's jet was the GR-1 strike version of the Tornado. Built by a consortium of western European countries, the Tornado was designed for World War III in Central Europe. Its war would be fought below 300 feet and above 600 knots (680 mph), in the very teeth of a Soviet air defense system specifically designed to stop Tornados, Aardvarks, Mirages, and Strike Eagles from reaching their targets in Eastern Europe and the western Soviet Union. These fliers lived at the focus of the scrum[2] and suffered the losses to prove it.

Flight Lieutenant Teakle:

I was born in a small town south of London called Beckenham in county

---

[1]Royal Air Force—RAF. Land-based air force of the United Kingdom.

[2]scrum—Massed formation in which rugby players hurl their unpadded bodies at each other.

Kent but grew up just outside of Belfast, Northern Ireland. When I was 15, I sat some aptitude tests for the air force but didn't have the hand-to-eye coordination to be a pilot. They offered me navigator then. I got my O-levels and A-levels[3], didn't go to university, and joined the air force as a navigator straight from school when I was 18 years old. We can join the air force at 16 with six O-levels and fly. I could have gone to university in Belfast, but I was quite keen to get out and see the big, wide world. The majority of fliers join before they're 20 with A-levels only.

All pilots and navigators are officers, so I began my service with initial officer training at RAF Henlow. I finished there in April 1979, and moved on to RAF Finningley for initial navigator training to earn the coveted nav brevet[4]. That initial training includes two months of ground school in meteorology, aeronautics, pure navigation, dead reckoning navigation, and instruments before going on to the initial phase of flying. That pure instrument flying is done sitting backwards in a British Aerospace HS-125 Dominie. After a visual navigation phase in Jet Provosts[5], I was streamed into the multiengine world and back to the Dominie for radar navigation training.

I went on to the Vulcan bomber for a short time before being switched to the Victor tanker. My first operational assignment was on Ascension Island with the Victor force to refuel Vulcans during the Falklands War. As the first nav off Victors to be cross-posted to the fast jet Tornado force, I left Victors while still flying from Ascension in 1985.

Fifty hours flying in the British Aerospace Hawk at RAF Chivenor and 60 hours on the Tornado at the Tri-national Tornado Training Establishment at RAF Cottesmore prepared me for my final training at RAF Honington. I was posted to No. 15 Squadron at RAF Laarbruch in Germany and served with that squadron until the end of the war. I returned to Honington in 1988 for Qualified Weapons Instructor training, which is similar to the American Air Force Fighter Weapons School.

The GR-1 Tornado is an all-weather, day-and-night, strike/attack bomber. It has no air-to-air role, but can carry a wide variety of weapons. We fly in pitch black and all weather to deliver them with extreme accuracy. It was designed purely to fly at low level and handles like a pig at medium level. The air force has always thought the

---

[3]O-levels and A-levels—Formal examinations for certificates of education in the United Kingdom. O-levels are taken at about 16 years old and a student can opt out of school then. A-levels are taken at about 18 and are required to enter university. Roughly eight percent of those leaving school go on to college.

[4]nav brevet—Navigator's brevet. Aircrew qualification badge worn by RAF navigators.

[5]Jet Provost—British-built, single-engined jet trainer similar to the T-37 (Tweet).

way to fight is at low level. We've been quite happy[6] down amongst the weeds.

We watched the Iraqi buildup on the border with Saudi Arabia and thought the Tornado F-3s[7] from Cyprus would go and hold the line. By the 8th of August, we had F-3s flying combat air patrol from Dhahran in eastern Saudi. We in Germany were called upon to provide 12 strike/attack aircraft as, we thought, a deterrent to show Saddam that we were serious. No. 15 squadron was put on alert fairly early in August, so, from then until the date we actually went, our required readiness went up and down like a whore's drawers.

We developed a very stringent syllabus to bring us up to "Gulf Combat Ready[8]." We had to practice operational low flying back in England since we hadn't done it for a few months given the restrictions in Germany. We did a lot of heavyweight work since aircraft perform differently with weapons aboard. We also had not tanked before—done any air-to-air refueling.

Our aircraft were repainted from the north European camouflage of green and black and brown to a sand colour with a shade of pink. It worked very well.

We and the British people thought the problems in Kuwait would be solved diplomatically. Nobody could envisage us actually going to war with a country that far away. The coalition power being massed against Saddam was so one-sided that nobody could believe he wouldn't capitulate and withdraw before the deadlines. Iraqi diplomats always gave us the little carrot of, "Yes, we are getting somewhere with diplomacy." We showed strength and solidarity with the coalition but believed surely people would not die out there.

We finally left on the 26th of November for Muharraq, Bahrain, to replace crews from 14 and 17 Squadrons. They'd been up and down in readiness states so many times that they'd lost their combat edge, so we were sent for a six-month stint.

We were treated very, very well by the civilian population in Bahrain. There's a great expatriot community of Brits that live there who took us to their hearts. The living conditions were fantastic as we stayed in the Sheraton Hotel in Manama, the capital. The standard of

---

[6]No, they weren't really happy as in joyous. Happy in British English also means satisfied or contented.

[7]Tornado F-3—Interceptor version of the Tornado.

[8]combat ready—Just what it says. British combat fliers train in their aircraft but are not ready to fight until checked out in their new unit's specific mission. A new theater means a new environment and, therefore, more training required. Same as mission ready in the USAF.

the food, the swimming pool, the fact that there was booze in Bahrain, made it quite difficult to reconcile the luxury we lived in with the job we eventually did. But it was nice to come back to a few beers in the hotel.

We'd taken over an old RAF building left over from our time there in the '60s. There was a very tight command and control chain, so we went straight into arrival briefs and nuclear, biological, and chemical protection procedures. We were very worried that Saddam might do something silly with chemicals.

Then it was straight into a week's training workup before we were considered combat ready there. It concentrated on air-to-air refueling, low flying in the desert, and airfield attacks on Shaikh Isa on the south side of Bahrain.

Cooperation with the Americans was very good. We were lucky to have Shaikh Isa down the road, so we were able to get the American intelligence reports, which were far better than the British ones. Plus, everybody down there was read into Desert Storm, so it was much easier to go there and chew the breeze. They were very envious of our living conditions, but, as our commanding officer said, "Any fool can live in discomfort."

We lost some aircraft in that training. A Tornado and a Jaguar crashed while low-flying in the Oman, and we lost another Tornado crew back in the U.K.[9]. They were practicing a loft maneuver with eight bombs on, and they hadn't realized that, when they pitched over, the momentum of the extra weight would pull them down into the sea. We lost three other aircrew in a midair collision over the North Sea. We lost some good friends during the buildup.

Our primary mission was to deliver the JP-233. It's a very useful munition for depriving the enemy of their airfields. It craters runways and taxiways while sowing antipersonnel minelets. The coalition wanted us there for that weapon as the spearhead of the offensive counter air[10] campaign which would obviously be the initial thrust of Desert Storm. JP-233 comes with 30 cratering munitions, weighing 28 kilos each, that explode under the runway, causing the surface to heave. It also sows antipersonnel mines that are very cunningly designed. If a bulldozer blade hits one, it tips and fires a shaped charge slug through the blade and into the cab. The system is two of those canisters slung under the jet and jettisoned after use.

---

[9]U.K.—United Kingdom. England, Wales, Scotland, and Northern Ireland.

[10]offensive counter air—OCA. Taking the battle for air superiority to the enemy by attacking his aircraft and their supporting infrastructure on the ground and over his territory.

We communicated with our families by the ubiquitous bluey[11]. It's an airmail letter form that the forces send free through a British Forces Post Office. Since we lived in a five-star hotel, it was also very easy to lie in bed and pick up the phone beside you to make a call home.

We felt an overwhelming sense of support from the British people. Prior to Christmas, we had Red Cross parcels with Christmas puddings, soap, and toilet rolls (quite reassuring to us there in the Sheraton). There were sackfuls and sackfuls of mail addressed to "An Airman in the Gulf" or to "A Flier". We had whole schools writing us and little old ladies sent their pension money so we could buy things. Little kids saved up their pocket money to send us sweets. It was quite touching. I especially liked a poem we received from a guy who'd flown from Muharraq in the Second World War. Never once did we receive any hate mail. We also received personal photographs of semi-dressed women, which were pinned up in the flying clothing section[12].

In January, we went to a regime of sleeping during the day and flying at night to prepare for the war.

We came in to fly a standard training mission on the night of 16 January. I knew something might be up because I was one of the three fliers read into the plan, but very few others did. Our boss called in the crews of the eight ship he was to lead and told us we were going for real. But we weren't allowed to tell anybody.

We were still in the mindset that it was just another training mission. The war didn't seem real at that stage.

We changed into our kits, went out to the jets and the ground crew said, "Do you want us to take these bombs off, sir?" "Nope." "Well, you're not allowed to go flying with those on, sir." They had practiced loading and downloading real weapons, which were always taken off before we flew. When we left them on that time, they knew immediately that something was up as well. They went and checked the weapons again and, all of a sudden, we were god-like creatures. "Would you like a drink, sir?" "Is there anything I can do for you before you go, sir?" "Are you sure you're going to go?" "What time, sir?" "Is the jet all right?"

From that moment on, the rapport between ground and air crews was outstanding. There's always an element of friction since we "take their jets out and break them." But that changed to, "The jet's not going to break for you and, if it does, it's *my* problem. It's *my* fault if the jet's not good enough for you." There was a change in emphasis so that we

---

[11]bluey—Blue British airmail letter form.

[12]flying clothing section—Part of a British flying unit responsible for the fit and maintenance of the flier's survival kit. Same as USAF life support.

were no longer the flyboys who would break their jets—they were the guys who provided us with the assets to take to war. They really felt that their aeroplanes had to keep us alive.

We got airborne with everybody waving us off, tanked in the Olive refueling trail, and dropped off some 60 miles south of the Iraqi border. We updated our navigation kit with radar fixes on a couple of small masts along pipelines.

Our mission was to attack Tallil Airfield by cutting off the hardened shelter accesses to the runway. I lead the back four that night as we spotted triple-A some 40 miles from the target. They had been stirred up by the initial American attack[13]. The JP-233 had to be delivered straight into that while flying straight and level at 600 knots and 200 feet. We all came out on the other end of that first drop in anger for the JP-233.

We were exhilarated on landing and the ground crews were ecstatic as well. The shifts had changed while we were out, but the night shift wouldn't go home until they counted eight jets. There was hugging and handshakes all around. That was a tremendous welcome.

We took quite a few losses at Muharraq, starting with one on the morning of the 17th to an SA-16[14] missile while doing a loft maneuver. One flew into the ground while another was shot down by a German/French Roland missile. That made for three of our 12 Tornados at Muharraq lost in the first 54 sorties of the war.

There was a perception at the time that all those losses had been to triple-A because it wasn't until after the war that we found out the truth. So we decided to introduce tactics to suppress the triple-A. The first guys were getting through scott-free but waking up the defenses. So we planned to send two JP guys in first, wake up the defenses, and then put some air-burst thousand pounders[15] on them. Having killed all the gun emplacements, we'd finish it all off with more JPs. So an eight ship would carry JPs on the first two, then four guys lofting eight one thousand pounders each followed by two guys bringing up the rear with JP.

We really didn't like those gunners much and planned to put 32,000 pounds of explosive into the air over them.

On the 20th, we prepared for those new tactics. The target was Al Jarrah, which is just north of the 32nd parallel. The lead navigator was our wing commander, who briefed the mission from my planning. We were no more apprehensive than usual when we walked out to the jets.

---

[13]See chapter 3.

[14]SA-16—Best Soviet-made, shoulder-launched, heat-seeking, surface-to-air missile.

[15]thousand pounders—1000-pound, high-explosive bombs. See MK-83.

Things went awry almost from the outset. We walked[16] as an eight ship and lost one on the ground to a system malfunction. We took off with seven and almost immediately lost another guy when he turned around with an airborne malfunction. We met up with our tankers at the normal place over Dhahran and the tanking went without any problems at all until we encountered bad weather at the final bracket[17]. The severe air turbulence prevented two guys from taking fuel so we were down to four jets: two with JPs and two with bombs.

However, Squadron Leader Gordon Buckley, "Buckers," and I were three minutes behind the other three. We decided to push on our own to kill some of those gun emplacements so there wouldn't be the same intense defenses the next time that airfield was attacked.

AWACS called and asked us to look for a downed American aircrew so we were vectored to the area where those guys were supposed to be. We flew an orbit there with our lights on with no luck. We then pushed for the target again at 480 knots and 200 feet.

This is a transcript of the Tornado's intercom that night. Buckers is the pilot (P) and Paddy is the navigator (N).

RRRrrrRRRrrrRRRrrrRRRrrrRRR [SAM radar warning]

Paddy (N): Turning in three minutes, avoiding the SAM 3 site, heading 350.

Buckers (P): Roger.

N: Crossing various lines of communication over the next couple of minutes.

P: Roger.

N: Head in for the fix[18]. Okay, good mark coming down the (radar scope) scales showing about three-quarter mile of error. That's about what I expected.

P: Lights on the left[19]. Looks like a campfire.

AWACS: CHOCTAW, PICTURE CLEAR[20].

P: Awright!

---

[16]walk—To leave the flying clothing section in flying kit and go to the aeroplane. See step.

[17]bracket—Refueling connection made when a British pilot flies the plane's probe into the refueling drogue.

[18]Advisory call alerting the pilot that the navigator is concentrating on the radar scope and not external lookout.

[19]Very obvious through the night vision goggles.

[20]picture clear—Radio call meaning, "The radar screen is free of unknown or enemy aircraft."

N: Crossing all those roads, railroads, and rivers now.

P: There's a lot of movement down there. Do we come back this way?

N: No, we go west of here.

P: Good. Stepping the height down and speeding up. How's the fuel?

N: We're running on mins[21], no combat[22]. We'll have to punch the underwings [fuel tanks] off in about 1000 kilos [of fuel] time.

P: How far away is the target now?

N: We're hitting it in eight minutes. We're about 60 miles south at the moment.

P: Good. I wonder what aircrew were down. Makes you wonder doesn't it?

N: Yep. I'm going head in for the pre-target fix. I'll use it as a confidence check (of the navigation systems).

AWACS: Choctaw, picture clear.

N: Fix is spot on.

P: Roger.

RRRrrrRRRrrrRRRrrrRRRrrrRRRrrrRRRrrr

N: Target is at your 11 o'clock[23] 35 miles. The rest of the guys are approaching the pre-IP turn.

P: Setting up the escape heading of 255 degrees.

N: Turning shortly and pushing the speed up to 600 knots.

P: When are the others on target?

N: About 30 seconds.

P: They're going to make [the defenders] really annoyed before we get there.

N: Yep. Turning shortly 335 [degrees]. The fuel checks at 5200 kilos.

We saw the first lot of bombs go off, which really did stimulate the triple-A. It wasn't like the first couple of nights when it fired straight up in the air, almost unaimed. The tracers weaved around at the heights we were flying. It was aimed. They were getting clever and not just firing their guns in the air.

Beep b beeeep [another radar warning]

---

[21]mins—Minimums. Could be minimum fuel, minimum weather limits, etc.

[22]combat fuel—Reserve fuel above that required to complete the route.

[23]clock position—To maintain a common reference, positions around an aircraft are labeled relative to a clock face, with 12 o'clock marking straight ahead. Something "at 11 o'clock" is at the aircraft's left front and something "at six o'clock" is directly behind.

P: There goes the triple-A[24].

N: Visual.

P: There's the JP [weapons] going.

N: Yep.

P: There go the second lot [second attack]. Where are the thousand pounders?

N: In 30 seconds.

AWACS: CHOCTAW, PICTURE CLEAR.

P: Boom! Boom! Boom! Boom! [watching thousand pounders exploding] Ha! Ha! Ha! Still triple-A there though.

N: Okay. Speeding up—use your burners. Low loft [attack option] selected.

I got to work finding the offset points on radar. We had calculated the positions of radar-significant points on the ground, such as bridges or fences. We can pick up the corner of a fence on the radar. On the run in, I designated those points on the radar to update the navigation computer, which, in turn, worked with the weapons systems to release the bombs at the proper moment. I worked the first offset, a nice little bridge over a river, and was very happy with it. The next offset was the perimeter fence, which showed up lovely. The final one was a HAS.[25]

N: Marking the bridge [on radar].

P: Switches live, low loft light's on.

N: Good mark on the second offset, going offset three.

P: Speed's 600 knots. Maximum dry (without afterburners) power thrust.

N: Marking the HAS—beautiful!

zzzt

ZZzzzzzt

We ran in toward the target and tapped the burners to get 600 knots so that we wouldn't highlight ourselves with burners in the loft. I selected the weapons, eight free-fall bombs, and selected the low loft attack profile with a pull-up at 22 seconds time to go. We had about a minute to run to the target.

P: How is it on time to go?

---

[24]Radar warning receivers give both audible and visual warnings that last as long as the radar beam stays on the airplane. Crews may miss the visual display if the radar pulse is too short.

[25]HAS—("haz") Hardened aircraft shelter. Reinforced concrete shelters that both protected airplanes and attracted laser-guided bombs.

N: Looks good, 59 seconds to run.

P: Looks like we're here, mate.

N: We are not here! (*Buckers wanted to pop early. The flack was getting very close.*)

P: Okay, okay.

N: 50 seconds.

BELFAST CHECK. [The Tornado leader checked on his formation.]

BELFAST TWO.

BELFAST THREE.

N: BELFAST FIVE APPROACHING.

N: 40 seconds. I know it (triple-A) looks close. You're alright, 35 seconds.

P: Okay.

N: 30 seconds to run. Pulling in five, four, three, two, one—pull!

At 22 seconds to release, we pulled up into the triple-A. The loft had seemed fine in planning because we were going to pull up at three and a half miles from the point of impact and not overfly the target. But that was not three and a half miles from the edge of the airfield. We pulled up over the perimeter fence right in amongst the triple-A that was being aimed. It looked very white and came from all around. It passed below us and above us and on both sides of us. I could see machine gun fire and 23mm as well. There was light everywhere. It felt as if we were on the inside of a Christmas tree.

We both committed to release by pressing the weapons release buttons and felt the bombs go when we were about 3000 feet up and very slow.

N: Bombs all gone.

meemeemeemee

N: It's going off all around us. There go the bombs [explosions].

N: Height is 3000 feet. Run out heading 255. [We're] in the recovery.

N: Jettisoning the underwing tanks. Right, they've gone.

meemeemeemeemeemee

N: [We're] in the descent back down to low level, passing 1500 feet. Don't look out, just fly the recovery.

Pilots must fly the recovery heads down and on instruments only. The 135 degree roll over on our back and three-G pull back to low level is extremely disorientating. They mustn't look out. I said, "Don't look out!" but Buckers took a little peek outside, saw all the lights around us and didn't know which way was up or down. That left us in a dive toward the ground. We were also low on fuel and needed to get rid of our tanks, so I banged those off.

P: [The triple-A] is still going off around us! hhmmhhmmhhmmhhmmhhmmwhoop!whoop!hhmmhhmm

N: Don't look out, mate. Just fly the plane. We're passing 700 feet and still going down—easy, easy!

N: Start levelling off mate, we've 300 feet to go.

We managed to get wings level and bottomed at 150 feet from the desert floor. There was a lot of heavy breathing.

A flier makes a distinctive and not too attractive sound while fighting to stay conscious under high Gs. Imagine Darth Vader with constipation.

whoop!whoop!
hhmmhhmmhhmmwhoop!whoooop!hhmm

N: Wings level now, 150 feet. Ease the height up, Buckers. That was bloody close!

P: I don't ever want to do that again. That was awful!

N: We were right up amongst it.

P: We don't get paid enough for this.

N: 500 feet. Good attack.

P: Well done, mate. Christ, [the triple-A] is still going.

They continued firing at the same strength for three minutes after our pass. There were so many guns that they circled the entire field.

AWACS: BELFAST, CAN I VECTOR YOU FOR OBSERVATION?

BELFAST LEADER: NEGATIVE, MINIMUM FUEL.

P: Look at that [triple-A]. Can you see it?

N: Yeah. It still looks close doesn't it?

P: I tell you, it *was* bloody close!

N: FIVE'S OFF TARGET, EGRESSING.

P: I can see my cold is going to get worse soon, mate.

On the way home, Buckers said he didn't want to do that again and that his cold might get worse so that he couldn't fly the next day (sic).

N: Captain B, my stomach's gone all squirty[26].

P: My stomach's on the floor at the moment. . . . Oh God, I think I want to die.

N: I think we almost did.

P: And it [the bombs] didn't stop the triple-A. We got so bloody close that all I could see were red and white lines going all around us; above, below and to the side. It was amazing. Bloody amazing.

---

[26]Quotation from British TV programme, *Blackadder Goes Forth.*

We were running short of fuel so we manufactured a few shortcuts by trimming corners on our return route and heading direct for the tanker. The twin store bomb carriers created a lot of drag and caused us to burn fuel at a greater rate than we would have wished. We decided to jettison them. Luckily, the carriers came off okay and tanking went well on the way home.

We decided we'd much rather go back with JP than try another night loft delivery against an airfield like that. As it was, we went to medium-level and laser-guided bombs to get away from the triple-A.

We shared the Sheraton with the press. One morning at half past six, Tony Birtley rang us and said, "It's over. Come and have a beer." He bought the hotel's supply of Heineken and had a party in his room. I had one beer and left as I was totally drained by the war. I slept for the rest of the day.

I'd received notice of my promotion and new posting to Headquarters Royal Air Force Germany at Rheindahlen. I had to be there on the 18th of March and so had to come back fairly schnell[27].

There was quite a welcoming party in the big servicing hangar at RAF Laarbruch. Very emotional. Highly charged. Tremendous.

The POWs, who had been released a week earlier, were there as well. Seeing those guys was almost as moving as seeing my wife and Kimberley.

Paddy's pilot was awarded the Distinguished Flying Cross for their night loft mission.

Sonia Teakle would identify closely with her American cousins. She married a flier, moved to various new postings, lived in married quarters, was part of the tightly knit military family, and saw her man off to war. There's no cultural gap when the subject is a woman's concern for her family.

Sonia Teakle:

I was born in Swansea, South Wales, and moved to Germany with my family when I was 10. After returning to England, I met Ian at RAF Finningley in 1980. We got married in 1982 and lived in our own house at first. Since then, we have lived in married quarters for six and a half years. A flight lieutenant's quarter tends to be a three-bedroom semi[28] and are normally pretty good.

---

[27]schnell—German word meaning fast, quick.

[28]semi—Semidetached house. Duplex.

We move every three years but there aren't many postings abroad anymore and those are mainly to Germany. There are a few exchange tours to the United States and Australia, but they are very far and few between.

We are a very close knit family in the air force. When the husbands are away, we get together quite often or go out for meals. We don't sit in our houses alone night after night, certainly not. My friends are mostly military though we certainly have civilian friends from when we owned our own home off-base. It's normal for most of our friends to be part of the squadron.

Our eldest two children go to boarding school in England simply because they don't want to change schools every three years. It was their decision to go and so they have a stable education. Boarding schools are common with service personnel but not with the general population. Kimberley stays with us and attends RAF schools.

The guys work long hours and go away on detachment quite a lot. They go to places like Sardinia, Goose Bay, Canada, and Las Vegas in the United States. It's hard to feel sorry for them, and it's a shame we can't go with them more often. I did go to Las Vegas with him once. It was absolutely brilliant and I love the States. We traveled about to San Diego, Los Angeles, and San Francisco. The people were very friendly, there was so much to see, so much to do. It's such a big country. And very cheap.

I made nothing of the invasion of Kuwait at the time. Then Paddy came home one day and said he had to go away to train to go down to the Gulf. I still didn't believe it would ever happen. The departure dates changed quite a lot between August and November so we simply had to accept the uncertainty.

I still couldn't believe it until he came home and said, "Right, we're going on the 26th of November." He left and I had to believe it. It was very difficult to accept that he went off to war even though that's his job. I understood that could happen but, when it did, the adjustment was still very hard.

We knew we were going to be apart for Christmas and decided to celebrate Christmas early. We arranged to have our own Christmas dinner on the 25th of November. It didn't really get off the ground. Kimberley burst into tears and said, "I don't want to have Christmas dinner—it's not Christmas! I don't want Daddy to go away!"

The next day, we sent Kimberley off to school after she said goodbye to him. We didn't make a big thing of it. I took Paddy down to the squadron, met the other wives whose husbands were leaving, the busses turned up, and off they went. Everybody was very emotional since we didn't know what would happen.

We still didn't think there would be a war.

We had the full support of the British people. There was no bad feeling toward the services at all. There were no protests. But it wasn't like in America. We don't have yellow ribbons or other signs you would see walking about.

Paddy wrote and rang me once a week and I wrote every day, sometimes twice a day. I could even ring him. I rang him one time and he answered immediately. I said, "I'm sorry, were you in bed?" He said, "No, I'm in the bath. There's a telephone right here in the bathroom next to the bath."

At about 20 to 2 on the morning of January 16th, an uncle of mine rang up from Wales: "Did you know the war's broken out?" I rang a friend of mine, Lynn Woods, with the news so she came around to sit with me. Helen Peters and Jane Brough came around as well so we watched the news coverage all night.

At about half past five they showed crews coming back off the first mission. The first guys they showed were off 15 Squadron; they were the guys from the four ship Paddy was with. But they only showed three crews. Paddy and Gordon were missing and I started to panic. Luckily, the telephone rang. It was Paddy to say that he was back safely. He said they were the first crew to land and had avoided the press. I was very relieved and hoped he would show his face on camera the next time.

By eight o'clock, the house was alive with people. At about quarter to 11, everybody went home so I could have an hour's sleep. Then the news announced that a Tornado had gone missing. I looked out the bedroom window and saw the station commander's car pull up at Helen Peter's[29] house across the street. That could only mean one thing. The station commander calls in full uniform for one reason only. I knew then who was missing. I left it a little while and then went across to be with her. We sat glued to the telly and made endless cups of tea like the Brits do.

I didn't want Kimberley to see it on the television when she came home so I sat her down and said, "You know Mr. Peters and John Nichol? Their Tornado has crashed." She asked, "Are they dead?" "I don't know but I don't think so. They probably managed to get out and we just have to wait." "What about my daddy? Could something like that happen to him?" I said, "Of course it could but we must hope it won't."

The press were desperate to interview Helen but she wouldn't give an interview. The press were let into the camp to interview some of the wives and I sat near to Liz Weeks as she was asked how she would cope with that situation. She said, "I hope I'm never put in that position." Her husband went missing the very next day.

---

[29]Flight Lieutenant John Peters was shot down and captured.

It was a very rough time for the squadron but we all stuck together.

Four days after Helen's husband went missing, he was paraded on TV. Helen had been told earlier that the men were prisoners of war so she knew they were alive anyway. They looked pretty bad but we were relieved to know they were alive. Some of their injuries were from the ejection but they were also beaten quite badly. It could have been worse.

Once the war started, I didn't get a letter for about two weeks. He still rang to say he was okay but it wasn't until about a fortnight into the war that Paddy sat down and wrote that he found it all too emotional to put his feelings down on paper. He just couldn't talk about the war early on.

Ceri, my son, was in boarding school and accepted the situation. It was quite a big thing that his dad went off to war. My eldest daughter, Sarah, found it quite difficult to accept since she was also very friendly with the single guys on the squadron. She was quite upset and very emotional. Kimberley missed Paddy an awful lot and kept asking, "When's Daddy coming home?" All I could say was, "I can't tell you when but he will be home one day, hopefully." She didn't fully understand what could happen though she knew where he was and what was happening.

A few wives found it quite difficult and went back home to England to live with family.

We had to carry on as normal for the children but the television was on all the time so we could catch a glimpse of our men if possible. They did show Muharraq quite a lot since the reporters were there in the hotel. But we didn't spend all our time sitting in front of it watching. For example, I went to aerobics three times a week and the wives went out together very often.

We had a wives' briefing every morning at a quarter to 10 where the air force told us what our husbands' squadrons did in the last 24 hours. That news was at least hot off the press and we knew it was true. We couldn't believe everything in the news on telly. Our station commander, Neil Buckland, gave those briefings and was absolutely superb throughout the whole war.

Every Friday night at RAF bases, there's a men-only happy hour. No ladies allowed apart from serving officers. They meet to talk about aircraft with their hands, the usual things. But the station commander bent the rules so that, while the husbands were away, every Friday night was ladies' happy hour. All the wives and children went to the mess where they laid on food, drinks, and meals for the children. He was unbelievable, such a lovely bloke.

The support from the RAF was superb. It helped immensely.

I received quite a lot of supporting letters from friends and even people I didn't know. The girls whose husbands had gone missing received thousand of letters of support. People sent letters to the squadron simply addressed, "To the Wives." It was brilliant.

The best moment was Paddy's phone call saying they would not fly any more. We were very excited and had another party, more champagne.

The prisoners of war came back first to a very emotional welcome, joy. They looked fine but painfully thin. That was an excuse to have yet another party.

I started cleaning the house when I knew Paddy was on his way home. I hadn't done more than tidy up for months when I'm normally so house proud. But I just couldn't be bothered to think of house work until then.

There were hundreds of people waiting, the band, the children with their Union Jack flags. Then I saw Paddy. I couldn't believe it. He'd lost about a stone or a stone and a half in weight (14–20 pounds) and looked lovely and slim, nicely suntanned. We clung to each other for awhile.

We drove to the hangar where everybody on Laarbruch waited to welcome him and eventually got back to the house. It was decorated with balloons on the trees, posters on the walls, Union Jack flags everywhere. Somebody said, "Right, let's all go back to Paddy's house for a party!" And they did.

We just sat together all the next day and couldn't believe our luck at being back together. We'd lost three lovely guys from Laarbruch. I was one of the lucky ones whose husband came back.

9

Sandy[1]

Captain Paul Johnson, PJ, took one of the more unusual roads to a fighter cockpit. He left a civilian career to fly jets as the best way to provide a stable life for his family. That late start at flying makes him, in his early thirties, one of the few "old" men profiled in this book. PJ's story is especially interesting because it shows how much attack pilots are committed to other fighter pilots as well as to the troops on the ground. He also has a few things to say about the A-10's durability.

With the significant exception of the Harrier, the Hog is the only up-close and personal jet left in the inventory. In fact, it was the first aircraft that ground soldiers ever surrendered to.

The true expression is a bit more colorful, but it's said that attack pilots have certain highly prized parts of the male anatomy made from solid brass. They have to because, if you spend enough time in the A-10's world of close air support, you will get hit—hard.

Captain Johnson:

My father was a preacher so we moved around, but I call Dresden, Tennessee, my home. I became interested in agriculture while in high school since that's a rural area and my friends and family were involved

---

[1]Sandy—Callsign originally used by attack aircraft specializing in search and rescue in Southeast Asia. Sandy One is always in charge during a rescue, and just hearing his callsign makes a downed flier's whole day.

in farming. I even wound up with a degree in agriculture. I worked at that for about five years after college but finally decided that I needed to make a living instead.

A very good friend of ours, Elliott Lambert, had been a Guardsman[2] all his Air Force life while flying heavies in Tennessee. Elliott really encouraged me to take a shot at getting into the Air Force though Tricia wasn't too keen on it to begin with. He took us down to Columbus AFB in Mississippi to look around. The only base we knew then was Millington Naval Air Station and it was grim. Columbus isn't a garden spot, but, compared to Millington, the facilities were excellent. So Tricia was willing to go for it.

We got accepted for pilot training and it's really been neat ever since.

We went to pilot training at Laughlin AFB in Del Rio, Texas, where I was rated fighter qualified[3]. I just knew I was going to have to come back as a T-38 IP[4]. But we got lucky and were assigned to A-10s at Myrtle Beach, South Carolina, instead. We arrived in February 1987 and spent 4½ years there.

I was preparing to go to Fighter Weapons School in August 1990. The plan was to come back to Myrtle Beach, rather than have to move, so all was right with the world. We were happy. Then everything came unglued in August, and the wing started preparations to deploy. I faced the decision of going to weapons school or deploying with the squadron. My gut call was, "Hey, I'm going with my squadron." That's a standard pilot reaction, he's going to go wherever his squadron goes. The jets were configured for the trip but we had not been given a departure time when the squadron commander came back from the DO's[5] office at about 1700 on the 14th of August. He called me aside and said, "We're going to Saudi Arabia and you're not." He was afraid they would get to Saudi Arabia and just sit there. He was right.

That decision killed me, it absolutely killed me. I sat in on the deployment brief while they got ready to take off direct for Moron, Spain. With Syph, Steve Phillis, I was an experienced instructor in the squadron so it just killed me to see them go.

---

[2]Guardsman—Member of the National Guard.

[3]fighter qualified—Fighter, Attack, Reconnaissance (FAR) ratings are subjective judgments of Air Force pilot training instructors that a new pilot is good enough to handle any plane in the inventory. A FAR rating is required before assignment to fighters or instructor duty.

[4]IP—Instructor pilot. Pilot qualified to train other pilots. Selection as an Air Force pilot training instructor was not generally considered to be a good deal.

[5]DO—Operations officer or ops officer—Air Force unit's second in command and the flier directly in charge of flying.

The next day, I left on the drive to Nellis AFB while the squadron took off for Moron. They arrived to some really tense moments. The only thing between the Iraqis and the Saudi oil fields were the 82nd Airborne Division and two squadrons of Hogs. The 82nd was "the speed bump division[6]" so right after that speed bump came King Fahd Airfield and the Hogs. That was it. We were the closest Air Force unit to Kuwait so there were some very tense moments when they, no kidding, thought the Iraqis were launching. They kept four airplanes sitting on alert with Mavericks but they didn't even have any cluster bombs early on.

Fortunately, I had three days on the way to Las Vegas to get my head on straight and adjust my attitude. As time went by, I realized that going to weapons school was the right thing to do. So, while the squadron sat over in Saudi for Desert Shield, filling sand bags and sweating through the morale roller coaster ride, I flew at Nellis.

Fighter Weapons School was over in mid-December and the DO sent word that he wanted me over there and he wanted me there ASAP. I came home from school, had about five days with my family and then left Trish again on Christmas day.

At King Fahd, we had hot showers, we had a bathroom in the building, and we had air conditioning, so we were not nearly as bad off as a lot of people over there. I thought life was good but the guys who had been there since August were getting pretty tired of it. At least we were flying routinely. They had gone through about four months of very little flying and without firing the guns because they didn't have anywhere to shoot. The Saudis didn't have ranges. By the time I got there, they had some ranges where we were dropping Mk-82s and shot a fair amount of TP[7].

I arrived on New Year's Eve and took over the weapons shop while getting spun up on flying in Saudi. The January 15th deadline was fast approaching. Morale was on the upswing and everybody was getting pumped up and prepared in anticipation of something actually happening. Yes, there was nervousness, but I didn't hear any bellyaching. The guys worked hard at getting ready since they needed maps for farther north than they'd trained. They built maps for Kuwait and eastern Iraq that included the contact points[8]. We distributed final versions of the spe-

---

[6]speed bump division—The 82nd Airborne when deployed to Saudi Arabia. Airborne forces are too lightly armed to stop a serious armored attack.

[7]TP—Target practice cannon shells. Inert practice rounds that match the ballistics of live rounds without causing the cleanup problems of high explosives and depleted uranium.

[8]contact point—CP. Easily identified spot on the ground used for rendezvous and navigation. Coded and classified so that all a fighter needs are orders to fly to "B123" and call "F4X22" (a typical ground controller callsign).

cial instructions, read file items, bomb parameters, and the weapons we would use. The guys were really getting serious. You could see it. They were dead serious about business even though they didn't know any more than anybody at home did. We knew the deadline was January 15th, but only a very few guys knew any more than that.

The guys had a good idea of how everybody at home felt. Videotapes from families were the big salvation. We had TVs and VCRs in the squadron and back at the hooch, so we watched movies and ball games as well as those tapes. NFL games, for example, made it to Saudi Arabia about three to four weeks late. We also had the *Armed Forces News Service* on TV so we saw *Headline News* several times a day. Letters from wives and girlfriends brought word that support was excellent and everybody was really behind us.

I had a unique perspective on the support from home and knew how firmly the country supported us since I'd stayed in the States for most of Desert Shield.

We finally got CNN piped straight in just before the war started. That was interesting because then we could watch the same *Headline News* the folks at home saw and knew how the media presented our story. While everybody in the States was glued to Bernard Shaw and all of the fireworks going off in Baghdad, those of us who were not briefing to fly that first morning watched the same thing in our hooch.

It was neat to see the anticipation build up in the squadron as we prepared for war. Our Ops officer had flown helicopters, Super Jollys[9], in Southeast Asia but nobody else in our squadron had flown in combat. The average line pilot was about 28 years old. The commander of another squadron spent nine months in Hanoi as a "guest" of the North Vietnamese; the wing commander, Sandy Sharp, flew F-4s in Southeast Asia, and our DO also flew there. That was it for combat experience in the wing.

I flew against GCI radars on the first day, didn't fly the second day, and led a Scud recce[10] on the third day. I was down again on the fourth day of the war and sat SAR[11] alert on the fifth day.

SAR has always been a secondary mission for the A-10, which is a follow on to the old A-1 Skyraider that flew search and rescue in Southeast Asia. They were the first guys to wear the SANDY callsign. It's a very historic callsign and some of the most spectacular stories out of

---

[9]Super Jolly—Version of the H-53 Jolly Green Giant heavy lift helicopter.

[10]recce—("recky") Reconnaissance. Finding means killing to attack pilots.

[11]SAR—Search and rescue. One of the most dangerous and rewarding missions fliers draw. A Special Operations and A-10 specialty.

Southeast Asia come from the work those guys did picking up downed fliers in Thailand, Laos, Cambodia, and Vietnam. The A-10's relatively low speed means we can escort helicopters, we have good loiter time so we can stay in the target area, our awesome firepower is required for suppressing defenses, and our 11 pylons can carry all kinds of ordnance. The special ops guys planned on flying search and rescue at night when they would go in solo. But if it came to flying SAR during daylight, they and everybody else wanted A-10 escort. We learned later that A-10s can fly electronic search at night just as well as we can during the day, so we have SAR capability at night too.

I was already scheduled to spend two weeks as a planner in Riyadh after that SAR mission. No real pilot volunteers for staff work, and I was going to go kicking and screaming while leaving bloody fingernail tracks in the desert. I thought I'd spend my last turn on the schedule watching CNN in the squadron. We wanted to be on the regular schedule attacking targets rather than sit SAR alert and not fly.

We went to the squadron to brief after a night with three alarm reds[12] for potential incoming Scuds. We'd rolled out of our bunks three times to put on gas masks and go to the bunkers. Randy Goff, "Goff Ball," my wingman, figured we had about 2½ hours sleep before that very early brief.

Navy Lieutenant Devon Jones, "Boots," is a Tomcat driver who went to war on the Saratoga *with VF-103. He and his RIO[13], Lieutenant Larry Slade, "Rat," escorted a Navy strike headed for Al Asad airfield just west of Baghdad before dawn on 21 January 1991, the fifth morning of the war. PJ and Boots discuss their missions:*

Boots (0330 hours): Our mission as a single F-14 was to escort a single EA-6 on an HVU station. We briefed at midnight for a 0300 launch to make the 0600 target time. There was one Tomcat for each EA-6 so we briefed with them, pretty standard. We launched as briefed and rendezvoused at the tankers over Saudi Arabia on the Raisin refueling track.

PJ (0400 hours): We started in life support to dress out. First came the stiff and uncomfortable charcoal flight suit as part of our chemical warfare protection. Then came a G-suit, essentially a blood pressure cuff from the waist down, stuffed with appropriate survival gear, escape and evasion maps, extra water bottles, snack food, and anything else we

---

[12]alarm red—Warning of incoming attack.

[13]RIO—("ree-o") Radar intercept officer. A flier who operates the radar and weapons in a two-seat naval fighter.

could cram in there. Then came the nylon mesh survival vest, which has a bunch of pouches and pockets for a survival radio, smoke flares, a compass, ammunition, first aid kit, and all kinds of gee-whiz items that every Boy Scout would love. There's also the holstered 38-caliber revolver. That survival stuff stays with you if you punch out[14] of the airplane, and you should also have the seat kit from the ejection seat. It holds more survival gear like a life raft, another radio, more water, mirrors, knives, etc.

The parachute harness fits over the survival vest and clips onto the parachute, which is, in turn, part of the ejection seat. The parachute harness itself isn't heavy, but all the buckles, straps, nylon webbing, survival equipment, and so forth, add to the 30 pounds of gear and makes the lot feel bulky.

Boots (0430): The tankers dragged us north and dropped us off about a hundred miles from the border. The weather was lousy from 8000 feet through the mid-20s and forced us higher as we crossed the border. We drove into our HARM axis and the EA-6 launched on his first target at 0600. We then pressed in as he looked for a TOO[15] shot.

PJ (0530): We waddled out to find our jets parked in the blackness so we could crank[16]. It was still dark, and I mean *dark*. We had black revetments surrounding the airplanes, so it was *dark* out there.

The crew chiefs waited with the airplanes prepped and ready. Unlike most A-10s, the search and rescue airplanes were not heavily loaded. We had two canisters of CBU-58 or CBU-52 cluster bombs. We also had two pods of willie pete[17] rockets for target marking plus the AIM-9s and the ECM pod. Instead of combat mix[18] in the guns, a mix of armor-piercing and high-explosive shells, we had straight HEI[19] loads. We didn't carry Mavericks on search and rescue. We planned to be the on-scene coordinators and call in firepower as needed, so we didn't want to hang a lot of drag on the airplanes. Loiter time was more important than a full weapons load.

---

[14]punch out—To eject. To bail out. To take the nylon letdown.

[15]TOO—("tee-oh-oh") Target of opportunity. Target selected by the fliers versus one that is preassigned.

[16]crank—To start the engine as in crank the motor's handle. No, they don't really crank a jet's handle.

[17]willie pete—White phosphorous. WP rockets explode in a thick cloud of white smoke and intense fire. They're used for either target marking or burning a flammable target.

[18]combat mix—Different types of cannon shells loaded together to allow attacks on a wide range of targets.

[19]HEI—High-explosive incendiary. Cannon shells that are essentially high-velocity grenades.

One of us had jet problems and had to step to a spare. By the time we were finally ready to go, we got word that KKMC[20] was closed for bad weather and we couldn't get there. We shut the airplanes down and went back inside to stretch out on a couch or the floor or a chair or wherever for a snooze.

Boots (0605): As we turned west for the egress, I saw a bright white plume as a SAM broke from the clouds at two o'clock to us and a mile out. It was a huge telephone pole that was still burning at 25,000 feet, so it had to be an SA-2 from an unplotted SAM site. I rolled hard right and pulled down into it. At EA-6 airspeeds and that altitude, unfortunately, we don't have a lot of G available[21], so I wasn't able to put much of a turn on it.

Its proximity fuse detonated near the tail. There was a big explosion and the airplane became uncontrollable. It departed violently, went out of control, and began spinning. My head banged off the canopy a couple of times, my mask ripped loose so I couldn't talk to Rat, and things went dark. Rat tried to talk to me but didn't get a response because my mask was gone. I groped for the lower ejection handle between my legs as we passed approximately 10,000 feet. It took three tries to get it all the way out, and I learned later that Larry pulled his handle at the same time.

Out we went into the night. The canopy came off as my shoulder straps tightened automatically and the rocket singed my hands[22]. There wasn't a whole lot to see. I just went violently out into the black and stark reality. I separated immediately from the seat and the parachute opened right away. I had a good parachute plus a million thoughts in my brain, none of them good.

I couldn't see or hear anything as I hung in the straps; a severe contrast to the noise and forces of an out-of-control jet. After a couple minutes, I saw the silhouette of my RIO a few hundred meters on my left and a little lower. I yelled to him but lost sight of my crewmate when we descended into another cloud layer.

I didn't see Rat again until the POWs were released.

A little later, I heard and saw my airplane hit the ground in a huge fireball. In the meantime, our EA-6 saw us go down and made the ap-

---

[20]KKMC—King Khalid Military City. No-frills military complex centered on a 12,000-foot runway 40 miles south of the point where Iraq, Kuwait, and Saudi Arabia come together. A forward operating location.

[21]An aircraft's turn performance depends on its design, airspeed, and the density of the air it's in. High and slow equals unresponsive.

[22]Unlike Air Force fliers, Navy jocks usually fly without gloves.

propriate call to the CSAR[23] people. Unfortunately, somebody got the co-ordinates wrong and searched 30 miles south of us.

I came out of the last cloud layer expecting about 8000 more feet of ride, but the ceilings were only 200 feet near the target. I was just hanging in the pitch black when the ground came up and whacked me. More reality.

I picked up my parachute and my seat pan and tried to get my bearings. I looked for signs of cars, trucks, airplanes, whatever. There was nothing—no lights or sound other than the burning airplane. I balled up the orange and white parachute and hid it under the green seat pan before moving away from it.

I made a radio transmission that I was on the ground, all right, and heading southwest, but I didn't reach anybody. I started out in the wrong direction, east, looking for references and calling my RIO on my survival radio. That went on for 45 minutes until the sun came up in my face. Oops.

PJ (0730): Word came back in about an hour that the weather was improving so we launched for the FOL[24]. Start-up went quickly as we cranked the engines and aligned the inertial navigation systems. I had to make a 90-degree turn coming out of the revetment, which was only 10 feet wider than the wing tips. So I tiptoed out of the revetment with that 43,000-pound beast, taxied to the runway with Goff Ball, and took off.

It was early morning by then, around seven or eight o'clock. About 30 minutes out, I called KKMC and asked for the weather observation. They came back and said, "STANDBY FOR TASKING." My initial reaction was, "Rats, they have another reported Scud and we're going to get diverted to look for it." So I asked, "WHAT KIND OF TASKING?" They said, "SAR TASKING" (as in, "Search and rescue tasking of course—what else did you expect?"). I was nearly dumbfounded at the thought that we were really going to do SAR.

Boots (0730): Now heading northwest, my objective was simply to get as far away from the wreckage as I could and find a place to hide. I turned around and saw the footprints I'd left from my seat pan. In survival training, we learned that a pilot got rescued in Vietnam after leaving some tracks in the wrong direction and then covered up his footprints as he backtracked, so I started walking on rocks to hide my footprints as much as possible. Those pieces of training creep into your

---

[23]CSAR—Combat search and rescue. (noun) Those units that rescue downed airmen in combat. (verb) Recovering downed airmen in combat.

[24]FOL—Forward operating location. Marine or Air Force bare base close to the action, used for refueling, rearming, and emergency recovery.

head in that situation. I saw plenty of fresh tire tracks, footprints, and litter so I knew the place was at least traveled. It looked like West Texas.

PJ (0830): They passed me the information they had: callsign—SLATE 46; aircraft type—F-14 Tomcat; coordinates; helicopter callsign—MOCCASIN O5; AWACS callsign—YUKON. After a quick look, I realized he was well west of anywhere we had planned to be during the war.

We were going to need gas so I called YUKON to coordinate for a tanker to rendezvous with us as we flew west.

Boots (0900): I walked for two or three hours. It was so flat that what appeared to be 400-foot hills a mile off turned out to be 3-foot mounds at a hundred yards. But I also realized the only ridge I could see was at least 15 miles off, so I wasn't going to reach it. After putting a quarter mile between me and the latest set of tire tracks, I stopped at a couple 2-foot mounds near a blue water tank and shallow wadi. That was the only protection I was going to find, so I dug sideways into a mound with my knife and hunkered down. I didn't expect a rescue attempt during daylight and so planned to stay put until nighttime.

PJ (1015): We dodged weather that you don't expect to see in the Middle Eastern desert—thunderstorms, lightning. YUKON made a bad call and sent the tanker and us away from each other until he figured it out. The resulting rendezvous was classic, straight out of the movies. We were within a thousand pounds of fuel of having to bingo back to the FOL when suddenly, we broke out of the clouds, looked over on our left side for a mile, and saw the tanker. We slid over, got our gas, and were ready to go. We'd been in the air over two hours already.

So we came off the tanker and I called YUKON again. We were ready to cross into Iraq and start the search but the AWACS controller said the helicopter had been up there searching with some other A-10s but nobody had been able to make radio contact. It didn't look good. But he did have a reported Scud location he wanted us to check, naturally.

Boots (1030): I saw the first Iraqi vehicle at around 1030. It was a farmer's stake bed truck that stopped at the blue tank before they drove off to the south. I stayed hunkered down. I felt pretty well hidden in the horizontal against anybody on foot, but I was very exposed from the air. My green flight suit and the freshly turned dirt really stood out against the light brown of the desert. So I camouflaged as well as I could by sprinkling light-colored dirt around and piling brush over the top.

PJ (1030): Randy and I thought the SAR was over and we were on a wild goose chase Scud hunt. So we pressed over the border into Iraq and started searching for the reported Scud location. I looked down, saw one and thought. "Yeah! There's more: there's three or four—there's half a dozen—man there's 15 or 20 of those things down there!" But that was just too many Scuds. Randy and I kept looking and looking to identify those things. YUKON wanted confirmation 'cause he was going to divert the world there, as in send strike packages after those things. We dropped a little bit lower, a little bit lower, until finally I couldn't stand it anymore. We had to figure it out. So I dropped down for a low pass at about 1500 feet and saw the livestock running. I saw the goats and figured out that our Scuds were Bedouin tents. No kidding. Our Scuds were long, skinny Bedouin tents.

We called YUKON and said, "DON'T SEND ANYONE TO ATTACK THESE TENTS." It was time to come back out to the tanker. We gassed up and prepared to go back to KKMC and sit SAR alert all over again.

Boots (1130): A black scorpion latched onto my sleeve and I flew out of hole, knocking my hard-worked camouflage everywhere. In fighter terminology, I went one-v-one[25] with the scorpion and squished him. I set about repairing the damage and working on more camouflage.

PJ (1130): YUKON said, "WELL, WE'D LIKE YOU TO GO BACK AND SEARCH SOME MORE FOR THE SURVIVOR." I really had mixed feelings. I thought we were being sent on another wild goose chase into Iraq but I said okay.

We turned toward the survivor's probable coordinates. He was about 130 miles from the Syrian border in a desolate expanse—I mean empty.

We started searching by radio from high altitude, 18,000 to 20,000 feet. The problem was, we didn't have any Intell updates on what threats were out there. The F-14 had been part of the strike war attacking an airfield near Baghdad from the *Saratoga* in the Red Sea—a totally different war from our operations. He escorted a strike package since they took their escort downtown.

The only thing we saw in the area was an airfield off to the east and even it was desolate, just strips of concrete with a few taxiways coming off the end and lots of bomb craters. We continued tiptoeing north through all the desolation and started getting indications on our radar warning receivers that the Iraqis were looking at us.

We got to the survivor's reported position and called on the radio: "SLATE 46 THIS IS SANDY 57. SLATE 46, HOW DO YOU COPY?" Goff Ball was getting frustrated because his radios were in bad shape, especially his UHF radio, which was the one we used for searching. He could hear me but couldn't hear the other end of the conversations with AWACS, the tankers, or anybody. That drove him nuts for the entire mission because he was in the middle of Iraq trying to keep situational awareness by me filling him in secondhand.

---

[25]one-v-one—One versus one. One airplane in a fight with one other airplane.

Boots (1205): I looked at my watch and it was 5 minutes into a prebriefed 10-minute block during which we were supposed to try radio transmissions. I wasn't expecting a rescue before dark and so had the radio off to conserve the battery. I decided to give it a whirl even though I didn't expect anybody to be up on the net[26] in daytime. But I heard voices and gave my callsign. Lo and behold, somebody answered me.

PJ (1205): We weren't critical on fuel yet but we couldn't stay up there too terribly much longer. Then we heard a weak but very readable call: "THIS IS SLATE 46." I really didn't expect him to answer; we'd been at it so long that I just really didn't expect to hear anything. So I repeated, "SLATE, THIS IS SANDY." He called, "SANDY, THIS IS SLATE." He was extremely calm and matter-of-fact, like he was sitting in an easy chair watching the ball game while chatting with me on the radio.

That bothered me, it really did. That guy was too cool.

We started the authentication process. It's a series of questions that the survivor must answer correctly so we can determine that he is who he says he is. We didn't have any of that information in our cockpits so we had to relay the questions and answers back and forth to the Navy. We finally determined that this cool voice was our man.

Then we had to find him. My direction-finding equipment wasn't telling me anything so I didn't know where to look. SLATE couldn't see us and he sure wasn't going to hear an A-10 up that high. And poor Goff Ball, he didn't hear a word at all. So I drove west a little bit while listening to the signal strength. It got weak so I turned around and so on until I got close enough for the automatic direction finder to pick him up. The direction finding equipment pointed north so I thought, "Great! Like I really want to go further into Iraq." We were already a hundred miles deep, in daylight, without escort, on the fifth day of the war. But the needle pointed north so we flew deeper and deeper into Iraq.

About the time the direction-finding gear showed us close to passing him, I asked if he could hear A-10s. No, we were too high. So it was time to go down folks; we dropped below 10,000 feet and drove around in our search pattern until he suddenly said, "I THINK I HEAR YOU—YOU'RE NORTH OF ME." So we turned around and drove closer to him while working through the scattered puffy clouds. I expended one of the self protection flares that we used to decoy missiles. It's nice and bright so he spotted us and started vectoring us in: "OKAY, COME LEFT, HARD LEFT, HARD LEFT, HARD LEFT, ROLL OUT. I'M AT YOUR TWELVE O'CLOCK." I marked his position on the inertial navigation set. I also looked around to memorize the terrain because I still couldn't see him even though we were down at 500 feet.

---

[26]net—Network. Collection of individuals or units using a particular radio frequency.

And we were northwest of Baghdad.

Boots (1220): It was an A-10, of course. He moved north as we authenticated and dropped a flare. I spotted him at about six or nine thousand feet since they weren't camouflaged, they were that green-black color. I vectored him to a hundred- or two hundred-foot pass[27] to mark my position even though he never saw me. That was definitely a morale booster.

While talking to the A-10s, I made a mistake that became important later. I described my position as 5 to 8 miles north of the wreckage and a quarter mile from a blue water tank. We were on a clear freq so everybody heard it.

The A-10 said he had to head back for gas on the Strawberry refueling track. All I could do then was hang out like I was in a small town with no place to go.

PJ (1230): Then we violated a cardinal rule of search and rescue. We found the survivor and had to leave him. We were low on gas, I mean *low* on gas. We *had* to hit a tanker because we couldn't make it to any of the emergency fields. So we called AWACS and said we needed the tanker to come north to meet us right now. They said: "ROGER, THE TANKERS ARE ESTABLISHED IN THE TRACK SOUTH OF THE BORDER." I said, "NO, YOU DON'T UNDERSTAND. I NEED THAT TANKER TO TURN NORTH NOW! BRING HIM TO ME!" They did. The tanker popped out of his orbit and, on the fifth day of the war, that KC-10 drove into Iraq. Those guys roamed all over the country later in the war, but on the fifth day of fighting, going low and slow for some Hogs inside Iraq was a pretty gutsy thing to do.

In the meantime, MOCCASIN O5, the MH-53 Pave Low chopper, had been back getting gas and listening in. Captain Tom Trask, the aircraft commander, called, "SANDY, THIS IS MOCCASIN, HAVE YOU GOT COORDINATES FOR ME?" I didn't have a lot of confidence in those coordinates, but he wanted to start inbound. MOCCASIN was fully prepared to start in by himself since he had such a long way to go. There was no lack of guts that day.

I asked AWACS if we had any other A-10s around because I wanted more firepower. But the nearest Hogs were 40 minutes away, MOCCASIN didn't want to wait, and I wasn't in the mood to wait. We went for it. MOCCASIN headed in while Goff Ball got on the tanker. We dropped off the tanker, he hooked south for the border and we pressed to catch up with MOCCASIN.

I called YUKON to say we wanted F-15 CAP since I didn't want a Mirage or MiG busting in on the middle of the rescue. Ten minutes later,

---

[27]A-10s are large and look black from the ground, so they're always perceived as flying lower than they actually are.

two Eagles checked in and asked where I wanted them. I said, "YOU KNOW WHERE THE THREAT IS SO WORK IT OUT WITH AWACS." That point shows that most search and rescue work is coordination. SANDY TWO, the leader's wingman, is supposed to work all those details out on the secondary frequency while SANDY ONE always stays up on the survivor's frequency. We couldn't do that 'cause Goff Ball's radio was messed up. So we ended up with two F-15's, the AWACS, the tanker, MOCASSIN 05, the survivor, and us all on the same frequency. The radios went to pot as usual.

Boots (1245): A second civilian truck rolled up to the tank. They got a drink and stretched for a few minutes. Then they left the tank and drove straight at me. I must have been closer to a trail than I thought because they passed 20 yards from me. You'd be surprised how low you can shrink down when you have to. All I could hear was my heart pounding.

They were a couple of lucky farmers to show up when the Hogs weren't around.

PJ (1315): We caught up with the helicopters (MOCASSIN 05 and his backup) intending to escort them from up high so as to not draw attention. The clouds put an end to that idea and forced us to drop below 3000 feet. We had to escort them with a daisy chain—sort of a low-altitude orbit around the helicopters. They were down in the dirt at 20 feet with their gear raking the ground.

There was no way to sneak in. Pilots had asked about changing to a lighter camouflage paint scheme and I knew the New Orleans A-10s, the Reserve guys, tried to repaint their airplanes some lighter color but it didn't happen. I don't know why not. I've never heard an explanation for why the airplanes didn't get repainted. By the time I got there, that was a dead issue that had already been fought over. The guys rolled their eyes and shook their heads when I mentioned camouflage. It wasn't going to happen. So the A-10 made a wonderful target: It was a black cross flying around in the desert sky.

The Iraqis could definitely see us. We would hit a vehicle in a convoy and they'd stop, all the doors would pop open, and everybody would bug out. Think about the psychological impact. They'd drive along, not hearing anything, not seeing anything, and suddenly a vehicle in the column would be vaporized by a Maverick. Then they'd spot the little black crosses up there. It didn't take them long to figure it out, and they were terrified of A-10s. I think part of that was because we were one of the few airplanes they could actually see. That also meant we were highlighted for the defenses.

An EPW[28] report said the A-10 was one of the most feared aircraft.

[28]EPW—Enemy prisoner of war.

The most frightening part of the whole sequence was the A-10s orbiting before we chose targets. The Iraqis were petrified because they didn't know what our targets were. Once we rolled in, they knew we weren't going to miss very often and the target was going to be destroyed. But that was okay if, "he's not attacking me."

Boots (1400): At about 1400, I got contact with the A-10s again. We went through the signal mirror procedure and they told me to look for the helicopter. I got a tally ho on the Hogs at about three miles but I still didn't see the helo. They were flying some sort of squirrel cage pattern over him.

PJ (1400): MOCASSIN was too low to hear the survivor so I guided him in. The radios were really garbaged with the Eagles saying, "OKAY, WE'RE GOING TO ORIENT EAST-WEST, etc., etc., etc." I finally called, "EVERYBODY ON THIS FREQUENCY EXCEPT SANDY, MOCASSIN, AND SLATE, SHUT UP!" You could have heard a pin drop. That was lousy radio discipline and not very professional, but it worked.

Then we saw a military truck coming onto the scene and I asked SLATE how far it was from him: less than a mile. We pressed in quickly as SLATE called that it was headed straight for him. Everything was coming together nicely with a vulnerable helicopter getting ready to land and the survivor getting ready to stand up for the tricky part, the pickup. I didn't know who was in the truck but he couldn't be there.

Boots (1410): The Iraqi army truck drove onto the scene from the south. He was moving fast and kicked up a good cloud of dust. I was hunkered down behind the little bushes and just saw the canvas top on the truck. We don't know what he was doing there, but he was driving straight for me like he was homing in on my radio. I was about to point it out when the A-10s attacked.

PJ (1410): I rolled in for a strafe shot and missed, an airball, because I didn't take the 35 knots of crosswind plus his speed into effect[29]. I keyed the fox mike[30] radio and said, "SANDY TWO, TAKE THE TRUCK." Goff Ball rolled in and caught a piece of him so he stopped. I rolled in for another pass and got up-close and personal. I probably would have fouled on a gunnery range because I was much closer than 2000 feet when I put about 200 rounds on him. That smoked him. Goff Ball also rolled in again and shot him just to be sure.

---

[29]A-10s had never been adequately upgraded since their introduction in the mid-1970s. Their gunsights were simply fixed marks on the heads up display with an indication of the wind's vector. Some Hogs were modified with computing weapons systems similar to those designed into the F-16, but the improved jets didn't make it to the war.

[30]fox mike—Phonetic alphabet for "FM." Usually refers to a radio used by ground forces and the aircraft that support them.

Boots (1412): Lead rolled in first and shot at close range. It looked like he was 100 feet up and at 200-foot slant range though it was obviously farther. Pretty amazing. I guess he missed because dash two rolled in behind him to shoot and there was a good puff of smoke from the truck. I couldn't see much near the truck because the shells kicked up a huge cloud of dust. Lead rolled again and I saw flames in the dust cloud. The truck was gone. I had a great seat for the show.

PJ (1415): SLATE saw the helicopter and took over the vectoring: "MOCASSIN, COME HARD LEFT, 40 DEGREES LEFT, OKAY, ROLL OUT. I'M ON YOUR NOSE." We were concentrating so hard on the truck that we didn't notice MOCASSIN slowing for his landing after getting out of the way during our attack. He slowed to a hover taxi as he passed 50 yards from the burning truck.

The first time I saw Devon Jones was when he stood up about 100 yards from the burning truck. He'd literally dug himself a hole, pulled the earth in after him, and stuck his antenna out the top. He looked like a little sand flea coming up out of the ground and running over to the helicopter. MOCASSIN jumped up, pivoted around, and started booking south.

Boots (1415): In the meantime, the helicopter came in from the east, behind me. He was right on the deck at 20 feet. I called him in until he was within about 30 yards before I popped up, a crewman waved me in, and off we went. I didn't know who was in the helo and I didn't care: I was gettin' in.

I was very tired and hungry. The doc on board gave me a quick lookover while we pressed south. When the adrenaline wore off, my entire body ached. I was a hurtin' unit.

PJ (1420): Nobody said a word. Finally, AWACS couldn't stand it anymore and said, "SANDY, UNDERSTAND YOU'RE SUCCESSFUL?" We still didn't know what happened to the backseater. When they punched out, SLATE saw his backseater in the chute, but the 80-knot wind at altitude separated them. He never made radio contact with the backseater and that was the great unknown for the whole mission. It turned out that he was picked up and went to Baghdad as POW just before we made contact with Devon.

Gas was becoming a factor again because we had a long way to go to the border and were still escorting in a daisy chain[31]. MOCASSIN finally had to continue alone but that was no problem because he had searched that same area all morning by himself. We hit the tanker for the

---

[31]A faster aircraft, such as the V-22 Osprey, would have eliminated the need for the tricky, fuel-wasting daisy chain escort pattern that requires fighters to orbit a helicopter at very low altitude.

fourth time that day, again in Iraq. As soon as we got on the boom, the tanker turned south and we pressed for the border.

We'd been in the air about seven hours and only then did I even think about using a piddle pack[32]. Things had just been a little bit too busy so I hadn't had a thing to eat, I hadn't used a piddle pack, nothing.

Boots (1600): We went due south and landed at Al Jouf where some special operations forces and an Air Force medical team were based. I was hurtin' bad enough that, even being a carrier boy out for months with 5000 other guys, I couldn't find the energy to even think about the nurses. I felt like an imposition but they were glad to have me since I was their first customer.

We went through the medical exam and intelligence debrief, they gave me some MREs (which are bad in the worst circumstances) and I passed out on a cot.

Of course, they had to wake me up for a Scud alert a couple hours later.

I got to meet some of the guys from the helicopter the next day before an S-3 flew out to bring me back to the *Saratoga*. I got back in the air a couple of days later and back into Iraq shortly thereafter.

PJ (1600): MOCASSIN called as he crossed the fence so it was officially over. Total mission time was 8 hours and 50 minutes, takeoff to landing.

I cannot describe the feeling of being at the focus of that big team effort to make sure one guy didn't go to Baghdad, but I fully appreciate why the SANDYs in Southeast Asia loved their jobs so much. There was intense personal satisfaction. Tom Trask, the MOCASSIN pilot, and I met at the parade in New York and figured out that somewhere between 40 and 50 people were directly involved.

I then had to go to Riyadh and work in combat planning for two weeks. I would have thought the people in Riyadh wouldn't want whining Fighter Weapons School grads hanging around complaining, because nobody was happy to be there planning the war 36 hours down the road. But the whining got us nowhere.

The A-10 had a very good reputation because it had demonstrated the flexibility to respond in certain situations when some the other systems had not. The A-10s were the first to respond to the Scud threat, for example. Flexibility was the nature of the A-10 mission. We expect to plan our next mission while sitting in the cockpit being rearmed and refueled with the engines running from the last one. That's the way Hog drivers live. Most pilots go into a premission brief to cover the plan as it will be flown. In close air support, we go into a briefing and cover op-

---

[32]piddle pack—Heavy baggy with a sponge used for inflight relief.

tions because we don't know targets, callsigns, who we will support, or any of that. Then you go to the line of scrimmage and call an audible. Our system develops a flexible mindset, which was one reason the A-10 could handle some of the strange stuff it was assigned.

There was a sign over the A-10 desk that read: "FRSRA-10G." We shot down some helicopters, which qualified us for the F (fighter); R because we had flown tactical reconnaissance over the Republican Guard; SR for strategic reconnaissance during the Scud search; A obviously for attack; and then G for the Wart Weasel[33] mission since they started sending A-10s to take out SAM sites.

We certainly weren't crazy about that Wart Weasel stuff but we were successful so we bought the job. They wanted somebody carrying iron[34] to blow the SAMs because they weren't turning on their radars[35]. The F-16s, who had that mission as part of the Weasel team, didn't go to war with their F-4s. The best way to attack the SAMs was with precision munitions like the Maverick, and the A-10 had the best Maverick expertise in the tactical world. We used the G-model Maverick with its 300-pound conventional warhead against the SAMs.

When I got back from those two weeks in Riyadh, my boss said, "Okay PJ, you've been giving us those dumb SAM suppression missions, it's your turn." They got even with me. The ordnance load was two G-model Mavericks, four MK-82s (500 pounds each), AIM-9s, the ECM pod and the gun. That's an awful lot of weight and brought our max level flight speed down to 280 knots at altitude. That was also the first time I flew with John Whitney, "Whit," who was my number two. Number three was Greg Weidekamp, "GQ," and number four was Larry Butler, "Spock."

We launched and proceeded northbound. As usual, we hassled with the weather and were really getting tired of it. The Weasels were on station to ram HARMs down any radars they could find as we went into our orbit at 18 to 20 grand[36] over the target. There was a moisture layer at

---

[33]Wart Weasel—An A-10 hunting surface-to-air missiles. Weasel refers to a surface-to-air missile hunter. That mission was handled superbly by the F-4G Wild Weasels, but their normal F-16 wingmen stayed home. The F-16s didn't work out. So A-10 Wart(hog) Weasels went out to kill SAMs in place of the F-16s, while the real Weasels protected the Hogs.

[34]iron—Heavy aircraft weapons such as "iron" bombs. Conventional, high-explosive bombs. Simply iron (steel), explosives, and a fuse, these are essentially the same unguided weapons dropped in every war since WWI.

[35]Weasels usually fire radar-homing missiles at SAMs. The SAM operators learned very quickly that the only way to survive with Weasels around was to shut off the radar so Weasel missiles wouldn't have anything to guide on.

[36]grand—One thousand feet. Eighteen to 20 grand is 18,000 to 20,000 feet.

about 15,000 that I could see through, but we had to get below it for the IR Mavericks to work. I located the target and rolled down the chute but my Maverick malfunctioned. So I switched to orchestrating everybody else.

We had 80 knots of wind out of the west so my wingmen were getting blown too close or too steep or too low to get their ordnance off[37]. Weather is pretty variable with winds that strong and it changed rapidly on us. My first judgment error was missing the weather change until the thicker stuff started moving in below us. I decided to work the target through holes in the undercast to put MK-82s on the target. That's when I began the real buffoonery.

We should have just called a King's X[38] and gone home. Instead, I rolled in, couldn't achieve anything even close to bomb parameters, and so put the gunsight on the radar. I threw about 150 bullets out there and pulled off. At that point, I decided we were done. We were going home. I bottomed out at 5000 or 6000 feet, which meant I was alone and within range of everything but small arms. Two, three, and four were stuck on top of the weather as I started climbing up on my recovery. There were no tracers. I'd seen no ground fire, no air bursts, nothing.

I was suddenly hit with a sledge hammer. There was a really loud pop like someone broke a balloon in the cockpit. I yelled rather loudly: "One's hit! One's hit! One's hit!" Then I decided to key the mike[39] and tell everybody else.

The airplane rolled hard right about 120 degrees as the nose dropped through the horizon. I looked out and saw a real ugly sight. There was a huge hole blown through my right wing with some fire as the residual fuel burned in the ruptured wing tank. The housing was blown away from the gear so that I could see my right tire, along with a whole lot of dirt, since I was inverted and not very high. I pulled on the stick but the airplane wouldn't respond, it would not roll at all. I figured it was time to step out of the jet so I reached for the ejection handles.

We think a shoulder-fired SAM detonated inside the wing.

The right engine had stalled, spit all the garbage out, and then wound back up—my compliments to General Electric and Fairchild! When the engine relit by itself, I got enough thrust to control the air-

---

[37]An airplane is always affected by the wind, even during a diving attack. Wind from behind forces the jet forward, thereby increasing the dive angle and vice versa. Weapons must be released at specified flight parameters so the changed dive angle (or groundspeed or aimpoint or altitude) can ruin the attack. Computers can handle variable parameters, but A-10s didn't have computers.

[38]King's X—Calling a halt to a deteriorating situation before matters get worse.

[39]key the mike—Press the microphone button to talk on the radio.

plane. I recovered level flight at 6000 feet, unable to climb or turn right. Whit came down to cover me as I limped out of Kuwait in the heart of everybody's triple-A envelope with some of those guys taking pot shots at us. Luckily they weren't terribly good because I was stuck in about 10 degrees of left bank and couldn't jink at all. Whit protected me by killing triple-A sites as I tried to get to Saudi airspace and jump out. I jettisoned the bombs once we confirmed they weren't fragged the way the Maverick and ECM pod were. I could also look out and see the wing flexing a little bit so I just didn't know how long it was going to hang on.

We got over Saudi and she was still flying. Maybe I had a chance to at least get close to the field. My airspeed indicator was taken out when I was hit so Whit told me I was doing 190 knots; that's all I could get.

We were down to 5000 feet at max power sucking a lot of gas. I couldn't make it all the way back to Fahd. GQ rejoined with me as my most experienced wingman, and he didn't have enough gas to get back either. We at least had to get GQ a tanker, so a KC-10 came spiraling down through the clouds and through all the refueling tracks to get to us.

I was so slow that the KC-10 dropped his gear as speed brakes, slowed down, then sucked the gear back up. Q refueled and I slid over to the boom. With no hydraulics for the refueling receptacle, I couldn't latch on. So the boomer[40] overrode his safety systems to refuel me anyway and we took that boom places it had never been before. It was pretty ugly. The tanker crew was stunned to see that wreckage flying. I was able to get about 1500 pounds of fuel, which was enough to get home.

The next problem was lowering the gear. That really worried me because the missile detonated right next to the right main gear, which was also where the center wing and outer wing sections join. I didn't know what damage had been done there but I knew the wing might fold. I got ready to drop the gear and told Q to get away from me. He pulled over about a mile and a half to stay well clear of anything that might happen. I watched the right main gear as I dropped the gear handle, and they extended normally: klunk-klunk-klunk, three green indicators, gear's down and locked. I actually keyed the radio and said, "I LOVE THIS AIRPLANE!"

It took full left rudder and about two-thirds left aileron to land. The right tire shredded, but I didn't even know it was gone until I noticed that she was sagging on the right. The airplane was easy to control and I stopped straight ahead. I asked the fire chief if he wanted me to taxi to the end of the runway, but he said, "NO, BUT YOU MIGHT WANT TO SHUT

---

[40]boomer—Enlisted person who operates the boom on a tanker aircraft.

DOWN SINCE THERE'S ALL KINDS OF LIQUID DRIPPING OUT OF YOUR AIRPLANE." There was hydraulic fluid and fuel everywhere so I shut everything off and got out.

My only emotion was anger. I was really angry at myself for being stupid enough to get in that position. It was my fault that I got shot since I stayed in the target area too long messing around with the weather and then flew too low on a delivery pass. As the wing commander said, "Excellent job getting the airplane back, PJ, but what did you get shot for?"

The airplane really looked nasty. There was the shredded tire, the 12-foot hole in the top of the wing with lots of parts hanging out and the Maverick hanging kind of sideways. There were shrapnel holes in the Maverick, the ECM pod, everywhere. That's exactly the way it looked over Kuwait when I was at 120 degrees of bank and going down fast. The front and mid-wing spars[41] were severed clean through and the aft spar was damaged. The wing held together on a piece of that aft spar and the heavy lower wing skin, which is part of the wing structure. The aluminum wing skin on an A-10 is thick enough to be armor on any other airplane. The guys at our maintenance depot later said they repaired the engine by pulling the oil cap off, sliding a new engine underneath it, and putting that cap back on. Every part that rotated was trashed. They had trouble believing it produced any thrust.

My poor crew chief, Eric Staniland, said going out to the runway to tow his jet felt like going to the morgue to identify a member of the family.

She sure brought me home bent. Our maintainers put her back together and I flew her back to the States.

Later on in the war, we saw the Iraqis park their vehicles together and get away from them to surrender. They realized the most dangerous place to be was in an Iraqi armored vehicle 'cause they were going to get hit, and, when they got hit, they were going to blow up. So they stayed clear of their armored vehicles and surrendered.

We didn't fly much after the cease-fire. There were A-10s covering the surrender ceremonies at Basra and when Schwarzkopf was up talking to the Iraqis, but we mostly went back to sitting alert.

We flew home through Sigonella, Italy; Bentwaters, England; and Pease, New Hampshire. Pease was closed down and they've never had fighters, but, when they found out an A-10 unit would land in 24 hours, they rolled out their red carpet. They did a wonderful job. One of the Reserve tanker pilots from Pease owned a restaurant there. As he

---

[41]wing spar—Main wing support that runs the length of the wing and ties in with the fuselage.

brought us home from Bentwaters, he called and said, "You guys like lobster?" "Sure." "We'll see what we can work out." He had 24 lobsters waiting for us on that first night home.

We got back to Myrtle Beach on the 20th of March. The folks here had a pretty spectacular welcome home ready for us. I've tried to tell people that knowing we had America's support during the war was even more important than the homecoming. My wing commander talked about being spit on when he came home from Southeast Asia, so it was sure easier to walk out to an airplane without having to worry about my wife running a gantlet of protesters or my kid going to some school off base and hearing slurs and slams about the American military.

We had America's support and that made our job a whole lot easier.

For the rescue mission, PJ won the Air Force Cross, the nation's second-highest award for heroism under fire, while Goff Ball earned the Silver Star. Captain Trask and his MH-53 crew from the 20th Special Operations Squadron won the Mackay Trophy for "the most meritorious flight of the year by the Air Force."

It may be said that Patricia Johnson had an easy time during Desert Shield and Desert Storm. Her husband wasn't gone as long as he could have been, luck was on his side during the close calls, and she had a strong support system. She could spend her days with her children and was surrounded by friends who understood exactly what she was going through. So it may be said that she had an easy time, but don't believe it. For a wife and mother, sending your man to war is never easy.

Patricia Johnson:

Security is very important to me, so when Elliott told us about the security in the Air Force, I liked it after being skeptical at first. I also didn't have to work and could be with the kids.

Moving to Del Rio, Texas, the backside of nowhere, was an exciting and a little bit scary adventure for me. We ended up with many close friends on the base. You make lasting friendships in the military and we were almost as close as my Christian friends from church.

I enjoy the squadron life. Fighter squadrons are so small that you really get to know everyone real well. I'm the type that likes to stay home with the kids, so many of the girls are even closer to each other than I am. But it's good to know that they're there when you need them and that they understand what you're going through. If anything happens, your friends in the squadron will be there.

Paul was supposed to drive to Nellis on August 15th but said he'd go with the squadron if they deployed. I was prepared for that, but I kept praying that he'd go to Fighter Weapons School instead. I prayed that it would all be over before he got back.

The worst part of the build-up was simply not knowing what would happen. The uncertainty was so bad that most of the wives said, "Just take him! He's driving me crazy, he wants to be there, just take him! Get him out of here." There's nothing worse than a cooped-up, whining fighter pilot.

The worst night of my life was the night the guys heard they'd deploy to the Gulf. I answered a phone call from the squadron, a recall[42], so I knew he was going. I started crying and was in tears when he walked in. Paul asked what was wrong, and I said I got the word. He said, "They're going but I'm not," and walked straight to the bedroom to be alone.

I didn't know what to say to him, how to react, what to do. He was miserable. And that was the last night we could be together before his four-month school. We were supposed to go out and have a good time, but all he wanted to do was go to the squadron and be with the guys. I told Paul to just go and be with them; that's what he needed to do.

It took Paul two full days on the road to come to terms with being left behind.

I kind of withdrew from the other wives because my husband wasn't in the same boat with theirs. He wasn't getting ready to fight a war and didn't have to put up with the boredom and heat in Saudi. I had a guilt complex even though nobody made me feel that way. I was also seven months pregnant and didn't feel like getting out a lot anyway.

Paul finished Fighter Weapons School as a distinguished graduate just before Christmas and I got to go to the graduation. I still felt a little guilty about having him around when the other wives would give anything for 10 minutes with their men. They said, "Don't feel guilty, enjoy him while you've got him!" But the fact that he would leave again was always in the back of my mind. We spent the holidays with family in Tennessee before he left for the Gulf on Christmas Day. It was especially tough for him to leave his new daughter so soon.

The kids took it well, like Daddy was just on another TDY[43].

I drove into the church parking lot one Wednesday to see most of the people still sitting in their cars. I didn't understand until they told me that the war had started. We had a very short service so everybody could go home. Cindy Moore, whose husband, Jeff, worked on Paul's jet, reached over and took my hand and we never let go all through the service. I think she was even more upset than I was.

---

[42]recall—Bringing all unit members in to work on short notice, usually for a deployment or other contingency.

[43]TDY—Temporary duty. Relatively short "business" trip.

I also couldn't let the kids see me all upset. Some of the mothers really reacted to the news, so their kids did too.

Civilians felt so terrible that the war started but, to the wives, it was almost a relief. It finally started so it would be over soon and the guys could get home. People couldn't understand us, but we had confidence that they'd end it quickly and get home.

One day, Elaine Highfill ran over with the news that Paul was on TV. I didn't know what was going on until we saw a report that he had helped rescue a pilot. Then the phone rang off the hook. Friends, family, people I hadn't seen in years, reporters, everybody called. I finally took the phone off the hook. As the guys say, I have a life too.

That went on the next day until the base public affairs office set up an interview. The media people poured in with camera after camera and microphone after microphone. I got really nervous but it started out to be painless. They were briefed that I wouldn't talk about my kids at all because I was afraid that would threaten their safety. But one reporter looked right at me and said, "What does your nine-year-old son, Chris, think about this?" It's too bad killer looks don't work 'cause he got one.

Chris, our oldest, was okay until the rescue mission when he saw Paul on TV. It then struck home that Daddy was really over there fighting a war. I had to stop watching CNN because Chris would see the war and start thinking about it. He was pretty depressed for a couple of days and especially didn't want to talk about it in public. He just wanted to block it out.

In a call a few weeks later, Paul said his airplane was shot but he was home safe. I thought it was like the damage a couple of the other wives had talked about, some bullet holes, no big deal to an A-10. I went to a squadron coffee later and the girls talked about the A-10 picture in the newspaper. We found it and there was Paul's plane with a big piece missing. He hadn't told me how bad it was, of course.

When Syph[44] and Sweetness went down, we got word that the jets were A-10s from our unit and the wives were called to a meeting at the war room on base. The vice wing commander told us who it was and went into detail on how to handle the media. Reporters even had the audacity to call Syph's home and questioned his fiancée until she hung up on them. The Air Force and the wives treated her as if she was already his wife, which really helped.

My opinion of that kind of reporter isn't very good.

---

[44]Syph, Captain Steve Phillis, was shot down while defending his wingman, who had bailed out and was being fired on in his parachute. Syph's family was presented with his posthumous Silver Star.

I heard about the cease-fire while driving home from church one night. I cried all the way home. Then it got frustrating again because the news ended and we didn't know when the guys would come back.

We didn't have to prepare much for the homecoming since that was handled by the wing commander's office. The families were separated from the crowd and the media so we didn't have to deal with the reporters, which was very nice. Paul was in the last cell of airplanes, which ended up late with maintenance problems. I was also a little extra anxious because he flew his repaired jet home. But he finally made it, safe and sound.

The kids made banners and hung them all over the house. They wouldn't let Paul sit down until they'd dragged him around the house to see them. The look on his face said it all—he was finally home.

10

They Can Run . . .

Captain Tony Murphy, ET, has led a charmed career, even for a fighter pilot. Simply flying the Eagle at Eglin AFB is enough for most jocks, but he managed to log over a thousand hours and a successful combat tour in his first three years as well. His story is proof that the Eagle owns the sky and that fighter pilots get surprisingly good, surprisingly young.

The McDonnel Douglas F-15 Eagle is a superb air-superiority fighter. It has the size and power to carry eight missiles at Mach 2.5 and yet can still turn at nine Gs in a close-in fight with the Vulcan canon. Originally designed with the lessons learned in Vietnam and with "not a pound for air-to-ground," Eagles have one mission: Clear the skies. Eagle drivers fear no one.

Captain Murphy:

I was born in L.A. in 1962 and grew up in a little town called Grants Pass, Oregon. It's real small, there was only one high school at the time. I didn't have any plans to go to college, and all I wanted to do was fly jets. I went to the Air Force recruiter and said, "I want to fly jets." He said, "You can't fly jets." I went to the Navy recruiter and said, "I want to fly jets." He said, "You can't fly jets." Then I went to the Marine recruiter and said, "I want to fly jets." He said, "You can fly jets but you've got to enlist first." I didn't think that was right. The Army bugged me the whole time about flying rotary-winged aircraft while I said, "I want to fly jets." I kept badgering the recruiters until finally, the Air Force said, "You need to go to college first." Now we were getting somewhere.

After I graduated from Grants Pass High School, I went to the local community college for a year to get some of the basics out of the way and then went to Oregon State, where I joined ROTC. I said, "I want to fly jets." They said, "Are you sure you want to fly jets?" I said, "Look, I'm getting a degree in mechanical engineering, I've got a private pilot's license, and I want to fly jets!" Maybe I wasn't being clear enough. They said, "We can help you out." So I went through the normal ROTC program, passed the physical, and they said, "Okay, we're going to give you a chance to fly." My commander at the time, Don Karpen, gave me a break since I didn't have the best grades and I wasn't exactly your model military guy. He got me an assignment to Shepherd AFB, Texas, for pilot training, which gives you a good chance to fly a fighter afterwards. That was my first big break.

I had dynamite instructors at Shepherd who really gave a shit about us fighter pilot wannabes. Abel Hamid, my Tweet[1] IP, was really inspiring. I had three IPs in T-38s who were also great. One of them was Rod Glass, one was Dave Hearn, and the third was a real character named Vito Posca. Vito was an Italian who led the Frake Tricolori, their aerial demonstration team. They taught me what I needed to know in the best way they knew how, plus they were fun to fly with. They had a grip, so to speak, on what was important and what wasn't.

I was not the best guy in the class by far. In fact, they tagged me to be a Tweet FAIP[2] until one of the flight commanders intervened to get me a fighter. I don't know what his reasons were, but that was my second big break.

Assignment blocks that time of the year always seem to be heavy in Eagles so I ended up getting an F-15 to Eglin AFB, Florida. I was pretty darn happy with an Eagle, as you can imagine, but Chris, my wife, wasn't too pleased about Eglin since Florida wouldn't accept her Texas pharmacy license. I didn't know that much about Eglin, but I heard it was a nice place and the Eagle's a great jet.

I had a good time at Holloman and then went through land survival and water survival on the way to Tyndall AFB, Florida, for RTU[3]. I had a

---

[1]Tweet—Cessna T-37 Tweety Bird basic jet trainer. Also known as the Flying Dog Whistle for its ear-shattering squeal, the Tweet has introduced Air Force pilot wannabes to jet flight for more than 35 years.

[2]FAIP—First assignment instructor pilot. Air Force pilot training instructor fresh out of pilot training. Technically proficient and fighter qualified, FAIPs were commonly nonvolunteers with poor morale because the assignment system did them no favors after that first assignment.

[3]RTU—Replacement training unit. Air Force squadron dedicated to training pilots in their fighters before sending them to operational squadrons. Counterparts of Navy/Marine RAGs.

couple of great IPs again in Tom Jordan and Jim Fitch. Jim Fitch taught me the first part and Tom Jordan, a patch wearer[4], took me through the latter part of RTU. They enjoyed flying and teaching so I enjoyed learning from them.

I ended up in the same squadron with a good friend, Bruce Till, who had been with us since UPT. By the time the war started, we had flown at Eglin for about 2½ years and were already working on our next assignments. I was a four ship flight lead and Bruce had made IP. The noteworthy point about those 2½ years was the nearly constant TDYs to Red Flag. We were always at Nellis AFB in Las Vegas. You can imagine the good large-force exercises and the awesome training we got from all those trips. We even called the war "Rag Flag" 'cause our training was so close to the real thing.

Our wing had a quick reaction plan that we'd used before so, when Kuwait was invaded, we knew a little bit about what to expect. That was a pretty frustrating time for us because the only guidance was: "Pack your bags and be ready." We figured we were going someplace and it would probably be the Middle East. The wives found out in the middle of August, which was unusual; they normally know our deployment plans before we do. Their "hotline" wasn't working very well at the time. We watched TV and figured we would go so we were excited as hell, as you can imagine. I was really proud to see the guys chomping at the bit to go.

It was evident that only one squadron was going and not every member of that squadron would get to go. That was kind of ugly. I didn't understand the selection logic and there were some hurt feelings. Nobody wanted to be left behind.

Toward the middle of August, we briefed the deployment and were sent home to spend some time with our families. Then we went through a couple of iterations on whether the whole squadron would go at once and when we would leave. We ended up sending 12 jets at a time a day apart.

We sent an advanced team to our deployment base and they called back to say, "Hold the deployment, there's no place to stay." There was some stupid problem with the Saudi contractor who said we could not occupy the rooms that were waiting empty for us. We delayed an Eagle deployment because the civilian contractor wasn't ready, which added to the perceived indecision in a lot of areas. That took a couple of days to work out, but, in retrospect, we were lucky to have rooms at all.

Some guys had to go say good-bye to their wives four times 'cause they were spares or the departure dates changed. In that whole shuffle,

---

[4]patch wearer—Fighter Weapons School graduate who wears the FWS patch on one shoulder. Also called "target arms" because the FWS patch includes a prominent bull's-eye.

there were five days when we had to sit by the phone just in case the plan changed again. Poor Chrissy, she was about ready to kick me out the door 'cause I was frustrated and getting on her nerves. That was a very common feeling. One wife said, "I just wanted him to get out. He was leaving little ping marks[5] around the house." What do you talk about when you're supposed to stay in your house but you're going to war? What do you talk about? You talk about the war. There was a lot of frustration on my part when they decided to send two cells and I had to wait for the second cell. I wanted to be the first one to take off, of course. There were some beefs over that because we were afraid we wouldn't get to go for some reason or that something would come up to trap us back here. That was an emotional roller coaster.

We stocked some oddball stuff. We received messages from the advanced team to bring things like liquid soap and lots of toilet paper. We also picked up a sling shot for rats. We thought there were rats all over the place so we might as well have some target practice. We figured whatever was on the jets was gonna have to hold us for a while so they were loaded with three fuel tanks, all the missiles, some MREs, chem gear and two or three bags of your own in bay five[6].

I was so busy preparing for the real departure brief that I didn't get much of a chance to say good-bye to Chris. She grabbed me some lunch at Burger King and gave it to me just as the brief started. All I could do was give her a quick kiss and say, "See you in a couple months, maybe, I hope." That was our good-bye.

We'd covered that brief two or three times already so it was just a review. Then, as we stepped, it started pouring down rain. We needed lots of time to arrange the two box lunches, luggage, Walkman, tapes, the flight plan, and all that stuff, but it was pouring. What a mess.

We took off and I immediately had problems with the cooling and pressurization system. It was hotter than heck in my cockpit with the cabin pressure fluctuating—not exactly something you want to cross the pond with. I was all ready to go and might have to abort. I milked the jet to the first tanker since I had time to see if I could get the thing fixed, but my ears didn't appreciate the pressure fluctuations. My wingman had a problem too, so he ended up turning around with one of the airborne spares and I took the other spare on my wing. My problem cleared up and the jet ran fine for the rest of the trip.

We flew out over the water, hit one tanker, he left and another one magically appeared from someplace. We refueled from him a couple

---

[5]As in pinging off the walls.

[6]bay five—Storage space behind the seat of a single seat F-15.

times and then he left. They handed us off like that until we showed up in Saudi on our own. At least the weather wasn't too bad. Most of the ocean crossing was at night and I got to deal with piddle packs for the first time after drinking all the juice in the lunches.

We were over the Mediterranean when the sun came up. Africa, with the sand and the beautiful coast, drove home the fact that we were in a different part of the world. We really knew we were heading for some-place different when we crossed the Nile and part of Egypt. Our base was in the northwest corner of Saudi Arabia, not far from the Red Sea and just a few miles from Jordan. I wondered where the heck we were going most of the time since that was the first ocean crossing for me and most of the guys. We flew it in one hop, 13½ hours straight into Tabuk.

Once we hit the Saudi coast, the last tankers left and nobody would talk to us. The regional controllers weren't up on freq[7], approach control wasn't up on freq, the tower wasn't on freq, so we just found the base and landed.

The only Americans there were the 12 guys in our advanced team. They gave us a bottle of water and a towel and said, "Welcome to Tabuk." I was ready: "Let's get these babies on alert! Give me something to eat and we'll be ready to go!" We were in another country to go to war so most of us were fired up.

The Saudis gave us room keys and then had a big feast in their squadron. We shared the squadron with the Saudi F-5s but they only gave us two rooms out of that huge building even though we were two-thirds of their operation. That was less than optimum. But they had that big feast for us and their wing commander welcomed us to Saudi Arabia. Our commanders told us some of the rules like no shorts, no booze, don't lift up your foot to them or give them the okay sign because they'll get upset. Then it was off to our rooms.

I figured we were going to war so we should be in tents and it should be hot, dirty. But we had a shower between two guys and each of us had our own little room with a bed and air conditioning. Even when we doubled up after the other jets landed, we were better off than most. It wasn't like Nellis, but we weren't there for Red Flag, so I wasn't complaining at all.

The contractor didn't even cook the food there; he brought it all from somewhere else. We never did identify any of it, even after we bit into it. So we didn't eat much except MREs[8]. Then somebody collected

---

[7]freq—Frequency.

[8]MRE—Meal ready to eat (or meal rejected by everyone, if you like). High-calorie field rations that replaced the Vietnam-era C rations.

Chapter 1:
Air Force Capt. Anne Armstrong in the cockpit of her C-5 Galaxy (below) and her father, George Armstrong (right).

Chapter 2:
Navy Lt. Phil "Chauncey" Gardner and his F/A-18 Hornet.

Chapter 2: *Chauncey and his wife, Deborah.*

Chapter 3: *Marine Capt. Dave "Dyno" Diest, his wife, Vicki, and son, James (right). Dyno's pilot, Capt. Paul "Droid" Andrus in the pair's A-6 Intruder (below).*

Chapter 7:
At left, Air Force Capt. Merrick "Genghis" Krause (right) and Joe "No Cap" Seidl stand beside their F-15E. Below, Genghis and his wife, Dr. Shari Krause, reunited after Desert Storm.

Chapter 8: *Royal Air Force Flight Lt. Ian "Paddy" Teakle (second from right) with his four ship in Muharraq, Bahrain, just before a sortie. Back row (left to right): Flight Officer Glyn Harley, F/O Tony McGlone, Squadron Leader Gordon "Buckers" Buckley (Paddy's pilot), F/L Steve Barnes, and F/L Mike Barley. Kneeling: F/L Bruce McDonald and F/L Dave Cockerill.*

Chapter 8: *Paddy in the cockpit of the Tornado prior to a sortie (above) and with his wife, Sonia, in Thailand after the war (right).*

Chapter 9: *Air Force Capt. Paul "PJ" Johnson was flying this A-10 when it took a direct hit. Despite the severe damage, the A-10 got PJ safely back to base and was repaired. PJ flew the same plane home to the United States.*

Chapter 10: *Air Force Capt. Tony "ET" Murphy with his F-15 Eagle (right). ET and his wife, Christine, celebrate his April 1991 homecoming (left) after Desert Storm.*

Chapter 11: *Marine 1st Lt. Lance "Jolt" Hoyt shows off the ordnance on his F/A-18 Hornet. Jolt and his flight leader, Capt. Rick "CJ" Sturckow, survived an ambush by two ZSU 23-4 anti-aircraft guns.*

Chapter 12: *(Above, left to right) Capt. Pete "Abner" McCaffrey, Capt. Evan "Ivan" Thomas, Lt. Joey "Boo Boo" Booher, and Capt. Bill "Psycho" Andrews were four of the F-16 pilots who bombed Iraqi ground troops to allow the exfill of eight Green Berets. Psycho was later shot down and captured. U.S. Army Sgt. 1st Class Mike "Buzz Saw" DeGroff, shown at right during his homecoming at Fort Campbell, Kentucky, directed the F-16s' bombing from the ground.*

Operational Detachment Alpha 525 training in the desert during Desert Shield. Due to personnel changes, not all of these men were involved in the February 24th mission. Left to right: Rob Gardner, Dan Kostrzebski, Buzz Saw, Charlie Hopkins, Jim Weatherford, Terry Harris, Rick Rice, Brad Herran, and Jimbo Hovermale.

Chapter 12: *Psycho and his family at home in Germany before the war—wife Stacey, daughter Shannon, 2, and son Sean, 5.*

Chapter 13:

Air Force Capt. Rob "Rob-San" Donaldson and his F-117 Stealth Fighter at Khamis Mushayt, Saudi Arabia, in February 1991.

Rob-San, his wife, Millie, and children, Katrina and Michael, at Nellis AFB, Nevada, at Christmas 1991.

Chapter 14: *Army Capt. Mike Klingele, an Apache helicopter pilot, greets his family upon his return from Desert Storm. Left to right: Mom, Dad, Mike, sister Vicki Fontinel, and sister Joanne.*

Chapter 15: *Marine Capt. J. Scott "Vapor" Walsh's AV-8B Harrier was shot down over Kuwait on his last mission of Desert Storm. His mother, Caroline (above), and father, Jim (right), welcomed him home in Cherry Point, North Carolina, after the war.*

all the MREs for a war reserve and we were left with no breakfast, the hideous lunch, and the unrecognizable dinners.

When the sun went down, the flies left and the mosquitoes showed up. A truck came by to fog the place, which concerned us because we'd choke on that stuff. You'd run into your room to get away from the truck but so would the mosquitoes. They were so bad that I could hear them through ear plugs at night.

We quickly settled into a four-day rotating schedule. We'd fly during the day, then fly at night, then pull alert and have the fourth day off. The day flights usually went eight hours with the night missions briefing around midnight. That change kind of screws up your circadian rhythm so you'd spend the second day trying to get some rest and eat. We never got used to that. The alert days were spent with four guys ready to launch in five minutes from a little shack with beds, a TV, a VCR, a bathroom and a kitchen. We didn't get scrambled very often and then it was usually to replace somebody with a problem out on the CAP that we manned 24 hours a day.

The days off were spent catching up on sleeping and eating. The Saudis eventually allowed us to use their sports facility for four hours a day when they didn't want it. They didn't want Americans and Saudis using the gym at the same time. It was an awesome gym: nice Olympic-size pool, weight room, bowling alleys, volleyball, basketball. It was nicer than any gym I had ever seen at any university. We'd also use that time to catch up on letter writing.

Our routine training was very limited. We were only allowed to download a few of our jets (take the live missiles and the tanks off) to get in some limited training. We couldn't work below 5000 feet because some attack guys had pranged one at low altitude. Somebody else crashed a jet after a gun jink so we were no longer allowed to practice gun jinks. That took away BFM[9], which we used to practice all the time. We would sometimes fly against the Saudis in their F-5s, but they put so many restrictions on us that we really didn't get anything out of it. We tried to avoid working with them as time went on. We were reduced to practicing two versus two against each other until the Navy in the Red Sea wanted to practice sending big strike packages against the ranges near our base. They sent messages tasking a four ship of our Eagles to defend the ranges. That was the cat's meow because we got to practice radar work and four ship employment. Those Navy strikes combined air-to-air escorts and bombers trying to hit us so we never knew what to ex-

---

[9]BFM—Basic fighter maneuvers. Simple attacks and defenses that fighter pilots learn as the basis for more fluid fights. BFM is practiced as a warm-up to more intense dogfight training.

pect. It was real good training for a mass raid. The training high point was working with the Navy; those guys were really good.

We knew we had a pretty healthy amount of support back home. We also heard about the protests from people we trusted, through newspapers, and through the small amount of "bad" news that made it past the Saudi censors to our TVs (we never got American TV). We perceived that the press emphasized the negative and not enough of the positive. People back home said, "You guys would not believe the support here at home with the flags and the ribbons." Once the war started, the support became incredible.

We got a ton of letters for Any Soldier. I got a couple of letters addressed directly to me from strangers, like a church in Seattle and the grade schools in my home town. The kids went nuts, all four classes, and I became their literature project or their art project. They sent art and tons of letters asking, "Is the desert hot? Are you scared? Have you ever met Saddam Hussein?" They were really cute letters. I had a foot-and-a-half-high stack of letters from those classes. I visited them after the war to let them eat some MREs and try on a G-suit.

We had Brit Tornadoes at Tabuk that changed their paint scheme to basically desert tan. It worked great, you could never see a Tornado. Our paint scheme didn't change at all 'cause the sky was nice and blue, the shade Eagles are painted to blend with.

Frustration built as Desert Shield went on. We didn't know when we were going home. There was a rotation plan. There was no rotation plan. The replacements are coming. They're not coming after all. The rest of the wing never deployed. It got to the point where you couldn't believe anything you heard.

We knew a few days in advance that war might happen. We started planning certain missions that we suspected we would fly and it was obvious that tensions were increasing. Saddam wasn't going to back down and neither would we.

Then the war started.

I was not involved in the first 24 hours' worth of big packages. Those were the missions where every flight got a kill or two. After that first day, opposition was very sporadic. I drove around Iraq trying to find trouble but there was no action. It was really frustrating. We had air supremacy so quickly that the Iraqis just didn't want to fly. It was boring. But we were very careful to not do something so stupid that our wingmen were either uncomfortable or didn't come back.

Our missions varied from DCA[10], where we flew a race-track pattern

---

[10]DCA—Defensive counter air. Interceptor operations that prevent enemy fighters from interfering with friendly air operations. Interceptors form a barrier designed to protect the areas and orbits behind it.

to protect the AWACS and tankers behind us, to a sweep where we drove around Iraq looking for trouble. We even flew in the cons[11] to advertise, "Here we are, come get us." We didn't get any takers.

We sometimes went out just to cause trouble. One time, we went up north of Baghdad to see if anything popped up and saw some air strips that we didn't know were there. Sure enough, there was an IL-76[12] sitting on one of them. We told AWACS about it and another base nearby with three Cubs[13]. AWACS wanted us to take them out. Attack is not our job—there's a lot of dirt down there that we want nothing to do with. But they directed us to destroy those targets so the flight lead tried to figure out how we were gonna do that. He decided that the number three man, my flight lead, would strafe the IL-76 while I went along to look for SAMs.

So we tried to figure out how to shoot at the ground—that was funny. Three rolled in while I flew above him looking for SAMs. He squeezed the trigger and drilled the IL-76's wing. There was a big ol' fireball and I thought, "Whoa!—that was pretty good for the first chance at strafing!" He came off of the target and put out a ton of flares in case somebody shot at him.

Then we went after the three Cubs. One and Two rolled in on the Cubs on one side of the airfield and then Three cleared me in on the last one. I rolled in not wanting to push it 'cause I'd never strafed before. I shot a little ways out and ran the pipper[14] through the target. I pulled off and saw the bullets run along the ground, go through the fuselage and then continue on the other side. A SAM site got active then, so we broke off the attack and went looking for more familiar targets.

We were bored because we could do our job by staying away from all that flak on the ground, which in itself was another nice point about flying an Eagle. I accepted that things were tapering off and I wasn't gonna get a kill. I just tried to stay smart and do my job.

On 7 February, third week of the war, my job was to keep enemy fighters from reaching Iran. The squadron had 13 kills already and that looked like it for us. Those patrols were already routine. I went in an hour before the briefing to find out who my tankers were, where they were gonna be, and what freqs they were gonna be on. Then I checked

---

[11]cons—Contrails. At the right combination of temperature and water vapor, jet exhausts leave white trails in the sky. Fighters normally avoid the "con level" so as to not be highlighted against the sky.

[12]IL-76—Russian IL-76 Candid. Large cargo aircraft that looks amazingly like the Lockheed C-141 Starlifter.

[13]Cub—Russian AN-12 Cub. Medium-sized turboprop transport similar to the C-130.

[14]pipper—Gunsight.

on who the AWACS controllers were, what freqs they used, and where they were gonna be so that I could look at their radar coverage. They sometimes got so far away that we couldn't talk to them or they couldn't see beyond us. I had the wing commander, Colonel Rick Parsons, on my wing that day. He was one of the very few of us with previous combat time, had been in the Eagle before, and had a reputation for being proficient from what most of the guys said. I felt comfortable with him when I flew on his wing and I imagine he felt just about as comfortable with me.

He showed up for the brief, we went through the new threats, and assigned responsibilities. We launched and headed for the Iranian border, which was all the way across the Arabian Peninsula. We had to fly about an hour and 15 minutes or so to get on station and hit a tanker early because it's nice to have lots of gas. So we had more gas than was originally planned when we dropped down to the mid-20's and started our march north. Colonel Parsons looked level with his radar for long-range scan while I looked down low to make sure nobody slipped below us.

He called a contact at 70 miles or so, which was unusual. I hadn't yet seen a blip on my scope anywhere over Iraq. I changed my radar's search to match his and sure enough, I locked that guy up[15]. There was one blip at low altitude moving to the southeast. I wanted to see what else was out there, so I broke lock and picked up another group roughly 40 miles in trail[16] and going in the same direction. We checked all the identification systems on our aircraft to find out who they were and didn't get any friendly responses.

These radio calls were recorded by Colonel Parsons' Eagle. They were Chevron Two One flight, so ET was CHEVRON TWO ONE or LEAD and his wingman answered as CHEVRON TWO or just TWO. BUCKEYE is a radar controller aboard the AWACS.

Elapsed time: 00:00.00
LEADER (L): CHEVRON CHECK[17] RIGHT TO THREE SIX ZERO (degrees).
L: CHEVRON TWO ONE, ADDITIONAL CONTACT[18] THREE FOUR ZERO (degrees), SEVENTY [miles].

---

[15]radar lock—To automatically follow a target on radar.

[16]trail—One airplane or formation of airplanes following behind another.

[17]check turn—Small turn of less than 90 degrees. Usually a course correction.

[18]contact—To see or be seen on radar.

Headings and distances such as "three four zero, seventy" are verbal shorthand for the target's location. Read this call as, "Chevron Leader sees more targets bearing 340° from me and 70 nautical miles away."

Wingman (W): CHEVRON TWO, SAME.

L: CHEVRON CHECK FARTHER RIGHT TO ZERO TWO ZERO.

L: BUCKEYE, CHEVRON SHOWING TWO GROUPS (of bandits), TWENTY MILE SPLIT.

ET turned the formation to intercept the lead bandits and fed tactical information back to the airborne radar controller.

L: BUCKEYE, CHEVRON TWO ONE, CONFIRM NO FRIENDLIES IN THIS AREA.

AWACS: THAT'S AFFIRMATIVE.

L: CHEVRON.

ET confirmed that they were the only good guys in that area.

AWACS: WE'RE NEGATIVE RADAR ON YOUR CONTACTS.

L: CHEVRON, THREE SIX ZERO [degrees], FORTY MILES, HEADING ONE THREE ZERO.

W: CHEVRON TWO, SAME.

Time: 00:01.30

L: CHEVRON TWO ONE SHOWING MULTIPLES, LEAD GROUP.

W: CHEVRON TWO, SAME.

L: CHEVRON TWO ONE, THIRTY MILES.

W: TWO.

L: CHEVRON TWO ONE, ZERO ONE ZERO, TWENTY FIVE. CONFIRM THEY'RE IN OUR AIRSPACE.

AWACS: THAT'S AFFIRMATIVE.

The bandits were too low at that range for tracking by AWACS radar. ET and his wingman sorted the targets themselves while telling the controller exactly where those bandits were. They then confirmed that the approaching fight would take place west of the Iranian border. Iraqi aircraft found sanctuary in Iran, but they first had to get past the Eagles.

Time: 00:02.26

L: BUCKEYE, CHEVRON TWO ONE, COMBAT ONE [jettison wing tanks]. CHECK FARTHER RIGHT TO ZERO FOUR ZERO, CLEAN [no contacts].

W: CHEVRON TWO, CLEAN, LOW [no contacts below us].

L: CHEVRON TWO ONE, ZERO FOUR ZERO, FIFTEEN.

AWACS: BUCKEYE'S CLEAN.

L: Chevron two one's got 'em heading one two zero, (turn) hard right to zero seven zero.

L: Buckeye, are you contact on Chevron?

AWACS: Buckeye's gettin' intermittent hits[19] sir.

L: Copy, keep us in the right country.
   Chevron, nose about ten miles low.

W: Chevron two, same.

AWACS: You've got about twenty-five miles to the border.

Time: 00:03.57

L: Chevron. Pushin' it up [accelerating].

L: [Bandits are] Ten miles in trail.

W: Chevron two, blind[20].

L: Chevron's high at your right three o'clock.

W: Chevron, visual[21].

In the last maneuvering before the fight, ET turned the formation to fine-tune the intercept, made absolutely sure that the fight would occur on the correct side of some line on a map, and accelerated.

Time: 00:05.08

L: Chevron, fox[22]!
   Tally one, low.

Time: 00:05.35

W: Chevron two, fox!

Each Eagle launched an AIM-7M Sparrow radar-guided missile.

AWACS: Fifteen miles to border.

L: Chevron.

Time: 00:05.53

L: Chevron splash[23] one!

L: Chevron's got another one on my nose, three miles.

W: Chevron two, same.

Time: 00:06.11

L: Chevron, fox!

---

[19]hits—Radar returns the controller can see on his screen.

[20]blind—Radio call meaning, "I can't see the friendly aircraft."

[21]visual—Radio call meaning, "I see the friendly aircraft."

[22]fox!—Radio call meaning, "I'm firing."

[23]splash!—Radio call meaning, "The target has been shot down."

AWACS: Border, five [miles].
L: Chevron.
AWACS: Check wreckage within border.
L: Chevron's comin' right.
Time: 00:06.48
L: Chevron, second fox!
Time: 00:06.53
W: Chevron two, fox!
L: Chevron, got an additional one. Looks like there's four.
W: Check our location.
Time: 00:07.20
L: Chevron, fox on a third!
Time: 00:07.34
L: Chevron, splash a second [bandit].

The sky was now full of missile trails, 840-mph jets, and several fireballs. Elapsed time between the first of six missiles and the last of three kills: two minutes and 26 seconds. Chevron flight witnessed two hits and saw the third smoke column when they turned around.

W: I don't think so.
L: Chevron's coming right to west.
W: Head's up for trailers.
L: Chevron, hard right!
AWACS: Still clean.
L: Roger. Chevron's splashed two confirmed, possibly three.
W: Say again for two.
L: I saw two go down, maybe three.
W: They might be our missiles.
L: I saw the fireballs.

The bandits were very low, possibly below 100 feet. It's very difficult to tell if an explosion is a missile hitting the ground or a missile hitting an airplane, which then hits the ground. But missiles don't leave a column of burning jet fuel.

Time: 00:08.27
W: Chevron two is contact [on another bandit], three three zero, twenty five. Twelve hundred feet [altitude].
L: Press[24]!

---

[24]press—Radio call meaning, "Continue your attack. I'll cover you."

Three bandits from the lead formation didn't reach the border. Chevron Two spotted more bandits 25 miles northwest and ET told him to go for it.

W: I'M AT YOUR RIGHT FOUR O'CLOCK, SLIGHTLY LOW.

L: CHEVRON'S VISUAL.

W: BUCKEYE, CONFIRM WE'RE IN THE RIGHT AIRSPACE?

L: CHEVRON'S GOT TWO [bandits], SIDE-SIDE, TWENTY MILES.

L: CHEVRON ONE IS ELEVEN POINT EIGHT [a fuel quantity check].

W: CHEVRON TWO IS FOURTEEN [14,000 pounds of fuel remaining].

L: CHEVRON IS ZERO BY FOUR [zero radar missiles and four heat seekers remaining].

W: TWO IS TWO BY FOUR.

L: CHEVRON.

W: BUCKEYE, CONFIRM CONTACT WITH CHEVRON.

Time: 00:09.19

L: CHEVRON, COMBAT TWO [jettison the centerline fuel tank].

W: TWO.

    TWO'S MANEUVERING, HEADING ZERO EIGHT ZERO.

L: CHEVRON SAY GAS?

W: CHEVRON TWO IS THIRTEEN.

L: COPY THIRTEEN.

W: BUCKEYE, CHEVRON, CONFIRM WE'RE IN THE RIGHT AIRSPACE.

AWACS: RIGHT AIRSPACE NOW.

L: CHEVRON, OUR CONTACT IS THIRTY [degrees] RIGHT FOR TEN MILES.

AWACS: CHEVRON STATUS?

W: CHEVRON'S TEN-MILE TAIL CHASE.

ET shifted from the first fight to the second. The centerline tanks were empty, so they were jettisoned. He counted the remaining missiles, turned to intercept the next targets, and checked their position with AWACS. They were 10 miles behind the bandits heading east.

Time: 00:10.18

AWACS: CONFIRM WESTBOUND?

W: HEADING ONE ZERO ZERO [nearly due East]. TARGETS ARE HEADING ONE ZERO ZERO, FORTY-FIVE HUNDRED FEET.

AWACS: I'VE LOST YOU. IF YOU'RE HEADING WESTBOUND, YOU'RE IN IRAQ.

W: ROGER, COMIN' BACK.

L: CHEVRON, SKIP IT [let the bandits go].

L: CHEVRON ONE'S VISUAL IN YOUR LEFT NINE O'CLOCK HIGH.

W: VISUAL.

Nuts! The second set of Iraqis managed to get across the border while Chevron intercepted the first ones.

L: BUCKEYE, WE NEED TO GET A TANKER AS FAR NORTH AS POSSIBLE AT
THIS TIME.
AWACS: CHEVRON, YOU FADED [didn't understand].
L: GET A TANKER NORTH! AS FAR AS POSSIBLE! CHEVRON COME LEFT TO
TWO THREE ZERO. CLIMB IT UP 460 (to 46,000 feet).

Now low on gas, ET called for a tanker to meet them while also climbing to conserve fuel.

Time: 00:10.58
L: WAS THAT A RUSH OR WHAT?
W: YEAH!

We pitched back around to chase the second formation, but we were low on fuel. So we headed home. We were 200 to 250 miles from the tankers on the other side of the Iraqi border and 600 miles from home. We climbed to 46,000 feet and slowed down to conserve gas while I tried to get a tanker as far north as they would go. A KC-10 gave us gas rather promptly so I began feeling a lot better with that full load of internal fuel. I told AWACS we were RTB[25] and he said, "WAIT A MINUTE. YOU'RE SUPPOSED TO BE HERE FOR SIX HOURS AND YOU'VE ONLY BEEN HERE FOR TWO. WHAT'S GOING ON?" I answered, "WE'VE GOT NO ORDNANCE OR EXTERNAL TANKS SO WE'RE GOING HOME." They scrambled a couple guys from our base to pick up the remainder of our patrol.

You can imagine the whole experience was pretty much of a rush.

About 50 miles out from the base, we made the standard call to say how many tanks we dropped and how many missiles we shot. When I called that I shot four missiles, they figured something had happened. By the time we got home, there were 150 people on the ramp trying to figure out what happened. I flew the traditional two victory rolls for my kills, landed, and taxied up to the ramp. Everybody congratulated us and asked all kinds of questions.

We were sure to spend some time with the crew chiefs. They get really motivated about their jets, and we get excited telling them how it went. They take great care of the jets so we enjoyed talking to them about "their" kills.

Colonel Parsons and I made our report to the command section in Riyadh and then had to repeat the story about every half hour for the

---

[25]RTB—Returning to base. Going home.

guys at Tabuk. I finally got to see some action and felt like I could stay there another month to wait for more. But I was bored again in a week and ready to go home.

We heard about the cease-fire but continued flying even farther into Iraq than ever. We were asked to identify helicopters but weren't allowed to shoot them. Again, the boredom was there, and we had to be careful so we could bring everybody home. There was a cease-fire but we could get shot anytime. We flew missions up until a few days before we came home.

Getting home was frustrating. We were one of the first units deployed so we were pretty upset about returning so late. Then we finally got to launch for Zaragoza, Spain. Oh man, just seeing green was neat. We rolled into the ops[26] squadron and they gave us beer, chips, salsa, veggies, and dip—I couldn't believe how great that was. I didn't think such simple things would be that great but it was an incredible high to have a beer and be out of that country.

We flew a 10½-hour hop back to Eglin, where they had a big homecoming waiting. We shook a bunch of generals' hands and then got to see our wives. The wives were in a little white corral where the crowd couldn't get to us. We walked around in a daze at all the fuss. It was weird.

I dropped into McDonalds on the way home to get a whole bunch of stuff, but my stomach was so small from not eating that I couldn't even finish a Big Mac and fries. Then Chris and I sat down to relax and talk.

My circadian rhythm was messed up, so we woke up at about 3:00 a.m. to make nachos. Man, that was great! It was wonderful to open up a refrigerator and have a choice.

Our sleeping schedule was all out of whack but that was okay. We had a lot to talk about.

Captain Murphy earned a Silver Star and two Distinguished Flying Crosses for his double kills on the Iranian border.

Chris Murphy married a hometown guy who was a little different. He wanted to fly jets. She ended up living the unique and more than a little stressful life of someone in love with a fighter pilot at war. Military spouses sign up for the bad with the good even if they also manage to deny the bad until it corners them. Some wives make it, some do not. Some, like Chris Murphy, discover life's priorities early as they are tempered by the stress.

---

[26]ops—Operations. Section that controls the flying while other people handle maintenance, administration, supply, etc.

Chris Murphy:

Our families in Oregon were upset when we moved so far away. But that move was relatively easy for us because many newly married couples in pilot training were in the same situation. It was an adventure we embarked on together, but it was hard on our moms. They knew the move was good for Tony though my career had to bend around his at first.

I was determined to go ahead and have my own career, my own job, so I finished the requirements for my Florida pharmacy license. I worked full-time up until we expected PCS orders and backed down to part-time to enjoy Florida. That's when we found out about Desert Shield and got a lesson in balancing two careers.

When the pilot's wives were finally told about the deployment in the middle of August, I tried to figure out how to run everything without Tony having to worry about me; that would make his job easier. Then we were told that they may leave within two days and so had to stay at home and sit by the phone. That notice was canceled and the deployment was postponed. The same roller coaster went on for a week until they finally sent the first wave of F-15s.

Tony came home that night disappointed and upset at not getting to go with all of his "brothers." Those were the guys he trained with for so long and he felt he needed to be there with them—especially if they were going into combat. It was extreme male bonding. I was ready for him to go because he would have been miserable around the house. He was devastated, and I realized that he needed to go no matter what it put me through. That was something he needed to do.

I went to the squadron with his lunch on the day he left and it was just like an ant hill swarming with people. I really felt like an outsider, like I didn't belong there, and I just needed to let him go as quickly as possible. I think having that real quick separation, instead of a long tearful good-bye, was best.

I knew of a place near the runway where you could watch the airplanes take off. Many of the other wives and families were down there with the extra guys from the squadron. We watched them take off, which was one of the most exciting things I've ever gone through in my life. To have one jet after another storm out of there got a lot of women very upset, but I didn't have any tears of sadness. I was so excited and had such an adrenaline surge that I wanted to go with him. That was our family away from family. I knew they were the best group of people Tony could be with to do what needed to be done.

I was ready to let go.

I went back to work full-time at the North Okaloosa Medical Center. They were very understanding of all their employees who were involved in Desert Shield and Desert Storm. My boss pretty much created a position to keep me busy because he knew that's what I needed. It was a great way to deal with the stress and anxiety.

Of course, since I was the only person at home, I gave up cooking. I joined a fitness center and worked out routinely to reduce anxiety and stress. The only problem I ran into, which I couldn't seem to get over, was not sleeping well at night. That started the very first night and I would have to stay up a couple of extra hours to wear myself out or I would just toss and turn. I didn't have a sound night's sleep until the day Tony came back.

Our squadron's "wives' support system" worked really well since there were many women in the same situation, many of them with children. Groups of us tried to get together and go out to dinner or do something with kids every week or so. People kept tabs on each other.

We got frustrated at the lack of information, of course. I guess families should never know everything, but there was so much misinformation in the rumor mill that it was nearly impossible to cut through it and figure out the truth. There were rumors like: We couldn't use stamps with the American flag on them because the Saudis wouldn't allow it; the guys would be home for Thanksgiving; they'll be home for Christmas . . . you just never knew what to believe. We wanted good information more than anything, short of their return. The leaders in the squadron did try real hard to give us the information they had. Ken Burke held a wives' briefing for us a few weeks after they deployed and told us what he could about their living conditions. That information helped enormously with our peace of mind.

Public support from people we didn't know was great. They talked on the radio and TV, businesses put supportive words on their signs, and folks were willing to help any family that needed it. People in our neighborhood watched over me by keeping an eye on my house. They were wonderful. Whenever I was out in the yard, they asked if I needed anything. Friends would have groups of wives over for dinner to keep their minds on something besides war.

Our families were very supportive during that time. Their caring and love helped me so much. I didn't realize how worn-down my spirit had become until my parents spent the holidays with me. They both experienced WWII and were able to help me focus on positive thoughts and strengthen myself for the upcoming deadline in January.

I got home from work in mid-January and sat down to watch TV while I ate dinner. I got into the habit of eating near the TV because I hate to eat alone. Then news about the bombs going off in Baghdad came on with the CNN reporters saying they didn't really know what was going on. It was fascinating. I couldn't believe it was real, I really couldn't. At first, I thought the reporters blew it out of proportion and that there really wasn't much happening. Then I flipped through all the channels to see if they agreed and finally realized that the war had started.

At about that moment, the phone started ringing. Other wives, family, and long-distance friends called to check on me. A few of those friends didn't even know Tony was gone and called to see if he was involved. Some of the wives got together to watch the news as a group, but I needed to be alone. I was excited because I knew by then that we had to go through a war before they could come home. We had waited so long already that they might as well get it over with. I was worried, of course, but their job kept them up high where it was safer.

From that first news report on, I was glued to the TV. I fortunately didn't have to work the next day. I left the TV on for the next 24 hours and slept in front of it. I realized it would be good for me to go to work even though they would probably give me time off. I needed to get back into my routine as much as I could. But CNN was on every moment that I was at home and awake so that I could hear it no matter where I was in the house. That preoccupation with the news went on for a couple of weeks before I started to do normal things again like go out for dinner at someone's house without watching CNN.

After about the third day of the war, I talked to Tony, who said, "It's not that bad, so don't worry. We're up real high, and I survived the first three days." Calls were much harder to make and shorter during the war, so we had to rely on messages passed when other people got through. We really missed the phone contact during Desert Storm. Our phone bills were huge, but is was money well spent. My family and friends called to check on me so often that I often spent three hours an evening on the phone.

My neighbors and coworkers were very sensitive and always there for me if I needed anything. Those coworkers dropped by the pharmacy to let me know what they'd just heard since we didn't have a radio in our department.

In early February, I headed straight from work to the squadron for one of those wives' briefings. I wanted to get there early because one of the guys was back from Saudi, and I knew he'd be swarmed by wives. As soon as I stepped in, he pulled me aside and asked if I'd heard the news. They just found out about Tony's kills the day before. It had been at least a week since anyone in the squadron had gotten an airplane so we weren't even thinking about that anymore. I was shocked—I couldn't believe they were still seeing action in the air.

We didn't really react to individual kills like that, but we tried to figure out how the guys felt about it. Would anything change when they came back? Would some guys be jealous and tougher to get along with?

Killing is obviously not something you want your husband to do, but, then again, the Iraqi airplanes were a threat to our forces so we were just as obviously glad our guys won. I don't know how to handle what he does for a living otherwise. It's easy to deny the really serious part of the fighter profession because they spend many years training for something that may never happen. Many guys train for years and never see combat.

When the cease-fire was announced, the military said the first troops in would be the first ones out. We were all excited and thought that was great. But squadrons that deployed after ours came back first, so that policy obviously didn't apply to our husbands. We were devastated. I wondered if it would ever end. It began to feel like their deployment would continue forever and we wouldn't get back to a normal life. We went on another roller coaster where the return dates changed as quickly as they were set. We became numb and didn't believe anything. When it was announced that they would come home on April 12th I thought, "Yeah right, I'll wait until April 12th and, when I'm driving to the squadron to pick him up, I'll believe Tony's really coming home."

When we were convinced they were really coming home, everything became exciting, exhilarating. I cleaned the house and was full of energy again. Nothing was more important than spending time with Tony, so I reorganized my routine. I took a leave of absence from work as the first step in making some changes in our priorities.

I woke up the morning the guys got home with so much energy that it was amazing. Eglin AFB prepared a grand welcoming. I was afraid the wives would get lost in the crowd, but the squadron corralled us off in a little area so that we wouldn't get trampled. The maintenance airplane came in first and hundreds of folks got off to be surrounded by their families. Then the first jets came in and the pilots' names were announced as they flew over the runway. We were excited and couldn't believe it was really happening. As they climbed down from the jets, we jumped up and down thinking it must be a dream.

I hugged Tony very tightly and wouldn't let him go. He felt so good that I couldn't leave his side for the rest of the day—he didn't mind.

We called our families to let them know that, yes, Tony was really home and okay. We had so much catching up to do that we chatted away for hours. Then the very long day hit him hard and we fell asleep early that night. He was not gonna be out of my sight so, when he woke up hungry around 3:00 a.m., I followed him to the kitchen for nachos. We laughed at how silly that was.

We've made some adjustments in our lifestyle. My career is very important to me, but I don't need to work full-time anymore. It took too much time away from each other and we need to make up for 7½ months of separation. We're a lot more spontaneous now.

War reorganizes your priorities a bit.

11

The Inferno

Marine First Lieutenant Lance Hoyt, Jolt, flew the McDonnel Douglas F/A-18 Hornet with VMFA 333 out of MCAS Beaufort, South Carolina. Like many of these officers, that was his first flying assignment.

His Hornet is designated "F/A" in recognition of its two completely different missions. As a fighter, it's armed with Sparrow and Sidewinder missiles plus the Vulcan 20mm canon. It replaced the F-4 Phantom II[1] as the shorter-ranged, more maneuverable complement to the F-14 Tomcat. As an attack jet, it replaced the A-7 Corsair II for battlefield interdiction[2] and close air support. The Hornet is arguably the most maneuverable fighter we have and is rumored to be such a dream to fly that it probably should be illegal.

First Lieutenant Hoyt:

When I was five years old and my father was stationed at Elmendorf Air Force Base in Anchorage, Alaska, I distinctly remember the Blue Angels doing an air show in the old F-4s with all the noise they made. Literally from that point on, I wanted to fly. I never really lost the bug.

I grew up mostly in Idaho, near Mountain Home AFB, after my dad retired from the Navy. I went through high school there and then went

---

[1]F-4 Phantom II—Vietnam-era, multi-mission jet fighter. The Rhino.

[2]interdiction—Attacks on targets behind the front lines, designed to isolate the battlefield by cutting the enemy off from his support.

to the Naval Academy in the Class of '86. I wanted to fly jets but didn't want to fly from a carrier, so I made the choice to join the Marine Corps. It was straight to The Basic School in Quantico, Virginia, from the Academy, then flight school, F-18 training, and finally to my first duty station at MCAS Beaufort, South Carolina.

I hate carrier landings but had to take the Hornet to the boat during training. It was day and night landings that time but we went to a fleet carrier so the deck was much bigger than the training boat. The Hornet is actually a very nice plane to take to the carrier because it's so stable at slow speeds. Of course, easy is a relative term. But it's a lot easier to land an F/A-18 aboard a carrier than something like the A-4, and it helps for somebody who has jitters about carriers. I had myself all worked up because I had almost pitched an A-4 off the deck of the *Lexington*. But those daytime landings in the Hornet were almost fun. The nighttime traps were another ballgame. Those first night carrier landings were an experiment in fear. You fly those first traps without anybody in the back seat because the Navy doesn't want to lose instructors when students kill themselves on the backs of carriers.

A squadron doesn't treat you with kid gloves at all. From the moment I came aboard, they threw me in the jet every day, usually with the Skipper or the XO[3], to see what kind of a pilot I was. It's really their job to figure out where you need the most help, what areas you're weak in. They'll ferret that out and then pair you up with particular people in the squadron who are strong in those areas. They give you a lot of flight time when you first get there 'cause they want to get you combat-ready. It's the squadron's job to finish your training. I flew in my squadron for about a year before things got interesting in the Gulf.

When Kuwait was invaded, we were just getting ready to deploy to a CAEX[4] at Twentynine Palms, California. That's a desert warfare range where we fight mock battles that may last a couple weeks. It was a routine deployment for us that had been planned for a long time. We were going through our final workups in Beaufort, and startin' to pack up all our gear, when Kuwait was invaded. At that point, we really didn't think it was going to affect us at all, so we just kept right on marching with the deployment.

We got two weeks' notice to deploy but were told it could happen as early as a week from notification or as long as a month. Timing depended on when the airlift became available.

---

[3]XO—Executive officer. The second in command of a Marine unit.

[4]CAEX—("kaks") Combined arms exercise. Marine exercise to practice integrating all air and ground assault forces. Conducted at the Marine Corps Air Ground Combat Center at Twentynine Palms, California.

I had a big advantage in preparing to leave with Lisa being in the military. She had a lot more firsthand information on what was going on than most of the other wives did. She said sometimes that knowledge turned out to be a real disadvantage because it would've been better not to know certain things. We don't have kids, and she was going to stay behind, so there wasn't a whole lot to do other than make sure the wills were up to date.

We did rush out and get me some more life insurance. Every one of us in my squadron went through that.

The flying didn't really change because we had been working ourselves up for a desert warfare scenario anyway. The majority of the flying was putting wing fuel tanks on the jets before taking them up to make sure all the plumbing worked and also getting practice plugs[5] off of different types of tankers. A lot of us had never seen a KC-135 before, let alone done plugs off of those things. That's a whole different ballgame tankin' off those guys. It's rather difficult and there's a tendency to rip our refueling probes off. We eventually got real good at it over in Saudi 'cause we did it so often.

I only had about 300 hours in the F-18 when we deployed. I was the junior man, the bull lieutenant, in the squadron so I didn't really have a whole lot of flying time in the jet.

We had 16 pilots and only 12 aircraft so I knew I wasn't going to fly one across the ocean. We used two KC-10s so all the squadron's people and cargo fit with enough fuel to take all 12 jets across in one big package. The two KC-10s actually flew together in a cell so we took everything in one big lump. We left Beaufort at about 2:00 in the morning on the 21st of August and flew into Rota, Spain. We landed there to let the flight crews get some rest before blasting out the next day to Bahrain.

We had absolutely everything with us. We took enough parts to sustain the jets for 30 days plus the jets went over fully loaded with air-to air-missiles and some HARMs. We really didn't know what to expect when we got there, we didn't know what was going to happen, so the jets were ready to fight their way in if they had to. They could just send the KC-10s away, punch off the external fuel tanks, and go for it.

We landed at Shaikh Isa airfield on the Persian Gulf island of Bahrain. Shaikh Isa is actually the Emir of the country of Bahrain so the airfield is named for him. It was built on the island for their defense force, which consisted of 12 F-16s and 6 F-16 pilots plus some F-5s.

All the maintenance people, all the enlisted troops, ended up in tents without air conditioning while the officers moved into the Bahraini enlisted barracks. There were no spaces for the squadrons to work out of, so we unpacked our pallets and stacked the boxes up to make little

---

[5]plug—To hook up with an aerial refueling tanker.

work areas for the different divisions. We tried to keep them in the hangars where there was shade but, once we ran out of room, they were kind of stuck out wherever.

We arrived on the 23rd of August when it was just brutally hot. The temperature hit 130 in the day and, since we were on an island, the humidity was 90 or 95 percent. It was real hard to make things work—to get people to move. It was hard to make yourself move. It was so hot that guys burned themselves just by touching the airplanes. It was almost impossible for those poor guys to sleep because it was so hot. It was really bad for the first couple of weeks there.

Through the duration over there, our Marines never had air conditioning or heat in the tents. We shared the base with the Wild Weasels, who put their enlisted in tents too, but they hooked huge 40,000 BTU air conditioner units up to them. In August and September, they kept their tent flaps open. They said, "It's too cold in here, we're trying to let some of the cold out." The leaders ended up separating all the Air Force enlisted from the Marine enlisted to avoid skirmishes. Morale took a real nosedive when our guys saw how they lived.

At least the support from home was great. As soon as we got into Bahrain, the guys figured out how to get an AT&T USA direct operator. Support right from the get go was really good—a lot of letters.

I'd packed a TV and a VCR with the squadron's stuff. We really expected to be living in tents too, right out there on the flight line. But I brought those things anyway on the off chance we'd have a space somewhere to set up. We sent that word back home and everyone started sending movies and videos.

Every so often, you'd catch an old series from the States on the only Bahraini channel. We watched *Lost in Space*, the old *Dick Van Dyke Show*, the *Flintstones*. They played 'em in English with Arabic subtitles. *Dallas* was also big over there, and *Thirty Something* showed in the evening.

Most of our news came from the heavy transport aircraft guys who brought big bundles of newspapers. We'd get 'em four or five days old, but they were from the major cities. So that's where we picked up a lot of our news at first.

Then we got swamped with the Any Serviceman mail. The volume got so high that it started blocking out mail from home, personal mail. The postal service started holding that stuff since they were getting such a volume that they weren't able to deliver the personal mail. They had to start up two different systems: They would get the personal mail through first and then load in as much Any Serviceman mail as they had room for.

There was a kid who wrote us. I forgot where he went to school, but he was like 9 or 10 years old and lived in some big city. The letter started: "Hey, you guys are cool. I think you're big and bad. Do you have a $50 bill? I've never seen one. Could you send it to me so I can see what one looks like? I'll send it back, I promise." And then, "PS, oh yeah, kick Saddam's butt." We hung that one up in the ready room. It was so funny. His friend wrote too and said, "If you send Tommy a $50 bill, could you send me a $100 one so I can see what that looks like?" God, it was funny the way the kid wrote it. Nice try.

Our whole mission at first was to fly CAP over the Gulf. We had at least two Hornets airborne near Kuwait 24 hours a day. We worked with the Navy ships down there, mostly the destroyers and the cruisers. We were looking for anybody trying to sneak out and take a shot at the ships. The Navy was really worried about Exocets from the Mirages 'cause it was an Iraqi jet that shot the USS *Stark*. So that was the big concern. We flew CAP for the entire length of Desert Shield.

For practice, we also flew mirror strikes[6]. We sometimes coordinated with the British, who were also in Bahrain, because some of their first Tornado missions were going to be to take out the airfields. A lot of our missions were HARM shots to quiet down the SAM sites so they could get in. They would fly practice attacks on our airfield down south because they could buzz us real low to practice delivering their JP-233 anti-runway device.

The Brits had a whole different attitude on the deployment; they were going to have a good time. The Brits are great. Nothing seemed to upset them. They'd start flying about nine in the morning and then quit at three or four in the afternoon to start getting hammered. That was a day for them. If they didn't feel like flying, they didn't fly. I mean, they'd just go out and do what they wanted.

The French called to let us know that they had the same variant of the Mirage that they had sold to the Iraqis. I don't know if it was a guilty conscience over selling so much stuff to Iraq or if they wanted to get some training for their pilots as well. They asked us if we would like to do some dissimilar air combat training[7] to get some practical experience fighting those jets. We really expected to be going up against them and had already run some intercepts on Iraqi Mirages coming out of Kuwait City. We agreed to that right away. But the French actually quit playing with us after about a week because they weren't winning the fights. They

---

[6]mirror strike—Air strike dress rehearsal, whereby the attack is flown up to the enemy border and then turned, or reflected, back into friendly territory. The flight planned for enemy airspace is simulated over friendly lands.

[7]dissimilar air combat training—DACT. Mock air-to-air combat against an aircraft type other than your own. DACT is the whole idea behind advanced fighter schools such as Top Gun and exercises such as Red Flag. It's also a very big part of the reason why Allied fighter pilots proved to be unbeatable.

said it was a little too demoralizing for their pilots to continue that way.

The U.S. initially wouldn't even let the French fly in the war 'cause they had the same Mirage that the Iraqis flew and we didn't want to shoot down the wrong ones. Later on, we let them come in but only after we'd cleared everybody else out. We didn't want a "friendly" kill.

As the war progressed, we spent most of our time on battlefield interdiction bombing. We still had to stand alerts though, so we didn't always know where or what the targets would be. But at least we flew with the same guy almost all the time over there. That was really nice because you got to learn how you both operated. You knew what the other guy was going to do. My flight leader was a Marine named Rick Sturckow, "CJ." He was a young captain with almost three years in the squadron. CJ was sharp, real sharp, very professional, a real tactician—especially for a young guy. He took his flight leader responsibility dead seriously and was a great guy to fly with.

CJ and I stood CAS alert on the night of 17 February. The weather was extremely bad and most standard missions were gettin' canceled because they wouldn't be able to find the targets. At about two in the morning, we got word that there was a lucrative target 20 miles south of Kuwait City. It was reported to be 30 to 40 tanks out in the open like an assembly area. You know, a nice juicy little target.

The call came to launch us so we ran out to the Hornets and were rolling down the runway within 10 minutes, just like we're supposed to. We were loaded with five MK-83s apiece. Both jets had forward-looking-infrared (FLIR) pods so we could pick targets out at night.

Since we flew over the water first, we had to check in with the picket ships in order to fly through their airspace. We worked our way inland and contacted the DASC[8]. They told us a couple of other aircraft had seen what they believed to be 30 or 40 tanks in some kind of an assembly area. They were supposed to be out in the open, not dug in, not camouflaged, just out in the open. They told us to go in there to see if it was a lucrative target because, unless they heard otherwise from us, they were going to launch more F/A-18s from our base.

The weather was, if anything, worse than we'd had back at homeplate[9]. There were several layers of clouds and real low vis[10].

---

[8]DASC—Direct Air Support Coordination Center. Marine "traffic cop" that directs fighters to their targets by radio.

[9]homeplate—One's airbase.

[10]vis—("viz") Visibility. Three-statute-mile visibility is normally required for low altitude, nonradar, visual flight. Under those conditions, a Hornet would fly over a target less than 25 seconds after it could theoretically be seen. Some attack jets even fight in two miles vis, which is really sporting.

We both decided that it was worth going under the weather to try and find that target because they were getting ready to launch a whole lot of jets behind us. There was no need sending all those jets up there, wasting all the time and effort and getting people shot at, if it wasn't going to be workable.

As soon as we got across the border and went lights out, CJ suggested I drop back into a radar trail[11] and follow at about 4 to 8 miles or 30 to 60 seconds behind him. He would pass over the target area to see what he could find and then talk to me on the radio. If he saw something good, he'd try and talk me onto it. I'd bomb the same target he did.

I fell back in trail as we crossed the border of Kuwait. We had the latitude and longitude of where the tanks were supposed to be punched in the inertial navigation systems. Our basic game plan was to go underneath the clouds, use the radar to find the target and, once we found it, to slew the FLIR there and take a good look. If it was good, we were going to drop on the first pass over the target. Due to weather, we were planning on dropping all five bombs on one pass.

We ended up punching through the clouds and sure enough, just like the aircrew who found the target told us, we broke out at 6000 feet. But they hadn't told us about the next cloud deck underneath. It started at 3000 feet. We were running out of time as we got closer to the target, so CJ decided that he was going to punch through that deck alone to see where it bottomed out, you know, give it a chance. He still couldn't see anything on his radar that looked like an assembly area of tanks, so we marched in.

We got underneath at about 900 feet but were over an area of burning oil wells. We were underneath the clouds, but the air was full of real black, smoky haze from the oil fires. Picture this: We had a very significant cloud deck above us but only 1000 feet off the ground. We were only underneath it by about a 100 feet, plus we were being illuminated by all those oil fires. I remember looking up through the top of the canopy and seeing the shadow of my jet moving across the cloud deck—that's how bright it was. It looked surreal.

I'd seen the fires quite a few times but never at night like that and certainly never that low or with a ceiling over my head. Pilots always feel like we've got a lot space around us, but, when we were down underneath that deck, I felt very closed in and extremely uncomfortable, claustrophobic. It looked like a movie set. It just didn't look real; it just wasn't real.

---

[11]radar trail—Trail formation with one aircraft at a specified distance directly behind another. Radar is used to stay in position when the wingman can't see the leader such as at night or in the clouds. The trailing distance can be specified in either time or distance.

Some of the guys described it as Dante's Inferno with all the bright orange fires down there. If you could picture hell, that was it.

I thought, "If I can see the cloud deck that bright above me, I can imagine what the underside of my jet looks like to the gunners."

We didn't see anything and turned back out over the water. It turns out the other jet never flew over that area themselves. The "target" was something they'd seen with their radar from out over the water! They'd never actually gone over that spot themselves.

We were running out of gas at that point because we were real heavy and flying low[12]. CJ decided to go back and make one more pass to look at that other possible target he'd seen on radar. He was going to try and find something worth putting ordnance on, and then we would blow home.

I set myself up in about a 5-to-6 mile trail on CJ as we turned back around to go feet dry. We waited until a little later to go through that very bottom deck this time 'cause we didn't want to expose ourselves down there any longer than we had to. We decided to wait until the last minute, dip down through that bottom deck real fast, and give the FLIR a chance to look around to see if there was anything worthwhile.

CJ got underneath, came up on the radio and said, "I've got something down here. I don't see any of those tanks they're talking about but it looks like I got some trucks on the road, like a little convoy." I was already underneath that bottom deck, watching my shadow streak by on the clouds, very, very head's down[13] in the cockpit. Between watching the radar display, manually swinging the FLIR with the other display, avoiding flying into the ground, and trying to find something to hit down there, I wasn't spending a lot of time looking outside. I looked out as much as I could to see if they were shooting at us, but I didn't see anything.

CJ called 'in' on his target to drop everything. I looked in front of me and saw his hits as he came back up on the radio: "Those look like some good hits. Just go ahead and lay yours down right there." I watched where his bombs detonated and aimed for his explosions.

The Iraqis had let him drop his bombs and come off target. Then they just watched me as I came in. My first warning was the RWR gear going off with Gun Dish radar indications meaning a ZSU. At the same time, I saw a bunch of bright red flashes immediately off my left side. I

---

[12]If you really want to burn fuel quickly, fly a heavy jet very low and very fast.

[13]When you're looking outside the aircraft, your head is "up" and you can see what's going on. When you're concentrating on sensors, gauges, etc., in the cockpit, your head is "down" and you can't keep track of what's happening outside the aircraft. In combat (actually any time for that matter), the idea is to limit the head's down time.

looked over and saw a four set stream of tracers aimed in front of and a little bit above me. It was a real, *real,* close range shot, a quarter to a half mile at the most. It looked like just one vehicle firing a continuous burst: He held the trigger down like he was going to empty everything he had at me!

We'd flown into a ZSU trap!

It was very strange, it was like I really wasn't thinking anymore. I remember just watching myself react to the bullets without a lot of conscious thought. I made a quick judgment on the bullet's path and figured that pulling up would only run me into them: I pushed full forward on the stick to fly underneath the stream of bullets. I could hear the sonic crack as they went over the top of the canopy and really thought there were going to be holes in my vertical tails, that's how close they were! He didn't try and follow me but deliberately aimed a long burst at one spot in the sky hoping I'd fly through it.

I got underneath that stream of bullets and then my next thought was, "You better pull up or you're going to smack the ground here in just a second." So I snatched back on the stick as hard as I could and put a six-and-a-half-G pull on the jet. It was still completely laden with bombs because I hadn't thought to jettison the ordnance, I didn't have time to think of it. I was completely overwhelmed at that point.

I bottomed out at a 150 feet above the ground and the ZSU's buddy in front of me opened fire directly off my nose. I saw the burst coming straight at the nose of the airplane. I couldn't pull up or I'd fly right into it, so I racked into a six-G level turn to the right. I was completely focused on the HUD to keep myself from hitting the ground.

I was level with some of the oil fires. I remember thinking, "I'm really low, too low!" I got away from the ZSU on my nose and ended up flying straight past a couple of the fires to try and hide in there. I grabbed a quick look around, didn't see any more triple-A, and decided I'd had enough. I hit the blowers and stood the jet straight up to punch through as many cloud layers as I could before I ran out of airspeed.

I still had all my ordnance on the jet, all the fuel tanks, everything. I still didn't think about getting rid of all that stuff. I flopped over at a 130 knots and went for the water.

It was nearly five minutes before I could talk on the radio to let CJ know what was going on. He called me since he'd seen some ground fire down there when he came off target. He saw the tracers come up through the clouds as they shot at me and so called, "Hey Jolt, are you still with me?!" Initially, I couldn't even click the mike because I was so focused on staying alive. "Are you still there? Can you hear me? Are you with me?" Finally, I found I could click the mike but I couldn't say anything. He said, "I think that's you clicking the mike. If that's you, give me a couple clicks." So I popped the mike twice and he said, "Okay great. I know you're still here. If you're okay, give me two clicks." Click–click and he let me settle down. He knew it had been kind of close down there.

CJ set up an orbit out over the water and let me know where he was. Then he took us home. I ended up bringing all five of those stinking bombs back to Bahrain. It took us 40 minutes to fly back to our base but I never really settled down on the way. He tried to calm me down, but I was still pretty psyched up when we got on the ground.

That was one of the few missions where I was still shook up when I got out of the jet. None of them had been that close before, and I was usually okay by the time I'd flown home. But that time, I just wanted to go find a corner to sit in and settle down. I ended up going back to the barracks and just sat wide awake in bed. It was 10 hours before I fell asleep. I just sat there thinking about it.

Have you ever watched a puppy when it sleeps? When the puppy starts dreaming, his little feet wiggle as he dreams he's running. Since there were six or seven of us per room, somebody was asleep in each room all the time. Once combat started and we were shot at, you'd watch guys having those puppy dreams. They'd be sound asleep flying their jets, their hands on a stick or throttle. You'd see them flying along and then, Oh no!, they'd call out SAMs and actually relive that stuff as they slept. I really hadn't had any bad dreams until that night, but sleep came real hard for the whole rest of the time I was over there. I relived that flight several times in my sleep. It made a real impression. To be that close and not get hit really stuck in my mind.

When the ground war kicked off, we came down much lower than our normal 10,000 feet plus. We killed artillery, tanks, anything that we thought would affect the troops. We were also able to use the canon. We were down low enough to where our 20mm was effective. We found that, if we could concentrate enough BBs[14] on a tank, we could at least get a mobility kill[15].

We could also bomb a tank from high altitude, which wasn't supposed to work. Even a near miss would take the turret off a tank, especially the T-72s, and you could actually see the turret go skidding across the desert. The 72s lost their turrets real easy—if you got any weapon fragments inside the tank, the turret came off.

Once a cease fire was called, we basically stopped flying. The

---

[14]BBs—Bullets.

[15]mobility kill—Immobilization of a vehicle. On the modern battlefield, an immobile vehicle is as good as dead. There are also firepower kills (knock out the main weapons) and catastrophic kills (the target blows up).

group commander kind of shut everything down to give everyone a rest, though we still kept some alert crews going for a couple of days until it looked like, no kidding, it was over. From that point on, we fixed the jets and got everything ready to go home. The squadron ended up coming home almost a month to the day after the cease-fire was called.

I got home a little bit earlier than the rest of the pilots since I was responsible for moving our stuff. The cargo airlift was available before the tankers, so I loaded up all our gear and jumped on the plane to escort the cargo home. I ended up being the first pilot from the entire air base at Beaufort to come home. I had my own one-man welcome home. All the wives came out, which was really neat. They all showed up and were waiting at the tower when I came in. The crowd was full of wives, neighbors, and friends. Lisa let them all know I was coming home.

We knew we had a lot of support, but we really had no idea what was going on back home. I didn't fully understand until I hit the States. Of course, we didn't get stateside news in Bahrain. The CNN we saw was the international version, so they showed almost no news from the US at all. The papers would talk about it, but we really had no idea what was going on over here. So, when I got in the car with Lisa for the 10-minute drive home, I was amazed that all the stores had their windows painted, the billboards were all done up, flags and ribbons were everywhere. She kept telling me, "You're not going to believe what it's like back here. You're really not going to believe it."

We got to our house where Lisa had a big banner over the whole garage. We've got 26 big old oak trees and she tied yellow ribbons around every one of them. It was really something, really something to see. It was sometimes hard to look at it all; it was almost overwhelming.

It was hard to get used to all the attention we got. I have a couple of brothers who are much older than me and who joined the military when Vietnam was going on. That's the period when my father was in the military too, so I knew how it was when they were in. To come back and get the kind of support and welcome home we did was almost uncomfortable. It took a long time to learn how to take having people come up to me, pat me on the back, shake my hand and say, "Thanks." I felt real awkward when people did that. For example, we went out to dinner the next night at a little seafood restaurant in Beaufort. We were eating dinner when some people came to the table and said, "Did you just get back from Desert Storm?" I don't know how they knew but they said, "Great! You're drinking free the rest of the night!" We had guys offering to buy us dinner, and all they wanted to do was shake my hand and say thanks. It was real awkward.

It took five airlifts to get all the people back, but every time a group came home to Beaufort, the town turned out. The energy never went down; if anything, it came up. All 24 jets from both squadrons came home at the same time and that was the big, huge welcome home. We had people from all over South Carolina come to Beaufort for that. It was really neat. The poor pilots had to endure a bunch of speeches on that one since the governor was there, the mayor was there, etc. Those guys flew for 11½ hours, stepped straight out of the jets, made a pit stop, formed up and marched. They were just bleary but it was a great end to the whole thing.

CJ and Jolt were awarded single-mission air medals for that flight among the oil fires.

Navy Lieutenant Commander Lisa Hoyt was a dentist assigned to MCAS Beaufort with her fighter-pilot husband. She combines the perspectives of a wife, a career woman, and a military officer into a character that's a bit more independent and resilient than even the legendary military wife. And that's resilient indeed.

Lieutenant Commander Hoyt:

I was raised in the Chicago area and went to college and dental school for eight years in Nebraska. After a couple years in North Carolina practicing dentistry, I joined the Navy. At Quantico, my first duty station, someone asked me if I wanted to go to the Marine Corp Ball on a blind date—that's how I met my husband. We dated for about four months until Lance left to start flight school and it was two and a half years before we ended up living in the same place. We were married during that time and finally ended up in Beaufort together in September 1989.

There's a lot of separation in the military family's life, but I don't think it's as difficult for us as it was for some people. We don't have children, I have a full-time job, and I have my own life. I don't rely on my spouse for my source of independence or anything like that—for my sense of who I am. I'm very busy so, when he's gone, I get a lot of projects done that I might not get to otherwise. When he's home, I like to spend as much time as I can with him.

We enjoy military life. We like the idea of moving some place new every three years, learning about an area and gettin' to do as many things in that area as we can. I don't think we've ever complained about having to move. Actually, we're the kind of people who fit into this lifestyle, and having no kids makes it very easy.

I was probably one of the first of the spouses to know about the deployment to Bahrain because I found out at work rather than from Lance. Basically, the guys couldn't tell their wives at first but I knew because I happened to be the dental liaison for the squadron.

It was really funny because the guys had been in the officer's club two days before whining: "We never get to do anything fun. We're not going to get to go." I thought, "You guys just wait . . ." And then it happened; they got orders to deploy. I was most concerned with what I had to do at work to get them ready and would worry about dealing with it at home later.

I didn't have time to worry beforehand because we were very, very busy at work getting two squadrons ready to go. It got to the point where we almost wished they would leave because the leaders kept saying, "We're leaving today, no we're leaving next week, no we're leaving yesterday!" We just wanted them to have a date to leave because it was driving everyone crazy.

I also didn't have time to sit down and miss him after the squadron left because we got other people ready to go too. We had to pay attention to the other units. Whenever Lance left on routine deployments, it was difficult for me to get motivated for a week or so, and it was the same thing that time. But I was also involved with work and didn't have time to feel sorry for myself. It really took a little while for everything to sink in.

I watched the news more during Desert Shield. I normally don't watch the news, I'm not a television watcher, but I definitely tried to catch the news at least once a day after Lance left. Thank God for CNN.

Some of the wives complained about their husbands being gone and not being able to visit or thought, "Oh my God, what's going to happen to him?" I'm practical by nature and I felt that Lance knew that if anything happened to him, I could take care of myself. So I prayed to God that nothing would happen, but it wasn't that frantic kind of hoping because-I-couldn't-survive-without-him type of thing. Some of the other wives, with children, who had been with their spouses longer, had much more trouble with the deployment. It really disrupted their routine and many spent lots of time writing letters.

AT&T discounted phone calls for people calling Saudi Arabia or calling from Saudi Arabia. Bahrain wasn't included in that, so we all called and complained. A few of the operators there were so wonderful. They went ahead and discounted our phone calls for us and said: "Hey, that's just our little part that we can do because you guys are making the sacrifice."

I go to church on base at Parris Island and a lot of people there kept track of me. If they didn't see me in church for a few weeks, they checked to see how I was.

I went out of town on the weekends a lot for company. There's another wife here who doesn't have kids, so we did a lot of things together. And my best friend lived in Fayetteville, North Carolina, so I visited her on some weekends. Once the war started, I didn't go out of town much. As a matter of fact, I was supposed to take a vacation in January and ended up not going just because I didn't want to be far from the telephone. The deadline was approaching, and I decided I didn't really want to go away.

I went to the officer's club for a dental clinic function one night in January. As I walked into the bar, I saw everybody standing around the television watching the start of the war.

It was almost a relief and kind of exciting too. I knew it was both exciting and scary for my husband. Who knew what was going to happen? We didn't have any idea and I wondered when I would hear from him.

I went home and watched the news for a while, but I didn't stay up all night like some people did. I was just too exhausted. There was also a certain amount of emotional relief for me because something finally happened after they had been there so long. The men were really frustrated.

I received some phone calls from friends and family that night to tell me that they were thinking about me.

The next day, I heard that the U.S. forces had lost an F-18. It was initially reported as a Marine Corp F-18, so we all held our breaths. Then the CO's wife called me and said everyone from our squadron was back on the ground and was safe. Okay fine, but I still wouldn't believe it until I heard my husband's voice, and I didn't know when he would call me. Then about noon that day, the first day of the war, he called me and I got to talk to him for five minutes. He was fine!

I remember thinking to myself, "This is some war where your husband goes out and drops bombs and then calls you to say he's okay." It was really strange.

I wasn't any better informed because of my job, but I would say I probably had a better understanding of the things they were doing. Lance is very good about explaining things to me, and I'm around military people all day. A lot of pilots don't tell their wives much about their jobs.

I got into a routine of getting up early so I could catch the 6:30 highlights on CNN before I went to work. I came home at lunch every day to watch the news and then I had CNN on all night long at home.

CNN was a big deal for information during the war, not just for me but for everyone. There were some nights when I didn't go to bed; all I did was stay up and watch CNN till two or three in the morning. It was difficult. So my routine was: get up early, watch CNN, go to work, go home at lunch, watch CNN, go back to work, come home in the evening and work around the house while watching CNN.

The information didn't always turn out to be true, and the rumors that spread amongst the wife community were rampant. That was another reason why I stayed away from a lot of the wives' functions. It was detrimental to my emotional well-being. I couldn't deal with the constant fretting and the generation of stories that weren't necessarily true. They'd just magnify everything. I remember, when the ground war started, a lot of the wives thought all our guys would be fine. They didn't realize that the F-18 is a major ground support aircraft, which is actually more dangerous than the bombing from 20,000 feet that they had been doing. Ground support is far more dangerous. Some wives thought that, once the ground war started, our guys would be home really soon and that they weren't going to be doing anything risky.

I'm kind of a high-strung person, but I always managed to keep a pretty even keel when I talked to Lance. Even though things were difficult at home, I didn't let on because I didn't want him to worry about me. I wanted my husband to know that if anything happened to him, I could take care of myself. During the whole war, I knew that he could get in his cockpit and forget about me for however long his mission was. He didn't have to think about me in a life-or-death situation. He told me that was the biggest gift I could give him the whole time he was gone. There were some other wives who complained to their husbands about them not being home and that they had to do everything on their own. The husbands didn't need to hear that.

That was a very emotionally charged period for both of us. We weren't exactly getting along when he left, and there were some real doubts in both of our minds about whether we would stay together. Even though I was going through those emotional struggles, I didn't mention a word of it to him and didn't want him to have that added emotional burden. Not all of our calls were pleasant and happy conversations, but I tried to maintain an even emotional keel for him. It was very important to me to not create the impression of being a distressed wife while he was gone. I showed enough of that to let him know I was concerned but not so much that he would have to worry about me.

Lance wasn't going to tell me about almost being shot down, but he can't keep anything from me. He wrote his brother a nine-page letter to tell him about it and asked him not to tell me. Then Lance told me about it anyway during our first call after that night.

It's almost surreal to think of your husband doing those things. Even though I probably have a better understanding of his flying than a lot of wives do, I still don't have any life experience to compare it to. I worried that I offended him by not being more upset about it, but I couldn't allow myself to be. I knew my anxiety would bother him.

I know the wife of one of the pilots who was hit but not injured was tremendously upset when she found out about it. My feeling about Lance was: if he's okay and fine now, that's great. He got through whatever it was he had to go through so there's no reason to fret over it.

I was glad when the war ended, but I didn't believe it would be over for us until my husband had his two little feet back on the ground in Beaufort. I don't like to get my hopes up only to be disappointed. All I could think about was his coming home soon.

It worked out great since Lance came home first. Everybody "hated" me because he was the embarkation officer for the squadron. He had to pack up all the gear and fly home with it on the 14th of March while the pilots who flew planes came home on the 2nd of April.

He called me from London and said, "I feel like the weight of the world has been taken off my shoulders. I am so glad to be out of there."

That gave me one more day to straighten up the house and tie yellow ribbons around the trees in our front yard. I felt badly for him because he was alone, and I didn't think there were going to be lots of people around to welcome him when he arrived. I didn't want him to feel like nobody cared. But the other wives were there when he landed, too, which was really great.

So anyway, the day he came home, I still refused to look too excited. But I *was* excited and everybody laughed at me because I was just so calm when they said I should be climbing the walls. I said, "Well, I won't believe it until he steps off the plane." We were standing out by the control tower when his plane taxied in. The other wives yelled at me to run but I just turned around and said, "Lieutenant commanders don't run." I kind of sauntered out there and had about 50 more feet to go when he stepped off the plane.

I started running and sobbing, and it was truly better than the day we were married. It was far more exciting. It was great, you know. After all the months of not knowing whether he was going to come home or not. . . .

We didn't get to go home for about three and a half hours but that was fine. Everybody thinks, after you've been separated like that, all you want to do is run home and rip each other's clothes off. You don't. You have to refamiliarize yourself with each other.

On Lance's first day back, he slept late, and we went out to lunch and shopping. He missed those things. He said, "I was so sensory-deprived over there in terms of movies and bookstores and people." So he wanted to go out and do things. That was fine with me. Some people just wanted to stay home but not Lance. He wanted to get back into things as quickly as he could. First on the list: go to the mall and catch a movie.

12

Danger Close![1]

Captain Bill Andrews, callsign Psycho, trained to fight World War III from Hahn Air Base, Germany. He was prepared to lead his pilots in under the Warsaw Pact's radar at 540 knots (about 610 mph) to hit the most heavily defended, highly mobile targets any pilot has ever faced. He knew a lot of them wouldn't make it back. But his deployment to the United Arab Emirates put Psycho and his wingmen in the completely different environment of medium-altitude attacks against a dug-in enemy. Their success is a tribute to the flexibility and skill that defines the Western fighter pilot.

Psycho's jet was the F-16C. Designed originally as the lightweight complement to the F-15 Eagle, the Falcon is a multirole airplane equally at home on an interdiction run or a close-in dogfight. It was the most numerous jet in Desert Storm and flew more sorties than any other type.

Captain Andrews:

I was born on Long Island, New York, attended high school in central New York State, and went directly from there to the Air Force Academy in 1976. After graduating with the class of 1980, I went to pilot training at Columbus, Mississippi, hoping to get a fighter. Like a lot of other new pilots, I ended up staying there for an additional three years as an in-

---

[1]danger close!—Formal warning given to attack pilots when friendly troops are closer to the target than the normal minimum safe clearance of one kilometer.

structor in T-37s. After Tweets, I got an EF-111 to Mountain Home AFB, Idaho, that I was pretty excited about. Anything tactical was a good deal as far as I was concerned. I was in the right place at the right time for my next assignment since it was our squadron's turn to get a Constant Carrot[2] F-16. After F-16 training, I reported to Hahn Air Base, Germany, in July of '89 and checked out as a flight lead and an instructor pilot.

By listening to the *Armed Forces Network*, we got all the news from America and knew what was going on back home during Desert Shield. Our fingers were crossed that there wouldn't be any kind of fight, that Saddam would come to reason and not really take it to the point where we would go to war. There was also a bit of wishing that we were in Saudi because it's tough to be left behind. But we knew we were pretty lucky to be back in Germany with our families while everyone waited during the Shield.

Around September 1990, I started training my guys pretty hard just because it looked like some of us might get tapped to go to Saudi. We got into the books on Iraqi equipment and used a little bit more of the high- to medium-altitude tactics that I thought we would probably use down there as opposed to punching through the front lines at low altitude and trying to skirt around the SAMs. We practiced the real simple kind of stuff, like what to do if you had a SAM launch while you were up at high altitude. In Germany, we'd always planned on running in as low and fast as we could to hide behind rocks[3] and scrape the SAMs off on the ground. But there's nowhere to hide at 15 or 20,000 feet so you have to have some specific maneuvers practiced, rehearsed, and understood to dodge those missiles while applying your electronic countermeasures.

We also got the homefront ready as I made all the guys in the flight go and get wills, take out some life insurance, and turn over the budget and the checkbook to their wives if they did all that kind of stuff themselves. As it turned out, we were lucky that I guessed right and the guys in the flight were pretty well prepared.

Then came November and December of 1990. The 10th Tac Fighter Squadron was told to get ready to deploy for Desert Shield and the 496th Tac Fighter Squadron, my squadron, transferred all seven of the guys in my flight over there to beef them up. I asked to go with them but we were obligated to keep the infrastructure of the 496th intact while we deactivated so, as a flight commander, I was stuck. I said bon voyage to my guys and tried to rebuild 'A' Flight with new guys.

---

[2]Constant Carrot—USAF personnel assignment program designed to reward the best fighter pilots with choice assignments.

[3]rocks—Small hills.

Coming down towards the goal line and deployment, the wing leadership decided to send more pilots with the 10th. They needed another five and I was picked.

My wife, Stacey, was really supportive. She basically said, "I know you have to do what you have to do."

An interesting thing about deploying out of USAFE[4] is that we were organized and prepared to fight in place. All of our air bases in Europe are well equipped with aircraft shelters, squadron shelters, etc. Our maintenance was designed to fight right out of our backyard, and we didn't have deployment plans like the units from the States. The war was supposed to be on our turf. So, while most of us were preparing to deploy, we sent some guys to the desert to figure out exactly what we needed to bring.

As one of the add-on pilots, I didn't get to fly an F-16 to the Middle East. I was reassigned to the 10th in mid-December and we left at the end of the month on a C-141 that took us down to Spain. We hopped on another C-141 at Torrejon Air Base near Madrid for a night flight to the Middle East. We landed at Al Dafhra in the United Arab Emirates at about 3:30 A.M. on New Year's Eve to join the 363rd Tac Fighter Wing, which already had two F-16 squadrons from Shaw AFB, South Carolina, in place. We slid right in with our F-16s and brought the 363rd up to a full three squadron wing.

Our officers lived in mobile-home-size hooches fairly close to the airfield. A typical hooch had three rooms plus a bathroom and kitchen; we put two guys in each of those three rooms. Our enlisted weren't quite so lucky. They moved into 10-man tents in a big tent city that sort of surrounded the hooches. The population of the tent city was somewhere around 3000 and it was complete with chapel, post office, and chow tents. We had air conditioners in all the tents and hooches.

The officer's club was the center of our social life. It was built before we got there in a big prefabricated building. My favorite feature was the white board covering the walls and ceilings that everybody scribbled on to their heart's content. It also had a couple nice little wooden bars the guys built from scratch to serve beer. Before the war, there were pretty good parties on Friday nights, and, on the morning after a party, they'd open up the front and back doors so that the base fire truck could blast out the whole club. The UAE was a little different from Saudi on that sort of thing.

The squadron building and the wing building were full of boxes and boxes of letters addressed to Any Service Member; there were ban-

---

[4]USAFE—United States Air Forces Europe. The American Air Force command in Europe.

ners hanging all over the place saying how the people back home were with us. The support from home was really impressive, it was overwhelming. The Shaw guys had become kind of used to it, but it was a real shock for us to see all the stuff people sent. It really gave you a strong sense of purpose and made the pride just burst out in you. We felt pretty good about what we were doing and were glad that most Americans were behind us. Some guys developed a writing habit and answered quite a few of the letters. The ones that really touched the heart said, "Thanks for defending me." You felt proud when you read something like that.

We had quite a few combat-loaded jets on alert (in case Saddam tried a surprise attack), so it was important for us to get up to speed quickly and pull our share of the load. The F-16s from Shaw deployed in August so they had their tactics and plans fairly well thought out. It was simply a matter of those earlier arrivals bringing us up to speed and then getting a little bit of flying under our belts. Their flight leaders took us on missions to acquaint us with the high-altitude tactics that they had been working on. It was similar to what I'd put my flight through, but our practice in Germany had been very restricted by the limited air space. You don't have much room for jets to work with in Germany. So we went from simple blocking and tackling drills in Germany to more realistic scrimmages once we got to the theater.

We planned on running in large packages of 24 to 40 strike aircraft with a full bag of support airplanes including F-15 sweep, jammers, Wild Weasels, AWACS, tankers, and all that. We expected to run in at 15 to 30,000 feet and to release our bombs in the mid-teens. As the defenses wore down, our bomb release altitudes could get lower, assuming the situation required better accuracy. We couldn't be as accurate up high as we are down low.

The waiting and not knowing what would happen continued while we settled in. We read an English newspaper everyday called the *Gulf News*. It seemed like they alternated between pessimistic headlines and optimistic headlines, which we referred to as "war days" and "peace days."

When we first got to the desert, we didn't know anything about the plans and really didn't know what to expect. Once we were briefed on the Desert Storm concept of operations, everybody went from a great deal of apprehension to, "Yee haw, let's go kick some butt!" We knew the Iraqis were going to be overwhelmed by our air power because it was a good plan. Everybody was very confident about the end result.

On January 16th, guys went to bed mumbling, "Hey, the Stealth Fighters are briefing[5] and some B-52s have launched from the U.S." We

---

[5]briefing—(verb) Preparing for a mission.

were all thrilled at the news. Those of us who weren't flying in the first wave woke up to the sound of something like 40 afterburners taking off over the tent city, 20 seconds apart. That was some sort of oh-dark-thirty[6] launch. Our fighters had a couple-hour flight before their sunrise time on target. It took eight minutes for all the jets to get off so, if you hadn't heard any rumors, you were pretty certain that exciting things were finally happening. A few guys stayed in bed, a lot of guys went outside to watch them go and cheer, and quite a few other guys dragged themselves down to the O-club to watch CNN.

My first mission came on Day Two, and I was number 33 out of 40 strikers against Tallil airfield in southern Iraq. For the first couple of weeks, our standard load was two Mk-84s—2000-pound iron bombs—two drop tanks, Sidewinders, and an ECM pod. We ran into a lot of bad weather and had to do some snaking around to stay out of the clouds. It really was a pretty quiet mission for us. The whole place was blanketed in clouds, so we decided to go with our backup mode of dropping the bombs using our radar. We hit the airfield through the clouds by identifying the target with our radars.

We started out with strategic interdiction missions, where we hit the Iraqi infrastructure with those large raids. After about two weeks, we shifted our focus to the Republican Guards on the Iraq-Kuwait border and pretty much stuck with that till the end of the war. Those later strikes were flown by independent four ships so we could keep continuous pressure on the Republican Guards and other ground units in southern Iraq and Kuwait.

We went through the inventory of weapons by dropping Rockeye[7] until we ran out of them and then switched to some of the older CBUs, CBU-52, 58, and 72. We also mixed in some 2,000-pound and 500-pound iron bombs. We covered the entire spectrum except Maverick and strafe. We also dropped some CBU-87s at the beginning but decided to hold off and save the rest of them until the ground offensive began. Those were our best, absolute best, weapons, and we wanted to save them for when we really needed them.

U.S. Army Sergeant First Class Robert M. DeGroff, Buzz Saw, was a weapons specialist in the Fifth Special Forces Command, Operational Detachment Alpha 525—The Shark Men. Green Berets. They were recalled from leave to their base at Fort Campbell, Kentucky, and deployed

---

[6]oh-dark-thirty—Any very dark time of the early morning.

[7]Rockeye—Cluster bomb containing 256 small shaped charges that behave like bazooka shells when they detonate.

to King Fahd in Saudi. The Shark Men infilled[8] at 2200 hours on 23 February 1991. Their mission was to reconnoiter the Basra-to-Baghdad highway because they were world-class experts at sneaking around on the bad guys' home turf.

Buzz Saw and Psycho alternate view points for the rest of their story:

Buzz Saw: We moved forward to King Khalid Military City and went into a reverse training cycle where we stayed up all night and slept all day. We played poker from ten o'clock at night until six in the morning with bullets as chips. Then we got the word that we were going in on the mission we'd planned during our isolation[9]. It was time to get as much sleep as possible, eat real good, and start hydrating.

Psycho: There were MiGs airborne during a few of the mass raids, but they never survived the F-15 sweep. That's the way it's supposed to be. Nobody in our wing was ever engaged by an Iraqi fighter.

That was a bad winter for aircraft. It was sometimes clear but many days were undercast, forcing most of the F-16s in the KTO[10] to bomb by radar or drop visually through a hole in the clouds; unlucky for the guys who found themselves underneath the clear weather. And there were times when we had to bring all of our bombs back just because the weather was unsuitable. That happened a lot during the ground war. If there had to be a ceiling, we preferred it up around the high teens[11] to give us plenty of room.

A lot of the media coverage came from cameras in laser pods on Strike Eagles, Stealths, or F-111s. The coverage from our HUD cameras isn't as spectacular and doesn't make as much of an impact on TV. When you're on a dive bomb run, you pickle the bomb off and pull out. You never see what happens through the camera in the HUD because you'd be crazy to stick around. So you didn't see that much press about the F-16s or F-18s because we didn't have any of the cosmic videos to give the media.

Buzz Saw (2000 hours, 23 Feb): After refueling at Rahfa, we left in a pair of Special Operations MH-60 Black Hawks[12]. Each of us had 150 pounds of gear, including a basic load of 420 rounds of M-16 ammuni-

---

[8]infill—Infiltrate.

[9]isolation—Green Beret teams plan missions while sequestered from everyone else. They won't say a word about the mission when away from their isolated area.

[10]KTO—Kuwaiti theater of operations. Desert Storm war zone.

[11]teens—13 to 19 or 13,000 feet to 19,000 feet.

[12]Black Hawk—UH-60. Transport and utility helicopter. Replaced the UH-1 Huey. Special operations version is designated MH-60.

tion and our 9mm Berettas. There were also a pair of grenade launchers and two MP-5 suppressed 9mm submachine guns.

It was important to get there quickly because our hide sites took six hours to dig. But we were recalled–Abort, abort, abort—just as we crossed the border northbound. Then, just as we got back to the refueling base, we were sent out again—execute, execute, execute! That indecision wasted almost two hours.

On the way in, my bird hit a dune and ripped off the rear wheel. All of a sudden, we were vertical as the pilot tried to climb but—BOOM! it was too late. That was exciting but no real big deal so we didn't worry about it.

The delay put us out of GPS[13] coverage so the pilots could only get us to where they thought we needed to be. We ended up 1500 meters from the hide sites and, when my bird touched down, the ripped tail dug into the soggy ground. Instead of just rolling out of the chopper as it flew away, we squished into the ground while the pilot used a lot of power to rip the tail out of the mud.

Everything was pitch black, and I couldn't believe I was 150 miles deep in Iraq. We started moving, wet, muddy, with the heavy equipment, and had to rest often to rebuild the strength to go on. And believe me, we were in spectacular condition. We were really behind the power curve by the time our leaders chose the hide sites.

We noticed animal tracks everywhere. That really concerned us because domestic animals meant people.

We broke up and got to work on the hide sites. Ours went into a bend in a chest-deep irrigation ditch that ran about 300 meters east to Highway Eight. It was a tarp supported by metal poles screwed together into a square. There was five-fifty cord[14] interlaced like shoestrings to tighten the tarp. A pole with conduit spread out like an umbrella held up the middle, and we piled dirt on top. We left the rear open this time, because we were concerned about being surprised by people or animals and so wanted a back door. The space ended up 9 foot square and 4 feet deep. The other site was 150 meters northwest of us.

At dawn, we saw that there were people everywhere. Women were carrying wood, children were playing, there were cars driving up and down the road. We hadn't realized that many of the civilians left Baghdad and were camped on the sides of the main highways. There were tents all over the place—the people were like ants coming out of

---

[13]GPS—Global positioning system. Constellation of satellites that allow users to fix their position very accurately if enough of the satellites are within view.

[14]five-fifty cord—Very thin, strong nylon cord with a 550-pound tensile strength. Similar to the cords used on parachutes.

the woodwork. They were everywhere. We were surprised we hadn't stumbled into them during the night. Then the animals started grazing nearby. We were getting pretty nervous.

Psycho (Morning, 24 Feb): The February 24th flight started out to be a fairly routine mission. We were supposed to hit armored formations in the KTO by working with F-16 Forward Air Controllers, callsign POINTER. POINTERs had been the traffic cops up there in the KTO while locating the lucrative targets with high-powered binoculars. Some of the direction I got from those guys was good, high-quality stuff. Spotting an armored battalion from the air was relatively easy because the Iraqis used big half-moon revetments in either circular or wedge formations. Their entrenchments and vehicles were easy to pick out. However, it was difficult to tell what kind of vehicle was in a revetment, whether it had been hit or not, or if it was a decoy. It was helpful when a POINTER would look through his binoculars and tell us, "The one at twelve o'clock is a tank." We would set up a wheel[15] over the target and pick off the armored vehicles that POINTER spotted by dropping our bombs one or two at a time.

I was scheduled to lead that late afternoon four ship made up of the guys I had been flying with throughout the war. We flew roughly 35 missions together. My number two man was Lieutenant Joey "Boo Boo" Booher. He was an F-16 guy right out of pilot training. Number three was Captain Evan "Ivan" Thomas, also an F-16 guy right out of pilot training, but he had been flying F-16s for about three years at Hahn, was a four ship flight leader and a real good man to have leading the back element. My number four man was Captain Pete "Abner" McAffrey. He had done a tour as a T-37 instructor at Del Rio, Texas, and was a good number four man. He kept a good eye out behind the flight.

Buzz Saw (0900 hours, 24 Feb): We heard the kids' voices real close by. We got quiet, woke up the guys who were sleeping, and Ski took out a suppressed 9mm. I speak Arabic and heard one of the girls say, "Enemy." Next thing you know, two little girls were looking right inside our observation hole. They saw us, we saw them, and I took the 9mm out of the site and could have shot them. The commander, CWO Richard "Bulldog" Balwanz, said, "No, don't shoot." That was a relief! You could see the fear in their eyes as they ran away.

It was still only 0900, so Bulldog got on the radio and called for immediate exfilltration. But there was no way to get an exfill[16] so we aban-

---

[15]wheel—Circular flight pattern centered on the target that allows any of the fighters to attack from any angle.

[16]exfill—Exfiltrate. To withdraw.

doned both of the hide sites along with the excess water weight, most of the food, and the comfort items. The sites were too close to the road to defend, so we pulled west along that ditch about 500 meters and set up a hasty hide above surface. We continued doing the mission while the eight of us waited to see what was going to happen with those little girls.

Psycho (1200 hours): The mission director assembled our mission materials, maps, line up card, authenticators—all the queep[17]. We checked out other classified material: the survival packets, escape and evasion maps, blood chits, etc. Blood chits were plasticized pieces of paper with an American flag at the top and a half dozen Middle Eastern languages saying: "I'm an American pilot and I mean you and your people no harm. If you help me and provide me with medical care, you will be rewarded kindly by my country." That was an accountable item because we obviously didn't want them floating around.

We would be loaded with two drop tanks and triple ejection racks holding a total of four CBU-87 Combined Effects Munitions (CEM). Cluster bombs. Those were our absolute best area-coverage weapons. They had wonderful radar fuses that seemed to work just about every time. When they broke open, a couple hundred bomblets spread out and hit with multiple effects, just like its name. Each bomblet has a shaped charge so, if it hits an armored target, it penetrates like a bazooka shell. It also has fragmentation and incendiary effects so it can take out a soft target with shrapnel and fire. Our jets were very accurate and the CEM never seemed to malfunction, so we were always happy to carry them.

Buzz Saw (1205): Just after our 1200-hours intelligence report, "Oqnod" (our generic name for Iraqi men) spotted us while herding his cattle. We said, "Salam a lekum," which means "peace be upon you," and he wandered off. When he got out of rifle range, he made a beeline for the road and we knew we were in trouble.

Psycho (1245): As usual, we started briefing 45 minutes before it was time to step out to the jets. The battlefield was divided up into a checkerboard grid system. We were to contact a Fast FAC[18] in a certain grid but didn't hold our breaths because you could end up with a target just about anywhere in Kuwait or southern Iraq. Our briefing wasn't very long, maybe five or ten minutes. Everything had become very standard for us, which was the point behind flying together all the time.

---

[17]queep—Pile of authenticators, line up cards, maps, printouts, and other papers required on every flight.

[18]Fast FAC—Forward air controller. Fighter aircraft (such as the F-18 or F-16) used to control air-to-ground attacks in place of the slower, traditional FAC planes like the OV-10 Bronco and the OA-10 Warthog. See FAC.

Buzz Saw (1300): We called for immediate exfill since contact was imminent. The reply told us that CAS was 20 minutes out and they were working on exfill. Charlie Hopkins was on our left flank with the binos saying, "Well, there's 15 soldiers in the ditch at the road . . . there's a full 80-passenger bus startin' to unload. . . ." The rest of us couldn't see the road, so we just listened to the numbers multiplying. We got into the escape and evasion[19] mode where each of us carried only the essentials we were assigned and prepared to blow up sensitive items. I carried the GPS system and the PRC 90 radio plus the normal weapons, etc. That stripped us down to about 45 pounds each from the 150 pounds we started with. We piled the rest on top of a pound of C4 plastic explosive and prepared to defend in place.

Psycho (1329): We waddled out to the jets loaded down with all of our queep, survival equipment, and flight gear. I started up, checked over all the aircraft systems thoroughly, warmed up the inertial navigation system, and checked the flight in on the radio.

Buzz Saw (1350): About 30 Iraqis came toward us in the ditch. When they spotted us from 50 yards out, our commander held up his weapon and shouted: "Kaf!" which is stop in Arabic. We said something like, just leave us alone and we'll get out of here. They took off running down the ditch. I guess they were done with their initial assessment.

Psycho (1404): We taxied towards the end of the runway and checked out our ALQ 131 jammers and radar receivers to be sure they were ready to go. A heavy load of bombs always meant afterburner take-offs 'cause we needed the thrust. So we took off in burners and I led a sweeping turn over the field to allow the wingmen to join up. After the rejoin, we tested our two boxes of chaff and flares because, if they didn't work, that jet would turn around.

Buzz Saw (1405): They really started massing on the road about then. We were being flanked by a platoon of 35 off to the right and another platoon off to the left with a larger group 600 meters away on the road. We were in our hasty defense formation, but, when I saw the number of people coming up that ditch, I personally knew it was all over. There was no way we could defend against that many troops. There were just eight of us, too many of them, and we had no close air support.

We had a saying that when death is inevitable, dying just isn't that hard. Well, that's bullshit.

Every time we called, the CAS was still 20 minutes out.

Psycho (1425): It was an almost relaxing flight up towards the tanker refueling tracks and the battlefield. We started in the UAE so it

---

[19]escape and evasion—E & E. Resistance techniques used to avoid capture or to escape.

was a pretty long haul over water. We flipped it on autopilot and enjoyed a nice hour-long cruise up towards the air refueling.

Buzz Saw (1445): The commander ordered the fuse pulled on the abandoned gear and we started running the 400 meters to the end of the ditch where we were going to stand and fight. The Iraqis were already around the pile of stuff when the C4 blew one minute later. Then we started receiving heavy volumes of fire. You could hear the cracking overhead; there were rounds deflecting all around us as we ran up the ditch. We still had not opened fire.

Psycho (1504): We coasted in near Dhahran, Saudi Arabia, and sorted out which tanker was ours. There was a lot of traffic in the vicinity of the tanker tracks, so it still took a little bit of sorting on the radar to figure out which one was ours. There could be half a dozen tankers in one orbit.

A bunch of other flights were also scheduled for our tanker at the same time. They were F-16s that had dropped four Mark 84s, the 2000-pounders, so they *needed* post-strike refueling. An F-16 can't carry drop tanks with that load so they were very low on gas.

Buzz Saw (1505): We got to the end of the ditch and the close air support was still 20 minutes out. I waved good-bye to my good buddy Ski over on the left flank and he waved good-bye to me.

Rounds bounced all around and cracked overhead. We got into our 360 degree defense, and Bulldog gave the order to fire. I started with the 40mm grenade launcher and everybody else opened up as well.

Iraqi fire got much heavier after we started firing back. Me and Jimbo would drop grenades in the ditch, they'd come out of there, and the other guys would just knock 'em down. We knocked 'em down at 400 meters plus with open sights on M-16s. Out of the eight guys on the team, we had five snipers. Any Iraqi who stood up got his ticket to paradise punched real quick.

Psycho (1528): About the time the first four ship finished and we were ready to plug in, another four ship came screaming up looking for post-strike gas while crying that they were real low on fuel. I figured there were three or four more four ships after them and it was going to be a hell of a long time before we could get on the boom, so I took us to a different tanker. I spent nearly 10 minutes negotiating with a couple of KC-135s until a KC-10 told them to give us some gas and they'd work out the other flights later. It was fairly frustrating and irritating. Some days worked very smoothly and other days were terrible. Scheduling problems somewhere down the line caused the refueling problems but you either persevered to make it work or you went home.

Buzz Saw (1557): Then we finally heard jets fly over. We began to feel pretty good until we realized we'd lost the antenna from the aircraft radio. We could not make commo with the aircraft. We could hear them but they couldn't hear us. That's when it became really hopeless.

Psycho (1600): We checked in with the EC-130 airborne command post to see if he had any news for us. We also called AWACS so they could check our IFF and be sure they had us on radar. That coordination took the time from dropping off the tanker until we crossed the border. We contacted POINTER and he gave us coordinates for the target. I typed the coordinates into the INS, thought, "Holy shit!" and then checked with my number three man to be sure we'd both typed them in right. On missions up until then, I'd looked at the HUD and seen five or six minutes remaining to the target. My eyes just about popped out of my head this time 'cause the INS showed something over 25 minutes north to the target, which Ivan confirmed.

Buzz Saw (1600): There were 8 or 10 soldiers flanking us on the right. The commander called me over and said, "Buzz Saw, take them out." I took a guess at the range, fired, and hit a guy with that 40mm grenade while he was running at about 350 meters. That shot must have been directed by God and sure impressed the hell out of the Iraqis. They had to think we had some kind of laser-guided guns as well.

Psycho (1602): We were going through some amazing mood swings. The mission started out sort of ho-hum because we'd been attacking Iraqi armor out in the open for a couple of weeks already. It was just another day at the office. Then things got real frustrating at the tanker as I thought, "Geez, are we ever going to get our gas?" Fuel was getting tight and I was getting mad at a tanker pilot and mad at the other flights coming in. We put all the frustration behind us instantly when we figured out where the good guys were. Our hearts jumped right up in our throats.

Buzz Saw (1602): We could hear the jets talking among themselves: "HAVE YOU GOT 'EM, HAVE YOU GOT 'EM? NO, I CAN'T SEE 'EM, I CAN'T HEAR 'EM. LET'S NOT WASTE THESE BOMBS. LET'S TAKE OUT THIS RADIO STATION." The jets flew 4 or 5 kilometers down the road and we heard the bombs go off.

That made the civilians real nervous. They had gathered around pointing us out to the soldiers and some of them mixed in with the troops by carrying old Enfield rifles. In fact, Ski's first shot took out ol' Oqnod, who'd come back with a rifle and was guiding troops. But the sound of the aircraft flying over cleared out the civilians. I guess they figured it was getting serious.

We knew it was just a matter of time before we ran out of ammunition. The commo men were desperately trying to contact the aircraft, but it was futile because they just couldn't hear us.

Another bird came in as the Iraqis charged up the ditch screaming their war chant. We dropped some 40mm in the ditch, they came out of there, and we shot some more of them.

Psycho (1604): I scrambled for my maps and set us up for a maximum-range cruise since we were going to need all the gas we could get. There was no way we were going to land back at home, so I set up new joker[20] and bingo fuels to much lower numbers, just enough to make it back to the border. Abner called, "HEY, WHAT GIVES?" I said we'd either find a tanker on the way back or we'd land at one of the fields right along the border.

Buzz Saw (1604): I took out the survival radio figuring I might as well die trying. E & E training said run the beacon for 15 seconds first so I did that and then switched to 243.0: "MAYDAY, MAYDAY, MAYDAY. THIS IS GUARD, THIS IS GUARD. MAYDAY, MAYDAY, MAYDAY." GUARD was our callsign.

I heard, "GUARD, THIS IS BULLDOG, WAIT ONE."

I stared at the radio and the commo man stared at me. I threw the radio to him and he called, "SERPENT SIX SEVEN, THIS IS GUARD." Nothing. He tried again. Nothing. He looked at me and I looked at him and I said, "It must be me" (thinking there must be divine intervention after that grenade shot). I got the radio back and called.

Serpent Six Seven answered and we got big smiles on our faces. Now we had a fighting chance.

Psycho (1610): So we headed up north and saw Tallil go by, we saw the big Basra-to-Baghdad highway go by, we crossed the Euphrates River and were still going north. I didn't have a single chart that went that far north, so we flew to a point in space without knowing what to expect. On the way, we listened to a battle unfolding on the guard radio, the emergency frequency. It sounded like POINTER was talking to an army unit on the ground and we were flying into an emergency CAS situation. Some people are in a bind on the ground, and we were going to help them out. We ended up on the Basra to Baghdad highway southeast of Baghdad where a four ship of F-16s was already working with POINTER.

Buzz Saw (1613): It seemed to take forever to get the jets' eyes on us. When he finally had us, he ran in from north to south just as the Iraqis made another mass run up the ditch with that war yell. I watched in what felt like slow motion as the cluster bombs broke open and landed right on target two or three hundred meters away. The ground was shakin' and there were eight ecstatic guys. We started to realize that we had a chance to live through it.

Psycho (1616): We listened to a lot of chatter on the radio as we approached the fight and tried to piece the situation together by what we could hear. POINTER gave the standard big geographic references to

---

[20]joker—Radio call meaning "I only have enough fuel for one more attack."

small references target area description to Lieutenant Colonel Billy Diehl's flight, so I listened in while trying to draw a map of what he described. Then POINTER gave the F-16s bombing corrections and told them where he wanted their bombs. For example, they started out bombing a couple of miles from the good guys by hitting the trucks that were bringing Iraqis troops. Then they did a bit of hunting around for the deployed Iraqi troops. We heard the original four ship go winchester[21] when they had dropped all their bombs.

The F-16s on scene were talking about some triple-A in the vicinity and I thought to myself, "The ground war has just started and it sounds like it's going really well. The ground guys are advancing quickly and the end of this war seems to be in sight. I made it up to this point and now I'm going to dive into that triple-A. Geez, is my number going to come up today with the end so close?" I remember thinking that very clearly, and then I just said to myself, "Well, those guys need help down on the ground and we're going to do whatever it takes." I just kind of folded that doubt up and put it aside to concentrate on getting the job done.

Buzz Saw (1620): Bombs dropped all around us, but the Iraqis kept massing on the road at the end of the ditch. They'd unload everything that drove by including 80 pax busses. They just kept 'em coming. I asked the second sortie to hit the vehicles on the road but we had to start over getting him to find us.

Then the jets started getting triple-A from the north and they were concerned about that. The jets weren't dropping down low enough to see us.

He hit the vehicles on the road and got them all in one pass.

POINTER 73, the jet in charge, then called; "GUARD, ALL THOSE VEHICLES ARE NOW GONE, WHAT ELSE 'YA GOT?"

Those F-16s, I love 'em. They were great.

Psycho (1632): By the time we arrived, the F-16s were all just about out of gas so POINTER tried to describe the location of the friendlies to me before he was forced to leave. But the team was camouflaged and dug in so they were impossible to see from our altitude. We had some burning motorized transport on the main road running north to south with a small town and a pretty good amount of triple-A coming out of the town. Other than that, it just looked like scrub brush and some trees with lots of waddies. POINTER walked my eyes from a bend in the river to the town and then to a football-shaped field while I got frustrated trying to find their position. They gave us mirror flashes continu-

---

[21]winchester—Radio call meaning, "I'm out of weapons."

ously, but we were still unable to see them. The conditions were fairly bad with the sun getting pretty low and a lot of haze. You couldn't see much of anything if you looked from the east to the west, into the setting sun. When we finally did find the friendly position, we couldn't maintain contact while on the east side of our orbit. Every time we came around the bend north of the good guys, we had to pick up a visual again by working back through the references from big to small. It took 7 or 8 minutes before I knew exactly where the good guys were and we weren't going to drop anything until we had them. We weren't going to risk hitting our own guys.

I give POINTER a lot of credit because he stuck around on (fuel) fumes to be sure that I knew where the friendlies were. When he finally got my eyes on the good guys, he had to just bolt right out of there because he was real low on gas.

Buzz Saw (1640): Another bunch of vehicles came down the road, saw the Iraqis trying to flag them down, and boogied on south. They wanted nothing to do with our fight!

Psycho (1640): POINTER left and we were on our own talking directly with the special forces on the UHF guard frequency; his callsign was also GUARD. So GUARD told us he had been compromised by the Iraqis and that he needed some CBUs to the west of his position. We had already set up a four ship wheel over the top of the good guys, so I rolled in and dropped my first two at a fairly conservative distance out. Even though I couldn't see them, I knew where the good guys were. But I still couldn't see any bad guys. Individuals are really tough to spot from the 13,000 feet or so we were holding to avoid the triple-A.

Buzz Saw (1654): We needed them to drop the cluster bomb units closer. They were obviously concerned about the danger-close situation since they were already dropping within 400 meters of us. But there were a couple Iraqi platoons even closer than that who were chanting their war chant and outflanking us. We needed bombs within a hundred meters of us. Face it, if the F-16s didn't drop closer, the Iraqis would kill us. We trusted the pilots since they had always dropped exactly where I wanted them to.

The flight leader told me again that they were dropping cluster bomb units. I tried to get through to him that we understood what they were dropping and that we were behind hard-packed dirt in the ditch. I knew we wouldn't survive a direct hit anymore than the Iraqis had, but we were dead otherwise. They just had to walk the bombs in closer.

Psycho (1700): GUARD gave us corrections in hundreds of meters north, south, east or west from our latest bomb. As long as we kept somebody rolling down the chute most of the time it, was pretty easy to make corrections from a bomb. A couple of times, GUARD asked if we could drop any closer. We were really pushing it. I thought the CBU-was going off right on the edge of his perimeter, I mean the edge of the pattern was exploding right where he was, so I said, "NEGATIVE." He said, "WE'RE UNDER HARD-DIRT COVER." I don't think he realized those were armor-piercing bomblets, because no cover he could come up with would have done them very much good if we scored a direct hit on his position.

Buzz Saw (1700): I could tell by his voice that the leader was skeptical about dropping closer. He wasn't impressed by our hard-dirt cover.

Psycho (1703): I felt a lot of weight on my shoulders all of a sudden and thought, "Wow, I'm the guy in charge over the top of this mess and this is one serious responsibility." Every time one of us rolled down the chute, I got really tense again because we were bombing so close.

Buzz Saw (1703): The fighters came in again and I yelled: "Take cover! Take cover! This is going to be close!" We jumped down in the ditch and pressed against the near side of the hard-dirt wall. I peeked over the rim and watched the jets come down in "slow motion," just like in a movie. They dropped, the bombs broke open, and the pellets spread out like they were coming right at us. Awesome.

The earth turned to Jello as the bombs went off: BOOM! Boom-boom-b-boom-b-boom! BOOM! BOOM! Boom-boom-b-boom-b-boom-boom! The earth just shook while the pellets kept exploding right outside our ditch.

Psycho (1704): On one pass when Abner pulled off target, I said to GUARD, "Okay, WHERE DO YOU WANT THE NEXT BOMB?" He didn't say anything. "GUARD, WHERE DO YOU WANT THE NEXT ONE? GUARD?" Nothing. So all of us thought, "Man, this isn't good, that was too close." Then GUARD started talking about the next bomb and, oh man, we breathed a sigh of relief. Thank God . . . I don't ever want to do that again! I can understand how friendlies get nailed during close air support. The A-10s nailed some friendlies in that war and I fully understand it. I'll bet the guys have nightmares.

Buzz Saw (1705): I had a real sense of control with the F-16s. It was like watching them on a TV screen where you know how the show ends. If I told them to bring it in a hundred meters, that's *exactly* where the bombs hit. It was perfect; they were that precise. We got a personal return on the millions of taxpayer dollars it took to train those pilots.

Their skill gave us hope.

Psycho (1705): I have to hand it to GUARD, there were ground troops coming after him, but he was pretty darn cool during his whole radio description. I think I would have been frantic.

As we marched our bombs in closer and closer, the bad guys moved along waddies from both the north and the south. We bombed the northern waddi first and then we bombed the southern one. GUARD really got excited toward the end shouting, "GOOD HIT! GOOD HIT! THAT'S THE ONE I'VE BEEN LOOKING FOR!" Then another one of the guys rolled in to put a couple more bombs in there and got the same enthusiasm. Finally, GUARD said; "OKAY, NO MORE HITS. I'M GOING TO SEND SOMEBODY DOWN THE RAVINE TO COUNT THE CASUALTIES."

Buzz Saw (1709): Bulldog went back down the ditch to be sure they weren't setting up an ambush for the exfill chopper. He said it was really a mess. There were bodies and evidence of wounded having been removed within a hundred meters of us. And it was totally devastated down by the road. There was nothing moving there at all.

Psycho (1714): About that time, POINTER 71 arrived and went through the same frustration that I did in finding the friendlies. It was almost sunset as we went through the big to small routine. POINTER ended up looking at some other landmarks about 5 miles down the river that looked real similar to what I was describing. Finally, he just took a radar lock on my number four man and followed Abner down the chute to get an idea of exactly where the good guys were. Now I know what the FAC[22] goes through.

Ivan and Abner went winchester so I cleared them off and sent them south to find a tanker. We had only two bombs left in the lead element and were running low on gas. It was time to go. In the half hour flight back to the border, Ivan talked to AWACS and coordinated for a tanker to give us a little bit of gas so we could get home. By the time Joey and I crossed the border, Ivan and Abner were already hooked up and taking gas. We joined those guys on the tanker.

1744: Sunset.

Buzz Saw (1800): A single F-16 stayed overhead until he ran out of gas, so we were alone for awhile until the next jet called in. He said he had our beacon in sight so I told him to drop 500 meters south. But the 2000-pounders went off about five klicks[23] away. I asked if he still had my beacon. "YES." That meant the Iraqis had set up a fake beacon south of us to attract jets for their triple-A. I said, "WELL, OUR BEACON IS OFF, WE HAVE NO BEACON. DROP ON THE BEACON." No more fake beacon.

---

[22]FAC—Forward air controller. Close air support specialist who controls all the weapons delivered in his assigned area. Desert Storm saw many aircraft fill this role, from the traditional FACs (OA-10s and OV-10s) to the Fast FACs (F-16s and F/A-18s). The faster jets could reach their targets quickly but were forced to stay well above the ground fire, lacked endurance, and did not carry marking rockets. OA-10s, the FAC version of the A-10, were rugged with the best loiter and target-marking capabilities but could not survive in space defended by the better SAMs.

[23]klick—Kilometer.

It seemed to take an hour to get his eyes on us. Finally I said, "I KNOW THIS IS GOING TO SOUND STUPID BUT FLY FROM THE MOON TO THE SUNSET AND I'LL TELL YOU WHEN TO TILT AND LOOK FOR A MIRROR FLASH." Sure enough, he called, "GOTCHA!"

Psycho (1830): The sun was down when we headed back for Abu Dabi. We really felt proud of our part in the whole thing and the guys on the ground sounded like they were in good hands. We could hear the FACs talking between themselves as they sorted out the callsigns of several different flights that were inbound to help. GUARD had lots of company.

As we cruised home, we felt great because we knew that we'd helped out some good guys who were in a jam. I never had such mission satisfaction before or since because this was a case where we knew some guys were counting on us and we came through. We all felt happy as could be. When we got on the ground, our operations center called Ivan and said, "BY THE WAY, IT'S A BOY." His wife had their first baby on that day. So we went to the O-club feeling pretty festive.

Buzz Saw (1930): It was dark when the chopper came in expecting a hot exfill. But it was calm, so we just got on the birds and flew out.

Psycho (2000): Another flight lead came in later and seemed a little shaken. He had flown the same mission some time after us but found a different situation. All the FACs had bingoed out, so he blundered into the place by himself and had to establish who the good guys were without any help from anybody else in the air. That really shook us up and we were worried about those guys on the ground. We wondered if we should have gassed up and flown back to the fight even though we only had two bombs left. We were real worried, so we hopped in a jeep, drove back over to the squadron building, and asked Intell to look into it for us. They made some calls and said, "Yeah, they got all eight of them out." We started hoopin' and hollering and went back to the club to have a couple more beers in celebration. We felt great after that.

Buzz Saw: We owe those pilots our lives. We knew we were dead. They are the only reason we're here today. And they were real concerned about dropping those bombs that close to us. But they were so precise that, when I said put it 200 meters from my position, it hit at 200 meters. They had control and we lived or died on what they did.

There's eight very grateful men and a bunch of wives and kids. You know it. I'm indebted for the rest of my life to those guys.

Psycho: Three days later, I flew another routine mission with the same guys and was shot down about 15 to 20 miles west of Basra. I ended up getting captured by the Iraqis, escaped, and got captured again. The war ended the day after I was shot down, and the President was adamant about POWs, so I had a relatively short stay in Baghdad. I was returned on March 6 when the Red Cross flew us to Riyadh. We had a big homecoming celebration at Andrews AFB that was pretty nice. Stacey and my kids and my mom and dad and Stacey's dad . . . a whole bunch of folks were there for me.

Sergeant First Class DeGroff and the rest of the Shark Men of 525 earned a Silver Star and seven Bronze Stars with valor devices for that action. Captain Andrews was awarded the Air Force Cross, the Purple Heart, and the POW Medal for his last mission.

Stacey Andrews met Bill while he was a senior at the Air Force Academy. She married him and set off on that adventure known as the military family's life. Since she grew up in the military, moving every few years was normal. But war isn't normal. No matter how prepared a family might be for the separations, dangers, and uncertainty, some news will always arrive with numbing force.

Stacey Andrews:

Hahn Air Base, Germany, was different in that I had never been overseas before. It turned out to be a much tighter-knit community than I'd seen. The people would socialize often and the squadrons were always doing something together. The ladies would get all of our kids together if for no other reason than the language barrier made it difficult to become integrated in our communities. It was lots of fun and I was a bit surprised that we put 30 women together and they mostly got along. It generally doesn't work that well, but we had a lot of good people.

The leaders sliced Bill's flight off from the squadron and left him out when they formed the unit that would deploy for Desert Shield. He started to train a new flight and was on a routine trip to Spain when they decided that they needed to deploy five more guys and chose Bill. He called me from Spain and said, "Guess what Honey?" I was almost ready for that news if for no other reason than we had been preparing the other guys in Bill's flight for deployment. Bill almost had to fight his way into the squadron that was leaving, but that was okay. It was. All of his guys were going and I would never have tried to keep him back.

Packing him up and getting him out was pretty much my job. We were lucky to get Christmas together and discussed what would happen if (a) he's shot down and/or (b) captured. Ironically, we didn't cover the MIA option. We weeded through all that heavy stuff and were pretty well prepared.

There were rumors that the wing expected 25 percent losses. Six pilots and planes stayed at Hahn as replacements.

We preferred to say good-bye quickly when he finally did leave.

Shannon was two at the time so she didn't really notice the big deal. Bill was normally gone for a month at a time anyway, so it was just Daddy going away again. Sean was five and he pretty much felt the same way: "Daddy's going off to a war. Is that like when he goes to Turkey for a month, Mom?" So we did treat it just like a deployment. One interesting thing Bill did before he left was buy a small bottle of Chivas Regal and a couple of glasses that we put on the shelf. He said, "Stace, when I come home, we're going to sit down and drink this. Stace, if I don't come home, you sit down and drink this."

The base had a wonderful area for the families to say good-bye in, so I said my see-you-laters to the rest of the folks, gave Bill a quick kiss and hug, and turned around and walked away real quick. I was already starting to cry. I went home, fixed the kids' lunch, and started getting into my deployment routine.

It took the usual two or three days to adjust and then we went right along with our old routine; Sean went to his kindergarten class and I spent time with the gals. It was business as usual. That was the best way to do it. We kept things normal so nobody would feel like it was abnormal.

The night before the war started, I sat up late listening to the radio and reading a book. At about one in the morning I thought, "Well, this is stupid, Stacey. You have to get up with the children in the morning so just turn it off and go to bed." I missed the beginning of the war by five minutes and was lucky that my closest friends waited until about six in the morning to call. I got a good night's sleep, which 99% of the base missed. When my girlfriend called, I promptly packed up my children and went over to her house to sit in front of the television for a couple of days of CNN. It was eventually time to go home and get back to normal.

Reactions to the start of the war were mixed. A lot of gals stayed glued to the TV, but the majority took a couple of days to readjust our way of thinking and then tried to keep things as normal as possible. One of the gals with a psychology education, Jeanne Long, started a support group on Saturday mornings for the gals to discuss things that were bothering them. A lot of gals went to talk or just to cry because we couldn't do that in front of the kids. We had a very good group of ladies for that situation.

Two squadrons were still at Hahn, and the guys who had been left behind were incredible, I mean just incredible. As well as being angry and/or relieved that they couldn't go, they were there for us any time of the day and their support was awesome.

My folks called about every five or six days and Bill's folks called at least once every weekend. The *Stars and Stripes* had wonderful stories of the support back home. Even the German community was with us. When the war broke out, a large group of antiwar demonstrators showed up outside the base. Two days later, the local community turned out with three times that number of people in a wonderful show of support. The news showed Germans protesting against the U.S., but the people we saw day in and day out were all there that day saying, "This is good. You guys are doing the right thing." Their support was very welcome, very very welcome.

The German press, like the American press, had a tendency to accentuate the negative and I was rather disappointed. But I don't pay that much attention to the American press when they get so negative either. I knew the German press was wrong because I could feel an outpouring of support from my neighbors when I could barely converse with them. For example, the gal next door would send her husband, Gerd, to shovel snow off of my walk, and he'd just nod and continue to shovel when I'd go out to say thanks.

I didn't listen to the radio as much as most people did. A friend asked me why not, and I told her there were only two things that would change my life. One of those things would be my husband driving up the driveway and the other would be the wing commander driving up the driveway[24]. Outside of that, there wasn't a darn thing I could do, so the best plan was keep my kids happy, keep my head on straight, and just stay strong. Those were the only two things that could change my life one way or the other. I was hoping for the first option, but it didn't work out that way. In any case, I didn't camp in front of the TV and gain 20 pounds on Oreos.

I explained the war to Sean so he had a little bit of a handle on it. The kids were talking about the war at school, and he brought home drawings of F-16s or other planes flying over ground that looked like the Iraqi flag. That's about the best that they could do at five years old to understand what was going on. He simply accepted that Daddy was fighting the bad guys. It was a difficult subject for me to talk about anyway, so kindergarten level explanations were enough.

Late one afternoon on a fairly normal day, a close friend of mine, Victoria Finnila, came over "just to visit." She was very cool even though she knew something was wrong. A while after Victoria came over, there was a knock on the door. It was Bill's previous squadron commander, Lieutenant Colonel Bill Harrell. It was not at all unusual for him to stop by and check up on any of the gals. So I didn't think anything of it except that he had kind of a long face on. Then I noticed that our wing

---

[24]Casualty notifications are made by a senior officer in the same unit if the family lives locally.

commander, Colonel Norwood, was behind Bill. That's when I got a clue that things were not all well. I don't remember much of what happened next, but Victoria told me that I just turned around and walked into the kitchen. At least I left the door open for them.

They followed me in and asked me to sit down. I remained standing and said, "No, you just say what you have to say and then you can just leave." I was rather impolite. Colonel Norwood said, "I regret to inform you that your husband has been shot down and is missing in action." I was kind of in shock and said, "Thank you Colonel Norwood, I appreciate your stopping by. Good afternoon." They just looked at me as I thought about it: "On second thought, that's probably not a good idea. Hang around for a little while."

Bless her heart, I called another close friend of mine, Susan Ferris, and asked her to come and get my kids. She said, "Sure Stace, you must have had a pretty bad day." She had no clue what had happened, of course. She asked if it could wait a few minutes, and I said I needed her to come right now. She said, "Well, yeah Stace, what's wrong?" "Bill's been shot down." She's so terrific and sensitive and kind . . . I might as well have taken a shotgun to the woman. I could hear her shaking on the phone.

Sean came upstairs and asked what was wrong. I told him Daddy's plane had crashed. His only reference for that sort of thing was a crash we had about a year earlier involving the dad of one of his friends so he asked, "Is that what happened to Daniel's daddy?" "Well yes, it is what happened to Daniel's daddy." "Is Daddy going to come home?" That's when I lost it. I said, "Sean, I don't know, I just don't know. We'll have to wait and see." He accepted that, and my daughter was too young to comprehend what was going on except that things were bad.

I had been through it with my best friend's husband's fatal crash a year earlier and couldn't take that again. So a week before Bill was shot down, I said a prayer: "Please Lord, if it has to happen, don't let it be any of my friend's husbands. I can't stand that again." Now I thought, "Thanks a lot for answering *that* prayer!" Talk about mysterious ways . . .

Victoria kept the crowd to a minimum that afternoon and stayed with me that night.

I felt a little better the next day, so Victoria put out the word that I'd like to see people. My gosh, the place was packed! For four or five days straight, until we got news that Bill was fine, there were people in my house constantly. It seemed that every person on that base, men and women, came by: "Can I help? What can I do? Would you like me to just hang out with you?" The support was incredible, and I wasn't allowed to do anything. These people were even taking out my garbage. They were terrific.

The war ended the day after he was shot down.

I couldn't allow myself to think he was dead because I just couldn't. At the same time, I couldn't allow myself the luxury of being sure he was alive because I would not do well if it turned out he was dead. I even snapped at some of the ladies who tried to be optimistic saying he must be alive. I apologized later.

Most of the base rejoiced that the war was over. Me and the rest of the ladies and most of the rest of the fliers were going, "Yeah. That's really nice." There was definitely no rejoicing in our group except that we wouldn't lose any more pilots.

We had a few hints that Bill was a POW. We knew he was alive when he hit the ground though his last words were: "They are attacking me now." An intercepted Iraqi transmission talked about a prisoner in the right general vicinity. But I could feel that the folks near me weren't giving him real good odds.

Sean's kindergarten teacher had been through a lot when her husband was a POW in Vietnam. I felt so sorry for her because she said she didn't handle Bill's loss very well at all. She had to turn Sean's class over to her aide. The class knew what had happened, so they made it Sean's day. But he came home that afternoon a wreck. He wasn't prepared for that much sympathy and negative emotion. I went with Sean the next day and thanked them for being so wonderful, but said we need to get things back to normal.

Four days after he was shot down, the wing leadership called to say that Bill was a prisoner. I told them to spread the word that there was to be a party at the officers club that evening! I went to the club and rang the bell[25]. I couldn't believe we were toasting that Bill was a prisoner of war. That was our day of celebration for the end of the war and it turned into a long night.

We hoped the POWs would be handled a lot better than they were in Vietnam.

Sean was real pleased to find out that his daddy was going to come home. All the negative emotion turned positive and, when I told him we were going to the United States to pick up Daddy he said, "All right!" He was just happy as a bug in a rug to be going to the States for Daddy.

Arrangements to meet the POWs at Andrews were really rushed. I wanted to meet Bill when they refueled in Spain on their way home and just get back to normal. But we had to go to Andrews for the big welcome. I was told it was a Presidential kind of thing, that is, out of our hands. We were treated like royalty when we got there.

---

[25]ring the bell—Military bars have ship's bells that are rung when someone is buying for the house.

After the hulabalu at Andrews, Bill's operation to fix his broken leg, and the hometown media interviews, we flew to Germany and got back into the swing of things. The house was decorated by the gals and those wonderful people were there to meet us. The entire German village we lived in saw the decorations and mobbed Bill; they were really great. A lot of his time was then spent going back and forth for medical stuff or therapy, and the kids loved having him home all the time.

After things settled down, all Bill wanted to do was get back to flying again. It happened so fast that it almost seems like a real bad week at work now.

Sue and I were running off at the mouth about the normal hassles of life. You know, the husband's never home, blah blah blah. We realized that we're not like most Americans. Like it or not, we are definitely different. Yeah, other people have really risky jobs and their home lives to cope with, but it's not the same. They were interested and supported the people in the Gulf with their yellow ribbons, but it wasn't usually personal. They go to work and might hurt themselves. Our husbands might not come home.

It was four or five days after our return to Germany before we sat down and drank that bottle of Chivas.

13

Shaba[1]

Air Force Captain Rob Donaldson, Rob-San, was destined to be a fighter pilot. His father spent more time over North Vietnam than many pilots manage to log in a year and more time in combat than any 10 Stealth pilots combined. Born overseas, graduated from high school overseas, and twice assigned overseas, Rob-San's life as an Air Force brat cum fighter pilot was fairly typical of that breed until August 1990. If America has a warrior class, Captain Donaldson was part of it when he took the fight downtown to Baghdad.

Rob-San flew the F-117 Stealth Fighter—a collection of proven technology from proven aircraft assembled under an ingeniously crafted skin. Like the colonials who built Old Ironsides *with Georgian iron oak, the armor of its day, Lockheed's Skunk Works used their hallmark Yankee ingenuity to craft the F-117. Stealth pilots think they did a damn good job.*

Captain Donaldson:

My Dad was a career Air Force fighter pilot, so we lived all around the world as well as all around the United States. I was born on the 6th of

---

[1]Shaba—Unofficial F-117 nickname, which is Arabic for "a ghost who walks at night and is not seen." The F-117 does not have an official nickname, but its pilots prefer to call it "The Black Jet." One proposed nickname was "Wet Dream," because it comes in the middle of the night and there's nothing you can do but clean up in the morning. F-117 pilots use names like Shaba, Stealth, or Nighthawk in more-polite company.

July 1959 in Munich, Germany, graduated from Balboa High School down in the Panama Canal Zone, and met my wife Millie there. I graduated from Arizona State University in 1981 with a B.S. in criminology and a pilot slot from ROTC. After earning my wings at Vance Air Force Base, Enid, Oklahoma, in 1982, I was assigned to OV-10 Broncos[2] at Osan Air Base in South Korea. Millie graduated from the University of Florida, and we were married after our long distance Ma Bell and American Airlines relationship.

We reported to Osan in January 1983. After six months in the Bronco, my squadron converted to OA-37s[3], which I flew for a year and a half before going back to OV-10s when we converted again. We left Korea in November of '85 for F-16 training at MacDill AFB near Tampa. At the end of our three-year F-16 assignment to Homestead AFB near Miami, I was offered the opportunity to fly Stealths. I reported to the 4450th Tactical Group, later the 37th Tac Fighter Wing, at Nellis in September of '89.

Stealth Fighter training was pretty simple 'cause we only take experienced guys. After a month of academics and a month of flying, you're checked out. I logged about 150 hours in the airplane during the year before the war, which was quite a lot compared to what guys used to get. They were lucky to fly 300 hours in a three-year tour, so I did pretty well. I had a little more than 400 hours when we came home from the war.

We followed the events of August 1990 on the news like most Americans. We didn't really think a whole lot about it, however, until the First Tac Fighter Wing was recalled from a Red Flag in a hurry, real pronto like. That raised eyebrows here and people followed the news a little bit closer.

We received deployment notification about 10 days prior to our eventual August 19th departure. It was an on-again, off-again plan since "they" didn't know where to put us. We planned on three different prospective bases in the Gulf region and got all the way up to putting on our survival gear for the flight over before one of those deployment dates was canceled. That got old after a while.

I was in the 415th Tac Fighter Squadron, which left first with 20 jets. We took off in pairs from our base at the Tonopah Test Range to meet KC-135 tankers and spent the first night out at Langley AFB, Virginia. I'm sure our 20 black jets made a good satellite picture on the ramp. We

---

[2]OV-10 Bronco—Vietnam-era, twin turboprop observation plane originally designed for counterinsurgency and now used by the Marines for forward air control and light attack.

[3]OA-37 Dragonfly—Souped-up FAC version of the Cessna T-37 Tweety Bird. Overpowered when empty, the OA-37 was sometimes called the "Killer Tweet."

were headed for Khamis Mushayt, a Saudi air base in southwestern Saudi Arabia by the border with Yemen and the Red Sea. We also carried two GBU-27s[4] each all the way from Tonopah to Saudi.

Our mood was pretty somber. There wasn't any horseplay or grab-ass or anything like that. An Intell briefer said things were serious and the hopes of the American people were riding on our airplane and its capability. That turned out to be a pretty prophetic statement.

We were briefed on what to expect by a guy from the TAC staff who had been an exchange pilot at Khamis Mushayt. He said no liquor, absolutely forbidden, no way–no how, but that turned out to be a big crock. He also told us about Saudi customs, their prayer, the Mutawa (religious police) and details like don't look at the Saudi women. It would be pretty sparse as far as the simple stuff like razors and toothpaste and towels and things like that go. Some guys made an extra supply run to the exchange, which they were kind enough to keep open for a lot of the troops going through Langley to Saudi Arabia.

Then he said the Saudis respect somebody they already know. Our wing commander said, "You just bought yourself a plane seat next to me so that you can do the talking when we land in Khamis Mushayt." Things went pretty smoothly 'cause he knew who to talk to as he stayed with us for three months.

We launched from Langley at four in the afternoon on August 20th. KC-10s took us all the way across in one 14½-hour hop with our crew chiefs and all our advanced party people on the tankers. We refueled every hour just to keep the tanks full, so that meant 14 air refuelings. The tankers were refueled twice by KC-10s out of the Azores and Moron, Spain. At times, our formation looked like two whales mating in the air with little black minnows swimming around nearby. That deployment was the only time I've ever taken a "go pill[5]" in my life. I took two of them. I also had my Sony Walkman hooked up and listened to all my tapes three times through. When it got light near Italy, I read a magazine while keeping an eye on the tanker.

That was some effort and it was flown largely under the cover of darkness. We wanted to keep our destination a secret. The news said we were going to Turkey, so I guess the Iraqis initially looked for us there. For the longest time, we were not allowed to tell anybody where we

---

[4]GBU-27—2000-pound laser-guided bomb designed solely for the F-117. Its specially hardened case and improved laser guidance system were designed to penetrate hardened targets.

[5]go pill—Upper prescribed by a flight surgeon that a flier had the option of using on an extremely long mission. Go pills caused problems with spatial disorientation and dependency and so probably will no longer be used.

were stationed, and we barred the media from our base. That worked out pretty darn good because the Iraqis looked for us in Turkey. We were very successful in keeping our location a secret from the Iraqis for a long, long time. But all you had to do was look in the zip code book to see that our 09671 return address meant Khamis Mushayt in Saudi Arabia.

Except for the Nile, Egypt was a giant sandbox, and Saudi Arabia was an even bigger sandbox. As we got closer, we saw the small city of Abha and then finally the air base at Khamis Mushayt. It blended in very, very well with the scenery and was a hard base to find even when you knew where to look. The Saudis do a good job with camouflage. Whoever picked that base for us did their homework just right. It was just like our base at Tonopah with the brown scenery, rocks, no trees, and high altitude.

Khamis is 6770 feet up in the mountain chain that runs along the southwestern coast of Saudi Arabia. Because it is so high, we were never too hot and never too cold. It was very pleasant and obviously had the best facilities that U.S. petro dollars could buy.

I think we caught the Saudis by surprise. I don't believe they were prepared 'cause they looked like some really surprised Joses when they saw our black airplanes. We got some bewildered looks as we taxied in, so they had obviously never seen F-117s. The only Saudi allowed in our area was their commander, Colonel Qhatani. We had our own security forces to guard the planes.

Since the airplane is black and sinister-looking and flew at night, the Saudis called us Shaba. That means, "a ghost who walks at night and is not seen." They were terrified of the airplane because they don't like the night.

The base was brand spanking new and the hardened shelters were just incredible. There were two-hole[6] and four-hole hardened aircraft group shelters. Each hole was big enough to hold two F-117s nose to tail. The shelters were set down flush with the earth so you didn't see any buildup. There were mini-boulders plopped on top so they also looked like the natural terrain around them.

The shelters were ultramodern beyond belief. They were super-hardened; they were chemically sealed; they were self-contained with water and power; they had briefing rooms, living quarters, and bath facilities. Each of the four-hole shelters could hold 100 to 120 people plus eight jets and cost around $600 million. The place was mind-boggling. We were the only U.S. aircraft to be stationed at Khamis Mushayt during

[6]hole—Aircraft parking bay in a hardened shelter. Think of a multicar garage with many feet of concrete on top and jets inside.

the war. That was nice since we had free run of our area. The other areas housed Saudi F-15s, Tornados, and F-5s.

The pilots and crew chiefs lived in those hangars. There were six 12-by-12 foot rooms and a big communal shower and toilet area on one side of each shelter. We had four guys to a room on bunkbeds. The other side had the cantina with its cooking facilities and a briefing room linked by closed-circuit TV to the other shelters. We chose to make the main briefing room into our lounge area with a TV, a VCR, and books. We only got Saudi TV in Arabic and some French.

We settled into a routine fairly quickly and put a couple jets on alert right away. Our combat mission planning cell, composed of our most experienced guys, got to work and was constantly farkling[7] the routes in and out of Baghdad as changes came down from Riyadh. On a normal day, the pilots would get up about 1:00 in the afternoon and go in for a 3:00 o'clock briefing. The first go took off at 6:00 or 7:00 at night, when it was dark over there, and then the next go would launch at about 11:30 or 12:00. The Saudis were very reluctant to let go of us, so we started with limited comm flights and then progressed to no communications at all. That's how we fight. Most of those flights stayed within 200 miles of our base, though several long missions went pretty far up north.

We did, however, use farley[8] freqs to BS with wingmen before the war. You'd brief him that the farley freq was 30-30, 29-92, or whatever so that if you just wanted to chat you could say: "Go farley," and he'd meet you on the prearranged frequency. Everybody had a different one and the funny thing was that we kept the ops officer and the squadron commander clueless the entire time; they didn't know the farley frequencies. We needed a frequency that nobody else could hear to yak because we were supposed to be no comm and all that kind of stuff.

We didn't really have a good idea how tremendous our support back home was until after we returned but, in the five months prior to Desert Storm, we did have a monumental amount of mail come in. There was Any Service Member mail with cookies, razors, gum, and things like that. It was just unbelievable, and we started to realize, "Wow, there's a tremendous amount of support back home for this whole effort." I ended up writing to a whole bunch of people.

Our only voice communication home early on was through ham radio operators. Our communications people set up in a bunch of tents so we could call back to the States about once every two weeks. You had

---

[7]farkle—To diddle; to make minor changes.

[8]farley—Unofficial; nonsense; under the table. Taken from the movie *The Three Amigos* by F-117 pilots.

to say "over" and you had to yell into the radio, but it was still nice to hear a voice from back home.

We started a pool betting on when we'd go back home. We'd only arrived on the 21st of August, but some guys thought we'd kick their butts and be home on the 1st of October. Some guys thought it would be a little bit after Thanksgiving, and nobody bet on any date past the end of the year. We all thought we'd be home for Christmas. We ended up decorating the main briefing room for Christmas.

Brigadier General Glosson came to Khamis in early September and told us there was a plan to attack Iraq first if it looked like Saudi was about to be invaded. That made good military sense. We were the only whole unit to be briefed on the plan; everybody else was kept in the dark. We had an F-117 guy in Riyadh working on the wartime frag[9], so we knew there was a plan for us to go get them, though we didn't know exactly when the war would start.

We'd come very close to going to war in September 1990. Saddam Hussein saw the buildup of forces on our side of the border and realized that the attack window was rapidly closing for him to take Saudi Arabia. Schwarzkopf said there was about a three-week period when he woke up every morning holding his breath 'cause we didn't have sufficient forces to stop the Iraqis from overrunning us. Saddam massed his troops at the border, so the plan was for us to get in the first lick before he could come south. But he held off and gave us another four months to build up.

At the afternoon briefing on January 16th, the wing commander, Colonel Al Whitley (who was also the first guy to fly the F-117) said, "This is it, we're going to go get them tonight." Simple as that. It was very quiet, very somber, very determined. Even after five months of preparation and practice, it was just phenomenal the way the first night of war went exactly like training, except that they shot back.

On that first night, I was the only allied aircraft in the skies over Kuwait. When you know you're the only guy out there, so every bullet and missile you see is meant for you, it brings out a real bagful of emotions you never knew were there. Except for the return fire, I just can't emphasize enough how much that first attack was like another peace-time sortie.

When it came time to fight, there was absolutely no change in the way we went about it down to the last detail. The tankers were the same and the rendezvous procedures were down pat with no communications at all, none. In wartime, everything went exactly as it had in peacetime.

---

[9]frag—Fragmentary order. Relevant piece of a day's air battle plan that each flying unit receives.

When the planners saw how effective the F-117s were, man they really cranked up the sortie rate on us. We started out with just two gos a night but they cranked it up to three gos a night, plus we brought over six additional airplanes with 10 more pilots from the training squadron. I ended up flying the first three nights, which just about killed me. We flew six-hour-plus sorties with some eight-hour missions going up to the northern border with Turkey. That was physically very, very demanding and I was a walking zombie after the third night. I settled into a routine of flying about every other night and mission planning for the other guys on the off nights. I ended up flying 23 missions during the 43-day war.

Once the war started, we weren't allowed to call home. But we had discovered an AT&T phone at a Saudi supermarket on base. There was normally a line of Saudis or third-country nationals waiting to use the phone, so I'd wait in line with them. I looked pretty ragged when I walked in with my salt-stained flight suit at about 8:00 in the morning after that first mission. I'll never forget the look that the locals in the supermarket gave me. I must have looked like I'd just come from Hell, because they all got out of line and gave me the phone right away. They stared at me with, I guess, a mixture of awe and appreciation. Nobody said a word. They saw the pictures from Baghdad on TV and knew what I'd just flown through. They always let me up to the front of the line after that.

I called my parents and said, "I don't know if I'm going to live through this thing. I just got back after my first night and it's going to be rough." My dad was a fighter pilot with three tours in Vietnam so he knew. He said, "Hang in there and do the best you can. You'll come out of it."

I also caught a whiff of the fact that the nation was behind us more than ever. People were glued to their TVs. I really didn't comprehend the scope of our support at that moment since I was so tired and the adrenaline had worn off. But it was important to know the country was behind us 100%.

Late in the war, I went to the 3:00 P.M. briefing and my Intell photo pack covered the Baath party headquarters in downtown Baghdad. The mission struck me as odd because there were a significant number of F-117s going after that target. It was not unusual for a couple of F-117s to go after the same target, but there were more than we'd assembled before. We figured the planners ran out of military targets and wanted us to take down Saddam's political structure. So I got together with my wingman, Major Lee "Gustaf" Gustin. We always took off in pairs, went to the tankers in pairs, and then split for solo attacks, so the formation brief by then was a two-minute thing.

He had the same target I did, but we had different DMPIs, designated mean points of impact[10], on the different buildings that comprised the Baath party headquarters. We were each assigned a spot on a building as targets. Each of us also had a TOT, time over target, as part of the simultaneous attack by many F-117s. The only way to bring that many silent jets through one spot and not hit anybody is implicit trust. We depended on each other to be on the altitude and the time that they should be—no deviation. We used the same inertial navigation system as the B-52 to make that work. It takes a long time to align, but I've come back from a seven-hour sortie with as little as 55 feet of drift. It's a pretty tremendous system.

After we had studied our photos and it came time to step, I went through my normal superstition thing of giving our female Intell officer a premission hug. I never missed that. Her name was Captain Jamieson, but we called her Dash. She was one of the guys, good gal, knew her stuff in Intell and real vibrant. That's the way it should be. She hugged the other guys too since it was a thing we all did for luck. Then I packed a bunch of stuff away that I flew for our security police people. I flew flags and footballs and shirts and panties and condoms and all kinds of things that folks could say had flown over Baghdad in an F-117.

We didn't bother with chem gear since the Scuds couldn't reach us. Our life-support gear was the same as anybody's with an Aces II ejection seat, so suiting up at life support and the bus trip to the jets was routine. Along with normal gear, we carried the EDTM, expanded data transfer module, which is the size of a small lunchbox. It's the computer heart and soul of the airplane. All the mission information is preprogrammed into that module, which plugs into the airplane.

My jet was in front of its shelter with the canopy open, electrical power on, and the cooling cart connected. The doors were open on the two bomb bays so that I could check the weapons. I had two GBU-10s, which were standard 2000-pound Mk-84 bodies with laser-guidance packages. They were normal laser-guided bombs. There was the standard writing on the bombs since the munitions guys or the administrative or support people or the crew chiefs wrote messages to Saddam Hussein. I guess we were just their mailmen.

After stowing my stuff in the cockpit, I inspected the rest of the jet. The critical part of the aircraft was the black coating called RAM, radar-absorbent material. That's why the aircraft is touch-sensitive, they won't let anybody touch it. Otherwise, the F-117 is a collection of good parts from other aircraft: engines from the F-18, flight control system from the F-16, an auxiliary power unit from the A-10, environmental control sys-

---

[10]designated mean point of impact (DMPI)—Exact spot on the target where an F-117's bomb will hit.

tem from C-130, landing gear from a Gulfstream. Then I climbed into the very roomy cockpit to strap in. The glass cockpit[11] has a fairly standard layout with a conventional stick and a seat that sits straight up like in an A-10.

The crew chiefs put out a fantastic, Herculean effort to maintain airplanes that made two round trips totaling 5000 miles or more each night. It was a super effort. I always told them what I was going after to make them feel like they were inside the airplane for the trip. They really got into that stuff, they loved it. After making sure I was strapped in, the crew chief gave me a final pat on the shoulder, a thumbs up, and said, "Go get 'em!"

As I taxied by, Gustaf slid in behind me in total radio silence. At the appointed time, we taxied out onto the runway and took off 20 seconds apart. We joined up and flew for about an hour to our refueling point. We "magically" appeared behind the tanker, still silent except for one radio check, but the tanker guys had already been briefed on who would meet them and at what time. We stayed with them for an hour enroute to the border and could talk to them through an interphone connection in the boom. They always asked about the target like the crew chiefs did.

Based on our separate routes, I dropped off first and pressed north. It was time to really get serious, so I ran the combat checklist, which included retracting the antennas. Antennas can be seen on radar so we pull them into the body; that also means an F-117 running silent cannot be stopped. All the way up, I played my favorite tapes on my Walkman (Heart and Def Leppard) and studied strike photos but put them away as I crossed the border with a lot of other 117s that I couldn't see.

My route took me south of Baghdad, around to the northeast and then across the city. I was going as fast as my foot on the throttle[12] would allow me. The 117 can really get going since it's pretty slick, but it's also hard to get stopped.

As I got closer to Baghdad, I saw a brilliant flash on the ground like one of the dozens of SAM missile launches I had seen. But that one was larger and I knew in an instant that it was a Scud missile launch right off the nose of my aircraft. It looked like the space shuttle 'cause it was slow to lift off as it gathered momentum. It passed a quarter of a mile off my right hand side; close enough to hear the rocket motor and see the bottom third of the Scud by the light of the booster rocket.

---

[11]glass cockpit—Instead of standard dials and instruments, modern aircraft display information on video screens. Much of the instrument panel space is taken up by that "glass."

[12]No, jets don't have accelerators on the floor. Fliers often refer to themselves as drivers, as in Eagle driver or Hog driver. Some carry business cards listing professions from Heavy Equipment Operator to Armor Recycler to MiG Parts Distributor.

I reached the southern outskirts of Baghdad, dropped down, and picked up speed. It was quiet. The lights were out like they'd been for about the past 40 days or so. Baghdad was just a big black hole with no lights except for some fires burning on destroyed targets. During the first week of the war, Baghdad turned into that black hole except for unbelievably long snakes of headlights streaming out of the city in all directions. Everybody had fled by then so it was pitch black.

I turned the corner to my southwesterly attack heading, descended even lower and picked up some more speed. Timing was critical. I got to my IP, the same kind of initial point everybody uses, and identified it on the night vision system. My inertial navigation set was pretty tight, so I expected to have my target in the field of view when I rolled out on final. The vision system was the equivalent of looking through a soda straw, but our key systems were so good that it works. We had the same image in the cockpit that you saw on TV.

I went through the same attack routine as any other fighter pilot. I made sure I was on altitude, on time, on course, and heading toward the target area. I was able to identify the target from a long way out on that particular night, and, as I got closer, I made one final check of the weapons switches to make sure everything was correct. There were still no shots from the Iraqis.

The 117s were the only aircraft allowed to go downtown to Baghdad because of our capability to get there undetected as well as deliver precision-guided munitions. They reduced civilian casualties and collateral damage by sending us.

I attacked with a dual door drop, released both bombs almost at the same time, and the jet jumped like a racing horse when those 4000 pounds dropped away. As I looked through the display about two seconds before my bombs impacted, I saw other bombs explode. My bombs hit just as many other bombs went off, which gives you a clue to the number of aircraft we had going through the same sky at the same time. It was a very compressed, nearly simultaneous attack, so we had a lot of bombs and F-117s going through the same piece of sky at the same time.

Sure as heck, just as soon as the first bombs went off, they started shooting like they did on all the other nights. I went through Baghdad on the second night of the war as well as on the last night and the triple-A was always the same intensity. It never let up.

I looked off my left wing to see a SAM lift off at me. It couldn't track me, so I kept on flying and watched as it passed behind my tail and exploded about a half mile off my right side. That missile didn't even raise my heartbeat, unlike the first night when my hiney puckered up tight.

We had the element of surprise in our favor though we still thought some guy would get hit by a golden BB[13]. But not a single F-117 took a hit during the entire course of the war, not a scratch, so we were lucky. Our tactics, our plan, and the execution played a large part too. When they don't know you're there, and they don't know where the punch is coming, it's awfully hard for them to defend against the attack.

I came off target and climbed to get out of everybody else's way and save a little bit of gas. It was time to pull down my mask and take a big gulp of water. I always saved some water because, even though I kept my cockpit cool, I was soaking wet with sweat. Tension and dry aircraft oxygen will always dehydrate you.

Gustaf and I joined up near the border and called CHOCTAW, the AWACS. I passed our callsign, THUNDER 21[14], and gave the code word for the day as we got clearance to come on across the border. They couldn't stop us anyway, so it was almost a courtesy call. To break tension, we'd occasionally play mind games with the AWACS controllers. Some 117 guys went through a silly routine from one of the movies we watched, and I laughed for 50 miles, it was so funny. We got back down and had another big laugh about the whole thing. Morale held up real well during the war. Real well.

We could afford the luxury of a bit more communication, so we gave the post-strike tanker a heads-up call. The same tanker had waited for us to return and they wanted to know, as usual, if we hit the target. After refueling, we climbed up and cruised the 600 miles back home to the base. I told Gustaf to go farley (go to the chat frequency) and found out that everybody had some good hits. The adrenaline rush wore off about then so it became a struggle to stay awake. I fell asleep on the way home during three separate missions. Lucky for me the Black Jet[15] has a great autopilot.

Since that was the first strike of the night, we landed at about 11:00 and taxied in. The crew chief marshaled me in and wanted to know right away if he could paint another bomb on the canopy rail, so I gave him the thumbs up. He got that wide grin on his face and gave me a thumbs up back.

I was always pretty beat after a mission, so it was a struggle to step out of the cockpit. I was dehydrated and the adrenaline had worn off. We each lost 15 or 20 pounds during the course of the war and my hiney

---

[13]golden BB—That one magic cannon shell with your name on it that hits you out of sheer dumb luck.

[14]Aircraft callsigns were often related. For example, F-117s were thunder, rain, lightning, ice, or some other weather-related noun. Tankers were fish such as shark. A-10 flights are often named after hogs, F-16s after snakes, and F-15s after birds of prey.

[15]Black Jet—Shaba. The F-117.

sure hurt after that flight[16]. I couldn't sit down, even on a padded seat. So I climbed on down the ladder and stretched out pretty good while I chatted with the crew chief. Then I looked around to see if I had any kind of battle damage or if I'd ripped off a bunch of RAM. After going through maintenance debrief and life support, Gustaf and I went to Intell to debrief the mission.

We told them the weather was clear and the standard defenses were up: surface-to-air missiles plus 23, 37, 57, 100, and 130mm cannons. Then we slid our tapes into the VCR and compared the points where the bombs impacted to the triangles marked on the building's photo. They were good hits, so Intell filled out their master target hit sheet that went to Riyadh every night.

I grabbed the helmet bag with the stuff that I had flown for the security police and spent some time telling them about the sortie and signing the bomb safety pin streamers they liked. After nearly an hour and a half of giving out the stuff I flew for them, I went to my room and fell asleep.

I woke up one morning at about 7:00 to all this hooting and hollering going on. I thought it would die down soon enough, but it didn't so I got up. There were a bunch of people out in the hallway hooting and hollering and drinking so I said, "What's the occasion?" "The war's over! The second wave has been turned back before the border!" I didn't believe them. I had three different people tell me the same thing before I finally believed it. Then I started hooting and hollering too.

We drank homemade wine and some liquor that had been saved for special occasions, so we got pretty well toasted.

We put some airplanes on alert as usual, but I still got about 14 hours sleep on each of the next four nights. I was that tired. We eventually stood down for six days to catch up on maintenance and give everybody a much-needed rest.

On about March 1st Brigadier General Glosson came back in an F-15E to tell us what a great job we did and that we'd go home in days, not weeks. Well, days turned into weeks—amazing how that works. I was very bitter about the delay. It was just one of those things that bugged me. We finally got out of there on the 30th of March.

My wingman for the flight out was Major Steve Edgar, callsign Fog Horn for his loud voice. Good guy, super guy. We took the ghutra and thobe Arab headgear (the Pizza Hut tablecloth and the fan belt) to the jets and put them on after we closed the canopies. The crew chiefs just went wild. They loved it and thought it was the neatest thing; more pi-

---

[16]Ejection seats cannot be padded. If they were, the seats would accelerate through the padding during an ejection and hit the occupant hard enough to cripple him or her.

lot humor. We put them on over our helmets so, with our visors down, it looked like we had great big outsized sunglasses. The crew chiefs brought their friends over to take pictures until we took them off for the taxi out. But the wing DO happened to see it and just went ballistic. He assumed we had our helmets off and were flying that way. By the time we got to our first stop at Zaragoza, Spain, the DO had already grounded Fog Horn so he couldn't fly a 117 back to the States. I stayed behind anyway because I had to take an F-117 to Madrid for the dignitaries since I speak Spanish. I met the second wave of the guys coming out of Saudi Arabia, gave my 117 to somebody else, and flew home on an EC-135.

We eventually made our way to Nellis. The transport from Tonopah parked in front of the base terminal where the band was going and all the wives and friends waited. Every arrival at Nellis AFB got the same reception whether there was one person or a thousand coming off the airplane. That was really nice. But the best part was seeing my wife and kids for the first time in 233 days.

Since then, the airshows have taken a lot of time, believe me. I flew the most combat sorties in the 117 and logged the most Desert Storm F-117 combat hours, so I've had several by-name requests for speaking engagements and air shows. They're a lot of fun, I've enjoyed it. We looked forward to a calm summer in 1991, but it didn't work out that way. The bosses asked for air show volunteers but ran out of them and started assigning that job. We even left four airplanes at Langley just to handle the East Coast static displays and air show requests.

We used to have our choice of assignments since it's a hard three years of commuting to a secret base. But now, with the cutbacks in the Air Force, we're being treated like any other fighter wing as far as assignments go.

My dad wrote me a letter that I got right after the war ended. He was a career fighter pilot so he knew what it was all about. He said thanks for putting to rest the ghost of Vietnam and the perception of the U.S. military as not being able to do anything right. Thanks for clearing up the record for the Vietnam-era people. That was one of the nice things about the homecoming: The nation finally welcomed home the Vietnam Vets as well as the Gulf War people. It seemed to me that it healed an old wound.

Rob-San earned a Distinguished Flying Cross and three Air Medals during Desert Storm.

Military families are used to separations, lousy hours, and jobs that can't be discussed at home. But most families aren't hit with those downers in quite the dose Millie Donaldson faced when her husband went into the black world of the Stealth Fighter. Three years of sending her pilot off to who knows where on Monday hoping that, if things went well, he might make it home by Friday would have been bad enough. Then CNN broadcast the fireworks over Baghdad.

How would you feel if your husband's "office" was illuminated by white hot metal, tracers, and missile plumes?

Millie Donaldson:

Rob and I are high school sweethearts—we go way back. After pilot training, we got married and went to Korea for what was probably the best assignment we've had. I really and truly enjoyed it. The moving around doesn't bother me because we've met so many neat people and we've made so many new friends. When we get close to three years in one place, I get kind of fidgety: okay, it's time to move, so let's go somewhere else now.

During our assignment in Las Vegas, the guys left on Monday around noon to take a 727 up to Tonopah and returned on Friday. It was a hard schedule to get used to at first because we are a close-knit family. It was probably harder on me than on the kids, but we all had to get used to it and I became very independent. Life goes on, so I was the mom and dad during the week, and Dad came home on Fridays.

Anybody listening to the news could tell what was going on in August of 1990. The guys couldn't tell us much, though, so when I asked Rob about their plans, he just said he didn't know. Yeah right. When they were recalled on a Saturday, we could figure out what was going on. They still weren't allowed to tell their wives where they were going or how long they'd be gone, so we just said our good-byes. See you whenever.

I guess my motto throughout that whole deployment was: Life goes on. For example, I tried to keep the same normal routine that I have with the kids. They were just starting school, and I kept them in their ballet classes and karate to make Rob's absence seem like a very long TDY. The hardest part of the whole deployment was the last part of Desert Shield when they wanted to know if Daddy would come home for Christmas. We just didn't know and the rumors didn't help. When we said our prayers at night, they would say, "Let Dad drop a bomb on Saddam and come home." Sometimes they floored me by saying those things. They had a good idea of what Dad did for a living.

I never talked to the kids about Rob's work, but they really listen when you don't realize it. They knew Dad was over there to fight and that there was going to be a war.

Support from the 37th Wing was great and the wives in our squadron got together often, especially for the holidays. Since Las Vegas is a big military town, there was a lot of support in the community. I never really felt alone with all those yellow ribbons everywhere, and I knew there was always somebody to talk to who understood.

It was almost two weeks after the guys left before we knew where to write them, and the letters took quite a while to get back and forth. I pretty much got a real short note every day just to say that everything was okay and he was doing fine. Around early November, I started getting a two-or-three-minute phone call about every two weeks. They went through the ham radios where you have to say "over" every time you finish talking. That became a joke among the wives: "I love you, over." "How are you doing, over."

I went home for the month of January 1991. As the deadline got closer and it seemed like something would happen, it was nice being home. Rob called me the night before his first combat flight to say, "Don't worry, everything's fine." I realize now that he knew something was going to happen.

I was on my way home at exactly 7:00 the next night when the guy on the radio said, "We are at war!" I got that real cold feeling all over. When I got home, we turned to CNN and got to see it firsthand like everybody else. I knew those first bombs had to be dropped on Baghdad by the Stealths. I couldn't say much and sat there praying everything would go okay and that Rob would come back safely.

Not even two minutes later, the phone started ringing off the hook as different friends called to encourage me. I told the kids when we said our prayers that night: "You knew Daddy was in Saudi and before they weren't fighting, they weren't in a war. But now they just started to fight so we really have to keep him in our prayers and pray that he'll be safe and God will take care of him." I was so proud of my kids, they took it so well. Sometimes kids handle life a lot better than adults.

I was glued to the TV during the first week of the war but that was too nerve-wracking. I decided to forget it and we flew back to Las Vegas to get back into our routine again. Support was the same though security tightened on the base. Otherwise, we kept to our school routine. Rob eventually got through with a real short call and said, "Don't worry—it works." He meant the stealth part worked. He started calling two or three times a week since he didn't have much time to write. I guess they weren't really allowed to call, but where there's a will there's a way with Rob. You know fighter pilots.

There were days during the war when I would get nervous and think, "Gosh, am I ever going to see him again? Does that plane really work?" Before the war, an article came out in the Las Vegas newspaper about the French picking up the plane on radar and that stealth really didn't work. I sent it to Rob in one of my letters but he said, "Don't worry. It does work and you don't have anything to worry about." I was confident that the airplane was doing the job it was supposed to do because Rob conveyed that through his phone calls and through his letters. I could see his confidence in the airplane. He knew the airplane best and told me not to worry.

I had just picked up my son from karate lessons in late February when President Bush came on the radio to say he'd just declared a cease-fire. I started screaming while driving down the street with the kids jumping up and down in the car! Right as I pulled into the house, Rob's parents called and we could barely talk to each other 'cause they were both crying and I was crying.

That was the greatest moment: to hear that there was a cease-fire. He was still alive!

Rob called three or four days after the cease-fire and told me they would probably be home in a couple weeks though he couldn't be specific. A couple weeks went by, and he said maybe in another couple weeks. Finally, eight Stealths came home on the first of April with the wing commander, the squadron commander, and a couple of other guys. Rob came home with the next group.

The homecoming was exciting. I was told they would land around 5:40 on Friday afternoon, so I had the whole day to get the house decorated and all that. But when I came back from aerobics around 12:30, there was a message saying they would land at 3:00. Oh my gosh! Panic city! We put balloons all over the outside of the house and hung a huge banner the kids and I made the night before: WELCOME HOME! YOU ARE OUR HERO! We had balloons everywhere, red, white, and blue balloons, and yellow ribbons. The counter tops were covered with all the gifts he'd missed from our anniversary, Christmas, Easter, even Halloween.

He was third off the airplane and we ran up to him and hugged him and kissed him! Rob couldn't get over how big the kids were but he'd been gone for eight months. His parents and I threw him a big surprise welcome home party two weeks later. We had relatives come in from Texas, Wisconsin, California, you name it. We made him open the door that Friday night and he was amazed at all the people who walked in. It was one big party the whole weekend.

There were a few things he had to get used to. For example, I'd traded both of our cars for a new Dodge van. When I let him drive it, Rob was so funny as he tried to figure out what all the switches did. But we mainly just hung around like everybody else who'd been gone so long, and he was happy to see that the house was still in one piece.

Rob showed me a very special letter his dad wrote:

Dear Robert, 28 FEB 1991
I started writing this letter (in my mind) at 4:30 A.M. today.

Neither Mother nor myself slept a wink last night because we were so elated and relieved that the cease-fire was declared.

There have been so many things I wanted to tell you in the past months and now is a good time to begin.

First, I want to tell you how very proud I am of you and the job you have done in Iraq. Although I wasn't flying with you, I have some appreciation of the courage and determination it takes to go on those kinds of missions night after night. And night after night, when we heard the news, I told Mother how lucky we are to have a son like you who is so unselfish to risk everything he has so that the rest of us (the world!) can live in peace. The debt we owe you can never be paid in full. All we can do is say THANK YOU.

Secondly, your place in Air Force history is firmly fixed. You and the other Stealth pilots will be honored as we have honored other great pilots such as the Flying Tigers, the Eagle Squadron in the Battle of Britain and many others. When the final story is told, I believe they will single out the Stealth as the key weapon that put Iraq out of the war before they could mount any kind of a coordinated air defense. But, as you well know, it wasn't just fancy high tech airplanes that did it. It still took pilots with lots of skill and plenty of guts to go out there alone every night and put the bombs on the target.

Thirdly, stay close and cherish the friendships and love you have with your squadron mates. In years to come, they will mean so much to you. Together you have experienced something that no one else, not even your family, can relate to. In future years, you will find that it is only them with whom you can really share what you have just gone through.

Fourthly, you and Millie will find it somewhat difficult to get your married life back to where it was. Everyone does. You have both been through a lot and have each made great sacrifices for which you consciously or unconsciously want recompense. It will cause some squabbles and take more time than you expect to get it all smoothed out. Just rely on the love you have for each other (and the children) and realize that time and caring will take care of all the problems.

I didn't mean this to be a long preachy letter but I did want to say "thank you" and to pass along some ideas. You and your friends have completely eradicated all that was wrongly heaped on the military from Vietnam. For that, I and all the vets of that war thank you again.

Take care, get home safely. We love you.

Dad

Part Four:

. . . And Then We're Going to Kill It. The Ground War

I saw a child's picture today
lying on the dirt floor
of a deserted Iraqi bunker.
It magnified the human side of war.
It could have been a picture
of one of my children,
if I had lived in a bunker.
It belonged to an Iraqi soldier who did,
and I saw it.
"He's got a picture of his kids in his wallet,
just like me,"
I used to say.
I saw the damn picture today
in a bunker
where men with children
waited to wage war.
It hurt me inside to see that picture.
Why didn't the guy just take it with him?
I came back to my hooch
and stared at the pictures of my children.

David Hafer   10 Mar 91
Air Force pilot
Kuwait City

14

In the Shadow of Death

Army Captain Mike Klingele deployed to the Gulf War as the commander of Charlie Company, 1st Battalion, 227th Aviation Regiment, First Cavalry Division, stationed at Fort Hood, Texas.

His Apache is arguably the most lethal attack helicopter in the world. Its eight laser-guided Hellfire[1] missiles could reach out 8000 meters while the 38 rockets and the 30mm gun gave his powerful machine plenty of close-in punch. The Apache's sensors displayed an infrared world on the pilot's helmet-mounted sight, giving it a better capability on the blackest night than lesser systems could manage during a clear day.

Captain Klingele is the only commander represented in this book, which highlights the fact that Army fliers become responsible for their people far sooner than do their counterparts in the other services. Through direct contact with both friendly and enemy troops, they also understand war on a human level that most jet pilots are thankfully spared.

Captain Klingele:

I was born in Quincy, Illinois, in February of 1960 to a very fundamental, basic, midwest Catholic family. I went to a Catholic school there

---

[1]Hellfire—Army's best, helicopter-launched, anti-armor missile. It homes in on a laser beam that's aimed by the launcher, an aeroscout, or any number of other lasers deployed across the battlefield.

through eighth grade and then moved to a public high school because they had a swimming team. I was going to try to pay for my college with my swimming skills. During my junior year, I got a letter from the swimming coach at West Point.

I knew nothing about West Point. I even thought the players in the Army-Navy football game were regular soldiers and sailors. So I went there on a recruiting trip to find out more about West Point, and that's what took me into the Army. I was leaning towards being an infantryman for the years I was at the Point, and then, for some reason, I went and got a flight physical. I decided to go aviation with infantry as my carrier branch. After one instructor assignment at West Point's Prep School, it was off to flight school.

Army rotary wing training starts off with about two weeks' of aeromedical stuff, and then aerodynamics, weather, and all the ground school stuff, before finally flying the TH-55, a Hughes 300. The flying was a joy and trying to hover was our first major challenge—the hard part.

We had a bunch of students out on this massive stage field, which was about the size of 20 football fields. We just ripped up the whole field, going wild all over and out of control, until finally the instructor pilots took the controls back to settle the aircraft down. Then they'd give it back to the student pilots and we'd go dancing all over the field again. Finally, we settled down and realized it wasn't that hard at all. From there, we transitioned to the UH-1 Huey for basic flying and the instrument stage.

My first flying tour was in Germany, where I flew aeroscouts[2] with the 4th Brigade (Aviation) of the 3rd Infantry Division. I came back to Ft. Rucker for the captain's course, the officer's advanced course, and got assigned to a research and development job. I wasn't too happy about that and tried to get an attack helicopter slot instead.

The Apache is an extremely sophisticated, high-speed aircraft, but, at the time, I wanted to fly the air cavalry mission that the Cobras were flying. It's also kind of an older, more vintage-model aircraft and requires a whole lot more finesse. So, for a variety of reasons, I asked for Cobras. The Army said, "No, but we'll be more than happy to give you an Apache." So I said okay (like I was going to say no?). I've been with the 1st Cavalry Division ever since.

I'd been there for about a year and a half when Kuwait was invaded. I was an Apache company commander with six Apaches, four

---

[2]aeroscouts—Helicopter scouts who search the battlefield and report back. They're the commander's eyes and, if teamed with attack helicopters, one of his most potent weapons. This mission is often flown by the OH-58 Kiowa.

Kiowa scouts, and 11 aircrews. Except for me and the two platoon leaders, all the pilots were warrant officers.

Kuwait was invaded while I was on leave after spending the month of May 1990 at the National Training Center[3]. At that point, we were still the only Apache unit to have ever gone there and really enjoyed some success. We'd come back for a major recovery phase in June and then more heavy training in July before I went on leave. I got home, saw all this crazy stuff happening on the news, and figured I'd be getting a phone call before too long. Sure enough, about two days later I got a call from my lieutenant, who said, "We've been alerted. It would probably be a pretty good idea for you to return." So I shot back to Ft. Hood and we got busy with the preparations for deployment.

We went to work on the extra training for that unexpected part of the world and obviously paid a little more attention to chemical defense. We went through a major helicopter gunnery exercise starting from individual work in the CMS[4] up through company live fire[5]. Money wasn't a problem all of a sudden, so we could meet all those unfinanced requirements that were normally left open.

There were a lot of mixed emotions during that prep period. Everybody was pretty pumped about deploying but there was also a very somber side. You realized that you were packing up for real that time and nobody knew what was ahead.

The 82nd Airborne Division went over first, I believe, and the 101st also went very early. Then the 24th Armored Division from Fort Stewart deployed just before us. We convoyed our support equipment and our ground vehicles down to the port at Houston and flew our aircraft there for loading on ships. We stayed on Fort Hood for about two more weeks before flying out on a 747 on September 28th.

For the first 10 days in Saudi, we were housed at the port, in big warehouses, waiting for our equipment to arrive. The heat was just unbelievable. I think all you could do was sit there and sweat because it was running up between 110 and 120 degrees in the middle of the day.

Then we went right out into the middle of nowhere. We're talkin' a 100 miles west of Daharan, Saudi Arabia, out in the desert where there's absolutely nothing. That's where we set up. There was a north-south-running two-lane highway, period. Actually, it was in an area where the

---

[3]National Training Center—NTC. Army's desert warfare training area at Fort Irwin, California. It covers nearly all of the Mojave Desert between Barstow and Death Valley.

[4]CMS—Combat mission simulator. AH-64 Apache simulator. Ultimate video game.

[5]live fire—Practice with real weapons and ammunition versus simulated, or dry, training. A company live fire includes all the unit's weapons firing together.

terrain went from very, very flat to pretty rugged, but there was still just miles and miles, as far as you could see or ever wanted to see, of brown sand. That's all there was.

The sand and the dirt was obviously kind of an enemy because it was terribly, terribly abrasive to the aircraft, more so than the sand at NTC. So the biggest headache was definitely maintenance.

It was also very powdery in our area. I mean, you'd get your stuff halfway clean (there was an accepted level of cleanliness there that normally would be terribly dirty) and then the winds would kick up. By the evening, everything you had would be covered with sand and dirty again. The sand was dirty. It was just endless brown blowing sand. It was just unbelievable, and it never ended.

To get there, we sent our ground convoy out a day early, and they made the trip to our grid coordinates in the sand. We then flew to our grid coordinates and there sat our trucks. We just picked a spot in the sand and landed. Starting from ground zero, we established communications with higher headquarters, secured the area defensively, and started building what we were going to live in, which, for us, was just basic tentage.

When we got to the desert, it was the same temperature-wise, but the humidity wasn't there. Fortunately, we'd made sure that all our tents had liners in them to help a little bit with the heat. Those were an absolute necessity because, if you didn't have a liner, your tent literally baked you. The normal routine was to get up in the morning and put the flaps up to get any kind of cool breeze going through because between about one and three in the afternoon, it was just ungodly hot.

We weren't sure what was going on at home. When we left, people weren't rallying yet like we understood they did after a period of time. A couple guys brought shortwave radios that could pick up the BBC, so we'd get some info from them. After a while, the *Armed Forces Radio Network* put up a radio station we could monitor. We got a lot of good information from that. Then there were letters from home and a lot of Any Service Member mail. Those letters were great. Some guys were far more conscientious about writing than the rest of us. They'd get a letter, read it, and sit down to write back. Quite a few pen pals were established, and I think a couple girlfriends were found. It was really great to get letters from kids and adults as well saying, "Hey, we're behind you!" That really meant a lot.

I had one girl write me and, as I read her first letter, I would have said it was the writing of maybe an eight-year-old. But the letter went on and on about who she was and about her family and how she had graduated from high school. She wrote, I'm 21 years old. I kind of thought, "Is this some kind of joke? What is this?" Then her second to last line was, "I won a bronze medal in the Special Olympics last week." I'll tell you, I almost started crying right there. It was just quite a letter and obviously caused me to do some inner soul-searching. I wrote her back and I mean she was absolutely faithful in her writing. I'd send her a letter and she'd write me back right now! and she'd write me again and again and again. Her letters followed me all the way through. It was really sweet.

Our mail was pushed out to the division and then our mail clerk would go there to pick it up. There were sometimes literally truckloads of mail. That was always something that was really kind of neat because the clerks started making multiple runs to handle it all. So our clerk would go get the mail with a little detail of men, come back, and sort it. I could pick up my field phone to the platoons anytime, day or night, and say, "Hey, mail's in, can I get a detail to go pick it up?" I always had volunteers there *right now*, ready to go; mail call was the highlight of the day.

It's not that we were bored, because we literally had so much work to do. Maintaining the aircraft and sustaining life out in the middle of nowhere in the desert required most of our time. Essentially, we got up at around 0630 to clean up and grab some breakfast. The dining facility was just a bunch of burners and ovens in a tent with a dust floor. If breakfast wasn't MREs, the little meals in a bag, it would be T-rations. Those are like big 10-man cans of something resembling the old C-rations, where scrambled eggs, for example, would come in a highly processed blob. The cook would cut you off a 3-inch cube of it. But any hot breakfast was a good breakfast. Then we'd get started on the life functions that were very difficult. Things like the water detail, shit-burning details, guard requirements, and mess hall cleanup took a lot of time.

You just kind of prevailed, you just drove on. Living was difficult but that was just living. You couldn't really ponder on that. The conditions were miserable, but I'm sure our conditions were better than the infantry guys or the Marines over in Kuwait who lived in dirt holes. Don't get me wrong—we had it a lot better than they did. We realized that and fully appreciated it. We lived on a dirt floor with a cot and the same sleeping bag for months. Luxury was having electricity, lights in your tent, powered by a generator that you had to constantly service. The Saudis contracted for wooden, three-stall showers with a tank on top that you poured water in. If things were going well, we got to take a quick rinse down, lather up, rinse off shower once every two days. It was usually cold as hell. It wasn't bad in the summer but it got cold in the winter. I'll tell you what, there was some shivering and squealing going on! It's pretty bad when you start dreading going and taking a shower but you know you have to.

The nearest phones were about an hour away. They were in a tent with tons of phones and you were scheduled for blocks of time. My unit would have, say, from two in the morning to four in the morning once every two weeks. You'd get 15 minutes on the phone. I realize my sister Vicki didn't think that was good enough. It was a no-win situation, who did you call? I've got three sisters, a mom and dad, and a brother, and my roommate Mary as well. I frequently called Mary because then it would get out on the network—everything. They were wired tight; they knew my every move.

Life was basic, absolutely basic.

The maintenance guys would jump on the helicopters in the morning and just go to town. I could talk to you for days on the problems they had. The eroding of the blades from sand was a significant problem, both main rotor and tail rotor. And any part of the aircraft that used the pressurized air system on the Apache was a big problem. The aircraft takes in outside air, pressurizes it, and uses it for a lot of the systems. That was a delicate system that really was affected by the dust.

The Army got those incredibly wonderful readiness statistics by drastically reducing the amount of flying we could do. And there was some creative maintenance. But we also had a captive audience, so to speak. Except for those life-function details, the crew chiefs were always available to maintain the aircraft. That helped. Long term, it took about twice as many maintenance manhours to fly the aircraft as it would in a normal environment. We had many of the same problems at NTC, but you don't see the long-term affects there. The OH-58[6] scouts did quite well overall since it's a very simple aircraft. The engines took it hard and the tail rotor blades took it a little harder than the Apaches, but, other than that, the aircraft did very well.

Once we were in place, our first objective was to develop individual and crew proficiency in that environment. When you start messing around with a helicopter in the sand, especially one like an Apache that weighs upwards of 16,000 pounds and has a pretty high rotor velocity, it gets exciting. That's especially true when you're working night vision systems and you try to land in the middle of your own dust cloud. I sent two instructor pilots out together on the first night flight because we'd experienced really exciting night system desert landings at NTC. The sand blows in the rotor wash[7] and obscures everything just as you try to set down.

They went out and did some work in the desert to get the feel of the system, see what visual cues were there, etc., so they could come

---

[6]OH-58 Kiowa—Small, single-engined, four-place utility helicopter. See aeroscout.

[7]rotor wash—Downward blast of air created by a helicopter's rotor.

back and brief us before we went out. We did everything we thought possible to give them visual cues for landing. We had blue landing zone lights on bean bags set out in an inverted Y shape. The pilot shoots his approach to the open end of the Y and could judge position and relative rates of closure.

It's kind of comical to look back on that first landing now. The crew chief stood about 50 feet in front of the point where they were supposed to land and tried to guide them in with his wands[8]. They flew their approach very slowly and very deliberately, actually well-executed, until they started to become obscured at about 30 feet above the ground and 100 meters from landing. That's normal, but, due to the fact that the sand seemed to be extra powdery, they were just completely enveloped. So essentially, we had an aircraft on a controlled approach crash path until they ended up getting to a point where they decided to abort the landing. They were going kind of sideways, crooked, and in all kinds of different directions.

Imagine, in that ball of dust with an aircraft coming down and the few little bean bag lights disappearing, you see two wands waving. Then they begin waving a little more furiously until finally, you see two wands fall down on the ground and a kid come running out of there. We all joked about that later and decided that the ground guide probably wasn't a good idea. But anyway, to make a long story short, they actually got the aircraft down on the ground after their eighth approach. I thought that was pretty good. A night vision system desert approach was one of the most challenging things we had to do. They learned a lot of lessons.

So we got everybody to the point where they could put the aircraft down in the desert on the night system without any problems . . . well, in a relatively safe manner anyway.

We got through the local area orientation and worked up to crew proficiency again. Then we started working teams where I'd send two aircraft out together. The scouts trained for reconnaissance. They'd gain and maintain contact[9] with the enemy and then hand over the target to the Apaches before moving to protect the flanks. They also focused on navigation because, in that massive area, you don't have any trees or creeks or anything to speak of. They got really good at time, distance, and heading[10], plus navigating at night. They could do some amazing things with a map. We also did some very limited gunnery.

---

[8]wands—Flashlights fitted with white plastic cones used to guide pilots at night.

[9]contact—To meet the enemy. Contact can mean anything from electronic detection to monitoring from a scout helicopter to fighting it out in the trenches.

[10]time and heading navigation—By flying in a known direction for a known time at a set speed, you can, theoretically, find your way around. But it's far from easy, and every low-altitude pilot has gotten hopelessly lost that way at one time or another.

A couple of us went to King Fahd Air Base, where the A-10s were, and did some JAAT[11] coordination with the folks there. We came back and flew probably half a dozen dry[12] JAATs but never got to use it in a real fight.

In the meantime, we jumped forward up by KKMC (King Khalid Military City). We had a definite defensive mission with companies up on the border all the time. We began practicing our unit's battle drills.

You could kind of tell from the news over the radio that things were happening, but we didn't know ahead of time that the air war was starting. Initially, we just continued to do our mission. The radio station went to constant broadcasting, you know, constant interviews and stuff. So needless to say, we were glued to the radio that first day. You didn't miss it. The initial reports we were getting were very, very favorable, so everybody was psyched about that. The guys were glad that we were doing something 'cause maybe that meant we'd get out of there sooner. All the reports we heard were just wonderful, but we were sad that it came to that point.

We weren't in it yet but that didn't cause any problems. It was the air war, the Air Force air war. That's how we looked at it.

As the war progressed, what we saw of support from home was just unbelievable, overwhelming. We only heard it over the radio, in magazines, and in letters, but you knew the support was just overwhelming, it was just unbelievable. That was *really* important, that was really important . . .

Then we jumped forward again up closer to the Iraqi border. We moved forward because the ground elements were moving forward—it was a function of staging for our next series of missions. We stayed with our division and were integrated into their plan.

We continued to do whatever training we could and to work the aircraft over to get them totally prepared. We were assigned several missions that we planned and then executed in a rehearsal fashion, well south of the border. One of them was going to be our first mission across into Iraq, where we'd cross friendly lines at about 0200. That's when the moon was completely down, completely dark. It was so dark in the desert that, if the moon wasn't up, it was difficult to find your aircraft

---

[11]JAAT—Joint air attack team. Attack helicopters and jets (usually A-10s) fighting together. Coordinated, rehearsed attack by helicopters and jets. Since the defense against helicopters with anti-tank missiles is very different from the defense against jets using cannons, missiles, and cluster bombs, the target is faced with the impossible job of switching tactics every 90 seconds or so. A real meat grinder.

[12]dry—Without weapons. A dry attack is simulated; in a hot attack, a practice or live weapon is released.

parked out in the dirt. You couldn't even see your hand in front of your face, which is the perfect Apache fighting environment. So we were to do a cross FLOT[13] mission approximately 10 kilometers into Iraq, hit some preprogrammed targets and some targets of opportunity, and egress back out to the assembly area.

We were told that we were going to fly that mission for real during early morning on February 25th. That's what we briefed, that's what we planned, you know, we went through all the planning and briefing for the early morning of the 25th.

Our mission changed and we were briefed that our crossing of friendly lines was supposed to be at 0700 on February 25th. Based on some of the information we had, that would've been okay. As it turned out, there was a good bit more resistance waiting there for us than we had anticipated or had been briefed. That mistake created some of the problems.

We planned a battalion mass attack, which meant the battalion would fly all 18 Apaches if possible. Seventeen of them were operational for that day, so Alpha company flew five Apaches and several '58s, Bravo company had six Apaches plus several '58s, and Charlie company, which was us, had six Apaches and four '58 scouts.

It was misting and overcast and gloomy. It was just a really nasty day with visibility running about 4 kilometers in our sector when we made our 0630 pitch pull[14]. We departed our assembly area, hit our pre-programmed route, and made our way towards our passage point. Upon hitting the passage point, we dropped off the scouts and proceeded Apaches only, with the battalion in line abreast formation and each company heading for its assigned sector. It was very important to maintain contact with your sister element, your flank element, meaning Bravo with Alpha and Charlie with Bravo.

Our scouts were not going to go forward of friendly lines because they're not as survivable as Apaches, especially during daylight. Their mission was to stop at friendly lines and wait there. They had a variety of sub-missions, such as downed pilot pickup. If one of our aircraft went down, there were two scouts designated to come forward to help rescue the crew. We also had two aircraft with sub-missions of dealing with surrendering Iraqis.

So we hit the passage point right on time. The artillery preparation

---

[13]FLOT—Forward line of troops. Imaginary line drawn along the positions of the friendly troops who are closest to the enemy.

[14]pitch pull—To lift a helicopter off the ground. Helicopter lift is controlled by changing the pitch, or angle, of the rotor blades. To take off, a pilot increases blade pitch by pulling on the lever that controls pitch.

preceded us and stopped on schedule. We started moving through our sectors and made contact. Several problems faced us right away. The minute those Iraqis saw us, some of them started coming out of their foxholes and surrendering while the guy next to 'em was sitting there trying to hose 'ya. Some guys were running around like crazy men, the whole gambit. We'd been briefed that there were some specific areas of resistance that had certain elements or pieces of equipment. Not much at all. We just expected some specific little pockets of resistance to focus on. But when we got in there, we found literally thousands of infantry dudes in a very, very thorough, deliberate, interwoven, mutually supportive defensive position. It was quite a bit more than we'd expected.

That first group of infantry was their forward element, their observation posts. Then they had their initial line of defense. Further back, at about the limit of our visibility, right at about 4 kilometers, we could see some hard targets[15]: some ZSU 23-4s, some tanks, some armored vehicles, several support vehicles, and some other equipment. Our report on that stuff to our higher headquarters surprised them 'cause it was so different from our Intell.

So there we were having a great morning so far. We dealt with all the dudes surrendering, we dealt with the dudes shooting us. We engaged some of their built-up positions, where they had heavy machine guns and things like that, with our rockets and 30mm cannon. We also engaged deeper into the hard targets.

I was in the front seat commanding the company and working our Hellfire system. Chief Warrant Officer Four Michael Butler was in the back seat, flying the aircraft. He had the gun slaved to his helmet's monocle eyepiece so that the gun was always pointed where he looked. I selected Hellfire missiles because I was hitting the hard targets in the distance—we were shooting different targets at the same time.

We had Iraqi infantry running crazy, laying on the ground, waving white flags, waving pieces of paper. Like good Americans, we didn't shoot anyone who appeared to be trying to surrender. We only focused on the dudes who were trying to bring us down. I mean, it got really interesting. There was a bunker line out about 3 or 4000 meters with a bunch of dudes going back and forth on the bunkers moving ammo. We shot rockets at them. Those guys knew the rockets were coming, but, and it was the most amazing thing I ever saw, all they did was lay down on the ground. After the rockets came in and blew up around them, they casually got back up and continued on with their business. Apparently, through all their fighting, they'd been hit by a bunch of rocket engage-

---

[15]hard target—Armored or reinforced object, such as tanks or bunkers.

ments and were almost casual about it. It was absolutely amazing. There was a simple solution to that—we just went up guns. There wasn't much they could do to beat the effects of the gun so that ended that problem.

It was going pretty much like NTC so far, except for all the gomers trying to surrender. I mean, having a bunch of shit come up at 'ya is a little different than laser tag but, all in all, it was normal. Things were a little more confusing 'cause we had a bunch of people out there wanting to surrender, but there wasn't much we could do about them.

The battalion commander told us to continue to our next battle position and then it was like a damn Rambo movie. Shit just started going off everywhere. There were main tank rounds[16] coming at helicopters, there was artillery everywhere, there were surface-to-air missiles everywhere, there was small arms fire everywhere. I mean, it just turned into a veritable hailstorm. Instantly. I wouldn't say it was a trap but we sure hit their trigger line or somethin'. It turned into a down-and-dirty fight.

I could see the six aircraft from Charlie company and the six aircraft from Bravo, but I really couldn't see Alpha due to the visibility. There were Hellfires flying off of all of them, rockets blasting, guns blasting, you know, it was just a variety of weapon systems going all out.

Our last Hellfire shot was typical. The target was a bastardized T-62.[17] It looked like a T-55[18] chassis with a '62 turret and barrel system. He was in my sector so he popped up as my target.

There are grips on either side of the target acquisition system TV screen in the front cockpit with triggers and buttons and switches all over them. It's purely a gunner's position and has nothing to do with the flying of the aircraft. The left side is for the weapons control and laser, while the right side is actually where you have your trigger and stuff like that. So it was a typical engagement where I put the crosshairs at the seam of the turret and the chassis. If you hit there, you can split the turret from the chassis. I announced to my back seater, "I have a target." He had the video screen in his cockpit set up to my picture so he could see everything that I was looking at, which is normal. It was out around 3000 meters away so we were outside the tank's range.

I pulled the left trigger, which sent out both the laser range finder and a laser designator. The missile-ready signal flashed up in the lower right hand portion of my screen, meaning the missile was looking at the

---

[16]main tank round—Canon projectile fired by a tank. A tank has a large cannon in the middle, the main gun, plus heavy machine guns. A main tank round is the 105mm+ shell fired by the main gun.

[17]T-62—1960s Soviet main battle tank.

[18]T-55—1950s Soviet main battle tank.

laser spot on the tank. Mike had to get the nose of the aircraft turned about 6 or 8 degrees to the right to get everything lined up within limits. Then I just pulled the trigger on my right hand grip. A missile came off of the right rail with an awesome explosion. It's just like there's something ripping off the side of the aircraft—it's a major explosion. I focused on the TV screen to make sure my laser spot stayed right where it was supposed to be.

The Hellfire hit the target in the left front seam of the turret. A T-55 or T-62 compared to Hellfire is no match. It just popped the turret right off the tank. The turret popped up and kind of flipped over and fell off to the side. The crew had seen a couple of other tanks around them go up in smoke and realized that they could do nothing about it, so they'd already jumped out. That seemed to happen fairly frequently, especially on night missions. When, all of a sudden, shit would start blowing up all around them, they would just get out and run. That's logical, it doesn't make too much sense to sit there in a tank when other tanks are blowing up and you don't know why. At those kind of ranges, they couldn't hear or see anything.

As the fight developed, I was gettin' less and less comfortable about our relative position. I didn't know the status of Alpha and Bravo but I knew we were in trouble. I keyed my uniform radio[19], which is what I controlled the company on, at the same time that I had a ZSU targeted for the next Hellfire. I was going hose it at the same time that I was going to tell the company to get the hell out of there: "Now! Egress immediately!"

As I keyed the mike, my back seater said, "I've got a flash at 10 o'clock." He started to turn the nose to the 10 o'clock position. I was still tracking the ZSU, 'cause my tracking system is independent of the aircraft, and keying the mike to get the company out of there. Then there was a violent rip in the aircraft from the missile impact.

The missile went into the number one engine on the left side, went through the center of the aircraft, and out the number two engine. The mike was already keyed so I called, "WE'RE HIT, WE'RE HIT!" Our wingman looked over and saw the explosion. We were at about 20 knots forward air speed and at about 40 feet above the ground when that happened. The aircraft immediately pitched a little bit nose low and was spun off to the left with no engine power.

I went into the classic slow-motion routine that seems to happen to everybody who's shot down. I looked at my caution warning panel and saw most of the 40 lights come on like a Christmas tree, just one light af-

---

[19]uniform radio—Radios are referred to by their frequency band. Since "U" is the first letter in ultra high frequency, or UHF, "uniform" is the shorthand term for that radio.

ter another. The aircraft started rolling over to the right, so Mr. Butler[20] put in right pedal to try to swing the nose to the right and put in full left and aft cyclic[21] to level the aircraft as much as possible. There was a little response to it but not much. The rotor RPM was obviously starting to decay, so he left the rotor pitch right where it was. Just before impacting the ground, he used the remaining rotor RPM to try to cushion the impact.

We hit nose low, rolling to the right and with the nose canted off about 20 degrees to the left. We slammed down hard. The landing struts and the seats collapsed like they're designed to do in a crash. All I remember is watching the impact happen until the side of the aircraft slammed onto the ground. At that point, my brain said, "Wow, this really really hurts!" and I blacked out.

When I came to, we were upside down, all the glass was gone in the aircraft, and I had already started unsnapping the harness. I fell to the ground, crawled out onto the sand, and turned to my back seater, who was stuck in the aircraft. His survival vest or something had become hung up in the wreckage. In the fog of it all, I just grabbed the front of his flight suit and started tugging on him in desperation to pull him out. He finally broke free and fell onto the ground.

I quickly looked him over; his right side, his arm and stuff, was cut up pretty good and he had blood all down his right side. So I looked right at him, I was holding his right hand with my right hand like shaking it, and said, "Are you okay?" He said, "Yeah, I'm okay."

At about that time, Lt. Rob Johnston and CW2 Ed Sanderline, our wingmen, crossed right over our heads and landed between us and the enemy. They laid down 30mm suppression fire while shielding us with their chopper. Another two-aircraft team swung in behind us and started putting in suppressive fire over the top of us. That must have been a pretty impressive roar with all those weapons firing, but it didn't register. It was there in the background, but it didn't register.

Mike took off running to the aircraft that landed. I reached down to pick up my map and some cards that had fallen off of my knee board, all the classified stuff. As I picked it up, there was a big puff of sand about three inches from my hand. It was then that I realized, "Those dudes are shooting at us! No shit!" I looked over and saw six machine

---

[20]Warrant officers are addressed as "Mister."

[21]right pedal and left cyclic—A helicopter's nose can be moved with the pedals on the floor while its roll is controlled with the cyclic (the stick to ordinary pilots) that sticks up through the floor. In this case, the Apache was turning left and rolling right, so the pilot used the right pedal to move the nose back to the right and the cyclic to counteract the roll.

guns and about 20 or 30 rifles 300 meters away in a trench line. How we didn't get hit I can't tell you 'cause they were just rocking and rolling! They were really pumping the lead out. It finally registered, "We probably ought to get out of here!"

That's when I ran up to our wingman's Apache. I went to the left wing and Mike went to the right wing. We climbed up on the wings and snapped onto the homemade lifelines we'd installed there. The Apache took off and flew us back 5 kilometers to a safe area. That was a heck of a ride with the two of us hanging onto the wings of the Apache. I remember tilting my head down so the helmet streamlined as opposed to trying to rip my head off. It was kind of a blur.

The scouts heard the call that we'd been hit so the two aircraft that were designated for downed pilot rescue had already started blasting forward. They met us at the rally point and flew Mike back to the Black Hawk that had a doctor on it. I got into the other scout since it was also my backup command and control aircraft in case my Apache went down. I called the company back to the forward area refueling point where we rearmed and refueled. We still had a job to do.

We got rearmed, refueled, and handed off to the ground armor brigade commander. They had their scouts out a little ahead of 'em and they had the Bradleys[22] and the M-1 tanks deployed on line. We stayed anywhere from a couple hundred meters to about a thousand meters behind them depending on how their formation was set up and where the lanes to fire between them were. It was a beautiful combination. We could talk back and forth with them and we could see out further than them 'cause we flew at about 40 feet or so. We could see quite a ways out there, especially with our optics, and report back what we saw, what we didn't see, what was going on. In one case, his scouts were going into what appeared to be a trap 'cause of the way the fire trenches were aligned and where the Iraqi infantry was. I called the commander and said, "Hey, we've got a visual on the enemy and they're waiting for your scouts." He called the scouts back closer to him, and the trench went up in flames minutes later.

A fire trench was a meter or meter-and-a-half wide, about a meter deep and, before they were burnt, there was just a thick black tar down in the bottom. The Iraqis would light that and you'd get a flame that was maybe 5 or 6 feet high and a huge line of smoke. Those trenches were anywhere from a couple hundred meters to a thousand meters long, so you'd essentially get a wall of fire and smoke.

The armored vehicle's thermal sights had a hard time seeing through the flames, but we'd come up a little bit higher to where we could see

---

[22]Bradley—U.S. Army's newest armored personnel carrier. Replaced the M-113.

right through the smoke. We could see dudes running around back there, lightin' trenches, moving equipment, and stuff like that. We'd fire right through it with our 30mm guns and rockets. The tankers and Bradleys would watch our fire go in and then they would fire into that sector too. So you'd get a big volume of fire that really was quite effective.

That battle went on for about four more hours until about 1300. Then we got pulled back to our assembly area because our big deception mission was over. That whole battle up the Wadi al Batin, right in the tri-border area along the border of Kuwait and Iraq, was a feint. We wanted them to think our major push was coming through there. Our mission was to go and make a major demonstration and make them think that that was where the main coalition attack was coming.

We were told our mission was successful because Saddam, in fact, sent as many as three divisions down to that sector when he saw us coming in. The real push was at least 80 miles to the west, so we went into reserve.

We waited, waited, waited, waited until all of a sudden, at the last minute, they said, "Go now! West and up!" We raced across the desert into Iraq following the path of destruction left by the Seventh Corps.

In a couple spots, there was some pretty amazing carnage. I mean, burned out hulks and tanks all over the place. The rest was empty desert. When we got to a spot south of Basra, and I mean literally in the middle of nowhere, they held us again. During that first night at assembly area John, we had nothing but helicopters. We slept on the ground or in our helicopters. No tents, no nothing. Our ground convoy caught up the next day. It was raining, cold, and nasty and finally I said; "Look, we've got to get some kind of shelter even if we have to take it down again in an hour." We ended up staying there for seven days. We were briefed that Schwarzkopf was holding us to come down like a hammer on the Republican Guard if they had any fight left in them.

One guy had a shortwave radio that could pick up the BBC, so we monitored that all the time. That's where we started hearing the bit about the talk of cease-fire and all that kind of stuff. The guys were pleased. Everybody was very pleased. We eventually went to work destroying abandoned equipment.

We finally went back down to a big assembly area in Saudi that the division recovered into. We started maintaining and repairing equipment until we were finally called down to the port. When the ships were loaded, we went to Khobar Towers down in the city of Khobar near Daharan. It was a huge development for something like 27,000 people that the Saudi government had built for the Bedouins. None of them moved in and it sat vacant for eight years. The whole place was empty so Army units moved through it on the way home.

We flew out on 17 April aboard a 747 "freedom bird." I was the plane load commander, which turned out to be the easiest job you could ever have. First of all, no one was going to be late for any of the manifesting or anything like that. You could bet your life that nobody was going to miss that flight. No complaining or anything, which was a first in the Army. Anytime I needed anything, I never had a single problem. Everybody was right there ready to help 'cause, if it meant getting on the plane a minute earlier, that's all that mattered.

The TWA crew was wonderful. When the plane started taxiing, everybody was psyched and there was a little bit of applause. We started our takeoff run and, when that baby rotated and lifted off the ground, the plane just roared. I mean, everybody cheered!

We flew to Gray Army Airfield at Ft. Hood, Texas. We downloaded the airplane, dropped off our weapons and all of our sensitive items like night vision goggles. We got on buses and made the 12-mile drive from Gray Army airfield back to main post. Along the route, there were just thousands of people cheering and hollering with banners and all kinds of really neat stuff. At the gymnasium, the old cavalry horse platoon we have was outside spinning around, shooting their rifles, and there were thousands of people standing around yelling and screaming. Then we marched into the gymnasium, which was all full of banners, and the bleachers were just full of people. The announcer said, "Here are your Desert Storm heroes!"

They dropped the rope barrier and people came screaming out of the stands: It was nothing but people crying and kissing and hugging and families. It was cool.

I felt great. My mom was the first one to see me, she was the first one to grab me, and then my sisters, then my dad. It was cool. We just bawled our eyes out, just bawled our eyes out. I always catch hell for being cold, but once you climb in the cockpit and close that canopy, all that other stuff has to disappear, it has to. It's just too damn busy and too dangerous in there to bring any emotional baggage along. And then they call us cold fish. The first thing Mary said was, "I never thought I'd ever see the day you'd cry."

That was a really, really good reunion, really good.

I got home and just wanted to lay around and be normal for a while. It was weird. I had literally lived in a tent with a dirt floor for seven months, so things like refrigerators, running water, toilets, they were a novelty. We'd had a latrine where you shit in a cut-off 55-gallon drum and then every day you had a shit-burning detail. We're talking basic life. Just having a carpeted floor was all of a sudden a luxury. Having lights that you didn't have to go out and start the generator for was also a luxury, it was wonderful!

It was quite a while before I could get out to see my sister Vicki in California. I went out and visited her and then went to the school where she taught kindergarten and first grade. I guess she had used my situation a lot in teaching, and they could also see her and read her emotions during the war, so the kids were waiting for me. The minute I walked in, they went crazy. It was really fun and I tried to be real close with them. They literally swarmed me, just physically climbed all over me. There were 20 or 30 kids and every single one of them wanted to be the kid on my lap. We'd sit down on the floor to have a little reading time or something, and they would literally maul me, which was really kind of cute.

They asked me about absolutely everything. "What did you do? How did you live?" The boys all asked me, "Did you kill anybody?" They were all excited about that. I just said, "Oh I don't know, I don't know if I did or not." Even the boys were amazingly affectionate. They just wanted to come up and hug me and hold me.

It was really kind of cool, really kind of cool.

Vicki Fontinel is part of a very close-knit, traditional family. Their lives changed dramatically when her kid brother went to war.

Vicki Fontinel:

I grew up in Quincy, Illinois, which is a little farm community right on the Mississippi River with about 50 or 60,000 people. Ours is a Catholic family, and I went to a Catholic grade school and high school before going away to college. The family is real close. We're all spread out now, but we're still real close at holidays or any time. We're on the phone all the time.

I now live in California with my two small girls. I'm a kindergarten teacher at Murwood School in Walnut Creek and have been for about 12 years.

I'm very close to Mike.

All five kids were home with my parents in the Ozarks on a vacation we had planned for early August 1990. All of us were going to be home for that week. My dad had been struggling with leukemia, so we knew that a family get-together like that was going to be important. We'd all just gotten down to the Ozarks when Kuwait was invaded. I guess they were calling the troops back without knowing who was going first 'cause Mike got a phone call that said he needed to go back to Ft. Hood. I remember my mom started to cry and my sisters started to cry and I started to cry. Mike was up about it.

My one sister can really cry, she can really get hysterical. She's also a veterinarian and Mike said: "You know Joanne, picture yourself in med school and you've been preparing for a surgery. You're really prepared, you're really good at it, and finally the opportunity comes where they've chosen you to do the surgery. Yeah, you're scared shitless, but it's your time, and you're thrilled to death." He said, "That's how I feel. It's my time."

My sister's so funny, she said, "Yeah, but there's no little liver or kidney going to sit up and start shooting at me when I do my surgery!" So we all laughed about that, but he was excited and, you know, ready to go, enthusiastic. We were really scared; I'm glad we were together.

The rest of us stayed in the Midwest for that week of vacation. That was kind of strange because our thoughts were with him. We didn't know if he was going to have to go right away or not. But the week went by and he hadn't gone yet, so Mary went back to Spokane where she's a nurse, my youngest brother Chris went back to work in a hospital, and the girls and I came back to California.

Mike stayed in Ft. Hood for a couple of months, I guess, before he was actually sent.

So then our school routine started but, you know, that underlying concern was still there. We thought about him every day. We talked about him. But there's so much I don't remember. It's like, I don't know where the memory is. You could ask me about something very specific and say, "Don't you remember? You did this, this, and this?" I don't remember, it's just gone, so I couldn't really even say exactly when he went. I guess I blocked it all out.

My mom and dad called to say Mike was gone. My parents are very private people, especially my dad. Emotions weren't talked about a whole lot. They're strong, real strong, and there's a lot of internal stuff going on that you just don't know about. They were just real matter-of-fact. They're both very prayerful people too, you know, so we talked of turning to prayer now that it was out of our hands.

Mike can be real matter-of-fact too. Everything was very calculated; he was packed and ready to go and everything was okay.

My whole focus became different—it was on him. He was in my thoughts all the time and we constantly watched CNN. As the news of my brother being there filtered out in the community of friends, at church, and at school, the support system began to build up with everyone asking and everyone caring. The focus became even more intense as life became wrapped up in caring for him, worrying about him, sending him letters, giving him support.

We did hear from him quite a bit and other people who were writing him heard a lot from him too. He was real matter-of-fact when writing thanks for the support. I kept saying, "Is there anything I can send you?" I remember at one point he said, "I'm being really well taken care of, there are lots of letters, lots of food, but there was one thing I need." He said, "I need hangers." I remember writing back saying, "You drive me crazy! You need to have your shirts hung up?! Where are your priorities?" He's very organized and everything was just right in its place. He later told me how it was easier to live with things in their homemade furniture than back in the bags.

There weren't a whole lot of emotions in his letters. He talked a lot about missing the family and how important we were to him, but he's much like my parents in that he doesn't talk easily about those things. I hear pilots are bred that way.

I'm sure I learned that war broke out from CNN. I worried immediately that Mike was involved in that first part and then I remember feeling a little safety after hearing that he wasn't. I said to my dad: "Now he's a captain, right Dad? He's in administration, right? They're not going to send him out first are they? He's going to be back making decisions . . . ?" And my dad said, "No, Vicki, he's the one that will be leading his men." I remember getting extremely bent out of shape over that, just shaking, just totally, physically, breaking out in shakes.

I spent a lot of that time in my own living room with my kids watching me cry. They saw me crying a lot while CNN was on. It got to the point where we walked in from school, it went on, and they became sick of it. Little kids hate news on TV.

Of course, the first part was a jet war, not a helicopter war. I relied on Caroline, another teacher at my school, for a lot of those explanations because of her husband. He was almost like having a military briefing person explaining everything to us. So he would explain it to her and she would explain it to me. I knew that her son was in combat before Mike was. I'd met Scott maybe twice. I was extremely worried about Caroline from watching her. With my family being so far away, I'd have to say that she's my mother figure here, and I love her like a mother. She's a wonderful woman. So it was tough watching the stress that she was coping with, and seeing her perspective as a mom also showed me what my mom was going through. At that point, I was probably a little more focused on Scott and worrying about him since Mike wasn't flying in the war yet.

I'm sure my daughters knew what was going on. Nicole was 11 and Lauren was 8, so they were well aware. I talked about it a lot and there were times when they got scared by watching me. Kids handle stress differently, and they would escape from the whole thing. They'd go out and ride their bikes to get away from what was going on. They cared a lot and I knew they were real scared right with me.

A lot of that concern was uncertainty caused by the way personal information from Mike came back to us. Mike had a roommate, Mary

Barton, renting a room from him. They became very good friends. She stayed at his house during the war and kind of ran things for him. She had a lot of ties with the military 'cause she worked on base and she was friends with some of Mike's buddies' wives. When she got information, she called my parents. She called me quite a lot too. She was really good in that, when she found out something, it got back to us. But it wasn't always factual. So there were times when we felt like we were up and down on a roller coaster. She kept saying, "That's what I heard. I'm doing the best I can but I don't know for sure." That rumor mill was how we got information.

For example, when Mike was shot down, it originally came back to her that his hand had been blown off and his pilot was wounded too. That wasn't true. There was a hand injury a week or two after he was shot down, but it was a small accident. It had nothing to do with fighting and was after the war. So bits and pieces like that just weren't true. We also didn't find out that Mike was shot down until two weeks afterward.

I didn't really know what Mike was doing during the air war. I never talked to Mike, though my parents did and Mary did. I was thinking he was on standby—I really didn't know what he was doing.

My day started in prayer for him for at least an hour. I woke up thinking about him, praying for him. I read my Bible more than usual during that time. Then I watched CNN before I went to work.

Once I got to school, Mike was there, practically. The faculty knew about him and asked every day; parents knew about him and asked every day. My children in my classroom knew about him. My class adopted his company; we wrote to them, and we sent Christmas packages to them. We heard back from individual soldiers, so there was always the question, "Who got a letter? Let's read the letter." Then we'd come home and watch CNN. At night again I'd sit in bed, after the kids had gone to sleep, and just sit and pray for him. I wrote to him all the time, sent him stuff all the time. He was in every part of my day.

Caroline and I talked about the letters that we had gotten. We'd read them back and forth to each other and look at pictures that they had sent. We cried a lot together, we hugged a lot together without saying much sometimes. I remember one time we were at a faculty meeting, that was the morning some Harrier, like Scott's plane, had been shot down. Caroline was just a wreck. I was sitting next to her at the meeting when in came this note. It was handed to her and she completely fell apart. I rushed her out behind the school and she looked at me and she said, "It wasn't him!" She said, "The news came almost as if it was him. There's almost no difference between sorrow and joy anymore." Our emotions were going back and forth all the time, all the time.

Public support through all of that was just overwhelming. I live in a cul-de-sac of 10 homes and I would say eight of them had flags outside the whole time. That was typical in our community. Flags were flown, yellow ribbons were everywhere. Our school was just unbelievable since we had immediate ties with two pilots. Meals came in to me, wonderful cards came in to me, parents stopped in to see me all the time saying, "Mike and Scott have been added to our prayer chain at church." I wrote one time to Mike saying, "There's every denomination praying for you and Scott. Whoever God is, you're covered." The support in Walnut Creek and Danville was just overwhelming.

I didn't know how to talk to the kids about some of the things happening over there at first. I guess because I'm teaching in California, I'm really sensitive to people of different ethnic and religious backgrounds. I'm almost paranoid about different things in that I can't push the flag or prayer, and I have to present touchy subjects very factually. But you know, kids were always coming in saying how they were praying at home with their families and how concerned they were about Mike. It ended up that we talked every day about praying for peace and trusting Mr. Bush and the respect we had for Mr. Bush. That was a year of wonderful lessons and patriotism. It got a lot of families talking about patriotism and religion and dealing with the kids' fears. I'd hear from parents: "Megan's really crying at night, she's so scared for Mike." "We prayed at dinner last night for Mike."

There was more fear during the ground war. When fear comes into your life, you grab hold stronger onto the thing that's the most important to you and that was Mike. I've been through a divorce, which I thought was going to kill me, but the ground war was even more fearful for me.

I was really afraid of Mike being captured since I really think those people over there are crazy. I saw those prisoners and the torture and I was really afraid that he'd be captured and that crazy stuff would happen to him.

We had no way of keeping track of Mike's unit so there was the uncertainty again. And people were more supportive to me when the ground war started. People that were just acquaintances really wanted to get as close to me as they could and help me as much as they could.

When CNN reported that an Apache had been shot down, Caroline's husband wanted to know right away, "Was that Mike?" I said, "I haven't heard, I haven't heard a thing from anybody." Then I called my mom and my sister but nobody had heard anything, so I didn't think about it anymore. About two weeks later, Mary Barton called Joanne who called me. Joanne reached me right before six in the morning and told me that Mike had been shot down two weeks before, that his hand had been shot off but the report was that, as of now, he's okay. That was it.

I was in a stupor. I didn't know what to do. I had to start getting ready to go to work but I was just crazy. I remember walking around my house for a while. I got down on my knees and cried. I was just crying and crying and crying. Then that automatic mode came in of: My God, I've got to get ready and take my shower, get ready for work, get the kids up. I told them, "Uncle Mike's been shot but we know he's okay."

I had a conference that morning with the family of a little boy in my room who was having trouble. We had scheduled it a week before; the father was going to go into work late, the mother was going to get a baby-sitter for the little kids. That meeting was supposed to be at 7:30. I completely forgot about it. I showed up at 8:00 and there at my door was this man in a suit and the mother all dressed up. I completely collapsed. I was crying hysterically. I just couldn't believe that I was so out of control. I explained what had happened and those two people were *so* wonderful to me. In fact, they've become really good friends. They were just there for me.

I remember going into Caroline's room and telling her what I had just heard. Within minutes, half of the faculty was in there with me. I somehow got settled down and went in and taught. A lot of the kids cried, but I was crying too. I was just so scared.

Caroline kept saying, "Vicki, that was two weeks ago, he's okay now." I was talking crazy about being captured and this and that. It didn't sink in that I should've been calm. The time to have been frantic was two weeks before. That whole reality of him being hit still landed pretty hard.

A lot of the guys didn't understand how hard it got at home, but I think he did. Mike was really close to me through my divorce. I fell apart and he supported me. There were other times when my sister has had trouble and my mom gets real emotional from time to time. He's watched us and will make jokes like, "We know how the Klingele women are." So he knew how the Klingele women were doing, he was well aware of that. In fact, in a couple letters that he wrote to children in my class, he talked about how he was doing, and that things weren't too bad, but that he didn't want to say too much because he knew that Mrs. Fontinel was reading those letters. He would often say, "You Klingele women . . ." and shake his head. We Klingele women were on the phone all the time, we can really get each other worked up! He understood and tried to protect us.

It was so hard on my dad too since his health was poor anyway. Mike knew it was hard on Dad and I'm sure that weighed heavily on his heart. His health really changed when Mike went to war. I think it was just too much. Once Mike left, Dad got progressively worse and he died a year later.

This is a little out of order because the war had been over for a week by the time we heard that Mike was hit. I still didn't relax too much 'cause I just wanted him to come home; I was afraid that it was going to start up again. Then there were many return dates thrashed around, many reservations made and canceled. I really wanted to be in Texas when he got home. So did my mom and dad. In fact everybody did, all my brothers and sisters. All the news came from Ft. Hood through Mary Barton. I basically said, "I don't care when it is. Give me a day's notice and I'll be there."

The homecoming was so absolutely wonderful . . .

It was amazing to me that the experience I was going through one time happened several times a day. People just parked car to car along the whole route, from the airfield to that gymnasium, with banners and music and balloons. It was just unbelievable and it happened several times a day for weeks as the troops came back. Some people did it every day to support the people coming back. There were big banners hung from the freeways and cars were parked on the on-ramps and down the roads that the buses passed on their way to the gym. People waved flags and banners and cheered them on.

I can remember my heart saying, "He's really down here now, he's really here." I think 10 or 12 buses went by just full of troops that day. We were just waving and crying unbelievably. Then they all marched in, but I couldn't tell which one he was, they were all dressed the same. When they were dismissed in that gym, hundreds of guys at the same time, everyone scattered. Joanne and I were together running around looking for him. It seemed to me like everyone had found their soldier while my sister and I were still running and running. We finally found him and just held him, all of us. He just cried and cried and cried. It was *so* good that he was really there.

Then he got his composure right back and it was, "Okay, yeah, I'm home okay. What's for dinner?"

We made him a good ol' roast beef-and-mashed-potato dinner and a special dessert. We stayed home that night and sat in his living room while he just talked and talked and talked. A few questions were asked, but he mainly just talked until really late. He talked about their way of life, and about some of the cities he had been in, and people that lived there, and the standard of living, and that he was just so thankful to not have sand. He walked around on the carpet or got a drink of water or a soda and said, "I can't tell you how good this feels." The next morning, he must have taken a shower for an hour and said again, "I can't tell you how good a shower feels with scalding hot water."

He and Dad sat out on the back porch for a long time that morning. Dad wore Mike's hat, the one that matches the desert uniform. I have a great picture of my dad sitting in his bathrobe on the deck with that hat on. Then we tried all the simple things that Mike liked, Pizza Hut, tuna casserole, the mall.

But that stuff wasn't important to him anymore. He talked about changes in priorities and how important his family was. His career had been critical, but relationships are really important now. I know he really wants to be married and have a family now. The 16-hour days and that total commitment to his career and his job and his men are still important, he's a real focused guy, but he's searching for something else.

A couple of weeks later, he came out to see me. He did the normal brother things of fixing stuff around the house for a while. Then it came time to go to school. He wanted to be with the people who supported him. The first couple days, he just hung out in the classroom. He helped me with lessons and art projects and pasting and gluing and cutting and all sorts of silly stuff. At recess, he'd go out and play dodge ball. You'd hear the kids yelling, "Captain Mike! Captain Mike!" He brought in those little brown food bags (MREs) and took groups of maybe eight kids to sit and discuss that bag. They'd all taste it for maybe a half an hour then he'd get another group of eight and do the same thing. They spent hours going through the food. The whole school was there for autographs and brought cookies in to him and presents in to him.

The parents were the same. So many parents came in and grabbed him and hugged him and said, "You don't know me but I know you!" He put a nice ending on it and kind of gave them back a piece of the support they'd sent to him.

Little kids are so wonderful. They'd run to him like he was their long-lost dad or uncle and they just hugged him and kissed him and he absorbed it all. I remember calling my mom saying, "He needed this so badly." He was just showered with love and affection and care and pride. When we got home on Friday, he went up to the bedroom that he was staying in, laid face down with all his clothes on, and fell asleep for three hours. The kids wore him out.

One day while he was here, Mike wore his uniform to school. There was a traffic jam on the freeway as we were driving home so traffic was stopped. A pickup truck pulled up next to us and there were these two guys in their 20s or early 30s in that pickup truck. They looked over at us and the driver said to Mike, "Were you over there?" Mike said, "Yeah." The guy put his thumb up and said, "Thanks, dude!"

That was really touching.

15

Never Present Me with a Flag

Marine Captain J. Scott Walsh, Vapor, flew the McDonnel Douglas AV-8B Harrier with VMA 542 at MCAS Cherry Point, North Carolina. At 27 years old, it was his first flying assignment, although he was already qualified as a division leader of four fighters.

His Harrier was an improvement on a 30-year-old British design for a vertical-takeoff-and-landing attack jet. The Marines fly Harriers from very austere strips pushed close to the front lines, so their living conditions were close to those of the troops they supported.

The single-seat "jump jet" carries virtually any conventional weapon from iron bombs to napalm to cluster bombs to a 25mm gun slung in two pods under the plane's belly. These fighters are close cousins of the Sea Harriers flown by the British in the Falklands War. Lightweight, single-engined, and barely supersonic when stripped down, Harriers couldn't take as much punishment as more conventional fighters. But they were accurate, fought within the sound of the guns, and were flown by Marines. That's what counts to a grunt.

Vapor's mission was as simple to express as it was tough to accomplish: Support the Marines on the cutting edge. Period.

Captain Walsh:

I was raised in California, the San Fransico Bay area, and went to UC Berkeley. Most of the men in my family served a couple years in the military. The opportunity to serve my country too, along with the challenge of becoming an officer, appealed to me. I looked at the different services, liked the Marine Corps, and joined.

I was impressed with the quality of the people in the Marines and originally planned to be an infantry officer. Flying came up later, after the Corps gave me some tests and asked if I'd be interested in flying. I thought, "Hey, I'll kick myself in the butt in a few years if I don't give it my best shot," so I went to flight school after college graduation in 1985.

At flight school in Pensacola, Florida, we were told we'd all be helo pilots since that was the big push at the time. But my timing was good, and I made good grades, so I landed a jet slot instead. I was overjoyed about that. Later on, in jet training, they said we'd all be Bronco pilots since that was the next big push. But it turned out that most of the guys were assigned F-18s and Harriers after getting winged. I received orders to VMAT-203 for Harrier training. After that RAG, I checked into VMA-542 at Cherry Point, North Carolina, just before we began work-ups for a six-month deployment to Japan, Korea, Okinawa, and the Philippines. We got back from that WestPac tour in June '90.

Our warning order to be ready to deploy to Southwest Asia came in early August. VMA 542 went right away 'cause we were very combat-ready after that WestPac tour. A lot of really experienced pilots from other units and the weapons school were attached to the squadron just before we deployed, which increased our readiness even more. We sent the A-team.

First Lieutenant Mike Kenny, "Pisser," and I share an apartment so we went home, packed our bags, and locked up. We were ready to go at 11 o'clock on the night of August 19th. The whole base was in an uproar since just about all the units were either leaving or supporting those that were.

I stuck a Domino's medium combination pan pizza in the cockpit with me 'cause I get really hungry when I fly. It fits perfectly standing up in the cockpit next to the ejection seat. With the pizza, some Gatorade, and Snickers bars, I was good to go.

We followed KC-10s through a storm at night on that 8½-hour flight into Rota, Spain, with bomb racks, Sidewinders, full guns, and two drop tanks. The jets were really heavy. We didn't sleep much before leaving, so it was nice seeing the sun coming up over Portugal. After 16 hours on the ground, we launched for Bahrain and the Shaikh Isa airbase, a formerly secret base on the south side of Bahrain island.

Isa was a new base that wasn't operational yet, and the locals weren't sure how to run it. There was really nothing there but two empty hangars so we slept on the hangar deck[1] the first night. Since the base

---

[1]hangar deck—Floor of an aircraft hangar.

had just been built, the Bahrainis hadn't turned anything on yet and took a while to get all the systems running. The population of the base was a strange mix because the Bahranis do the flying but hire Pakistanis, Indians, Jordanians, Philippinos, and Koreans to do all the labor.

We landed at two o'clock in the morning and tried to sleep in the 100-degree heat with a 100-percent humidity. We got up, ate some MREs, and started building shelters as more units flew in. The F-4G Wild Weasels, Harriers, Marine F-18s, Intruders, and Prowlers really overloaded the base. But we all had to be on an island since the speed bump division wasn't going to slow Saddam down. The 82nd Airborne has to be light to get there first but, after four days, they were running out of food and water. They were resupplied from the prepositioned ships the Marines stationed at Diego Garcia as part of the Marine prepositioned shipping force.

If the Iraqis had come down the coast road from Kuwait, we would've blown the bridge to Bahrain and flown away.

We got a bonus when the Bahrainis gave us a barracks. They moved some of their people off the base so our pilots could have it. That comfort caused some morale problems 'cause we're used to sharing the same conditions with our troops whenever we deploy to an austere base. But we had a helicopter crash on a night flight and it turned out the pilot wasn't sleeping in the heat. We had to get the pilots a place where they could sleep before we lost any more of them. The Bahraini barracks was the only place with air conditioning.

There was a lot of construction going on at the base. They were building bunkers and fuel pits and maintenance spaces, chow halls, laundromats. Getting a real chow hall was a big deal. We could conserve the MREs then and were getting pretty sick of them anyway.

We were on alert 24 hours a day. Somebody was always cocked with cluster bombs and thousand-pounders waiting for a phone call. We didn't know if Saddam was coming or not, but we were ready for him. Not knowing what was going to happen was the hardest part.

After the First and Seventh MEBs[2] deployed on the Kuwaiti border and blocked the coastal road, we didn't have to hide on an island anymore. So we forward-deployed to King Abdul Aziz airfield about 100 miles south of the border. It was normally a soccer stadium with a small landing strip the Saudi royal family used to come see the national soccer team. The Seabees did a great job building taxiways, bunkers, a mess hall, etc. We went back to living in tents without air conditioners, and were back to stage one for comfort, but at least it was getting cooler.

---

[2]MEB—Marine Expeditionary Brigade. Approximately 17,000 Marines with 30 days of combat supplies.

We set up a weight room to stay in shape and kill time. Some sergeant wrote a letter to *Muscle Magazine* about the lack of weights in Saudi that got a great response. Thank God for Arnold Schwarzenegger 'cause he donated up a bunch of weights for us. He's king in my book!

Living in a tent out in the desert waiting for the Iraqis to either attack or pull out became tedious, to say the least. Standing alert seven days a week is boring, so we played sports to keep busy. We played volleyball and ultimate Frisbee[3]. It was a real leadership challenge to keep the morale of our Marines up so we started the Deadbeat Club in one of our tents. It had a little bar that served near beer and Cokes but, hey, it wasn't too bad. Folks back home sent tapes and mail, which really helped a lot.

We got news mainly from folks sending us newspaper clippings and listening to the Armed Forces Radio station. We eventually got a TV for CNN, so heck, we knew as much as anybody.

My mom's a school teacher who had whole classrooms writing to me. That kept me busy writing half a dozen letters a night. You just can't overestimate how important mail call was and gettin' something from home. Distant relatives, friends, people you didn't even know—they all wrote. Reading those letters meant a lot to us because it showed how the American people really felt—not what the press said they felt.

We knew the people back home really supported us. There were a couple peace demonstrations initially that we read about, but then strangers wrote to say, "You may see some demonstrations, but we want you to know that the people really support you." My folks sent clippings saying there was a peace demonstration by 2 or 300 people with a counter support demonstration of 10,000 people. They said it was typical that the vocal minority got a lot of press, but we had the people's support. We felt good about that, and I felt pretty good about why we were there.

We were on the cutting edge. I was doing my job, what I was trained to do, and I didn't want to be anywhere else.

The press put out a lot of misinformation on the effect the desert environment had on our men and equipment. If any of those reporters had bothered to ask or had looked at a map, they would've seen that the Marine Corps' largest training base is in the Mojave desert. We know how to operate in the desert and the aircraft held up just fine. There were some considerations we had to take into account, but we weren't learning anything new. For example, we knew to leave some of the avionics off until we launched so they wouldn't overheat on the ground.

---

[3]ultimate Frisbee—Full-contact Frisbee on a soccer field. Imagine rugby with a pie plate.

The worst thing was the dirt. Sand got into everything, but we didn't spend a lot of time washing airplanes; everybody had more important things to do. People were stretched pretty much to the limits pulling additional duty in the mess hall or on guard duty. And the terrorist threat had our attention.

Our Marines worked nonstop to keep "their" planes fully mission-capable[4]. We maintained a 90% to 95% FMC rate, which is really impressive considering the conditions. They didn't have air-conditioned offices or modern hangars like the Air Force, Navy, and other Marine Corps jet squadrons did; they worked in tents on sand and in expeditionary fold-out hangars. But even under those conditions, the troops wanted to work seven days a week. That wasn't safe, though, 'cause people eventually get tired and make mistakes. Our CO[5] actually had to order our troops to throttle back to a six-day week and ended up drawing a line in the sand between our tents and the work tents that we were ordered not to cross on our day off.

We didn't do a lot of flying, though we did enough to maintain proficiency. Everybody we took over there was combat-capable. The training we did was with our Marine ground units up north and with the British. When the Brits first came over, they were with our Marines, so we did a lot of work with the Desert Rats and the Scots Royal Dragoon Guards. They wanted to use us for close air support since they didn't have any CAS of their own. So, instead of flying dry missions at Twentynine Palms, we flew dry missions in Saudi.

That August-to-January lull was the hardest time because we were just waiting and training without really knowing what was going on.

At least we got rid of most of the "four letter" jobs. I wasn't worried about being the hurricane evacuation officer, navigation officer, maintaining rifle and pistol qualification, weight control, military appearance, or a bunch of the other irritants that take up so much effort in peacetime. But I was still in charge of NBC[6] training for our squadron with Corporal Frisbie and Corporal Milke. For the first time, it was easy to get people to do their NBC training without argument; they knew all about Iraq's chemical weapons history.

That's pretty much how it went until the war kicked off.

It was my section's routine alert when someone came down to wake us up and with: "Hey, you gotta get in your planes and launch.

---

[4]fully mission capable—FMC. Aircraft status code indicating that it is ready to fly without restrictions. All important systems work.

[5]CO—Commanding officer. Unit commander.

[6]NBC—Nuclear, biological, and chemical.

The Air Force launched its first strikes last night and the carriers are going now." It wasn't a drill and we were really going. We knew the war would kick off soon, but we didn't know exactly when. It was a relief, if anything, because we thought, "Okay, for better or for worse, we're going to get this thing over with." It was like a football team where you practice, practice, practice, and you wanna play a game finally. It almost got to that point, with our eagerness, since none of us had ever been in combat before.

I was nervous but it wasn't so much flying up there and getting killed as much as like the first time I landed on a carrier. I knew I could do the job, but I wanted to know how well I could do it. This was going to be something I had never done before although I had been trained. I wanted to do well because my fellow Marines and our country were counting on us. I wanted to make people proud of us—the Harrier squadrons, the Marine Corps, the military, our country, the whole world. Fear of failure is one of the greatest motivators. We also had tremendous camaraderie in the face of peril.

This was real.

That first ride was led by the CO to take out some artillery that was shelling Marines near the town of Kafji. We flew in from the Gulf and I ran my combat checklist 10 times with my head on a swivel[7] trying to be a good wingman by looking out for bogeys, SAMs, or triple-A. We talked to a Bronco—in fact, it was Guy Hunter, the guy who got shot down and showed up in the press as a POW. The Bronco pinpointed the artillery hitting our Marines and assumed his role of airborne FAC. Captain Curry and CWO-4 Hunter, in the Bronco, spotted the Iraqi artillery and called us in. It was an ominous feeling breaking out below the clouds at 7000 feet and going feet dry into Kuwait the first time.

We attacked feeling really exposed 'cause the weather forced us a lot lower than we wanted to be. I dropped my bombs on one of the artillery batteries and then we strafed with our 25mm guns until we were out of ammunition. Strafing at a 1000 feet wasn't real smart, but we were extremely aggressive after spending all those months in the desert[8]. We really left some fang marks[9] in the sand.

We got kinda crazy and were being stupid. I think it was the frustration built up after being in the desert for so long. There was a photo

---

[7]The wingman is primarily responsible for spotting threats to the formation while the leader concentrates on getting the job done.

[8]Fighter pilots are bred to be aggressive, but a bored and frustrated fighter pilot given the first opportunity to defend his comrades can take that trait to the extreme. Stay out of his way.

[9]fangs—Sign of overly aggressive behavior, as in letting the hormones take over.

of some graffiti on a bomb that said, "After five months in the desert—it's personal." That's classic.

The tempo picked up until we launched a section of two planes every five minutes at the start of the ground war. By the second day of that phase, I'd flown 38 missions and was going up for the second time that day.

We got up early as the Iraqi counterattacks were building against the Marine divisions breaching the barriers. The Intell guys had seen a lot of Iraqi movement. Their units that had prepared for a 4th MEB beach landing were coming back south along with some divisions from central Kuwait. The Iraqis finally figured out that there wasn't going to be a beach landing, but those units from northwest Kuwait obviously didn't know the Seventh Corps was comin' up behind them at that moment.

So we launched to hit a T-55 armored division comin' down to attack the left flank of the Second Marine Division. An F-18D[10] had spotted them and was working the target as a fast FAC. We staged out of a forward base or FARP[11] at Tanajib, about 30 miles south of the Kuwaiti border. We could reload with bombs and fuel in about 20 minutes, get a new Intell brief, and go back to the same area.

I launched on that second mission with cluster bombs and the gun. Major Dan "Salt" Peters led us out onto the 1500-foot runway for a short field takeoff. Salt said, "Rolling, rolling, go!" and I put the power in the corner[12] for max thrust. At 75 knots, I slapped the nozzles[13] into 55 degrees and the jet jumped off the deck. We flew the 15 minutes back into the target area in a combat spread formation of about a mile and a half line abreast at 15,000 feet.

There were two other sections of Harriers on the same tactical freq with the F-18D. We heard them going into the target up by Ali al Salim airfield just west of Kuwait City. We penetrated the clouds and joined up underneath.

The first section of Harriers came off target and the second rolled in. I could see their bombs going off with some pretty good secondaries. There were some vehicles burning on the ground, residue from our first

---

[10]F-18D—Two-seat F/A-18 Hornet. Normally used for training, although it's fully combat capable. The second seat allows one pilot to coordinate the fight on the ground while the other flies the jet. See Fast FAC.

[11]FARP—Forward arming and refueling point. Bare base operation for refueling and rearming only.

[12]in the corner—To push the throttles all the way to their stops, which are in the front left corner of the cockpit.

[13]nozzles—Variable exhaust nozzles on a Harrier that allow vertical takeoffs and landings. They're controlled by a lever in the cockpit.

attacks that morning. The cloud deck was at 9,000 feet, which forced us to stay down around 8000. We started a hard left turn at about 450 knots to get to the target area.

The visibility was very bad that day; you couldn't see things on the ground too well through all the smoke from burning vehicles and oil wells.

I never saw it coming.

The missile knocked the shit out of my plane! I got hit in the right rear hot nozzle, and the cockpit warning lights lit up like a Christmas tree. There was a big engine fire light staring me in the face, a flaps light, temperature lights, and all the hooters, the warning horns, went off.

My initial thought was anger: I was pissed off that those guys hit me. I couldn't believe it. We'd been shot at for a month and a half but they couldn't hit us, we'd always been able to get away. We thought we were better than that. And I didn't even get my bombs off.

It was probably a hand-held heat-seeker. The Iraqis had thousands of those things, which we'd see launching from the target during ingress and egress. But I didn't see that one.

Emergency procedures training took over when I saw that fire light, so I pulled my power back to see if the engine would respond. The RPMs decreased but the temperature increased. I really did have a fire.

I stayed in my left turn 'cause I wanted to get the plane pointed south. I thought, "If I gotta punch out of this thing real quick, I want to point south and get across friendly lines if I can."

I watched my engine temperature gauge as it went off the page and then clicked to zero. I knew I was burning—one glance over my shoulder confirmed that. All I saw behind me was red-orange flame and a big cloud of white smoke. I had streaming fuel burning as it came out.

I thought about the ejection decision and remembered what my dad taught me when I was little. Fuel burns, vapor explodes. So I thought, "If I was going to explode, I would've exploded by now."

That kinda went through my mind, and I decided I was going to stay with the plane. I also didn't want to eject over the target area. I don't think I would have lasted too long down there 'cause we'd been bombing the shit out of those guys for about three hours. I don't think they would've been too happy about a pilot landing in the middle of them.

I was going to ride the thing out as long as I could even though the flaps and part of the right wing were missing. The missile blew them off the jet.

I jettisoned my bombs and traded altitude for airspeed[14]. I set up a

---

[14]An airplane accelerates as it descends and decelerates as it climbs. That's the required tradeoff between kinetic and potential energy.

slow descent with the power pulled back trying to get south. The F-18, with Lieutenant Rob Scanio in front and Major Cronnen in the back, pulled right up next to me and called out battle damage. Salt turned back to join up too.

I gotta give those guys credit for flying cover on me in what was obviously a high-threat area; I'd just been hit there. They gave me a lot of support that I really needed. One minute you're King Kong, ruling the skies, reaping death and destruction on guys below you. Next thing you know you're on fire and everything's going to shit and you're wondering if you can even stay in the plane much longer.

We headed south and I told them to let me know when I got across friendly lines. I figured, hey, then I'd feel better about ejecting. I really didn't want to get out before then.

That was the first time I'd seen warning lights for fire, hydraulics, flaps, jet temperature limiter, or overtemperature outside of a simulator emergency procedures sortie. I always hated those simulators.

I had a hydraulic warning light with the pressure dropping. That really worried me. You need an engine and hydraulics to fly the plane. Everything else is just nice to have. I knew I had to land that thing as soon as possible 'cause, when the hydraulics went, I wouldn't be able to control the plane. You can't deadstick the aircraft.

The F-18 guys knew I had to land right away and said they'd guide me back to Tanajib. They said: "It looks like the fire's going down and you're losing a lot of fuel. You got hit in the right rear nozzle and it's pretty twisted up. Your wing's burning but it's holding together." I said, "The plane's flying okay, considering."

At that point, I knew everything I needed to know and had to land the plane as soon as possible. People ask me what kind of caution lights I had but I didn't care about the caution lights. I had so many warning lights taking priority that I didn't really care about the rest. I had a fire light and was losing hydraulics, so my job was to land the plane as soon as possible. That's all I was trying to do.

I wasn't going to make Tanajib, so the F-18 started lookin' around for a road to land on. I thought we should've overrun that central airfield in Kuwait by now, so I told the F-18 we'd try to make Ahmed al Jaber. They steered me in that direction since their navigation was obviously better than mine at that point.

Salt flew high cover for us.

I told the F-18 to fly ahead and check out the runway 'cause I knew we'd bombed that area. But we'd left one of the runways in good condition since we thought we might have to use it for a forward base if we advanced into Iraq. They said the left runway hadn't been bombed, so I rolled onto final and tried to get my gear down.

My gear didn't go down. I had unsafe indications that said the nose and mains had moved but weren't down and locked. The outriggers[15] hadn't moved at all. I tried the emergency blowdown procedure but didn't get any change in indications. So I thought, "If I can't do a normal landing with the gear, I'll do a vertical landing."

I was maybe a mile from the runway at about 1500 feet when I went ahead and tried to pull in some nozzles to see if I could make a vertical landing. As I did that, I think three of the nozzles moved but the one that got hit didn't move. The plane didn't feel right, it sideslipped and felt a little squirrely. Some type of vertical landing wasn't going to be a player at that point.

I went ahead and moved the nozzles back out and turned to downwind. I overflew the field and told the F-18 to join up on me. If I just had a gear indicator problem, well, maybe I could still land the thing.

I really wanted to save the plane at that point. Yea, the poor plane was damaged, but it was still flying, it was a valuable weapons asset, and we wanted to save the thing. I really wanted to do that. Anyway, the F-18 said it looked like my nose and mains (landing gear) were down but my outriggers were still up and in trail. That's a real bad combination to land with.

At that point I was thinking, you know, I wasn't going to be able to land like that and I'd probably have to punch out.

My mind got made up for me about 10 seconds later as I was pretty much abeam the field. The hydraulics finally all went out and the stick started freezing up on me. The plane kinda pitched up and rolled upside down. Next thing you know, I found myself with a frozen stick, upside down, 30 degrees nose down at about 900 feet.

The F-18 guys screamed at me to eject.

I went ahead and took a deep breath, got my butt all the way back against the seat and my thighs flat on the seat so the slap wouldn't break my legs, pushed my feet all the way to the pedals, shoulders back to the seat, and head tilted back slightly. I grabbed the ejection handle between my thighs with both hands.

I looked up through my canopy and saw that the plane was rolling and the ground was gettin' closer. I thought, "Boy I hope this seat works 'cause I'm goin' in right now." I pulled on the black and yellow striped ejection handle.

All hell broke lose. There was a big flash on the canopy from the detonation cord blowing a hole for the seat to go through. I felt myself being lifted and then I remember that feeling of being violently pulled

---

[15]outrigger—The very small landing gear that extend from the wingtips of a Harrier.

around. It felt like a thousand hands were trying to rip the flight suit from my body. It was really loud. I could see the flames from the seat's rocket motor blasting out between my feet.

All of a sudden, everything went calm for a second. I figure that's when I separated from the seat and the 'chute deployed. Then the 'chute blew open and I got an opening shock that just snapped the hell out of me. I remember seeing my toes and fingers coming up in front of my face and my neck got snapped so bad that I had some stiff muscles for quite a while. When I got violently tossed around again and started seein' stars real bad, I thought to myself: "DO NOT LOSE CONSCIOUSNESS!"

I was twisted up a little bit and still gettin' tossed around when I saw my plane hit the ground in a big orange fireball. Then, suddenly, everything was real quiet.

I just floated there in the 'chute and could only hear the canopy cords straining in the wind. Amazing. One minute you're in a screaming jet and then it's real quiet as you hang there in the straps. So much for King Kong.

I looked around and saw my plane burning on the edge of the airfield with the ground comin' up pretty quick. I figured I'd better go through the post-ejection procedures, so I checked my canopy. I was too low to get anything else done except grab the parachute releases.

My roommate, Mike Kenny, he's Mr. Skydiving. We had just had a conversation a week before on how to skydive. He talked about how you want to look at the horizon. Don't look down when you land, or you'll hurt your neck, and don't reach for the ground with your feet. So all that flashed through my mind real quick as I got into position to land.

There was a pretty strong wind blowing and I was going sideways. I thought, "This will work out perfect. I'll hit toes first, knees, hips and roll and everything." Well, about 10 feet up, the wind shifted or something, so I went straight into the ground.

I brought my feet up closer to my body and, as soon as they hit, I pulled on the risers and tried to twist my body to the side. I hit pretty hard but luckily it was soft sand. I kinda burrowed in and was getting dragged on my back by the wind. I popped the parachute harness releases, jumped up, looked around, and stood there for a second checking my body for pain. I felt pretty good!

I reached up to loosen my oxygen mask and got rid of the seat pan that had the life raft and some other things I figured I didn't need.

I looked around the airfield to get my orientation. I didn't see any friendlies, so I thought the best thing for me to do was start heading south. I knew that's where the friendlies were, so I turned and jogged south. I could hear bombs going off to the north.

Being all alone and real exposed was a very strange feeling. I felt really exposed and vulnerable, so I jumped in a bomb crater for some cover.

I got out my survival radio, pulled out my pistol, and tried to make contact with Salt and the F-18. They were flying above me, checking me out, so I waved to 'em. I raised them on the radio and told them, "HEY, I'M OKAY." They said, "GOOD, TAKE CARE OF YOURSELF AND YOU BETTER GET GOING." I said, "THANKS FOR YOUR HELP AND IF YOU MARK YOUR POSITION AND GET SOMEBODY OUT HERE, I'M GOIN' TO START MOVING SOUTH." They said, "ROGER THAT BUDDY, GOOD LUCK."

So I got up and started to move. As I headed south, I could see a couple folks moving around. I looked around and saw a trench that I jumped in to take some cover. I called the F-18 guys and said, "I GOT PERSONNEL TO MY SOUTH, CAN YOU GO CHECK 'EM OUT FOR ME?" They said, "ROGER THAT," and came back around. Salt went to high cover and I figured, "If these are bad guys, I have an F-18 up there and a Harrier with bombs and the gun that I can call in."

They said, "HEY, THESE GUYS ARE FRIENDLIES." They saw the inverted V[16] on top of the Humvee[17] and said, "TRY TO MAKE YOUR WAY TO THEM."

I got out of the trench and started to run south when I saw little flags around me. I looked at the flags and thought to myself, "Here I am, south of Jaber. That's an infantry trench and what's usually in front of a trench? Minefield. Damn."

I took a closer look around using my infantry training (all Marines are trained infantry), and it didn't have any indications of mines with the way the dirt was. I moved farther south until the ground changed and decided not to move any farther.

I dropped to one knee since I could see five Marines spread out looking around. I waited until they got closer and waved my helmet so the closest guy would see the reflective tape on it. He ran up to me and said we weren't in a minefield after all, but that it was Iraqi territory. They still held the airfield. Good thing I didn't land there.

It was real good to see those guys. They were a five-man patrol leading Task Force Sheppard from the First Marine Regiment. They were moving ahead when they saw my plane go down and came looking for me.

We all piled in their Humvee and they took me back to the task force, which was standing by on line. We passed by where my plane hit. The engine was sittin' up on the ground and the tail was kinda sticking

---

[16]An inverted "V" was painted on all coalition vehicles for identification.

[17]Humvee—Four-wheeled, all-purpose, all-terrain replacement for the Jeep. Variants carried TOW missiles, grenade launchers, or machine guns.

up in the air. The tail looked fine, but everything else was just smoldering. I felt bad seein' the squadron's tiger stripes on the tail sittin' there.

We drove through the drizzle to the front of the task force. They sent a patrol to scout the area but didn't expect to find a pilot! I gave an Intell brief to the task force CO on what was going on up in front of them while they called back to let my squadron know I was in friendly hands. They joked with me and asked if I wanted to head up north with them. They were in all the chem gear and I stood there in only my flight suit, G-suit, and helmet thinking, "What's wrong with this picture?" I felt kinda naked without a gas mask or a rifle.

So I told the CO I could do more good if I had a Harrier to fight with and that I wanted to get back to my squadron. About that time, two Hueys landed with orders for the regiment so they started moving out. I stuck with the Huey guys thinkin' they had to fly back to the base eventually, so I'd be better off with them.

The task force drove by in their amphibious assault vehicles, their light armored vehicles, Humvees, TOWs, and lots of trucks haulin' troops. You could tell they were pretty pumped up.

Then it was just me and the Hueys. I became the assistant door gunner on a Huey for an hour.

We landed near the First Marine Division Combat Operations Center just after the division won a brief firefight. Everybody looked at me in my dirty flight gear like, "Who is this guy and where did he come from?" It looked like I just dropped in for lunch. The Division Air Officer took me over to the commander, Major General Myatt. The general was very happy that they were able to rescue me and was also pleased with the CAS our Harriers provided. I asked to go back to my squadron, so he had the Hueys take me back to their base at Lonesome Dove. I caught a CH-53E ride from there back to Tanajib.

I finally got back to my forward base and spent the night. The next day, I hopped in the maintenance truck that made a parts run back to King Abdul Aziz. It was real good to see the guys; they're like family and it was real important to get back to them.

First thing they told me was to call my folks. One of the bad things about the media was that whenever a plane got shot down, CNN would find out and put it on the news. The people back at Cherry Point would have to call all the families and tell them that it wasn't one of us. Well, we'd lost Trey on the first night of the ground war and they delayed releasing that information 'cause the SAR effort was still underway. Then I went down and nobody called the family before it was on TV. That day, an A-10 went down, two Harriers, a Bronco, and an Apache. A lot of planes went down.

So my parents were at home calling the relatives of other squadron pilots to see if anybody had news about the squadron. They called Cherry Point and found out that it was me but I was okay. That news was pretty hard on them. Then I called and it was a big relief. I said I was going up tomorrow and they said, "You've done enough!" "No, no," I said, "we've got a job to do here, and I won't stop until it's over." Plus I said, "What's the odds of getting shot down twice?" They didn't think that was too humorous.

The doctor said I had a compression fracture of a lumbar vertebrae and cut up the tops of my feet pretty good. I'm kinda tall and so I caught the bottom of the dash on the way out. But he gave me an up chit[18] for the next day, and they put me on the flight schedule. The next day's flight operations were canceled 'cause the ground war had pretty much ended for us. The Marines had taken their objectives, so that was my last mission. Hell of a way to end it, but what the heck.

We stuck around a few more weeks and then flew to Rota, Spain, to meet the USS *Saratoga* and the USS *Kennedy*. We couldn't get any tankers for the flight home so the Navy offered a ride on their carriers. It was a great feeling going home and gettin' the hell out of Saudi. It didn't matter when you got home, just get out of Saudi.

We floated across on the *Kennedy*. It was a real pleasant trip, good food, air conditioning. That would have been a good way to go to war. Those Navy guys were all bitching about being on a ship, while we loved it like it was a Sheraton hotel. We'd had eight guys to a hot tent, so we thought the carrier was an absolute paradise, even with eight guys in a stateroom. Running water, air conditioning, movies, a gym. It was super. The Navy treated us well.

There were 22 Harriers plus the whole carrier air wing on the *Kennedy*. We launched at dawn to clear the deck for the air wing while still about 300 miles off the U.S. coast. I was really excited to be finally going home. And the launch was awesome with two entire carrier air wings and 22 Harriers blasting off for the flight home together. When I crossed the coast and saw the green forests and fields, I couldn't believe how beautiful it looked. The civilian radar controllers said, "Welcome home guys! You did a great job!"

My parents were waiting at Cherry Point with my girlfriend, Susan Anderson. It was real great seeing them. My mom cried, of course. They'd never seen me fly, so watching me come back from war in a Harrier was something else.

We waited for Pisser to get in and went to our apartment. Our parents had stocked the refrigerator and cleaned up, so that was real nice. We put on civilian clothes for the first time in like eight months, and I

---

[18]up chit—Medical clearance to fly.

thought that was pretty great. It felt weird at first though. Culture shock.

That was a good homecoming. It was good to get home. I was really proud.

Caroline Walsh raised her family in the American dream setting of Walnut Creek, California. Her paying job as a librarian (in addition to the real work of running a family) gave Scott the perfect outlet for his boyhood fascination with books. In time, that tame interest gave way to sports and eventually to combat aviation. Caroline then joined that exclusive sorority whose children simply ignore the dangers that eat at their mother's hearts. Her son was a fighter pilot and the country was at war. For a couple hundred thousand moms, it couldn't get much worse than that without tragedy.

Her perspective is a bit different in that Caroline isn't a military wife. She didn't see flight suits every day and become somewhat numb to the routine dangers as the immediate families tend to do in a form of emotional self-defense. She wasn't used to the constant good-byes that milepost the airman's life. After all, Scott was almost as gone in North Carolina as he was in Japan or Saudi. So she had more to get used to when the missions turned hot.

The war detonated in all of these lives, but a mom feels a unique pain when her child goes in harm's way.

Caroline Walsh:

Scott worked quite hard toward being a good Marine pilot, and I was naturally quite proud of him. I knew that's really what he wanted to do though I had quite a bit of internal turmoil about his decision because of my fears of his being harmed. I didn't want anything to happen to him, naturally you don't. That's what was inside me and why I really didn't want him to do it. When I saw that was what he wanted and I saw the happiness and contentment that was part of him, I realized that was the niche that he had to fill.

When I knew Scott was going to go into the military, my private fear was that something would happen to him. I remember saying to my husband Jim, "They'd better never ever present me with a flag."

When that war broke out, I'm telling you I lived in daily fear of that.

We learned of the deployment from Scott at a time when we were expecting him to come home on leave. He had just returned from over six months in Japan, so we wanted him to come home for a vacation.

We learned of the invasion of Kuwait, of course, and our military's involvement, but we didn't know that Scott would be going over immediately. We just knew what we heard on television. But then at noon on a Sunday in August, Scott called sounding very tired to me. I said it sounded like he'd just gotten up. Noon our time would've been three in the afternoon his time, so I thought that was very unusual. He said they'd been getting on Middle Eastern time for a week.

He called to tell me good-bye because they were flying out that night. He wondered what he was going to do about his phone and utilities. I always spoke very soundly to him, I never cried with Scott on the phone. That came later. I hung up and called his brother at work and said, "Quick, you've got to call Scott to tell him good-bye." Then my sister Susan called him, and then my mother, and as many people as possible called Scott to say good-bye.

Then all we could do was wait for mail from him and watch the news.

I don't care how old your child becomes, the worry is always there when they go in harm's way. The worry is always there. And the boys just feel invincible. They have to. But they don't understand the feeling at home. I remember leaning over the kitchen counter one time and telling my other son Mike, "I can't stand it!" You just can't stand the worry. It tears you apart. But we couldn't turn the news off; not knowing was worse.

Since we weren't at Cherry Point, the executive officer's wife, Kathy Leffler, contacted us and was just marvelous. She sent notes and photos and made calls to include us in everything the families did. The guys sent a newsletter from Saudi that the wives included in their newsletter. And any time the wives did anything for the guys, like stockings at Christmas time, they would be sure to include the bachelors. They were great.

The civilian support around here was absolutely unbelievable too. People always wanted to know how Scott was doing and what he needed. They would gather together whatever the papers said the men needed and send it to Scott's squadron. My classroom started to do the same thing and every child had a particular person in Scott's squadron to write to.

My eldest son was listening to his car radio that day in January when he heard that the war had started. He immediately came home and turned the television on. Jim came home, too, and Mike said, "Pa, come quick, the war has started." Jim just couldn't believe it. The three of us sat there together, watching the bombing on television, not knowing where Scott was. Jim said, "I wonder where he is?" I said immediately, "I KNOW HE'S FLYING AND I KNOW HE'S ONE OF THEM."

What bothered me the most was not really knowing for sure. You have your worst fears when you don't really know. When we'd get letters from Scott—and oh how we lived for those letters—I would realize that's how he was 10 days before. We would read them and read them and read them. Then the fears would start up again. Where is he today? How is he today?

I had to tell myself that no news was good news. At those times, when I couldn't stand it any longer, I'd pick up the phone and call Kathy Leffler to ask, "How are the fellas?" She'd say, "They're fine." She'd hear from her husband or the headquarters there and say, "They're fine. They're getting their packages. They're getting their mail." I found so much internal peace after I talked to her. She's a wonderful lady.

When the war started, the support around here just mushroomed. People came out of the woodwork and our phone never stopped ringing. All the relatives, many of Scott's teachers, his friends from high school and Berkeley all called and were extremely supportive. Every note and every card contained encouraging, positive words of support for us. Jim and I absolutely could not believe how people reacted. There was a banding together unlike anything we had ever experienced.

There were a few flags out on our cul-de-sac before the war started, but then I realized there were seven of them. And then there were 11. And then I counted 16, then 19. I think we finally had 21 flags on our little street. That display of patriotism started after a demonstration on the Golden Gate bridge against the start of the war. The next day, there were flags everywhere. There were flags on cars, shopping centers had flags out, there were signs supporting the people in Desert Storm. It really helped to see those flags as I went to and from school.

It's a very good thing that I was teaching school or I don't think I could have handled it mentally. School kept me busy. When you walk into a classroom, the world could fall apart outside and you'd never know it. Time flies because you're involved with children and you do not have 30 seconds of peace. You truly do forget many other things. When I walked into school, my mind immediately went to the kids and then, when I left, my mind immediately shifted to the war.

I beelined home every day, as did Jim. We never used to watch television during the day. That's just not part of us. But we couldn't get home fast enough and we would live for CNN when Scott was gone. We didn't sit in front of the television, but our home is set up so that we could get on with things and still be aware of it. My Jim and Mike would come down at seven in the morning and watch the briefings to find out what was going on.

My life was just school and the news. Jim and I did absolutely nothing socially because we wouldn't want to be away from home. I have to say Mike was very much the same way. We'd come directly home to compare notes on what we'd heard that day.

My very best friend and staunchest supporter, Lee Kinser, talked to me daily and gave me the support I needed. She would always say, "He's going to be fine 'cause he knows what he's doing. He's a smart pilot." Scott's friends said the same thing over and over. The Hindmarsh family, our oldest and dear friends, were so caring and supportive.

That support was severely tested when Harriers started getting shot down. We formed a telephone chain to reassure the pilots' families that the latest loss wasn't one of ours. Our contacts were Mr. Kenny (Scott's roommate's father) or Kathy Leffler. Then we heard of a Harrier being shot down and learned that it was from the 542 squadron. It was Trey. We were so saddened, my husband was so very saddened.

You see, Mrs. Vance, whose husband worked for Aramco in Saudi, made a Christmas dinner videotape of a small group of the men from the squadron. Trey was among them. Trey stood next to Scott in that Christmas tape. He seemed like such a nice young fella. Quiet spoken. Just a nice, quiet young man. We'd watched that tape so many times. My husband couldn't watch it after Trey died.

Then came that fateful weekend in February. I was on my way to school that Monday and heard the report: two AV-8Bs, an A-10, an Apache helicopter, and an OV-10 Bronco were shot down. Well, I thought I knew who the one Harrier pilot was, Trey, but I didn't know who the other one was.

I got that sickening, sinking feeling inside unlike anything I could describe. Something told me it was Scott. As soon as I got to school, I called my husband and told Jim what I'd heard. I said, "You've just got to call and find out who the other one is—I just know it's Scott!"

I was in my classroom at about 9:30 that morning when there was a faint knock at the door and it opened. My eldest son Mike was standing there. When I first saw him, my heart sank.

Then I saw the look on his face and it was partly a smile. I ran to him, put my arms around him and he said, "He's all right, Mom. You were right. It was Scott. But he's all right, Mom. He's been rescued."

I'll never forget his words. Never. Those were his words exactly.

My principal was standing right behind Mike and said, "Mrs. Stevenson will take your class." She said, "I'm here Caroline, you go on home."

I shook my head and said, "No, no, it's better if I stay here. My kids need me."

I remember Mike looking at me and saying, "You don't want to come home, Mom? Scott's going to call." I had that inner peace just knowing he was okay and said, "No, it's better I stay here." And I made the right decision because Scott couldn't call until the next day. Had I gone home, I would've been in such mental anguish I couldn't have tolerated it.

The children in my class were so understanding. Nobody left their seats. They were quiet. I went in, wiped my eyes and heard little David Robbins say, "We were going to talk about our math, Mrs. Walsh." I said, "You're right, David, we're talking about math." And I immediately continued with the math lesson. The kids always knew what to say. I'll never forget those wonderful children.

I didn't tell the kids about losing Trey until the next day. I just couldn't talk about it anymore.

I have to tell you that I work with the greatest bunch of teachers that ever worked together. One of them, Vicki Fontinel, is also the sister of the Apache helicopter pilot who was shot down.

Boy, when we heard on television that the war was over, we were absolutely elated! That war aged my husband and me. It aged us. But it was over!

Did things ever lighten up when the war ended! I am telling you, my husband and I felt such relief, such relief. It was miraculous. There was that wonderful elation and it was like we could finally breathe. The war was stifling, stifling. We were just overjoyed and then couldn't wait until Scott came home.

Once again, we got the news from Mrs. Leffler when she told us what group would leave first and what group would be next. All we had to do was wait while they came across the ocean on a carrier. Jim was very happy to learn that Scott would not fly across the ocean again. That always worried Jim, the idea of the refuelings and the long time in the air. That's very taxing to the body.

All I wanted was to know that he was back home somewhere, back on good ol' U.S. soil. It would sure be wonderful to be able to pick up the phone and talk to him.

Scott was going to land the week before my spring vacation so it was a bad time to leave school. But nothing was going to hold me back! The Lefflers made our arrangements and were absolutely wonderful to us.

The pilots came in real early so we went out to the hangar at Cherry Point at about seven in the morning. There we were, standing around bedecked in red, white, and blue, when I looked up to see the planes coming. Amazingly, just like that, they were on the ground.

I didn't know if I was allowed to run out to Scott so I sort of stood back until I couldn't wait any longer and just ran to him. We held on to him for dear life.

I said, "I love you Scott!" I was never-so-glad-to-see-anybody-in-my-life.

He just smiled so calmly and asked about his brother. He couldn't understand what all the fuss was about.

Lessons Learned

At the end of every action, military leaders write reports that summarize events and list the lessons they learned. That process went on thousands of times at the end of Desert Storm, with most of the resulting documents classified and filed away. I pulled these lessons from between the lines of these stories to give you one version of what went well or perhaps not so well.

Many of these points are negative simply because the good points could be covered earlier without fear of the consequences. In some cases, these conclusions oppose positions taken by the military leadership. Such disagreements between generals and captains are normal. Some people point to the political positions senior leaders feel they must defend versus the apolitical realities of combat as exclusively experienced by the younger officers and troops. Others call it the difference between experience and youth. In any case, these lessons were learned on the cutting edge and so are not always politically correct. Combat fliers don't have time for politics.

Rapid intercontinental transport is critical if we are to both withdraw from overseas bases and also deal with regional conflicts. We need more intercontinental transports. Our mothballed sealift ships weren't as ready as they were supposed to be, we had trouble finding sailors who could run their steam-driven engines, and we were very lucky to have the few fast roll-on, roll-off ships that Congress forced on the Navy. Our airlifters flew grueling and sometimes illegally long schedules to make the system work in spite of the equipment and command deficiencies. But the C-141s are worn out and the C-5s aren't far behind. Most cargo flew on standard pallets, which could be more efficiently moved by military versions of civilian air freighters while the C-141s and C-5s fly specialized cargo. Those conventional air freighters could even be tankers with cargo capacity.

We need more aerial refueling tankers. Fighter squadrons were ready to deploy in a matter of hours, but commonly cooled their heels for days waiting for the overworked tankers to show up. By the way, tanker crews haven't received enough recognition for the stamina and sheer guts they displayed in the early days of the war. I hope the fliers' appreciation showed through in these stories.

America cannot shoulder the same proportion of the Allied burden that it did in Desert Storm again. The air forces we deployed simply don't exist any more, while no future Saddam will allow us to build up for months when only faced with a speed bump division. But our forces are being reduced by Cold War standards that, for example, place little value on specialized airplanes to fly reconnaissance, missile suppression, or close air support. The Cold War is over, so regional conflicts such as Desert Storm are far more likely than WWIII in Central Europe. Armed forces should be structured accordingly. Lightweight, multirole jets, for example, proved inadequate. Inadequate equipment kills.

We rely far too much on the F-16. Viper drivers (F-16 pilots) are required to stay current in five missions and now must become true close air support experts since nearly 80% of the A-10s have been retired to the boneyard. The F-16 is simply too lightweight and fuel-limited for CAS, while her pilots, extremely capable though they are, have been tasked too heavily. The multimission panacea only works so far and is beyond the limits of that lightweight, single-engined airplane. Regardless of budget problems, extremely specialized missions require specialized airplanes and crews.

We don't pay enough attention to airplane survivability. A-10s were hit 70 times. If they had been F-16s or Harriers, we would have lost 50 of them behind the lines instead of four. The A-10s took that many hits because attack must be flown low and slow enough to identify friendly troops as well as targets. They also destroyed just over half of all the armor, vehicles, artillery, etc., hit by the Allies while sustaining that damage. Let me say that again: 144 A-10s accounted for half of the mobile ground targets destroyed by the Allies while only losing four jets behind the lines and two more during emergency landings. Of the damaged A-10s, 94% got back to friendly lines; less than 40% of the damaged F-16s made it out of Iraqi airspace. The modern battlefield is so lethal that speed is no guarantee, and staying high out of the defenses deprives soldiers of the support that means life or death to them. Airplanes in combat are going to be hit, so we need to design for that certainty.

Institutional prejudices interfered with common sense, again. For example, a commander of the American Tactical Air Command decreed that low-flying airplanes would look like trees. He ignored the expert advice found in his own camouflage studies and the obvious fact that gunners look up at airplanes. As a result, F-15Es, F-4Gs, F-111s, A-10s, and eventually even cargo jets were painted in very dark colors. Some of that mistake was corrected, but most of those planes went to war with camouflage designs that are as easy to see as the Blue Angels. At best, that thoughtless legacy caused several pilots to sit out the war in Baghdad who shouldn't have. At worst, it killed Syph. We're better than that, and good leaders know to listen to their experts. The British re-painted jets enroute to the desert as a matter of common sense. There's no excuse.

American Reserve forces were not always used as intended, al-though they did a fine job in spite of the handicap. Many Reserve and National Guard transport fliers, for example, were called to active duty without full support on the ground. Service obligations were extended several times at the last minute, which caused the added stress of un-certainty and disrupted their employers' efforts to hold the fort back home. Other Reservists were mobilized only to fill make-work positions in the States. Reserve and National Guard units should be mobilized with full support, the way they train, and in the manner specified by the in-tent of the law.

Allies will not always be there when you need them. Using just the B-52 example, Spain would not allow them in before the shooting started, so the first BUFF missions were 35-hour round trips from Louisiana. Turkey hesitated on clearance through its airspace and so aborted the second night's missions. Remember France's refusal to allow F-111s through enroute to Libya? The only resources we can always count on are the ones we own, such as the Navy and those based at home.

The homefront POW/MIA issues were handled poorly. Except for the well-staffed Air Force office, none of the POW/MIA affairs people had over a year's experience, and the Army even changed its senior of-ficer in that office a week before the war started. Individual casualty as-sistance officers and NCOs gave their all, but there was very little consistency or direction from the top. We spent months preparing for the war, but no discernible time preparing for that inevitable conse-quence.

There was too much eye wash. For example, senior officers flew combat missions just to fill that square while endangering other fliers with their limited proficiency. American leadership apparently deceived the British public about the circumstances of a friendly fire incident. On the morale level, the only time some units had good food in the mess tent was when VIPs were around. The good food, Cokes, etc., disap-peared with them. We're all on the same side and should be able to put the mission before individual careers, admit tragic though honest mistakes, and support our people well even if they're not VIPs. Such examples were given by junior officers to illustrate the point that few peacetime (bureaucratic) people managers made the transition to combat leadership.

Allied training was superb. Fliers consistently remarked at how much the war ran like a Red Flag exercise. One junior tank commander at the Battle of 73 Easting commented that he'd already been to war 15 times in training so he knew what to expect. Unwise cuts in training budgets will erase this critical force multiplier, which was the key to Allied dominance and which saved many lives.

Allied equipment was equally superb. High tech proved to be reliable and a life saver for both the Allies and the Iraqis. I expect a few ex-Soviet generals were relived that their 10-foot tall reputation was never tested in Central Europe.

Initiative and flexibility are the norm at the small unit level, but were also seen on a much larger scale. Tactics quickly shifted to medium altitudes when that proved more survivable (though at the expense of accuracy in some airplanes), unusual missions were quickly assigned as unexpected needs popped up, and leaders all the way to the Secretary of Defense were genuinely concerned that things were done right.

This summary pointed out a few areas that didn't go as well as they could have, but don't take that as an indictment of the system. Desert Storm was a very successful military action from the first deployments through the cease-fire. Compared to Vietnam and even operations as recent as Grenada and Panama, it was flawless.

Those improvements over our recent history were bought with the blood of Vietnam vets. Guys, we are truly grateful. Thank you. And welcome home.

Afterword

The Persian Gulf war proved that the military learned most of the lessons from Vietnam pretty well. While some things won't change (such as politics that become too important to military leaders after long periods of peace), the equipment, training, and congressional interference problems I saw during the Vietnam War weren't there.

Internal politics and overly conservative leadership aren't new. Senior officers' careers are on the line with every action of the junior officers in their command, and those leaders have to be careful not to offend the political positions of their superiors. Junior officers tend to be a little bit more foolhardy and reckless: Their recklessness is what wins or loses wars. At least that problem of politics in the military wasn't nearly as bad recently as it was in Vietnam.

Senior officers also quite often go into combat with preconceived ideas, especially those who haven't been in combat before. Although leaders have to keep the reins, junior officers are often better able to look at the situation and adapt. I coined a phrase that came back to haunt me when I became a commander: "Why let rank lead when ability can do it better?" That's still true today, because the junior officers soak in the environment and adapt better than their leaders. I suppose you could say the same thing about Congress.

Problems with bureaucrats in leadership positions are relatively minor. More important was the fact that Desert Storm was a change from the recent past in that we had the equipment and training to fight. There's no substitute for being prepared, but we have a history of waiting too long before accepting the fact that we may have to fight. America was behind the power curve going into World War I. We still didn't have the proper machines, the proper aircraft, or the proper training when we were dragged into World War II, even though fighting had gone on for two years by then. That war lasted a long time and allowed us to gear up. There was a lot of experience still left within the military when the Korean War started, but, due to the cutbacks after World War II, our equipment was inadequate again. When the Vietnam War started, our aircraft were again antiquated, and most of the leaders with combat experience were gone. Part of that problem repeated recently when we didn't have the transport aircraft or the bottoms, the ships, to carry out the deployment plans for Desert Shield and so had to depend on foreign ships and civilian aircraft.

As a generation of war fighters goes by, the bean counters and people without combat experience take over with their weird ideas on how to fight. For example, we went into Vietnam with aircraft and pilots who were only equipped to intercept bombers and who had never trained against other types of fighters. We took a beating. The leaders of that time didn't want to risk pilots in training, so we lost many more of them to Vietnamese MiGs instead. We solved that problem after Vietnam with good aggressor programs that trained our people to fight against Soviet tactics and dissimilar aircraft.

But now, with the cutbacks, we've eliminated most specialized aircraft like those aggressors. We'll have young Jonathan Livingston Seagulls trying to train in too many areas with their multirole jets. They'll end up doing everything average and nothing well.

The fliers and their families you read about in this book are the best young people America has to offer. I'm as proud of them as I am of the men I flew into combat with. These fliers, and the other service people with them, put the ghost of Vietnam to rest. Now it's our turn to see that they are ready for the next, inevitable, conflict.

> God Bless & Check Six,
> Duke

Representative Randy "Duke" Cunningham is the only Navy ace from Vietnam. He now represents California's 51st District in the U.S. House of Representatives.

'Nuff said.

THE END

Glossary

A-6   Intruder.

AC   Aircraft commander.

ATC   Air Training Command.

ACM   Air combat maneuvering. Fundamental dogfighting maneuvers. (Chapter 3)

aeroscouts   Helicopter scouts who search the battlefield and report back. They're the commander's eyes, and, if teamed with attack helicopters, one of his most potent weapons. This mission is often flown by the OH-58 Kiowa. (Chapter 14)

afterburner   Aft section of a fighter's engines that inject raw fuel into the exhaust for a very fuel-expensive burst of power. Reheat. Can. Blower. (Chapter 7)

aimed (directed) fire   Anti-aircraft fire deliberately aimed at a specific aircraft, as in shooting skeet. (Chapter 6)

Air Force Reserves   The American Air Force comes in three parts—active-duty, the Reserves, and the Air National Guard. (Chapter 1)

air spare   Airborne backup airplane. On critical deployments, spare airplanes and crews stand by to fill in for scheduled airplanes that drop out for any reason. Air spares take off with the group and fly to a predetermined point where, if they're not needed, they turn around and return home. (Chapter 7)

Air Training Command (ATC)   Air Force command that handles all pilot training among many other training functions. As a nonoperational, stateside command, ATC became stagnant with an overemphasis on tradition and politics. (Chapter 1)

aircraft commander (AC)   The individual responsible for the aircraft, crew, and its mission. He or she commands an aircraft just as a captain commands a ship. (Chapter 1)

alarm red   Warning of incoming attack. (Chapter 9)

Alex   England AFB near Alexandria, Louisiana. (Chapter 4)

ALR-67   RWR system on an F/A-18 Hornet. (Chapter 2)

ALS   Air Lift Squadron. A later identification for MAS. (Chapter 1)

APU   Auxiliary power unit. A small jet engine in the fuselage of a plane that supplies electric, hydraulic, and pneumatic power for ground and emergency operations. (Chapter 1)

attack   Though generically known as fighter pilots, attack pilots bring the fight directly to the enemy forces on the battlefield. Not fighters dueling high out of sight or bombers leveling whole acres, attack pilots fight in the teeth of the air defenses and often within easy sight of the friendly troops. One attack pilot was paraphrased as saying aerial combat was simply the irritating delay attack pilots have to put up with as they shoot down any fighters that try to interfere with their real mission of hitting ground targets. A pair of USS *Saratoga* F/A-18s dispatched a pair of Iraqi MiG-21s just that way before delivering their bombs as planned. (Chapter 2)

Aviation Officer Candidate School (AOCS)   Fourteen weeks of basic military training by Marine drill instructors. See *An Officer and a Gentleman.* (Chapter 2)

AWACS   Airborne Warning and Control System. Heavily modified Boeing 707 airframe sporting a radar disk on top that monitors huge volumes of the sky. Used to spot enemy aircraft and control the battle from behind friendly lines. (Chapter 2)

bag   External drop tank for extra fuel. (Chapter 7)

bandit   Confirmed hostile aircraft. (Chapter 2)

barrage fire   Unaimed anti-aircraft artillery fired in the air to create a lethal barrier over the ground unit. (Chapter 6)

base   That part of the normal landing pattern perpendicular to the runway, just before the turn to final approach. (Chapter 1)

basket   Aircraft that use probe and drogue refueling, like Navy and Marine aircraft as well as helicopters, plug into a cone-shaped receptacle, the basket, on the end of the refueling hose. (Chapter 2)

bay five   Storage space behind the seat of an F-15. (Chapter 10)

BBs   Bullets. (Chapter 11)

BDU Olympics   Intramural bombing competition using practice bombs (BDUs) on small, nontactical weapons ranges. (Chapter 4)

BFM   Basic fighter maneuvers. Simple attacks and defenses that fighter pilots learn as the basis for more fluid fights. BFM is practiced as a warm-up to more intense dogfight training. (Chapter 10)

bingo Radio call meaning, "I'm out of fuel and must go home now." A low fuel state. (Chapter 4)

Black Hawk UH-60 transport and utility helicopter. Replaced the UH-1 Huey. Special operations version is designated MH-60. (Chapter 12)

Black Jet Shaba. The F-117. (Chapter 13)

blind Radio call: "I can't see the friendly aircraft." (Chapter 10)

blood chits Leaflets with phrases printed in many languages promising rewards for helping downed airmen. (Chapter 3)

blowers Afterburners. Cans. Reheat. (Chapter 2)

bluey Blue British airmail letter form. (Chapter 8)

B/N Bombardier/navigator.

board Runway length-remaining marker. All runways have signs showing how much runway is left, so the nine-board indicates 9000 feet remaining. (Chapter 3)

bogey Unidentified and possibly hostile aircraft. Could be friendly, neutral/civilian, or hostile. Treated as hostile for monitoring but will not be attacked unless confirmed hostile. See bandit. (Chapter 2)

bombardier/navigator (B/N) Half of an attack jet's flight crew, the B/N is responsible for everything but the piloting. B/Ns navigate to the target, find it on radar, designate it with the laser, clear the pilot to release the weapons, and then find their way home. (Chapter 3)

boomer Enlisted person who operates the boom on a tanker aircraft. (Chapter 9)

bracket Refueling connection made when a British pilot flies the plane's probe into the refueling drogue. (Chapter 8)

Bradley U.S. Army's newest armored personnel carrier. Replaced the M-113. (Chapter 14)

bravo alert Airlift contingency status that keeps a crew ready to lift off in less than three and a half hours for up to 48 hours at a time. (Chapter 1)

break/broke (verb) As in "break turn," the act of making a max-performance, last-ditch, everything-she's-got turn to avoid being hit by a missile. (Chapter 2)

briefing (verb) Preparing for a mission. (Chapter 12)

BUFF Big, Ugly, Flying, um. . . Fellow. "Affectionate" nickname for the B-52 Stratofortress. (Chapter 6)

buffoonery To behave like a lower primate (apologies to those buffoons who know the real correlation between fighter pilots and even hairier primates). Some would say flying fighters isn't exactly smart in the first place, so comparing the low points to ape behavior is considered insulting by real buffoons. (Chapter 2)

bull's-eye Common geographic reference point. Usually refers to the common reference used by radar controllers to point out enemy aircraft such as, "Bandit, bull's-eye one six zero (degrees) for 30 (nautical miles), heading south at 35,000 feet. (Chapter 2)

buster Hurry. Signal to go to full speed. Used by pilots when entering the target area or when bandits are present. (Chapter 2)

CAEX ("kaks") Combined arms exercise. Marine exercise to practice integrating all air and ground assault forces. Conducted at the Marine Corps Air Ground Combat Center at Twentynine Palms, California. (Chapter 11)

CAG Carrier Air Group. Unit composed of all aircraft stationed on a carrier. "The CAG" usually refers to the wing commander who leads all the aircraft assigned to his carrier. (Chapter 2)

cans Afterburners. Reheat. Blowers. (Chapter 2)

CAP Combat Air Patrol. Interceptors roaming assigned areas looking for trouble. Interceptors sweeping in front of a strike to clear the skies of enemy aircraft. Fighter patrols to gain and maintain air superiority. Allied fighters did a spectacular job and never lost an escorted friendly to an enemy fighter. (Chapter 2)

cat Catapult.

CAS Close air support.

CBU Cluster bomb unit. Lots of little bomblets within one bomb casing. CBUs are further specified by their numerical designation, such as CBU-58 or CBU-87. (Chapter 4)

CENTAF Central Air Force. Command headquartered in Riyadh and at McDill AFB, Florida, that controlled essentially all Allied flying in the Kuwaiti theater. (Chapter 4)

chaff Radar-reflecting strips of metallic foil released in bunches to confuse radar. Bundles of chaff are released in clouds designed to blind enemy radar and decoy radar-guided missiles. (Chapter 2)

check turn Small turn of less than 90 degrees. Usually a course correction. (Chapter 10)

chock (noun) Block of wood or plastic wedged under a tire to prevent it from rolling. (verb) To put the chock in place. (Chapter 1)

chop Light turbulence, like driving on a rough road. (Chapter 2)

chute Diving attack flightpath. Probably a reference to everything coming together in one direction, as in a coal chute. (Chapter 3)

clock position To maintain a common reference, positions around an aircraft are labeled relative to a clock face, with 12 o'clock marking straight ahead. Something "at 11 o'clock" is at the aircraft's left front, and something "at six o'clock" is directly behind. (Chapter 8)

close air support (CAS) Attacks in very close proximity to, and in direct support of, friendly ground forces. This job is the toughest a fighter pilot can draw with the greatest chance of being shot down, killing friendly troops, or earning the Medal of Honor. Both Air Force Crosses won in Desert Storm were earned on attack missions. (Chapter 4)

CMS Combat mission simulator. AH-64 Apache simulator. Ultimate video game. (Chapter 14)

CO Commanding officer. Unit commander. (Chapter 15)

combat fuel Reserve fuel above that required to complete the route. (Chapter 8)

combat mix Different types of cannon shells loaded together to allow attacks on a wide range of targets. (Chapter 9)

combat ready British combat fliers train in their aircraft but are not ready to fight until checked out in their new unit's specific mission. A new theater means a new environment and, therefore, more training required. Same as mission ready in the USAF. (Chapter 8)

comm out Without communications. Executing a plan without using radios so as to reduce the chance of detection. (Chapter 4)

command post Command and control center on a base that handles the flow of aircraft, keeps track of the crews, etc. (Chapter 1)

conformal tanks External fuel tank that are molded, or conformed, to the sides of an airplane. Most common on the F-15E. (Chapter 7)

cons Contrails. At the right combination of temperature and water vapor, jet exhausts leave white trails in the sky. Fighters normally avoid the "con level" so as to not be highlighted against the sky. (Chapter 10)

Constant Carrot USAF personnel assignment program designed to reward the best fighter pilots with choice assignments. (Chapter 12)

contact point (CP) Easily identified spot on the ground used for rendezvous and navigation. Coded and classified so that all a fighter needs are orders to fly to "B123" and call "F4X22" (a typical ground controller callsign). (Chapter 9)

contact To see or be seen on radar (chapter 10). To meet the enemy (chapter 14).

CP Contact point.

crank To start the engine as in crank the motor's handle. No, they don't really crank a jet's handle. (Chapter 9)

crew chief Enlisted person who "owns" and babies a jet. When given a darn good reason, crew chiefs grudgingly lend their jets to fliers, who invariably break something that the long-suffering crew chief must fix before the next ham-fisted flier shows up. See plane captain. (Chapter 5)

crew rest The mandatory rest period a flier must have between duty days. Twelve hours off is required, although transport crews lived on 10-hour breaks for part of the crisis. (Chapter 1)

CSAR Combat search and rescue. (noun) Those units that rescue downed airmen in combat. (verb) Recovering downed airmen in combat. (Chapter 9)

Cub   Russian AN-12 Cub. Medium-sized turboprop transport similar to the C-130. (Chapter 10)

CVIC   Carrier Intelligence Center. "CV" stands for carrier, fixed wing. (Chapter 2)

DACT   Dissimilar air combat training.

danger close!   Formal warning given to attack pilots when friendly troops are closer to the target than the normal minimum safe clearance of one kilometer. (Chapter 12)

DASC   Direct Air Support Coordination Center. Marine "traffic cop" that directs fighters to their targets by radio. (Chapter 11)

DCA   Defensive counter air. Interceptor operations that prevent enemy fighters from interfering with friendly air operations. Interceptors form a barrier designed to protect the areas and orbits behind it. (Chapter 10)

designated mean point of impact (DMPI)   Exact spot on the target where an F-117's bomb will hit. (Chapter 13)

dets   Detachments. Deployments from the main unit or base for temporary operations somewhere else. (Chapter 3)

Diego Garcia   British island in the southern Indian ocean. It served as an unsinkable aircraft carrier for bombers, tankers, and transports. (Chapter 6)

dissimilar air combat training (DACT)   Mock air-to-air combat against an aircraft type other than your own. DACT is the whole idea behind advanced fighter schools such as Top Gun and exercises such as Red Flag. It's also a very big part of the reason why Allied fighter pilots proved to be unbeatable. (Chapter 11)

division   Navy and Marine term for four aircraft in formation. See four ship. (Chapter 2)

DO   Operations officer or ops officer—Air Force unit's second in command and the flier directly in charge of flying. (Chapter 9)

downrange   Final destination. In this case, it refers to the Persian Gulf area of operations. (Chapter 1)

downstairs   Lower level of a B-52 cockpit. Two crew members ride in the lower level and eject downward.

downtown   Metropolitan Baghdad or another heavily defended area. Fliers in Southeast Asia referred to a flight over Hanoi as "going downtown." Desert Storm fliers used the same term for heavily defended areas. (Chapter 7)

downwind   The part of a normal landing pattern that is parallel to the runway but flown in the direction opposite to landing, en route to the base turn. (Chapter 1)

dry   Without weapons. A dry attack is simulated; in a hot attack, a practice or live weapon is released. (Chapter 14)

dumb bombs Bombs without guidance. Opposite of laser-, TV-, etc., guided smart bombs. (Chapter 7)

E & E Escape and evasion.

EC-130 E (for electronic warfare) version of the C-130 light transport that jammed enemy radar and communications. They were a real showstopper for the Iraqi defenses. (Chapter 6)

ECM Electronic counter measures. Fighting electrons with electrons. Much of a modern war is fought with "electrons." This war of radars, radios, and jammers is critical to putting bombs on target. (Chapter 3)

egress To leave the target area. (Chapter 2)

element Air Force formation of two airplanes within a larger formation. A two ship. (Chapter 5)

engine running offload/onload Most military transport airplanes can load or unload in a hurry with the engines running. (Chapter 1)

envelope Flight regime of an aircraft or missile as in the altitude, airspeed, and range capabilities. (Chapter 2)

EPW Enemy prisoner of war. (Chapter 9)

escape and evasion E & E. Resistance techniques used to avoid capture or to escape. (Chapter 12)

EW Early warning radar. (Chapter 2)

exfill Exfiltrate. To withdraw. (Chapter 12)

eye wash Window dressing. More glitter than substance. (Chapter 4)

F-4 Phantom II Vietnam-era, multi-mission jet fighter. The Rhino. (Chapter 11)

F-18D Two-seat F/A-18 Hornet. Normally used for training, although it's fully combat capable. See Fast FAC. (Chapter 15)

FAC Forward air controller. Close air support specialist who controls all the weapons delivered in his assigned area. Desert Storm saw many aircraft fill this role, from the traditional FACs (OA-10s and OV-10s) to the Fast FACs (F-16s and F/A-18s). The faster jets could reach their targets quickly but were forced to stay well above the ground fire, lacked endurance, and did not carry marking rockets. OA-10s, the FAC version of the A-10, were rugged with the best loiter and target-marking capabilities but could not survive in space defended by the better SAMs. (Chapter 12)

FAIP First assignment instructor pilot. Air Force pilot training instructor fresh out of pilot training. Technically proficient and fighter qualified, FAIPs were commonly nonvolunteers with poor morale because the assignment system did them no favors after that first assignment. (Chapter 10)

fangs Sign of overly aggressive behavior, as in letting the hormones take over. (Chapter 15)

farkle   To diddle; to make minor changes. (Chapter 13)

farley   Unofficial; nonsense; under the table. Taken from the movie *The Three Amigos* by F-117 pilots. (Chapter 13)

FARP   Forward arming and refueling point. Bare base operation for refueling and rearming only. (Chapter 15)

Fast FAC   Forward air controller. Fighter aircraft (such as the F-18 or F-16) used to control air-to-ground attacks in place of the slower, traditional FAC planes like the OV-10 Bronco and the OA-10 Warthog. See FAC. (Chapter 12)

fence   Boundary between the good guys and the bad guys. As John Wayne would've said, "When you cross the fence into Indian country, partner, you'd better have your guns loaded and your feces consolidated." (Chapter 6)

fighter qualified   Fighter, Attack, Reconnaissance (FAR) ratings are subjective judgments of Air Force pilot training instructors that a new pilot is good enough to handle any plane in the inventory. A FAR rating is required before assignment to fighters or instructor duty. (Chapter 9)

Fighter Weapons School (FWS)   The Air Force "doctorate" program in combat flying based at Nellis AFB, Las Vegas, Nevada. Similar to the Navy's Top Gun program, though twice as long and more detailed. Renamed simply USAF Weapons School. (Chapter 4)

filling squares   Meeting requirements, as in marking off the square blocks on a checklist. (Chapter 1)

final (approach)   Last part of a landing pattern before touchdown. Last part of a bombing attack before weapons release. (Chapter 1)

fire handle   An emergency engine shutdown system that cuts off all fuel, fluids, and ignition. On a plane with more than one flier, both confirm that the proper engine is being shut down to avoid getting that deafening silence from the wrong engine. (Chapter 1)

firewall   Reference to the fire barrier between the engine and the cockpit on old piston-engined fighters. Throttles were usually rods that stuck out of that firewall, so firewalling the throttle meant pushing it all the way to the stops without regard to the damage full power might do to the engine. It's better to bring back damaged engines than to not come home at all. (Chapter 6)

five-fifty cord   Very thin, strong nylon cord with a 550-pound tensile strength. Similar to the cords used on parachutes. (Chapter 12)

flight deck   On a carrier, the flight deck is the flat part on top covered with the semicontrolled chaos of flight operations. Aircraft take off and land on the flight deck. (Chapter 2)

flight lead(er)   Pilot in command of a formation of aircraft. Combat aircraft usually fly in fours or pairs with one flight lead commanding the whole formation and an element or section lead commanding the second pair if in a four ship or division. (Chapter 4)

flight plan (verb) To check the weather, notices, fuel requirements, routes, etc., and complete a flight plan. (noun) Standard form listing mission information and route of flight. (Chapter 1)

FLIR Forward Looking Infrared.

FLOT Forward line of troops. Imaginary line drawn along the positions of the friendly troops who are closest to the enemy. (Chapter 14)

flying clothing section Part of a British flying unit responsible for the fit and maintenance of the flier's survival kit. Same as USAF life support. (Chapter 8)

FMC Fully mission capable.

FOL Forward operating location. Marine or Air Force bare base close to the action, used for refueling, rearming, and emergency recovery. (Chapter 9)

Forward Looking Infrared (FLIR) Imaging system that produced an infrared view for fliers. That image was seen often on bombing video. (Chapter 7)

four ship Four aircraft in formation fighting as a team. Division. (Chapter 5)

fox mike Phonetic alphabet for "FM." Usually refers to a radio used by ground forces and the aircraft that support them. (Chapter 9)

fox! Radio call meaning, "I'm firing." (Chapter 10)

frag (verb) To be hit with fragmented pieces of an exploding warhead. (noun) Fragmentation (chapter 6). High-velocity metal parts from a bomb casing. Fragmentary order (chapter 13). Relevant piece of a day's air battle plan that each flying unit receives.

fragged (verb) To be assigned a mission that is listed in the frag, or fragmentary order. (Chapter 4)

freq Frequency. (Chapter 10)

Frog Soviet-made, short-range ballistic missile. (Chapter 4)

fuel flow A measure of how much fuel is being pumped to an engine. The fuel is supposed to be burned normally, but, if the engine is damaged, raw fuel may be pumped into the engine area, causing an extreme fire hazard. (Chapter 1)

Fulcrum MiG-29. Latest-generation Soviet fighter bomber. Roughly similar to the F-18 and the best fighter the Iraqis had. (Chapter 5)

fully mission capable (FMC) Aircraft status code indicating that it is ready to fly without restrictions. All important systems work. (Chapter 15)

FWS Fighter Weapons School.

G-limited Flight restriction on the acceleration, Gs, an airplane can stand. Such restrictions are usually the result of old wings beginning to crack at the end of their useful lives. No flier wants to go into combat in a limited jet. (Chapter 3)

G-model   Aircraft and missile variations are designated with suffixes, so a G-model B-52 is newer than a D-model but older than an H-model. (Chapter 6)

GBU-27   2000-pound laser-guided bomb designed solely for the F-117. Its specially hardened case and improved laser guidance system were designed to penetrate hardened targets. (Chapter 13)

GCI   Ground-controlled intercept. Under the Soviet system, fighters are held on a short leash by radar controllers and become very dependent on directions over the radio. Western fliers, conversely, are barely controllable in the best of times (sic) and so need only be pointed in the right direction with permission to fire. Western pilots are selected for initiative and individual skill, giving them a distinct advantage over pilots dependent on GCI. That also partially explains their formidable and well-deserved egos. (Chapter 2)

GCI site   Radar station whose controllers direct fighters very closely on intercepts. Key part of the inflexible Soviet-style air defense system and vulnerable to disruption. See GCI. (Chapter 4)

gear   Landing gear. The wheels. (Chapter 1)

glass cockpit   Instead of standard dials and instruments, modern aircraft display information on video screens. Much of the instrument panel space is taken up by that "glass." (Chapter 13)

go pill   Upper prescribed by a flight surgeon that a flier has the option of using on an extremely long mission. Go pills caused problems with spatial disorientation and dependency and so probably will no longer be used routinely. (Chapter 13)

go speed   On heavy aircraft, the copilot calls "Go" at a predetermined speed, meaning the aircraft is committed to takeoff. (Chapter 1)

golden BB   That one magic cannon shell with your name on it that hits you out of sheer dumb luck. (Chapter 13)

GPS   Global positioning system. Constellation of satellites that allow users to fix their position very accurately if enough of the satellites are within view. (Chapter 12)

grand   One thousand feet. Eighteen to 20 grand is 18,000 to 20,000 feet. (Chapter 9)

groove   Glidepath to a landing on a carrier. (Chapter 2)

grunt   Infantryman. (Chapter 4)

guard   Common emergency frequency that all NATO aircraft monitor. (Chapter 4)

Guardsman   Member of the National Guard. (Chapter 9)

hangar deck   Floor of an aircraft hangar. (Chapter 15)

hard target   Armored or reinforced object, such as tanks or bunkers. (Chapter 14)

HARM   High-speed anti-radiation missile. Very fast, very lethal air-to-ground radar homing missile used to kill radar sites. Follow-on to the Shrike carried by the original Wild Weasels in Southeast Asia. (Chapter 2)

HAS   ("haz") Hardened aircraft shelter. Reinforced concrete shelters that both protected airplanes and attracted laser-guided bombs. (Chapter 8)

heavy airlift airplanes (heavies)   Usually refers to transports, tankers, or bombers. (Chapter 1)

HEI   High-explosive incendiary. Cannon shells that are essentially high-velocity grenades. (Chapter 9)

Hellfire   Army's best, helicopter-launched, anti-armor missile. It homes in on a laser beam fired by any number of lasers deployed across the battlefield. (Chapter 14)

high value unit (HVU)   Navy term for an airborne asset worth protecting with its own escort. (Chapter 2)

hits   Radar returns the controller can see on his screen. (Chapter 10)

Hog   Warthog. A-10 Thunderbolt II's more common nickname. (Chapter 4)

hole   Aircraft parking bay in a hardened shelter. Think of a multicar garage with many feet of concrete on top and jets inside. (Chapter 13)

hook   (noun) Arresting gear tailhook on the back of a carrier-based airplane (chapter 2). (verb) To turn around in a pattern that resembles a fish hook (chapter 7).

HUD   Heads up display. Small glass screen on top of the instrument panel that displays critical flight and weapons data. Allows the pilot to fly and fight without the potentially fatal distraction of looking inside the cockpit. Allows "heads up" rather than "heads down" flight. The rapidly moving symbols seen in gun camera film were projected on the HUD and used by the pilot to control the aircraft. (Chapter 7)

Humvee   Four-wheeled, all-purpose, all-terrain replacement for the Jeep. Variants carried TOW missiles, grenade launchers, or machine guns. (Chapter 15)

HVU   High value unit.

IFF   Identification Friend or Foe. Electronic identification system. (Chapter 3)

IL-76   Russian IL-76 Candid. Large cargo aircraft that looks amazingly like the Lockheed C-141 Starlifter. (Chapter 10)

in the corner   To push the throttles all the way to their stops, which are in the front left corner of the cockpit. (Chapter 15)

in the weeds   Really low. If your job is to penetrate radar defenses and you aren't scaring squirrels out of the trees, you're doing something wrong. (Chapter 6)

infill   Infiltrate. (Chapter 12)

Intell   Intelligence. Department that briefs intelligence information to fliers. People who brief intelligence information. Intelligence information itself. (Chapter 3)

interdiction   Attacks on targets behind the front lines, designed to isolate the battlefield by cutting the enemy off from his support. (Chapter 11)

Intruder (A-6 Intruder)   Navy and Marine Vietnam-era medium bomber. Subsonic, two-seat, very accurate, all-weather workhorse also flown as a four-seat electronic warfare jet (EA-6B Prowler). (Chapter 3)

IP   Initial point (chapter 3). Known geographic reference from where the final attack run begins. Instructor pilot (chapter 9). Pilot qualified to train other pilots. Selection as an Air Force pilot training instructor was not generally considered to be a good deal.

iron   Heavy aircraft weapons such as "iron" bombs. Conventional, high-explosive bombs. Simply iron (steel), explosives, and a fuse, these are essentially the same unguided weapons dropped in every war since WWI. (Chapter 9)

isolation   Green Beret teams plan missions while sequestered from everyone else. They won't say a word about the mission when away from their isolated area. (Chapter 12)

JAAT   Joint air attack team. Attack helicopters and jets (usually A-10s) fighting together. Coordinated, rehearsed attack by helicopters and jets. Since the defense against helicopters with anti-tank missiles is very different from the defense against jets using cannons, missiles, and cluster bombs, the target is faced with the impossible job of switching tactics every 90 seconds or so. A real meat grinder. (Chapter 14)

Jet Provost   British-built, single-engined jet trainer similar to the T-37 (Tweet). (Chapter 8)

jockey   Airplane driver. Flier. (Chapter 6)

KC-135   Tanker or refueling aircraft based on the Boeing 707 airframe. Any aircraft with a "K" prefix is a tanker. They were some of the unsung heroes of the war. (Chapter 2)

key the mike   Press the microphone button to talk on the radio. (Chapter 9)

King's X   Calling a halt to a deteriorating situation before matters get worse. (Chapter 9)

KKMC   King Khalid Military City. No-frills military complex centered on a 12,000-foot runway 40 miles south of the point where Iraq, Kuwait, and Saudi Arabia come together. A forward operating location. (Chapter 9)

klick   Kilometer. (Chapter 12)

knot   Nautical mile per hour. A knot equals about 1.14 miles, so 480 knots equals about 550 mph. (Chapter 2)

KTO   Kuwaiti theater of operations. The war zone. (Chapter 12)

laser tag   Modern battlefield exercises are scored by computers and lasers. Each weapon has a laser mounted on it, plus an array of laser sensors to declare "kills." Also, hitting a target with a laser-guided weapon. (Chapter 7)

live fire   Practice with real weapons and ammunition versus simulated, or dry, training. (Chapter 14)

lock   Radar lock-on. To highlight a target by radar just prior to killing it. (Chapter 2)

loft attack   To release bombs while climbing so they fly a ballistic arc to the target like artillery. Designed to increase the distance between the bomber and a high threat target. (Chapter 7)

lost wingman   Planned and rehearsed turn away from the formation that wingmen use when they lose sight of their leaders in clouds. (Chapter 4)

low threat   Measure of the enemy's defenses, meaning "not too bad." Generally assuming an absence of radar-guided missiles or enemy fighters, low threat tactics are flown above ground fire versus high threat tactics, which are flown below radar coverage. (Chapter 4)

LSO   Landing signal officer. Specially trained flier on duty at the back of a carrier to ensure all landings are safe and to grade the landings. (Chapter 2)

MAC   Military Airlift Command.

mach   Aircraft speed relative to the speed of sound. Point 94 mach, for example, is 94% of the speed of sound. (Chapter 2)

main tank round   Canon projectile fired by a tank. A tank has a large cannon in the middle, the main gun, plus heavy machine guns. A main tank round is the 105mm+ shell fired by the main gun. (Chapter 14)

Marine Corps Air Station (MCAS)   Marine Corps base. (Chapter 3)

MAS   Military Airlift Squadron, a unit of the Military Airlift Command. (Chapter 1)

Maverick   AGM-65A/B/D/G. Short, stubby, TV- or infrared-guided air-to-ground missile carried almost exclusively by the A-10. Most have 125-pound shaped-charge warheads, but the G-model has a 300-pound blast warhead. It's a Maverick on steroids. Extremely lethal, the Maverick and the Sidewinder are sometimes referred to as "I wish you were dead" missiles. (Chapter 4)

MCAS   Marine Corps Air Station.

MCCRES   Marine Corps Combat Readiness Evaluation System. As-real-as-possible test of a unit's combat readiness. Similar to Air Force Operational Readiness Inspection. (Chapter 3)

MEB   Marine Expeditionary Brigade. Approximately 17,000 Marines with 30 days of combat supplies. (Chapter 15)

MEZ Missile engagement zone. One of the defensive rings around a naval battle group, the MEZ is an extremely dangerous place for hostile or unidentified aircraft or any aviator who's recently insulted a radar operator. See Robocruiser. (Chapter 2)

Military Airlift Command (MAC) The Air Force transport aircraft people. Superseded by the Air Mobility Command. (Chapter 1)

mins Minimums. Could be minimum fuel, minimum weather limits, etc. (Chapter 8)

Mirage Family of fighters built by France. (Chapter 5)

mirror strike Air strike dress rehearsal, whereby the attack is flown up to the enemy border and then turned, or reflected, back into friendly territory. The flight planned for enemy airspace is simulated over friendly lands. (Chapter 11)

MK-82 ("mark eighty-two") General-purpose, 500-pound, high-explosive bomb. (Chapter 4)

MK-83 ("mark eighty-three") General-purpose, 1000-pound, high-explosive bomb. (Chapter 3)

MK-84 ("mark eighty-four") General-purpose, 2000-pound, high-explosive bomb. (Chapter 2)

mobility kill Immobilization of a vehicle. On the modern battlefield, an immobile vehicle is as good as dead. There are also firepower kills (knock out the main weapons) and catastrophic kills (the target blows up). (Chapter 11)

mode four Classified part of the Identification Friend or Foe system that electronically identifies an aircraft to properly equipped radars (like those connected to missiles). (Chapter 5)

MRE Meal ready to eat (or meal rejected by everyone, if you like). High-calorie field rations that replaced the Vietnam-era C rations. (Chapter 10)

National Training Center (NTC) Army's desert warfare training area at Fort Irwin, California. It covers nearly all of the Mojave Desert between Barstow and Death Valley. (Chapter 14)

nav brevet Navigator's brevet. Aircrew qualification badge worn by RAF navigators. (Chapter 8)

Navy common Frequency used together by all Navy aircraft in an operation. Air Force slang for the emergency frequency all military aircraft must monitor, but only the Navy seems to use to chat. See guard. (Chapter 2)

NBC Nuclear, biological, and chemical. (Chapter 15)

NCO Noncommissioned officer. Senior enlisted person who does most of the work in the military, while allowing officers the ego-saving illusion of control. (Chapter 1)

net Network. Collection of individuals or units using a particular radio frequency. (Chapter 9)

NFO Naval flight officer. Navy or Marine flier who is not a pilot; B/Ns, for example. (Chapter 3)

nose Front of the airplane. "The targets are on/off the nose" means directly in front of the airplane. (Chapter 2)

nozzles Variable exhaust nozzles on a Harrier that allow vertical take-offs and landings. They're controlled by a lever in the cockpit. (Chapter 15)

NTC National Training Center.

O-levels and A-levels Formal examinations for certificates of education in the United Kingdom. O-levels are taken at about 16 years old and a student can opt out of school then. A-levels are taken at about 18 and are required to enter university. Roughly eight percent of those leaving school go on to college. (Chapter 8)

OA-37 Dragonfly Souped-up FAC version of the Cessna T-37 Tweety Bird. Overpowered when empty, the OA-37 was sometimes called the "Killer Tweet." (Chapter 13)

OCA Offensive counter air.

off Done with the attack and moving away. "Lead is off the target." (Chapter 3)

offensive counter air (OCA) Taking the battle for air superiority to the enemy by attacking his aircraft and their supporting infrastructure on the ground and over his territory. (Chapter 8)

OH-58 Kiowa Small, single-engined, four-place utility helicopter. See aeroscout. (Chapter 14)

oh-dark-thirty Any very dark time of the early morning. (Chapter 12)

on the boom Connected to the refueling probe (boom) that extends from the back of a tanker. (Chapter 6)

one-v-one One versus one. One airplane in a fight with one other airplane. (Chapter 9)

ops Operations. Section that controls the flying while other people handle maintenance, administration, supply, etc. (Chapter 10)

ordies Ordnance specialists. Weapons loaders. The guys who arm the airplanes. (Chapter 2)

outrigger The very small landing gear that extend from the wingtips of a Harrier. (Chapter 15)

outside the aircraft Figure of speech meaning attention is focused outside the cockpit while leaving the instruments, displays, weapons, etc., to other crew members. (Chapter 6)

OV-10 Bronco Vietnam-era, twin turboprop observation plane originally designed for counterinsurgency and now used by the Marines for forward air control and light attack. (Chapter 13)

patch wearer Fighter Weapons School graduate who wears the FWS patch on one shoulder. Also called "target arms" because the FWS patch includes a prominent bull's-eye. (Chapter 10)

PCS Permanent change of station. Permanent move from one base and assignment to another as opposed to a temporary assignment and return. (Chapter 6)

picture clear Radio call meaning, "The radar screen is free of unknown or enemy aircraft." (Chapter 8)

piddle pack Heavy baggy with a sponge used for inflight relief. (Chapter 9)

pipper Gunsight. (Chapter 10)

pitch pull To lift a helicopter off the ground. Helicopter lift is controlled by changing the pitch, or angle, of the rotor blades. To take off, a pilot increases blade pitch by pulling on the lever that controls pitch. (Chapter 14)

plane captain Enlisted man responsible for the care and feeding of a Navy or Marine aircraft. See crew chief. (Chapter 2)

plug To hook up with an aerial refueling tanker. (Chapter 11)

pond Ocean. Usually the Atlantic Ocean. (Chapter 1)

pop Pop-up attack. Climbing then diving maneuver that takes a bomber from low altitude to a diving attack. Pops usually include a turn toward the target, so a direct pop is one flown straight at the target without turns. (Chapter 7)

pounds of fuel Jet fuel is often measured by weight. The type used by most of these jets weighs 6.5 pounds per U.S. gallon, so 200,000 pounds was about 30,800 gallons. (Chapter 1)

preflight The aircraft inspection made prior to engine start. The preflight of a fighter takes the pilot a few minutes. The preflight of a C-5 takes both flight engineers about an hour and a half. (Chapter 1)

press Radio call meaning, "Continue your attack. I'll cover you." (Chapter 10)

punch off To drop or turn off. You can punch off (jettison) external fuel tanks to strip down for a fight or punch off a radio to silence it. (Chapter 7)

punch out To eject; to bail out; to take the nylon letdown. (Chapter 9)

queep Pile of authenticators, line up cards, maps, printouts, and other papers required on every flight. (Chapter 12)

radar altimeter Simple radar pointed down that displays exact altitude above the ground. (Chapter 6)

radar lock To automatically follow a target on radar. (Chapter 10)

radar trail Trail formation with one aircraft at a specified distance directly behind another. Radar is used to stay in position when the wingman can't see the leader such as at night or in the clouds. Trailing distance can be specified in time or distance. (Chapter 11)

RAF Royal Air Force.

RAG Reserve Air Group. Navy and Marine units that train qualified pilots in the specific missions of their new squadrons. (Chapter 2)

ramp   Multiple-acre concrete expanse where airplanes park. (Chapter 1)

recall   Bringing all unit members in to work on short notice, usually for a deployment or other contingency. (Chapter 9)

recce   ("recky") Reconnaissance. (Chapter 9)

Red Flag   Largest air war and interdiction exercise anywhere. Run many times a year on the instrumented ranges north and west of Las Vegas, this realistic training gave Allied pilots a real edge. (Chapter 3)

Reserve Officer Training Corps (ROTC)   Military scholarship program that pays for college and leads to a commission as an officer. (Chapter 1)

RF-4   Tactical reconnaissance version of the F-4 Phantom. (Chapter 4)

ring the bell   Military bars have ship's bells that are rung when someone is buying for the house. (Chapter 12)

RIO   ("ree-o") Radar intercept officer. A flier who operates the radar and weapons in a two-seat naval fighter. (Chapter 9)

Robocruiser   Guided missile cruiser with the Aegis system capable of shooting down everything in the sky almost simultaneously. (Chapter 2)

Rockeye   Cluster bomb containing 256 small shaped charges that behave like bazooka shells when they detonate. (Chapter 12)

ROE   Rules of engagement. Who can shoot what, when, and how. A sore point with the military, because politically imposed ROE allowed the Koreans, Chinese, and Vietnamese to use sanctuaries in past wars. (Chapter 2)

Roland missile   Very good surface-to-air missile built by a French and German consortium. (Chapter 7)

ROTC   Reserve Officer Training Corps.

rotor wash   Downward blast of air created by a helicopter's rotor. (Chapter 14)

Royal Air Force (RAF)   Land-based air force of the United Kingdom. (Chapter 8)

RPM   Revolutions per minute. Measure of the power being generated by a jet engine. (Chapter 1)

RTB   Return to base. Go home. (Chapter 10)

RTU   Replacement training unit. Air Force squadron the sole purpose of which is training pilots in their fighters before sending them to operational squadrons. Counterparts of Navy/Marine RAGs. (Chapter 10)

RWR   Radar warning receiver. Sensors that give fliers the direction and identity of radars that are looking at them. Very sophisticated radar detector that works on surface and airborne radars. Provides both audible and visible warning. To a flier in Indian country, this display of bad-guy radars is the neatest thing since hangover remedies. (Chapter 2)

SA-6   Soviet-built, low- to medium-altitude, radar-guided, surface-to-air missile. Bad news. (Chapter 3)

SA-8 Soviet-built, low-altitude, radar-guided, surface-to-air missile. (Chapter 3)

SA-16 Best Soviet-made, shoulder-launched, heat-seeking, surface-to-air missile. (Chapter 8)

SAC Strategic Air Command. One of the Air Force's major commands before the latest restructuring. SAC's mission was nuclear deterrence. They owned all of the Air Force's strategic nuclear weapons and the means to deliver them. (Chapter 4)

SAM Surface-to-air missile. Missile fired from the ground and guided to the target by radar, heat, laser, or some other energy. Soviet SAMs are designated "SA" and a number (such as SA-6); the higher the number, the newer and more deadly the missile. (Chapter 2)

Sandy Callsign originally used by attack aircraft specializing in search and rescue in Southeast Asia. Sandy One is always in charge during a rescue, and just hearing his callsign makes a downed flier's whole day. (Chapter 9)

SAR Search and rescue. One of the most dangerous and rewarding missions fliers draw. A Special Operations and A-10 specialty. (Chapter 9)

scanner A fully qualified flight engineer who moves around the airplane to check on trouble spots. (Chapter 1)

schnell German word meaning fast, quick. (Chapter 8)

scrum Massed formation in which rugby players hurl their unpadded bodies at each other. (Chapter 8)

scud Thin cloud layer. (Chapter 2)

Scud Russian-built, militarily useless terror weapon based on captured German V2 rockets. (Chapter 1)

SEAD Suppression of enemy air defenses. Reducing the threat to attacking aircraft. An attack is often led by aircraft that engage the enemy missiles and triple-A. Trolling for Jaws. (Chapter 3)

secondary explosion Detonation of something on the ground caused by an attack. (Chapter 2)

section Navy and Marine term for a formation of two aircraft. A two ship. (Chapter 3)

semi Semidetached house. Duplex. (Chapter 8)

Shaba Unofficial F-117 nickname. Arabic for a ghost who walks at night and is not seen. The F-117 does not have an official nickname, but its pilots prefer to call it "The Black Jet." One proposed nickname was "Wet Dream," because it comes in the middle of the night and there's nothing you can do but clean up in the morning. F-117 pilots use names like Shaba, Stealth, or Nighthawk in more-polite company. (Chapter 13)

ship Airplane. A four ship is a formation of four airplanes. (Chapter 4)

Sidewinder (AIM-9) Heat-seeking, air-to-air missile used in a dogfight between gun and radar missile ranges. Very lethal. (Chapter 2)

situational awareness (SA) How well an airman knows what's going on around him or her. The critical, unteachable, unmeasurable quality that good airmen have and poor airmen don't. Most fliers have it, while some—the lucky or the dead—don't. Opposite of clueless. (Chapter 2)

skipper Commander. The Boss. (Chapter 2)

Sparrow (AIM-7) Radar-guided, air-to-air missile used at long range. (Chapter 2)

speed bump division The 82nd Airborne when deployed to Saudi Arabia. Airborne forces are too lightly armed to stop a serious armored attack. (Chapter 9)

splash! Radio call meaning, "The target has been shot down." (Chapter 10)

squawk (noun) Electronic transponder that identifies an aircraft. (verb) To intentionally transmit that identification signal. (Chapter 2)

squirrel cage Basic acrobatics flown in a defined block of sky. From the outside, the plane looks like a squirrel running around inside a cage. (Chapter 3)

step To leave the life support section in flight gear and go to the jet (U.S.). See walk. (Chapter 7)

stick (of bombs) More than one bomb dropped at a time. (Chapter 3)

strafe (verb) To attack a ground target with a gun carried by an aircraft. (noun) The gun attack itself. (Chapter 4)

strike Long-range bombing attack made deep in the enemy's territory. (Chapter 2)

Super Jollys Version of the H-53 Jolly Green Giant heavy lift helicopter. (Chapter 9)

sweep To clear the sky. What interceptors do to the sky ahead of the strike formations they protect, as in "sweep the sky of MiGs." (Chapter 2)

T-38 Talon (38) Supersonic Air Force advanced trainer. Every Air Force pilot trained in that Northrop jet fell in love with it. (Chapter 1)

TA set Terrain avoidance radar. Radar display of the terrain in front of an aircraft that enables the pilot to manually avoid the "rocks." (Chapter 6)

Tacan Ground-based navigation system that allows fliers to navigate and find a runway without seeing it. In the air-to-air mode, it's used to measure the distance between aircraft. (Chapter 3)

TBS The Basic School.

TDY Temporary duty. Relatively short "business" trip. (Chapter 9)

terrain masking Flying "behind" terrain to avoid detection by radar. (Chapter 6)

The Basic School (TBS) Marine Corps basic officer training. All Marines start out at TBS and are trained infantrymen. The fliers have a very good idea what the guys they're supporting are going through. (Chapter 3)

thousand pounders   1000-pound, high-explosive bombs. See MK-83. (Chapter 8)

three wire   Aircraft carriers have five arresting wires strung across the touchdown zone. Catching the third wire indicates a good landing and is a point of pride with pilots. (Chapter 2)

time and heading navigation   By flying in a known direction for a known time at a set speed, you can, theoretically, find your way around. But it's far from easy, and every low-altitude pilot has gotten hopelessly lost that way at one time or another. (Chapter 14)

TOO   ("tee-oh-oh") Target of opportunity. Target selected by the fliers versus one that is preassigned. (Chapter 9)

Tornado F-3   Interceptor version of the Tornado. (Chapter 8)

TOT   Time on target. Exact time the bombs will detonate (interdiction). Timing is the primary means of ensuring safety from "friendly" explosions, and crews count on the effectiveness of earlier attacks to pave the way for their missions. Entire raids fit into 90 seconds or a few minutes. (Chapter 3)

TP   Target practice cannon shells. Inert practice rounds that match the ballistics of live rounds without causing the cleanup problems of high explosives and depleted uranium. (Chapter 9)

trail   One airplane or formation of airplanes following behind another. (Chapter 10)

trap   To land on a carrier and be stopped, trapped, by the arresting gear. (Chapter 2)

triple-A   Anti-aircraft artillery. Guns that shoot at airplanes. Everything from rifles to 130mm radar-directed cannons with time fuses. Over 80% of aircraft losses are usually due to triple-A. It was the primary reason coalition aircraft fought the war from above 10,000 feet. The nightly light show over Baghdad was triple-A. (Chapter 2)

Tweet   Cessna T-37 Tweety Bird basic jet trainer. Also known as the Flying Dog Whistle for its ear-shattering squeal, the Tweet has introduced Air Force pilot wannabes to jet flight for more than 35 years. (Chapter 10)

two ship   Two aircraft in formation fighting as a team. Section.

U.K.   United Kingdom. England, Wales, Scotland, and Northern Ireland. (Chapter 8)

ultimate Frisbee   Full-contact Frisbee on a soccer field. Imagine rugby with a pie plate. (Chapter 15)

uniform radio   Radios are referred to by their frequency band. Since "U" is the first letter in ultra high frequency, or UHF, "uniform" is the shorthand term for that radio. (Chapter 14)

up chit   Medical clearance to fly. (Chapter 15)

UPT   Undergraduate Pilot Training. Air Force pilot training program. Primary training is flown in the Cessna T-37, a very mild and forgiving jet, while advanced training is flown in the supersonic Northrop T-38. (Chapter 1)

USAFE   United States Air Forces Europe. American Air Force command in Europe. (Chapter 12)

VFA   Navy and Marine squadrons are designated according to their missions and equipment. V means heavier than air, F means fighters, A means attack, M means Marine and H means helicopter. So VFA-81 is a naval heavier-than-air squadron that flies both fighter and attack missions. (Chapter 2)

vis   ("viz") Visibility. (Chapter 11)

visual   Radio call meaning, "I see the friendly aircraft." (Chapter 10)

walk   To leave the flying clothing section in flying kit and go to the airplane. (Chapter 8)

wands   Flashlights fitted with white plastic cones used to guide pilots on the ground at night. (Chapter 14)

war clause   That line in most life insurance policies that voids the coverage during war. Military fliers have a hard time finding commercial life insurance that covers hostilities and crashes. (Chapter 6)

Wart Weasel   An A-10 hunting surface-to-air missiles. Weasel refers to a surface-to-air missile hunter. That mission was handled superbly by the F-4G Wild Weasels, but their normal F-16 wingmen stayed home. The F-16s didn't work out. So A-10 Wart(hog) Weasels went out to kill SAMs in place of the F-16s, while the real Weasels protected the Hogs. (Chapter 9)

weapons systems operator (WSO)   ("wizzo") U.S. Air Force flier who runs the navigation and weapons systems while the other flier flies the jet. B/N, RIO, RAF navigator, pitter, backseater. (Chapter 7)

weather   (noun) Specifically, bad weather that obscures vision such as fog, rain, or clouds. Fliers mention weather only when it's a significant consideration, as in lots of clouds, thunderstorms, bad visibility, etc. It can be a real showstopper. (Chapter 1)

WestPac   Western Pacific. Marines routinely deploy to Iwakuni, Japan, on six-month tours for training in Korea, Japan, the Philippines, etc. (Chapter 3)

wheel   Circular flight pattern centered on the target that allows any of the fighters to attack from any angle. (Chapter 12)

wheels in the well   To retract the landing gear into the wheel wells after takeoff. (Chapter 1)

Wild Weasel   F-4G Phantom II anti-SAM fighter. Descended from the F-100 and F-105 Wild Weasels, these fliers display the solid brass parts of their anatomies by hunting surface-to-air missiles. Other aircraft, such as the F/A-18 Hornet, have a limited Weasel capability also. Imagine trolling for Jaws. (Chapter 2)

willie pete   White phosphorous. WP rockets explode in a thick cloud of white smoke and intense fire. They're used for either target marking or burning a flammable target. (Chapter 9)

winchester   Radio call meaning, "I'm out of weapons." (Chapter 12)

wing spar   Main wing support that runs the length of the wing and ties in with the fuselage. (Chapter 9)

WSO   Weapons system operator.

WTI   Weapons and Tactics Instructor school. "Doctorate" in combat flying (British and U.S. Marine Corps term). See Fighter Weapons School. (Chapter 3)

XO   Executive officer. The second in command of a Marine or Army unit. (Chapter 11)

yo-yo   Dogfighting maneuver that resembles the up and down movement of a yo-yo as the attacking fighter tries to get behind a rapidly turning target. (Chapter 3)

yoke   Aircraft control wheel. Most large aircraft have control wheels, while fighters have sticks. (Chapter 6)

ZSU   ZSU 23-4 Shilka. Soviet-built, four-barreled, radar-directed, 23mm, mobile, armored, anti-aircraft gun system on a tank chassis. Bad news. (Chapter 7)